ANTÆUS
ON NATURE

Since 1970 *Antæus* has established itself as one of the
most successful and distinguished literary magazines
in the world. In more than sixty issues it has published
work by a wide range of internationally known writers
and also, equally important, writers who are beginning
to make their reputations. Contributors to *Antæus*
include W.H. Auden, Mario Vargas Llosa, Marguerite
Duras, Joseph Brodsky, John Fowles, Czeslaw Milosz,
Edna O'Brien, Richard Ford, Josef Škvorecký,
V.S. Naipaul, Italo Calvino, Seamus Heaney, Joyce
Carol Oates, Edmund White, Oliver Sacks, Peter
Matthiessen, Stephen Spender and many others.
Major issues of *Antæus* are now published in book form
by Harvill paperbacks.

AVAILABLE

Antæus: Journals, Notebooks & Diaries (including
M.F.K. Fisher, Mary Gordon, V.S. Naipaul, Edna
O'Brien, Ursula Le Guin, Lawrence Durrell and
Oliver Sacks)

FORTHCOMING

Antæus: Literature as Pleasure (including Richard Ford,
Josef Škvorecký, Joyce Carol Oates and Charles
Simic)

THE MUSIC OF THE SPHERES

The world thus shaped then is not at rest but eternally revolves with indescribable velocity, each revolution occupying the space of 24 hours: the rising and setting of the sun have left this not doubtful. Whether the sound of this vast mass whirling in unceasing rotation is of enormous volume and consequently beyond the capacity of our ears to perceive, for my own part I cannot easily say – any more in fact than whether this is true of the tinkling of the stars that travel round with it, revolving in their own orbits; or whether it emits a sweet harmonious music that is beyond belief charming. To us who live within it the world glides silently alike by day and night.

PLINY
Natural History

ANTÆUS

ON NATURE

Edited by
Daniel Halpern

COLLINS HARVILL
8 Grafton Street, London W1
1989

Collins Harvill
William Collins Sons and Co Ltd
London · Glasgow · Sydney · Auckland
Toronto · Johannesburg

Antæus is published in the USA by The Ecco Press
26 West 17th Street, New York, NY10011

BRITISH LIBRARY CATALOGUING IN PUBLICATION DATA

Antæus : *on nature, 1989*
1. Literature. Critical studies. Serials
I. Halpern, Daniel, *1945-*
809

ISBN 0–00–272027–2

First published in the USA by The Ecco Press in 1986

© *Antæus* 1986

Page 320 constitutes an extension of the copyright page

Printed and bound in Great Britain by
William Collins Sons and Co Ltd, Glasgow

CONTENTS

John Hay

The Nature Writer's Dilemma

You might think, after many years of teaching a class called "Nature Writers," that I would know what nature meant, but I do not. Perhaps this is of little importance. The word comes from the Latin, *to be born*, which is fundamental enough, and puts it under the heading of abiding mystery. Then we have the essential character of something, like a rock, or a child; plus physical power, according to the dictionary, causing the phenomena of the material world; or for one grand definition, the sum of the surrounding universe. When I hear it said in caustic tones that "Everyone knows man is a part of nature," I have only the vaguest idea of what that means either. The last time I heard such a remark, it came from a teacher of philosophy who did not seem to be particularly interested in what is often referred to as "the lower forms of life." There is reason to suspect the assumptions of the human brain when it becomes too elevated from the earth that nurtured it.

The dictionary also includes "the state of nature," which was long considered to be unregenerate, the opposite of grace, with the heathen and the wolves. The Judeo-Christian ethic has been blamed for putting man above nature in God's name. In this view, technology, ravaging industrialism, the will to exploit are an extension of overweening Christian arrogance. It is certainly true that most people still believe in their superiority to nonhuman life, though this may now be tempered by the idea that both of us share in an equality of inheritance, and that consciousness may not be man's exclusive property.

Are we unique? The ethologist Niko Tinbergen says it is difficult to prove scientifically. The question of why we need to feel unique might be more useful. How does the human spirit stand and survive in relation to the surrounding universe?

I find further difficulties in coming to grips with this subject because of my society, which sees the natural world not as a range of correlated lives and communities but as a province for plunder. The terms it appropriates, such as *ecology*, *the environment*, or *conservation*, may be politically useful to the cause, but they hardly guarantee an intimacy with its sources. Someone might go into a woodland area saying: "Great ecology you got here!" and care less about the trees.

For all our human claiming of the right to possess and dominate the earth, we have lost a great deal of our sense of it. A relationship which was once as direct as the food we put into our mouths has become abstract. We seldom know where the food comes from. If you approach certain publishers with writing which deals with nature, in other words, the world of life, the water we could not live without, the air we breathe, you might very well be advised to "put more people into it." But if you can't find nature, where will the people live? The subject is only au courant if backpacking, canoeing, sailing, and other acceptable activities make it so, added, of course, to writings with the authority of science, the accepted interpreter of all natural phenomena. We could identify very little without it. At the same time, the priesthood that can take us beyond Jupiter to black holes and quarks seems to alter common nature into a detached state most people can't take in.

So the contemporary nature writer can be forgiven if he is not quite sure on which shelf he is to end up. It may give him some confidence that his subject derives from the Latin *nasci*, "to be born," and so is the most important one he could possibly have, but he is subject, like all the race, to confusion. It may be better to hang loose and respect your capacity to receive unknown surprises than to wait on terms and categories, from whatever important direction they come.

John Muir, who was a religious man in spite of his rejection of his Scots Calvinist upbringing, said that he took a walk and decided to stay out past sundown, to conclude that going out is really going in. His wilderness has now become the cause for a more translated religion, so that those who want it saved but have never entered it, and might not like it if they did, talk about it as if it were some paradisal refuge at the end of the mind. Things are getting pretty desperate when you can no longer move out into the substance of where you ought to be.

A practical culture wants to know what things are, how they work, even, for almost anything under the sun, "What good is it?" Existence for its own sake — life forms that flow in the beauty of the wind, like a flock of sanderlings — becomes subordinated to labels. The facts may help us to feel sure about our control of circumstances, but they are a poor substitute for the deeper equations of earth and human life.

The American Indian saw the Word behind all manifested things, the primal, creative power. The Word was invoked through silence and dreams, through chants in healing ceremonies, and hypnotic poetry that mirrored the sounds of nature. Knud Rasmussen wrote down the words of a song which came spontaneously to a woman Eskimo from her "helping spirit," as Margot Astrov records it in her anthology, *The Winged Spirit*. The song went like this:

> The great sea
> Has sent me adrift,
> It moves me as the weed in a great river,
> Earth and the great weather move me,
> Have carried me away,
> And move my inward parts with joy.

Now, if a Western reader should read this as a poem for the first time, he might find it pleasing, fragmentary, even moving, but the depth and spontaneity which occasioned it would certainly pass him by, as, I am afraid, much of the Indian experience has passed us by. Rasmussen said that she was repeating these verses incessantly during a gathering in a big snow house; and that she was intoxicated with joy, a joy that everyone else in the house felt too. They began to state all "their misdeeds, as well as those of others, and those who felt themselves accused and admitted their offenses obtained release from these by lifting their arms and making movements as if to fling away all evil, all that was false and wicked was thrown away. . . ."

We do not often get catharsis of the soul, I am afraid, out of what goes under the general heading of Nature Writing, but one senses through this example just how narrow our view of the subject is forced to be. The earth's great weather is too often put down in terms of climatology, meteorology, predictable fronts, and clouds, such as cirrus, nimbus, and cumulus, which have little to do with tears or joy.

Writers who go beyond scientific nomenclature to talk about their thoughts and feelings, with nature as their foil, are invariably compared with Thoreau, as if he were the only writer we had who belonged in that classification. Thoreau tested the ideals of experience against the elements of his country world, and certainly derived much joy from it. That he was a poet and a literary craftsman, rather than an educator in outdoor living, may have put him in the nature-writer category by default, but there are a great many others who belong there with him. Wasn't Emily Dickinson invoking the Word behind natural phenomena? Surely *Moby-Dick*, a great mythic saga, belongs there, and would it be demeaning to Shakespeare, with his incomparable human range, to call him a nature writer, or to hear profoundly natural rhythms in Beethoven?

Clearly, the term *Nature Writers* is totally inadequate to start with if it only implies an interest in landscapes peopled by plants and animals but otherwise isolated from central human experience. We give the novelists charge of our demented psyches, our quirks and foibles, but the depth of human character seldom seems anchored in the known earth and its surrounding waters. Man is still on one side, Nature on the other.

If I am to stick solely to the discipline of natural history I suppose I have no right to bring in poetry, music, drama, and other arts, but the implication is that our subject may be starved for want of room. That diverse human experience should be kept out of it does not bode well for our earth relationship. (Naturalists are often thought of in terms of whether or not they like people, which assumes that their concerns with the natural world leave little room for human sympathy. It is a chilly gap, but I doubt that the naturalists created it.)

A writer like Edward Abbey, in his *Desert Solitaire*, defended Moab, Utah, and its beautiful environs with savage irony and sympathy, as if he felt he was going to be accused of bias. Too often the acceptable norm is natural history in its tamest and most factual form. You cannot go wrong if you are backed up by accurate nomenclature. Thus Gilbert White's *The Natural History of Selborne* is praised as much for its early use of precise observation and the scientific method as for the wonderful sense of peace and rooted continuity that pervades the book. We think of nature as a source of information we are entitled to have.

Nature is also a place, like Florida, to escape to (except that Florida appears to have become denaturalized) and it implies the danger, discomfort, and inconvenience which a whole civilization works to overcome; but as reality, as a part and parcel of this volatility, this deep turmoil, this trouble and delight we call existence, the term has lost credit. But we will come back to its truth through our own inadequacy, if nothing else. Primal law demands it. In the meantime, though I am obliged to an economy and a readership that insists on categories, I think I will stick with my confusion and the mystery of things, as if human domination never existed. How else are we to be born again? There is no help but to continue on this tack until I reach the far side of the horizon, if the food holds out. Nature undefined is what I know in myself. What better, more incalculable, capricious, and impossible guide could I have than that! This voyage is going to be interesting.

I

Noel Perrin

Forever Virgin: The American View of America

If there is one novel that nearly all educated Americans have read, it's F. Scott Fitzgerald's *The Great Gatsby*. If there's a single most famous passage in that novel, it's the one on the last page where Fitzgerald talks about Gatsby's belief in the green light ahead. He has in mind two or three kinds of green light at once. There's the literal green dock-identification light that Gatsby can see from his Long Island mansion, glimmering across the bay where Daisy lives. There's the metaphorical green traffic light: the future is open, the future is GO. And finally there's the green light that nature produces: the reflection from trees, and especially from a whole forest, a forest crowding right up to the shore of Long Island Sound.

In that famous last passage, the narrator of the book is standing in front of Gatsby's mansion at night—a summer night. He is looking across the bay, just as Gatsby used to do. There is a bright moon. As he looks, "the inessential houses began to melt away until gradually I became aware of the old island here that flowered once for Dutch sailors' eyes—a fresh, green breast of the new world. Its vanished trees, the trees that had made way for Gatsby's house, had once pandered in whispers to the last and greatest of all human dreams; for a transitory enchanted moment man must have held his breath in the presence of this continent . . . face to face for the last time in history with something commensurate to his capacity for wonder."

Fitzgerald says in this passage that it was just for a moment that men and women beheld the new world as a fresh, untouched place, a virgin world, a place where the future is open and green. But, of course, it wasn't. We still see it that way—or most of us do most of the time. Certainly that was how Jay Gatsby saw it sixty years ago. In the narrator's vision, there on the last page, that is how he, too, sees it: Long Island with the houses invisible in the moonlight, the island like a green breast, the breast of Mother Nature, inexhaustibly nourishing. As I am going to try to show in a little while, that is how most Americans still perceive the country now: morning in America, a green light ahead, nature glad and strong and free. Or at least we do in our dominant mood, and that's why the majority of us don't really worry much about acid rain, or recycling, or any of that. We have a consciousness below knowledge that the big country can handle all that.

But there are two things I want to do before I come to the relationship between human beings and nature in America in the 1980s: a short thing and a long thing. The short one is simply to make clear what I mean by nature. And the long one is to give some of the history of the encounter between us and nature since we got here. Because of course I am not claiming we feel exactly the same as Henryk Hudson's sailors did in 1609. We have changed, and the country has changed since then. A lot. All I'm claiming is that we still see the green light.

First, what nature is. Among other things, it's a word that if you look it up turns out to have twelve meanings, plus eight more sub-meanings. They vary so widely that Robert Frost could and did once write a poem on the subject. In the poem, he and an anonymous college official are arguing about what the word means in the epitaph that the Victorian poet Walter Savage Landor wrote for himself. Landor summed up his life thus:

> I strove with none, for none was worth my strife.
> Nature I loved, and next to Nature, Art.
> I warm'd both hands before the fire of life;
> It sinks, and I am ready to depart.

Frost and the administrator can't agree on what it was that Landor loved, and the result is a mocking little poem that begins

> Dean, adult education may seem silly.
> What of it, though? I got some willy-nilly
> The other evening at your college deanery.
> And grateful for it (let's not be facetious!)
> For I thought Epicurus and Lucretius
> By Nature meant the Whole Goddam Machinery
> But you say that in college nomenclature
> The only meaning possible for Nature
> In Landor's quatrain would be Pretty Scenery.

Well, what I mean by nature is more than pretty scenery, but slightly less than the whole goddam machinery. I mean everything that exists on this planet (or elsewhere) that was not made by man. It's what most people mean. Only the minute you look closely, it turns out to be very hard to decide what was made by man and what wasn't. A plastic bag or a beer can is easy: Both were made by man — though of course out of natural materials, since that's all there are. But what about a garden? Nature made the carrot, but man modified it, planted it, grew it. There are two wills in collaboration here — the will of the carrot to be orange and to taste carroty and so forth — and the will of human beings to have it be a large carrot that travels well, keeps in cold storage, and so forth. What about a lake that exists because someone has built a dam, a so-called man-made or artificial lake? What about a tree? Only God — or nature — can make them, as Joyce Kilmer pointed out. But then, there are hybrid poplars: designed, planted, shaped by human beings. Again, a collaboration. Almost the entire surface of England is such a collaboration, and most of the United States, too. Only a wilderness area is not at least partly a collaboration. Lots of the prettiest scenery *is*.

So what I'm going to call nature is everything on this planet that is at least partially under the control of some other will than ours. Pure nature is of course what exists entirely without our will. In terms of landscape, there isn't much of it.

That still leaves one big question unanswered. Is man himself part of nature? Our remote ancestors certainly were: They evolved without planning to. But we ourselves? Well, I think we're partly in and partly out of nature — and the balance varies from age to age. But for the moment I'm going to say we're outside of nature. Certainly we thought of ourselves that way when we came to America. The Dutch sailors did, the pioneer settlers did. The authors of the Bible did.

Now let me drop back a little, and talk history. Not as far back as 1609 — the Dutch sailors didn't leave much record of what they thought when they saw Long Island — but back to the eighteenth century and to a book called *Letters From an American Farmer*, which was written in the 1770s (though not published until 1782), and which was one of the very early American best-sellers. Basically, it's a report to Europeans on conditions in America just before the Revolution. Most of it is about what it's like to come be a farmer in one of the thirteen colonies, though there is one long section on what it's like to live on Nantucket and be a sailor.

At that time "America" was a strip of land about 300 miles wide, going south from Maine to Georgia. In the absence of airplanes, satellites, and so forth, no one knew exactly how much more land there was west of the frontier.

But the general feeling was that for all practical purposes this continent was infinite. As Hector St. John de Crevecoeur says in *Letters From an American Farmer*, "Many ages will not see the shores of our great lakes replenished with inland nations, nor the unknown bounds of North America entirely peopled. Who can tell how far it extends?"

St. John was wrong, of course. It did not take many ages to start inland nations on the shores of our Great Lakes. It took about two generations. Fifty years after he wrote the book, the inland nation of Illinois came into being. Another fifty years and Chicago was a large city, another forty and it had two million people. But he couldn't know that. He and everyone else in 1770 thought we would still have a frontier in, say, the twenty-fifth century, and that the still-growing country could absorb all the immigrants who might ever wish to come, that it, in fact, would always *need* more. "There is room for everybody in America," he wrote. And, remember, America had already existed for a century and a half when he wrote that: The image was firmly fixed that this was an infinite country.

The other thing that St. John took for granted was that pure nature is an appalling thing. He saw no beauty in wilderness whatsoever. Trackless forests did not appeal to him, and he considered frontiersmen corrupt and degenerate barbarians. What he liked, what he thought beautiful was the collaboration between man and nature that a farm is, and he considered that the best possible use of a person's time lay in taming wild nature.

> To examine how the world is gradually settled, how the howling swamp is converted into a pleasing meadow, the rough ridge into a fine field; and to hear the cheerful whistling, the rural song, where there was no sound heard before save . . . the screech of the owl or the hissing of the snake—

that, says St. John, gives him enormous pleasure. He explains to his European audience how the first thing an American does when he comes into a new piece of wilderness is to build a bridge over whatever creek or little river runs through it, and the second is to take his axe and chop down as many acres of trees as he has energy to do that year, and the third is to start draining swamps and other wetlands. And perfectly reasonable, too, since the woods, the swamps, and the rivers are infinite. But St. John's assumptions are that nature is not in any way sacred, or precious, or to be treasured just because it exists; on the contrary it is badly in need of collaboration with man, and only under our governance can it become the beautiful thing it should be. And he also assumes, as the Bible told him to, that nature has no other important function than to serve us. He even thinks that God intended the wolves, the bears, the snakes, and the Indians themselves to give way before us. He doesn't worry about their becoming extinct, because the continent is infinite — but I think if you pressed him, he'd say that had to be their eventual fate.

One other observation of St. John's demands mention, even though it has little to do with nature, only nurture. I mentioned that one long section of the book is about Nantucket, a place St. John greatly admired. It was a Quaker community, and already deep into whaling — the people St. John met there were the great-grandfathers of the people Melville wrote about in *Moby-Dick*. St. John also admired the women of Nantucket, who ran the farms while their husbands were off whaling — and whom he regarded as the most spirited, independent, and, incidentally, good-looking women in America — which for him means they were the most spirited, independent, and good-looking women in the world. But, he says, "a singular custom prevails here among the women, at which I was greatly surprised. . . . They have adopted these many years the Asiatic custom of taking a dose of opium every morning, and so deeply rooted is it that they would be at a loss how to live without this indulgence; they would rather be deprived of any necessary than forego their favorite luxury." Nantucket men, St. John says, didn't touch opium.

Now I want to move ahead to 1804, which was the year that President Jefferson sent Captains Meriwether Lewis and William Clark of the U.S. Army across the continent on foot, the first human beings, so far as I know, to make that entire trip across what is now the United States. It took them and their party of twenty-five enlisted men and a couple of guides two years to get to the Pacific ocean and back again. Plus, as usual, rather more money than the government had anticipated. President Jefferson budgeted the two-year trip for thirty people, including boats, a newly invented airgun to impress the Indians, all supplies, at $2,500. The actual cost of the expedition was nearly $5,000. But it did reach the Pacific.

After Lewis and Clark, no one could think that North America was infinite. They returned with maps and mileage estimates. The shrinking process had begun. But it was still huge — a place that takes you a year to cross in each direction — and it was still largely pure nature.

Lewis and Clark did not see the wilderness quite the way St. John did — partly because the region he knew was all woods, and a great deal of their time was spent crossing the Great Plains, the grassy open plains with herds of antelope and buffalo. What struck them was that nature had already made the center of America into a garden, just waiting for the settlers to come cultivate it. In fact, some of it God or nature had already cultivated for us. On July 10, 1804, going up the Missouri River, they passed a piece of bottom-land: 2,000 acres covered with wild potatoes. At any time, there were hordes of deer, wild turkeys, elk, just waiting to be killed. Lewis gave it as his professional army captain's opinion that two hunters could keep a regiment supplied with meat. On August 5, 1804, Captain Clark noticed how abundant the fresh fruit was. "Great quantities of grapes on the banks. I observe three kinds, at this time ripe." On August 16, 1804, Captain Lewis and twelve men spent the morning fishing. Here's the report: "Caught upwards of 800 fine fish: 79 pike, 8 salmon resembling trout, 1 rock, 1 flat back, 127 buffalo and red horse, 4 bass, 490 cats, with many small silver fish and shrimp."

Sometimes, when the captains climbed a hill for the view, a whole section of what is now Iowa or Nebraska would remind them of a giant stock farm back in Virginia. Lewis described one view in which there was a forest of wild plum trees on one side—"loaded with fruit and now ripe"—and on the other twenty miles of open grassland, smooth as a bowling green. "This scenery," he says, "already rich, pleasing, and beautiful, was still further heightened by immense herds of buffalo, deer, elk, and antelopes, which we saw in every direction. . . . I do not think I exaggerate when I estimate the number of buffalo which could be comprehended at one view to be 3,000." The wolves prowling around the edge of each herd even reminded him of the sheepdogs back in Virginia.

Again, the sense is that nature is so bounteous that we could never possibly run short of anything. Nor was this some special white prejudice. The Indians felt the same. Lewis and Clark watched several times while a small tribe of Plains Indians drove a whole herd of buffalo over a cliff, took the tongues and humps of a couple of dozen to eat, and left all the rest to rot. Why not? There was no more need to be frugal with buffalo than we feel the need to be frugal with, say, ice cubes. Don't think I'm blaming either Lewis and Clark or the Indians. Their behavior made perfect sense at the time.

Nature wasn't all bounty, though. For example, the whole region was swarming with grizzly bears: eating plums, waiting at the bottoms of cliffs for someone to drive a herd of buffalo over, and just generally enjoying life. They were not a bit afraid of American soldiers. And in fact a soldier with a single-shot rifle was in no way a match for a grizzly. By experience, Lewis and Clark found that about six soldiers equaled one grizzly. If all six shot, they were pretty likely to kill the bear with no one being hurt or chased up a tree. If fewer shot, there was apt to be trouble.

There was other trouble, too. When the expedition reached the Rocky Mountains, they found the peaks terrifying. Not beautiful (except snow-capped from a distance), not fun to be in. Instead, a place where you were very apt to starve to death, freeze to death, fall off a cliff. A typical campsite was by the mountain stream they called Hungry Creek—"at that place we had nothing to eat"—where they spent the night of September 18, 1805. A typical adventure occurred the next morning when Private Robert Frazer's packhorse, bought from the Indians, lost its footing and rolled a hundred yards down a precipice.

Most of the year, the only food you were going to find in the Rockies was what you carried in on your back, and when you ran out of that, there was no store to buy more at, nor could you decide to quit and hitch a ride back to Virginia, much less catch a plane to Denver. In short, not only was nature huge, but man was weak. Clever—clever enough to have invented axes and to drive stupid buffalo off cliffs—but weak. Nature, Mother Nature, was a worthy opponent as well as a worthy partner. In fact, let me make a sort of metaphor out of the grizzly and the buffalo, the two of them standing for wild nature. Both are physically stronger than men, and can run faster. One, the grizzly, is untameable, and more or less useless to us. So the thing to do is kill them, and that's a heroic and dangerous task: one part of subduing the wilderness. The other, the buffalo, is partially tameable, and very useful to us. Kill them, too, but not all of them, because we want them around to eat. Or else replace them with cattle, which are completely tameable. That's another part of subduing the wilderness—less heroic, maybe, but still a big job, and still nature offers plenty of resistance to the changes we make. The collaboration is not entirely on our terms, but partly on hers.

In sum, for the first two centuries that Europeans lived in North America, they saw the continent as a giant wilderness or desert—they used the two words interchangeably—the motto of Dartmouth College, *Vox clamantis in deserto*, translates to "A voice crying in the wilderness." They saw a vast, powerful, and immensely rich wilderness, which it would be the bounden duty of their descendants to turn into farms and gardens and alabaster cities, but which we would never entirely do, because the country was so damned big and the power of the axe and plow so limited.

All that began to change in the nineteenth century with the growth of technology. Railroads and steamboats were, of course, the first major manifestations. They made the wilderness accessible and the continent (relatively) small. In so doing, they produced the first few converts to a new point of view. Henry David Thoreau was one. Thoreau lived right next to the Fitchburg Railroad. He saw quite clearly the threat steam posed to untamed nature. Steam engines are bigger and faster than grizzlies. Steam saws can cut trees up far more quickly than forests can grow them. Steam shovels can drain an everglade.

Wilderness threatened became wilderness desirable — for the handful of converts. Thoreau was, as far as I know, the first American who publicly concluded that wilderness as wilderness — that is, pure nature — was a good thing to have around. In the 1850s he made a proposal that each town in Massachusetts save a 500-acre piece of woods which would be forever wild: no lumbering, no changes at all. Needless to say, he got nowhere, not even in Concord itself. It was still too much like going down to McDonald's and suggesting to the manager that he put 500 ice cubes in permanent deep freeze, against the time when ice may be scarce.

John Muir was a slightly later convert. It's a coincidence, but a nice coincidence, that the year in which he began to describe the western mountains as wonderful places, sacred ground, God's outdoor temples, was the same year in which the transcontinental railroad was completed. That was 1869. Henceforth the Lewis and Clark journey of a year could be done in a few days. Muir, like Thoreau before him, sensed the growth of man's power against nature, though in 1869 nature was still stronger. And, of course, Muir could be romantic about mountains in part because by now the country had been so much tamed that within one day's walk of most of his camping places in the Sierras he could borrow or buy flour to make bread with, sometimes even go to a regular store. He could even be worried about the ecological harm that overgrazing by sheep was doing in the Sierras, and eventually have some success in banning sheep from portions.

Ever since then, human power has grown at an almost geometric rate, while the forces of nature have remained static. The ascending line was bound eventually to cross the level one. It's not possible to pinpoint the year in which this happened, but it *is* possible to suggest a decade. I think the 1950s represent the swing point in man's relationship to nature, certainly in the United States, and probably in the whole world. During that decade we became stronger than our surroundings. Certainly not in all ways—such physical phenomena as earthquakes and hurricanes and volcanoes remain quite beyond our power to control. But in most ways. The biggest river isn't even difficult for us to bridge, or to dam. No other living creature can seriously dispute us, certainly not on a one-to-one basis. In Melville's day, six men in a whaleboat were generally a match for one whale—but not always; sometimes the whale won. By the 1950s, one man with a harpoon gun could do in any number of whales. There's not even any thrill to it.

More important than any of this, by the 1950s our science and our engineering enabled us to produce new substances and to distribute old substances on a scale equal to nature's own. For example, we can put sulfur dioxide in the air at a rate faster than the volcanoes do. One single refinery in Sudbury, Ontario, became the source of 5 percent of all the sulfur dioxide that entered the air of the entire planet, there to become sulfuric acid and to come down again as acid rain and snow. One fleet of jet airplanes could seriously affect the ozone layer.

We have earth-moving machinery that can rearrange a whole landscape. We have new chemical compounds that can affect the whole chain of life. Nature cannot easily absorb the effect of DDT or of Sevin; nature is no longer resilient. We can nearly eliminate whales, sort of half-meaning to, and we can all but extinguish peregrine falcons as an unintended by-product of raising crops. We really are what our ancestors only claimed to be: the masters of nature—or at least we're the dominant partner in the collaboration. To use one more metaphor, we are like goldfish who have been living in an aquarium for as long as we can remember; and being clever goldfish, we have discovered how to manipulate the controls of the aquarium: put more oxygen in the water, get rid of the pesky turtle we never liked anyway, triple the supply of goldfish food. Only once we realize we're partly running the aquarium, it scares some of us. What if we make a mistake, and wreck the aquarium entirely? We couldn't live outside it.

That has been the actual position since the 1950s, and it is what our rational minds clearly report. The green light has turned yellow, and there is a real possibility it will go to red. But it is not what our emotions tell us. Emotionally, almost all of us still believe what the Dutch sailors thought: that here is an inexhaustible new world, with plenty of everything for everybody.

And because of that emotion, which I, too, share, we have had a double response since the 1950s. One is to do our damndest to keep part of our continent still virgin—pure nature, wilderness. That's the nature-lover's response, the Sierra Club response, and sometimes the environmentalist's response. It's almost uniquely American. I have a friend, for example, who is a Spanish environmentalist, and I know from him that there is exactly one national park in Spain, the former hunting forest of the dukes of Medina, and even that is by no means a wilderness area. Spain is not virgin country. At the moment, about 2 percent of the United States is official wilderness, just about the same amount that is paved. And in a country this big, 2 percent is quite a lot: something like 60,000 square miles, twelve times as big as the state of Connecticut.

In terms of our whole population, to be sure, it's less impressive: If you put all of us in the wilderness at once, we'd each have a fifth of an acre. But it's enough to give a comforting illusion that pure nature is still going, independent of us. And most people who seek that illusion also want to downplay their separateness from nature, and to say that we have no right to meddle, our collaboration is deadly. We goldfish should stand back and let the aquarium run itself as it always has.

The other response involves a much greater illusion—or I think it does, anyway. And that is simply to deny that anything has changed significantly since the days of Hector St. John de Crevecoeur and Lewis and Clark. This is the response, for example, of the present United States government. We're still just collaborators with nature, people who hold this view say, more effective collaborators than we used to be, certainly; and if we do our part, nature will do its. Nature is still resilient; it can still absorb anything we do. Besides, we were meant to rule the planet—this aquarium was designed specially for us—and what we do was pretty much all allowed for in the original design.

One group wants to re-create the world the Dutch sailors saw, and the other denies that it has ever ceased to exist. If I have to choose, of course I choose to be one of the re-creators—to try to protect as much wilderness as possible. I'd like to get the proportion of untouched land up to 3 percent. I've even dreamt of 4 percent.

But neither group, I think, is right. Neither has really dealt with the fact that a generation ago the green light turned to yellow. If there is anything that is really, really worth doing in the rest of this century, I think, it's to find a third and better way of dealing with the relationship between man and nature.

Howard Ensign Evans

Remembering Pioneer Naturalists

A few years ago we decided to spend our declining years in a habitat of our choice, far from the screech of traffic, the aromas of industry, and the too-visible signs of what passes for progress. We had, after all, done our small bit for society, trying to instill in our students and our children something of the reverence we have always felt for that delicate and incredibly complex earthly wrapping called the biosphere. Now we wished to indulge in a final orgy of what Edward Wilson has called biophilia — more than a love, an *affiliation* with life in its broadest sense. There are others, of course, who have "moved to the woods," seeking like Thoreau to become inspectors of rainstorms and surveyors of forest paths. We selected a granite cliff in the Colorado Rockies, with a view across meadows and valleys to the Mummy Range, cresting at over 13,000 feet elevation. The area is called Glacier View Meadows, though the best it can claim is a distant view of a few semipermanent snow fields. We were greedy for as big a piece of the biosphere as we could absorb from our windows — fifty miles, more or less, to the south and east, and (from nearby promontories) nearly as far to the north and west.

But more than living among the rocks and chipmunks, we wished to relive some of the discoveries of the things around us. Outside, a Cassin's finch is busy at our feeder; a Cooper's hawk traverses the valley below; Abert's squirrels gambol on the rocks; in the spring the hillsides will sparkle with *Claytonia* (spring beauties); the valleys will ring with the songs of Wilson's warblers and the woods with the drumming of Williamson's sapsuckers. Cassin, Cooper, Abert, Clayton, Wilson, Williamson, and so many more: though long gone they live by having had their names attached to species that survive — and will survive, we hope, for a very long time. Their discoveries were made at a time when life in the wild was not easy, and some gave their lives in the search for a fuller knowledge of living things. They deserve to be remembered, and we resolve to remember them.

Now, as I write this in winter, the world is stripped of much of its vitality. Rocks, snow, pines, dead herbs and grasses whipped by a bitter wind. But still those most elegant of birds are about, the Steller's jays: breast and tail blue as the late evening sky, back and head like the night sky, white streaks about their eyes giving them a roguish appearance that suits them well. Their crests are the longest of any of our birds, composed of feathers that can be erected or depressed to suit their moods. Unfortunately they are not musicians, but they do at least produce an interesting variety of sounds, some of them resembling the calls of red-tailed hawks. In the summer they eat a great many insects, but the benefits they perform are outweighed by their appetite for the eggs of other birds. In the winter they supplement a diet of pine seeds with whatever scraps they can find, and they are regular visitors to our feeders. So adaptable are they that they thrive all the way from Alaska to Guatemala, but always in forested mountain country. Ornithologist Elliott Coues described them well: "a tough, wiry, independent creature, with sense enough to take precious good care of himself." Out our window, last fall, we saw a sharp-skinned hawk trying to catch a Steller's jay in a Douglas fir. The jay hopped about where the branches were thickest, rather than taking wing, where he would surely have been caught. The hawk left without a meal.

The jays are named for Georg Wilhelm Steller, who first discovered them in 1741. Steller was a German naturalist who was attached to a Russian expedition that left Kamchatka in two ships to explore the "Great Land" to the east, now called Alaska. It was headed by Vitus Bering (a Dane), for whom the Bering Sea is named. Steller discovered not only the jays but several other creatures that were later named for him: Steller's eagle, Steller's eider duck, and Steller's sea cow (now extinct). He found the jays during a landfall on Kayak Island (not far from present-day Valdez). He recognized them at once as relatives of the blue jays of eastern North America, which had been described a few years earlier. "This bird [he said] proved to me that we were really in America."

In fact Steller was able to spend only one day on the Alaska coast before Bering set sail for home. But they were busy hours, and resulted in the first scientific report on the plants and animals of Alaska. In the words of a biographer, "perhaps no other naturalist in history ever accomplished so monumental a task under such difficulties and in so little time." The return trip proved disastrous. Violent storms constantly drove the ships off course, and it was late November before they approached the Asiatic continent. In fact they did not make it, for they were shipwrecked on what is now called Bering Island. Bering died there, and most of the officers and crew were ill with scurvy. Remarkably, Steller and several others survived the winter and built a new ship from the remains of the old. They arrived safely in Kamchatka the following summer. But Steller was plagued with bad luck and died a few years later while wandering around Siberia, still finding plants and animals new to science. Fortunately his journals survived, so we may still share in his adventures. It is good to be reminded of him by so visible a bird.

Douglas firs dominate the view from three of the four sides of our house: stately, symmetrical trees, hung with shaggy cones, in winter decorated with globs of snow. To be sure, those that grow along the semiarid slopes of the Front Range cannot rival those of the humid Northwest. David Douglas, exploring Oregon Territory in 1825, was awed by these great trees; one that he measured was 227 feet tall and 48 feet in circumference. Our trees do not exceed 40 feet in height, though some in nearby ravines surpass 100. Douglas firs range all the way from British Columbia to northern Mexico, from sea level to (in the southern Rockies) over 10,000 feet, and from places with only 40 inches annual rainfall to places with well over 100. It would be difficult to find another tree adapted to such a broad range of circumstances. Douglas firs are tough in other ways. Over two hundred kinds of insects are known to attack them. Some of these are very destructive locally, particularly western spruce budworms and Douglas fir beetles. Some trees are killed, but others spring up to take their places. These are relatively fast-growing trees, but when well established they may live several hundred years.

Douglas firs are not really true firs, nor are they spruces, though they look superficially like both. The cones are very different: they are pendant, with bracts extending from between the scales. Each bract has a double end with a slender filament between: rather like the tail ends of tiny animals plunging into the cones to escape a hawk circling overhead. The scientific name, *Pseudotsuga taxifolia* (false hemlock with yew leaves!), reveals the puzzle the trees presented to early taxonomists. In the Northwest, these are timber trees of major importance; in fact they surpass all other tree species in the value of lumber produced. No one is likely to eye our trees for lumber. But as fuel, Douglas fir, along with ponderosa pine, keeps us twice warm, as the saying goes: once in the splitting and once in the burning.

David Douglas was not the first to discover the trees, but he was the first to send living material back to England, where the trees became important ornamentals. Douglas was born to a poor family in Scone, Scotland, in 1799. He was apprenticed as a youth to a gardener and showed so much talent that by the time he was 24 he had been hired by the Royal Horticultural Society of London as a field collector. The Society was actively involved in importing plants from many parts of the world to enrich British gardens.

Douglas's first trip was to New York and Ontario, with a side trip to Philadelphia, where he met Thomas Nuttall. On the next trip the Horticultural Society sent him, via Cape Horn, to join the Hudson's Bay Company's outposts on the Columbia River. As he roamed about the Northwest, and later California, he met with a variety of misadventures, but in spite of problems he collected specimens, seeds, and roots of many plants new to science. He was the discoverer of some of the Far West's most distinctive trees: sugar pine, western white pine, silver fir, Oregon white oak, and several others. The Northwest was then a land of dense forests of giant trees, peopled by Indians and by transplanted Europeans mainly involved in the fur trade. Douglas was a complex person, troubled by indecision and the fear of failure. One of his shortcomings was an inability to estimate altitudes. While crossing the Rockies, Douglas climbed Mt. Brown, which he thought to be about 16,000 feet, highest in the Rockies. It is now known to be 9,156 feet in elevation!

In a fit of pique, in 1833 Douglas resigned from the Horticultural Society and traveled to Hawaii where, at the age of thirty-four, he fell into a trap set to capture wild cattle and was trampled to death by a bull — a dismal end of a person said to have had more plants named in his honor than anyone else in the history of botany.

As soon as the snow is off the ground, or even before, Richardson's ground squirrels will be out in the meadows around us, restoring their burrows and going about the business of mating. The young will be born in May, when green vegetation is abundant and fresh. These are rodents of the high plains and mountain meadows, sometimes living as high as 12,000 feet elevation. Their alarm calls, a rapid series of high-pitched chirps, are as evocative of the high country as the croaks of ravens and the odors of sage.

These are not glamorous animals; they lack the beautiful tails of tree squirrels and the decorative stripes of chipmunks. But they are plentiful enough to insist on our attention, and like all animals they are exciting in their own way. They have scent glands on their backs which they use to mark the walls of the burrows and the undersides of bushes around their territories. When the young are about, the family members greet each other by "nuzzling." There are other scent glands on the head that produce a "friendly" odor, in contrast to that produced by the glands on the back. Individuals live several years, unless picked off by a hawk or a weasel — or squashed by a car. Females may occupy the same territory on successive years, and when they die may pass it on to a daughter. The damage they do to vegetation is negligible, though horsemen sometimes have unkind words to say about their burrows.

One of the surprising things about Richardson's ground squirrels is that they disappear so early in the season. Adult males disperse in early summer and are rarely seen after early July; most adult females have gone into hibernation by late July (if one can call it hibernation when so many warm days remain). The pups, however, remain active through much of August before curling up in the burrows for winter. It is important that the pups put on a layer of fat for the cold months ahead, and perhaps the early disappearance of the adults functions to leave more food for the young.

These ground squirrels were named for John Richardson, who discovered them in Saskatchewan in 1822. He had just returned from an expedition overland from Manitoba to the arctic coast, under the leadership of John Franklin. Both were officers in the British navy and had been commissioned to help define the Northwest Passage. Richardson was the physician and naturalist of the expedition, and a close friend of Franklin. The expedition achieved its goals but suffered greatly from cold and from shortage of food. For a period they lived on lichens, old shoes, and a boiled buffalo robe. Nevertheless Richardson persevered in collecting plants, animals, and minerals. A second expedition, in 1825–1827, was better equipped and surveyed a much greater length of the arctic coast; for several weeks Franklin and Richardson explored the coast separately.

In 1845 Franklin, then nearly sixty, undertook a third expedition, this one in two ships with 129 officers and crew. Richardson did not accompany Franklin, but a few years later he made an expedition of his own — in a vain attempt to rescue Franklin, who had never returned. It was eventually learned that his ships had been icebound for many months and all had perished, mainly from scurvy, in those days the scourge of all sailors a long way from fresh food. Richardson wrote of the third expedition that "they had forged the last link of the North West Passage with their lives."

Both Franklin and Richardson were knighted, but a more lasting tribute is to be found in the expeditions' legacy of plants and animals. There is a Franklin's ground squirrel as well as a Richardson's, and Richardson has also had several of the plants he collected named for him: Richardson's geranium (*Geranium richardsonii*) and rough alumroot (*Heuchera richardsonii*). Neither grows near our home, but closely related species of geranium and alumroot abound. Along with the ubiquitous ground squirrels, they will do to remind us of an explorer and naturalist who more than once risked his life in a noble cause.

Now and then, quite unpredictably, Clark's nutcrackers appear around our home in numbers, calling each other harshly from treetops. These are large, striking birds, mostly light gray but with black wings and tail broadly banded with white. Most of the time they live high in the mountains, close to treeline, but at times they seem afflicted with wanderlust and roam far from their breeding sites. Along Trail Ridge Road in Rocky Mountain National Park they can often be seen taking snacks from the tourists. Their usual food is pine seeds, which they collect by hammering cones apart with their powerful beaks. They breed very early in the season, often laying their eggs in March. Females have been seen incubating their eggs in snowstorms, with the temperature close to zero.

When pine seeds are ripe in the fall, nutcrackers collect them in great quantity and cache them for recovery during the winter and spring. The seeds are buried an inch or two deep, usually on cliff ledges or south-facing slopes. A single nutcracker may store as many as 50,000 pine seeds. Since they put only a few seeds in a cache, each bird must remember several thousand hiding places. Evidently they memorize large landmarks in the area as well as small landmarks close to the caches. They have even been seen uncovering caches under several feet of snow. It is estimated that it takes about ten thousand seeds to support a nutcracker from October to April — to say nothing of what may be required to feed the young. Even so, they bury many more seeds than they need; they must compensate for a considerable loss to rodents. When recovering seeds, they land at a selected spot, probe with their bill, then dig with sideswiping motions of the bill. When seeds are found, they are cracked open at the site and eaten or carried back to the nest in a pouch beneath the tongue.

We are sorry we don't see more of Clark's nutcrackers at Glacier View. Winter days are often cold enough at 7,800 feet; we can only wonder at their ability to survive and rear their families so much higher in the mountains.

These unusual birds were fittingly named for a remarkable man: William Clark. He and Meriwether Lewis became acquainted during the Indian wars, when they both served under "Mad Anthony" Wayne. When Thomas Jefferson purchased Louisiana Territory from Napoleon in 1803, he selected these two to head an expedition with the object of "exploring the Missouri and whatever river, heading into that, leads to the western ocean." Neither Lewis nor Clark had much formal education, but Jefferson arranged for a "crash course" in botany, zoology, medicine, and navigation for Lewis, then his secretary. In the course of the expedition, now a classic of American history, Clark quickly learned to be a superb geographer as well as an accurate observer of the environment through which he passed. His and Lewis's descriptions of the plants and animals they saw and collected were often so detailed that they can be easily recognized. However, it remained for other, better trained biologists to supply formal names and descriptions for the plants and animals they recorded. In his book *Lewis and Clark: Pioneer Naturalists*, Paul Russell Cutright has dutifully compiled a list of the biological discoveries of the expedition, covering forty-seven pages and including many species that were named for the two leaders.

It was on August 22, 1804, while crossing what is now Idaho, that Clark noted "a bird of the woodpecker kind which fed on Pine burs. Its bill and tail white the wings black . . . about the size of a robin." That he called it a woodpecker is not surprising, since the flight is undulating and the huge bill suggestive of a woodpecker. Specimens were collected and eventually found their way to pioneer ornithologist Alexander Wilson, who figured the bird in his *American Ornithology* in 1811, appropriately on the same plate with Lewis's woodpecker. Wilson called it "Clark's crow," a more suitable name since it is a member of the crow family.

It would take many pages to do justice to the discoveries of the Lewis and Clark expedition. Two genera of plants were named for them: *Lewisia* became the generic name of the bitterroot, or rock rose, the roots of which served the Indians as food (now the state flower of Montana); *Clarkia* came to be applied to another showy, pink flower, often called ragged robin (a member of the evening primrose family). Among the species named for the explorers were the cutthroat trout, named *Salmo clarkii* by Sir John Richardson, and the common blue flax of the Rockies, named *Linum lewisii* by Frederick Pursh. Sometimes others were credited with their discoveries. Lewis was the first to discover the poorwill, a bird that calls from the valley below our house on warm summer nights. He found a poorwill that appeared torpid, as if hibernating (in October, in the Dakotas). This was a novel discovery; in fact poorwills are one of the very few birds that do hibernate. But Audubon elected to name it *Caprimulgus nuttallii*, after Thomas Nuttall, a later "discoverer." Nevertheless, there are plenty of plants and animals around to remind us of Lewis and Clark — and of course Nuttall, too, is worth remembering.

To persons attuned to nature, there are few dramas more rewarding than the sequence of wildflowers that through the spring and summer spring from the ground, often in the most unlikely places. Can anything compare to the sight of the first yellow violets blooming along a woodland path? These most fragile of plants are yet hardy enough to bloom when nights are still frosty and snow still lingers in the ravines. Hereabouts, yellow violets (*Viola nuttalli*) appear in May, when (as our wildflower guide puts it) "crows are incubating, wood ducks beginning to nest." Despite their lack of odor, violets have a quiet charm and a distinctive flower shape that is theirs alone. In fact they need no odor, as they are self-fertile and have no need to attract bees. The violet's showy flowers rarely set seed; instead, inconspicuous flowers close to the ground that do not open are the ones that produce the seeds. Violets are edible plants, used by some tribes of Indians as greens and by early settlers for thickening soups or making violet tea. We may try them some day, though it seems a shame to pick such delicate plants. Violets are major food plants for the caterpillars of several of our local fritillary butterflies; perhaps we had best leave them for the butterflies.

It was Frederick Pursh who named these plants after Nuttall. Pursh had been hired to describe and name the plants collected on the Lewis and Clark expedition, and he also had access to many of the plants collected by Nuttall. Pursh came to regard the specimens as his personal property, and he carried them off to London. Said Nuttall of him: "It was not surely honorable to snatch from me the little imaginary credit due my enthusiastic researches made at the most imminent risk of personal safety." But Pursh got his comeuppance. Bitterbrush (*Purshia*) was named for him, as well as *Astragalus purshii* (a locoweed!).

Thomas Nuttall seems to have packed several lifetimes into one. Born in England in 1786 and devoted to natural history since childhood, he emigrated to Philadelphia when he was twenty-two and determined to spend his life exploring the plants of the New World. Although he had little training, he was employed by Dr. Benjamin Barton, author of the first American textbook of botany, to collect plants in the Northwest. Here he joined Astor's American Fur Company and traveled up the Missouri River, returning by way of New Orleans. He traveled in the wilds unarmed and was lost several times. Washington Irving said of him (in *Astoria*): "Delighted with the treasures, he went groping and stumbling along among a wilderness of sweets, forgetful of everything but his immediate pursuit. The Canadian voyageurs used to make merry at his expense, regarding him as some whimsical kind of madman."

Back in Philadelphia and disappointed that he was not asked to join Stephen Long's expedition of 1819–1820 to the Rocky Mountains, Nuttall set off on his own for the Arkansas River, where he collected many new plants despite a variety of adventures with the Indians. Soon afterward he was appointed instructor in natural history at Harvard, a position in which he flourished despite his lack of an academic background. After a decade at Harvard, he was off again to the West, this time teaming up with John Kirk Townsend and traveling all the way to the Pacific Northwest and later to California. (This was several years after Douglas's trip to these same regions.) One of his former Harvard students, Richard Henry Dana, found Nuttall on a California beach stuffing shells into his bulging pockets, an event recorded in his classic *Two Years Before the Mast*. Nuttall took passage on Dana's ship, returning east via Cape Horn. At the age of fifty-six he retired to England.

On their grand tour of the Far West, Townsend wrote of him: "Throughout the whole of our long journey, I have had constantly to admire the ardor and perfect indefatigability with which he has devoted himself to the grand object of his tour. No difficulty, no danger, no fatigue has ever daunted him."

Nuttall provided formal descriptions and names for many important plants, including western larch, Oregon ash, Rocky Mountain iris, and many others. And many were named for him besides the yellow violet. *Cornus nuttalli*, a dogwood, was named by none other than John James Audubon. Audubon was, of course, not a botanist, but in his painting of the band-tailed pigeon he included the food plant, which he named for his good friend Thomas Nuttall. Townsend reported in his journal that when his supply of quinine was exhausted, he treated several Indians who were ill with fever with an extract of the bark of this dogwood. Evidently it was effective.

A good many creatures other than plants also bear Nuttall's name: Nuttall's woodpecker, Nuttall's warbler, and of course the poorwill. As I write this a cottontail rabbit is sitting on the rocks outside staring in the window: *Sylvilagus nuttallii.* I can scarcely expect a more insistent reminder of a naturalist with whom I would have enjoyed a few weeks in the field—though I am sure he would have left me exhausted!

The prolonged melody of the Townsend's solitaire evokes wild mountain forests: a flute obbligato to the wind in the pines and firs. Solitaire: a word for hermit, a being that is self-sufficient and in little need of companionship. Solitaires, indeed, are rarely to be seen in flocks, and they disdain our feeders, surviving the winter perfectly well on juniper berries and the like. Not really beautiful birds except in song: gray, with a white eye ring, a dash of buff on the wings and of white on the tail. However, the young, after they leave the nest, are striking birds, completely covered with white polka dots, as if ready for a masquerade ball. When we first saw one we rushed to our bird guide, thinking we had spotted a stray from some other continent.

In the summer, males perch on the tops of tall trees, defending their nesting territories by pouring song over the hills. These are among the few birds that sing at almost any time of year. But in the fall and winter the songs are a bit more subdued, and in fact are produced mainly by the females, which have established feeding territories where there are good sources of winter food. Male and female solitaires look alike—in contrast to their relatives the bluebirds—and along with the similarity in color goes an almost equal vocal proficiency, though the songs differ in function according to the season. Like true hermits, solitaires go their own way, individualists in every sense.

John Kirk Townsend discovered the solitaire in 1836 while trekking through Wyoming. In his journal he remarked that he had found "a beautiful new species of mocking bird." Indeed, solitaires do resemble mockingbirds in many ways, although they are thrushes. Solitaires were only one of many novelties collected by Townsend in his travels in the Northwest. Others included Townsend's warbler, Townsend's big-eared bat, Townsend's ground squirrel, and the white-tailed jackrabbit

(*Lepus townsendii*). He was also the discoverer of the lark bunting, now the state bird of Colorado.

Townsend was a Philadelphia Quaker, trained in medicine but from youth fascinated by birds. When he was in his twenties he had an opportunity to join an expedition to the Columbia River, led by Nathaniel Wyeth (for whom the dwarf sunflower, *Wyethia*, was named). His companion Thomas Nuttall collected plants while Townsend concentrated on birds, mammals, and reptiles. (Nuttall named the common easter daisy of the Rockies *Townsendia grandiflora* as a tribute to the man with whom he had shared so many adventures.) Townsend's *Narrative of a Journey Across the Rocky Mountains to the Columbia River* tells of some of these adventures. He collected his snakes and lizards in whisky, the only readily available preservative. But the tailor of the expedition, named Thornburg, had a great thirst for "ardent spirits." One day Townsend was away collecting, and when he returned he found that Thornburg "had decanted the liquor from the precious reptiles which I had destined for immortality, and he . . . had been 'happy' upon it for a whole day." These specimens did not survive, but Townsend brought back a great many others. They were studied by (among others) Audubon, who duly included them in his monumental volumes on birds and mammals.

To be sure, a living thing is more than a name. But names are what we use to call forth the essence of what they are, and often something of the history of their discovery. "What is nature," asked Thoreau, "unless there is an eventful human life passing within her?" We enjoy our Clark's nutcrackers, our Richardson's ground squirrels, our *Viola nuttalli* for themselves and as part of a vast interconnected web of living things of which we, too, are a part. We enjoy them more for having found, in their names, a clue to their initial impingement on the human endeavor. It may not matter to a Steller's jay that his kind was discovered on the Alaska coast by a German naturalist who perished a few years later in the wilds of Siberia. But to us it makes the jays that much more worthy of our attention and admiration. May they continue to thrive; and may the memory of Steller, Douglas, Townsend, and the other pioneer naturalists endure as long as there are people who find joy in their discoveries.

Ann Zwinger

A World of Infinite Variety

I find myself in the midst of an index to the letters of John Xantus, written from Baja California where he was a tidal observer for the U.S. Coast Survey between 1859 and 1861, to Spencer F. Baird at the Smithsonian, for whom he collected. Xantus, a Hungarian, fled the 1848 revolution in his country and ended up in the United States Army, as unsympathetic a profession for this well-educated, thin-skinned, arrogant personality as one could imagine. Fortunately, through a combination of being in the right place at the right time and his knowledge of natural history, he came to be a collector for Baird, then Assistant Secretary of the Smithsonian, who was interested in building an unparalleled collection for the United States Museum of Natural History.

Unlike modern specialist collectors, Xantus snagged specimens from ocean to mountain, finny as well as feathered, four-legged hoppers, six-legged crawlers, eight-legged lurkers, flutterers and slinkers, as well as plants, minerals, and fossils. His letters record the breadth of his collecting activities, and the index reflects, in truncated form, that exhilarating variety. The index begins with Abalone and ends with *Zonotrichia*. Gila River comes before Gill, Theodore; three lights of the nineteenth-century natural history world are cheek by jowl in the index: George Lawrence, John LeConte, and Joseph Leidy; Ophurian comes before Oregon and Orioles; Rattlesnake precedes the schooner *Raymond*; the Smithsonian Institution follows Captain Charles B. Smith; and toward the end it's Whalers, Whimbrels, Whipsnakes, and Whistling-ducks.

The range of entries, characteristic of Xantus's activities, is also the range characteristic of the breadth of natural history. Where else can one range so widely and wander so happily into archaeology and anthropology, biology and botany, geology and history, taxonomy and zoology? And that only skims the surface of the subjects in my note cards. Which is precisely what makes natural history the far-ranging, fascinating discipline that it is for its practitioners — those batty people who like to tie together yesterday and tomorrow within the framework of today's natural world in which man walks, crab scuttles, lizard leaps, jack rabbit bounds, and beetle trundles.

It is impossible to write natural history without getting involved in history history, and especially so in a book of historical letters. Through Xantus's descriptive carping but observant letters, I have stepped back in time and space and come to walk in a natural world that I can never otherwise have known.

No wonder he bridled whenever Baird praised other collectors; Xantus was an alien in an alien world, and collecting was his definition of self. No wonder he never missed carping about an expense—he was nearly penniless because of penurious Coast Survey practices and the Smithsonian's own close-to-the-vest financing. No wonder his natural acquisitiveness endlessly found new species—not only was the nineteenth century a time of splitting rather than lumping, but there were so many new species to be named. To be credited with discovering a new species, or even more wonderful, to have one named after you, was a ticket to immortality.

A few years ago, when I stood on the beach at Cape San Lucas where Xantus had mounted his tidal gauge, it was not hard to imagine myself back in the nineteenth century. It was not difficult at all to read away the thin veneer of civilization that modern-day tourist-oriented Cabo San Lucas sports, and even less difficult when one gets away from the populated fringe back into the countryside on some of the remote ranches. I stepped back to 1860 and smelled the endless heat in July, watched the same vultures soar in the cool upper air, watched the same lizards scatter between bushes and the same kestrels peer, sharp-eyed and hungry, from the spire of a cardon cactus.

Another carryover is the collector's instinct. While ornithologists no longer go around shooting at everything that flies to get a specimen, as they did in Xantus's day, netting insects and pressing plants is still a very current concern of entomologists and botanists. An amateur in both, I respond to Xantus's enthusiasm when he first netted fish out of San Lucas Bay: "The first time I tried my large seine, we capture about 3000 pounds in a few pulls, and my heart bursted nearly when I had to throw them away, so beautiful they were." I felt the same way when I first saw a king angelfish and a Moorish idol.

The mid-nineteenth century was a prime time for naturalists in the United States. By that time, any city of any size was opening its own natural science institutions and building up its collections, from the New York Lyceum for Natural History on the East Coast to The California Academy of Sciences on the West. There was a wonderfully chaotic expansiveness about those early natural history societies, a sense of discovery around every corner that I, as a child of the twentieth century, rather envy.

Most naturalists of the time were generalists, fascinated by stars and starfish, *Chelonius* and *Chaenactis*, Gila monsters and *Gilia*, enthralled by lepidoptera and *Lepidium*, ponderosa and *Pondetaria*, and whether you can make a silk purse out of a pig's ear as someone at the Academy of Natural Sciences of Philadelphia did. Dr. Elliott Coues may have been an ornithologist but he wrote definitively on mammals. Baird was primarily a mammalogist but wrote up the birds *and* the reptiles for the Pacific Railroad Reports.

The spontaneity and diversity of these institutions is fascinating. They are not only interesting in themselves, but several were the forerunners of more sophisticated educational institutions such as The California Academy and The American Museum of Natural History.

Among the most venerable of the early natural history associations was The Academy of Natural Sciences in Philadelphia, an august body into which John Xantus was inducted on the strength of his collection of flora and fauna from Fort Tejon, California.

The Academy's early *Proceedings* are handsome leather-bound volumes complete with marbled end papers. In the very first volume, March–April 1841, with the president "in the Chair," the Academy acknowledged contributions received and papers given, and presented a treasurer's report — unique in that there was not a single figure given. That year the Academy received from contributors, and gave papers on, everything from owls, sugar cane, and the micaceous oxides of iron, to shells taken at 75 fathoms off the coast of Maine as well as off the coast of West Africa.

Two hippopotamus skulls were logged in, and William Gambel, after whom our delightful western quail is named, contributed a grebe. One paper compared old soil from the Nile Valley, dug three feet above the river, with newly laid sediments — an item which might be of interest to present-day ecologists since the Nile no longer floods below the Aswan Dam.

The wonderful variety of interests continued. Sixteen years later, in 1857, the Academy published a list of its members, italicizing the names of those who had passed on to the greater Academy in the sky — in other words, once a member always a member (like the Cook County voting list). There are over 350 names in that membership list, and included are some of the most prestigious naturalists and scientists of the day: Spencer F. Baird, then Assistant Secretary of the Smithsonian Institution and a life member of the Academy; Dr. Joseph Leidy, the great paleontologist; John L. LeConte, who wrote up the innumerable species of coleoptera coming into the Academy; and John Cassin, a successful publisher who catalogued the 26,000 birds in the collection of the Academy and wrote widely on taxonomy—in his spare time. Among those who sent him birds was John Xantus.

Also members of the Academy were many military men and members of major surveys. In addition to their duties, the Pacific Railroad Survey and Boundary Survey teams collected plants and animals. Baird exhorted the many surgeons at Western posts to "collect, collect, collect." These surgeons had an almost unlimited resource of enlisted men for various jobs and produced very well-prepared specimens. Dr. Elliot Coues contributed impressively in Western ornithology, as well as mammalogy and history. Dr. William Hammond, stationed with the United States Army at Fort Riley, Missouri (during the Civil War he gave distinguished service as Surgeon General of the United States), sent forty species of reptiles from that area. He was later immortalized in Hammond's flycatcher, a new species taken by his protégé, John Xantus, while he was stationed with the Army in California.

The Academy extended its member resource through a list of "Correspondents," outlanders which included such drop-dead names as John James Audubon and Thomas Jefferson. There were Correspondents from England and Brazil, Argentina and Sweden, Germany and Italy, including Alfred Malherbe of France and William M'Gillivray of Edinburgh. M. Malherbe wrote a distinguished treatise on woodpeckers, and Mr. M'Gillivray's name is associated with a charming warbler. The list even includes such foreigners as those living in New York and Maine.

In that same year of 1857 the Academy's *Proceedings* noted that Dr. A. Heermann sent thirty new species of reptiles from Texas; Heermann is better known for the somber-plumaged Heermann's gull. The Academy welcomed a collection of plants from lichenologist Tuckerman, a name familiar to hikers of Mt. Washington.

The 1857 volume is elegantly illustrated "on stone by Wm E. Hitchcock," and these lithographs, on heavy paper, carefully printed, distinguish many natural history publications, a thread which runs felicitously through much natural history publishing. This year's [1986] recipient of the John Burroughs Medal for Natural History Writing, *Gathering the Desert*, is as handsomely illustrated as it is written.

Early scientific illustrators were unparalleled for their portrayals of detail and their understanding of the natural world. For a wonderful afternoon, spend it looking at the illustrations in the Pacific Railroad Surveys. They are of the highest quality—exquisite, precise, and informative.

Because the Academy was so well-known, it drew contributions like a magnet. A single year suffices to show the range of scholarly and descriptive papers. In 1856 Dr. Leidy produced papers on topics ranging from tapeworms to extinct mammals, fish, and reptiles. Dr. Charles Girard, who assisted Baird at the Smithsonian, gave four papers on West Coast fish, and Edward Hallowell seven on reptiles. Robert Kennicott, who would become one of Baird's most famous collectors, described a new snake from Illinois. Lieutenant Beale described the first crossing of the American desert with the Camel Corps and recommended the beasts highly for their performance and weight-carrying ability (the Civil War and the ensuing railroads terminated this practical venture in cross-country transportation).

Also included in the 1856 *Proceedings* is a paper by a gentleman from Indiana, Rufus Haymond, who sent in a collection of and wrote a paper on "Birds of Southern Indiana." Another Haymond wrote on bats. Since I grew up in Indiana, the daughter of William T. Haymond, I felt a warm albeit tenuous connection with the Academy through one of their far-flung correspondents.

Although the Pacific Railroad Survey Reports were within the purview of the Smithsonian, Assistant Secretary Baird maintained close ties with the Philadelphia Academy. In their *Proceedings* he published the initial reports of many of the findings that would later be worked up in the larger, more definitive Smithsonian reports. For example, Baird published the first list of new species of North American mammals collected by Major W. H. Emory on the United States-Mexican Boundary Survey in the Academy *Proceedings* of 1857.

In the main, the important natural history associations were East Coast institutions. Besides the New York Lyceum there was the Boston Society of Natural History. Thomas Brewer was associated with the latter, and collectors all over the country, like Xantus, learned to collect eggs and nests, to blow, package, and ship them to him as he prepared a monumental publication of Oölogy for the Smithsonian—a publication, alas, that was never finished for the oldest publishing reason in the world: the plates cost too much.

I have the impression that in order to be encyclopedic these societies accepted, higgledy-piggledy, objects ranging from the bizarre to the sublime and the important to the ridiculous. One year the Boston Society of Natural History logged in everything from the "dried and inflated lungs of a snapping-turtle, and a frog intermediate between the imperfect and perfect animal" plus "two teeth of the sperm whale" along with a noddy tern, a gecko egg, and a section of an elephant's tusk with a musket-ball imbedded in it!

Natural historians have been known to express themselves quite pungently. The son of the president of the Boston Society, William Greene Binney, migrated West from the sedate halls of Boston. He later published a natural history journal and wrote a definitive treatise on land snails (he named *Bulimulus xantusi* after a specimen collected by Xantus near Cabo San Lucas). As an editor he was evidently plagued by a Mr. Orcutt who sent him minuscule shells to be identified. After what must have been a particularly exasperating incursion on his time and energies, Binney wrote one of my favorite paragraphs:

> The San Diego Pupa does not seem to me arizonensis, and I cannot spare eyes to determine it. In my books are enlarged views of the described species of Pupa, by means of which and a pocket lens you can readily make this out. I detest Pupa and Succinea above all things Conchological. I give you a camera lucida drawing of the outline of your shell—the aperture was still unfinished when the tube of my microscope slid down on the shell and smashed it, much to my delight.

The California Academy of Sciences was founded April 4, 1853. Unlike the Academy of Philadelphia's imposing and proper *Proceedings*, their first publication is a scant three-eighths inch thick, bound in paper—they've made up for any difference between the two institutions in the magnificence of their current museum and superb library.

There were only fifty-seven members in 1857 and, in true Western hospitality, the membership included men from all over the United States and Mexico—from Boston, Cambridge, Philadelphia, and New York—and included Louis Agassiz, Spencer Baird, Dr. Charles Girard, John Torrey, and Dr. Asa Gray, the most prominent botanists in the United States, and Theodore Gill, a felicitously named Smithsonian employee who wrote widely on fish, among them those that Xantus collected in Baja California. Alexander Bache, then head of the U.S. Coast Survey, was a member. Some members of the Academy served as tidal observers for the Survey on the West Coast.

There were forty-one resident members, among them William Gabb of the California Geological Survey, John Cooper who founded the Cooper Ornithological Society, and Dr. John B. Trask who went West with Audubon's son and became curator of the Academy's geology and mineralogy collections, and eventually its president.

In 1857 they discussed the boracic acid in Pacific sea water and published drawings and descriptions of new plants such as *Fritillaria*, *Abies*, *Ledum*, and *Penstemon* with the appropriate engraved illustrations.

At the annual meeting in 1864 there were fifteen members present. The financial report indicated that $815.35 was received from various sources, and that expenditures were $903.75, ending the year with $52.82 in the treasury, an expense sheet a modern natural history society might view with disbelief. Such modest expenses took their toll. Although fifty books and three hundred shell species were added, other collections remained static. The botany acquisitions were noted, but the collections were deemed "not in good condition for want of suitable cases." Things had not improved in five years. In 1859, when he was in San Francisco learning how to run the tide gauge before shipping out to Cabo San Lucas, Xantus noted that the Academy was

in a deplorable condition, they have only 11 . . . members, and each of them has to pay about $300 a year to defray the expenses of the society. Their once beautiful collection is entirely eaten up by the miriads of mice & rats, they even destroyed the labels of all the Rocks & fossil.

At their meeting of July 3, 1865, only eight members were present, but what members! Dr. John Torrey, Robert Kennicott, W. H. Dall (Baird's biographer), and Horace Mann made up half the group. The minutes closed with this quintessential natural history line:

This evening, at 7 o'clock, a magnificent rainbow was observed, the colors of which were unusually vivid.

Many early natural scientists were medical doctors, although many of them never practiced medicine. At that time a medical education was the best and in some cases the only scientific education available. Although they may have had special fields of interest, they tended to be competent in many, with a curiosity fired by all the unfamiliar species turning up in the newly opened West. By default they were primarily collectors and namers, and it is no accident that the names of so many familiar species in the West are those of these gentlemen who often found, studied, and identified the species.

Most maintained a faithful correspondence with each other. Spencer Baird estimated that one year he wrote three thousand letters. Longhand. Edwin Way Teale, in the Foreword to *The American Seasons*, when asked what naturalists do, replied with some spirit and perhaps a little exasperation, "They write *letters!*" As Joseph Kastner, in *A Species of Eternity*, described naturalists of the previous century in Europe:

> The world . . . was a small place and every prominent person knew all the others. Naturalists who never laid eyes on each other became intimate friends by virtue of the long and faithful letters they wrote to each other, year in and year out, until death ended their exchanges.

Quite obviously, being an old-fashioned naturalist involved energy, devotion, and enthusiasm. One followed the naturalist's path for the love of doing and the joy of learning, not for the profit. As an avocation, it enriched without impinging on the necessities of making a living. It provided intellectual challenges and aesthetic pleasures and pleasant friendships.

The picture, rightly or wrongly, that I have of old-fashioned naturalists is tinged with dilettanteism, of professionally amateur status. There is good reason that Jacob Bronowski called it "that quaint Victorian profession." Compared to the professions that are taken more seriously, a naturalist is rather a dabbler. Naturalists are wanderers and wonderers, and perhaps there is not time for that in the highly paced world in which we live.

Just when I felt comfortably ensconced in the long naturalist tradition that goes back to Aristotle and was happily following my avocation of nature writer, I got a nasty turn. Edwin Way Teale, the epitome of the old-fashioned naturalist, gave me a biography of William Beebe. Beebe was a scientist at The American Museum of Natural History and a prolific and well-known natural history writer.

His biographer, Robert Welker, found that natural science was fast becoming obsolete, and its practitioners with it. Welker felt that there was no longer room for a botanist or an entomologist, a limnologist or an ecologist in the research team concept in large universities and museums. He concluded:

> And of all such people, the naturalist is surely the oddest, a figure not merely old-fashioned but antique. A naturalist studies nothing less than the living world, perhaps out of love for it; and for such a man or woman, where is there a meaningful place?

I can cope with allergies and absent-mindedness, but to be an anachronism is too much. Was there no space for the naturalist's profession in a fast-moving, computerized, scientific world? I felt like an endangered species. Had I become the wafting cranefly, left behind on the evolutionary ladder, to be replaced by the lethally efficient assassin fly?

I began looking about in some desperation for others of my ilk. I expected to find, and did, that in the expanding frontiers of science, more and more scientists pursue more and more esoteric and restricted lines of research. As research becomes narrower, so the language becomes more and more precise. Oftentimes such scientists can speak to and be understood by only the few others in their field. This focusing down may be a necessary prerequisite for the kind of solid scientific knowledge upon which our continued existence as a viable genus depends, and this work may hold for the specialist the same joys and challenges as that of being a generalist naturalist holds for me, but their communication with an interested public, one of the glories of natural history, is limited. One of the things natural historians have done over the decades is to put into words an appreciation of the natural world and by so doing, lead others to care.

Fortunately, I also got some good news. Dr. Kenneth Norris is a Professor of Natural History at the University of California at Santa Cruz. Walking out in the desert, looking for the little night lizard *Xantusia vigilis*, we talked about the naturalist's trade. Dr. Norris considers himself first a naturalist, then a herpetologist (which he was) or a geologist (with his brother he did a definitive paper on the Algodones Dunes in California) or a mammalogist (which he is), a point of view more typical of a naturalist-generalist thinker who looks for big connections than a researcher (which he also is). He later wrote:

> By the way naturalists are definitely not extinct. People in my

field keep realizing, sometimes with a kind of surprise, that eye-to-eye contact with nature is the truest of experiences, and the simplest way to understand. I noted recently that people studying ultra high pressure phenomena, such as occur in the core of the earth, do so through pressure vises whose jaws are diamonds through which they can see that which they squeeze.

And imagine my delight when I discovered that there actually were courses in "Natural History" at respected colleges like Carleton College, where students get up at the crack of dawn to go look at birds and limestone cliffs and ponder what is growing there and why, who competently discuss soil development on alluvial fans in the Mojave deserts and how that correlates with the plants that grow there, and why the horned lark is singing in springtime by the third creosote bush from the right and where to look for algae on a quartz pebble.

I find this downright exhilarating because in my bones I feel there is a place for the old-fashioned naturalist in today's world. Whether these students become economists or diplomats, musicians or historians, they have discovered something that will give them sustenance and pleasure for the rest of their lives. And that is precisely what a college *should* teach: what to do with your tomorrows.

As I finger through page proofs and deal with Xantus's archaic nomenclature and his peregrinations through a place I know and love, it is with a comforting sense of connection. I index *Hylocharis xanti*, the white-eared hummingbird George Lawrence named after Xantus, and the tiny leaf-toed gecko, *Phyllodactylus xantii*, with an appreciation for Xantus's contribution to natural history, keenly aware that for the naturalist there is always something to be interested in: the tiny crab that hangs by one claw on the side of a tide pool, swaying with the gentle currents of tide out and tide in; the bouquets of pink *Malacothrix xantii* blooming across the sea cliffs.

It is no leap of the imagination but a personal reality to walk the same shores and watch the Sally Lightfoots scuttle out of sight like lightning, to delight in the brilliant origami-like tide-pool fish, to listen to the empty landsnail crunch under foot in a cool arroyo, to inhale the spicy odor of elephant tree bark and taste the frolicking freshness of sea air.

Xantus found a reason for living in the formal patterns of cactus spines, in the way in which a darkling beetle left parenthetical tracks in the sand. For him, as for me over a hundred years later, as for any naturalist, there is the joy of discovery and the sense of wonder. Xantus's specimens range from *Aphelocoma* to *Xanthodes xantusii* and come to imbue the index with a life of its own as a witness to a world of infinite variety and richness, of proven sense and reassuring order — the world of an old-fashioned naturalist.

Edward Hoagland

In Praise of John Muir

We must go halfway with John Muir. He was more of an explorer than a writer, more confident of his abilities in botany and geology than of what he could do with the eagle-quill pens he liked to use, while encouraging a friend's year-old baby to scramble about the floor, lending liveliness to the tedium of a writer's room. He was a student of glaciers, cloud shapes and skyscapes—a lover of Sitka spruce one hundred and fifty feet tall, of big sequoias, tiny woods orchids and great waterfalls. He put together his books late in life—he was fifty-six before *The Mountains of California*, his first book, was published—from magazine articles, most of which had themselves been reconstructed well after the events described, from notes jotted down in the field with wildfire enthusiasm but little thought of eventually publishing them. Though he was a wonderful talker, he was never entirely respectful of the written word and was surprised to find that there was an audience willing to read him, amazed he could earn a living by writing. Being one of those people "who give the freest and most buoyant portion of their lives to climbing and seeing for themselves," he wished more of his readers preferred to hike on their own two feet into the fastnesses he had described.

Henry David Thoreau lived to write, but Muir lived to hike. "I will touch naked God," he wrote once, while glacier-climbing. And, on another jaunt, lunching on his customary dry crust of bread: "To dine with a glacier on a sunny day is a glorious thing and makes common feasts of meat and wine ridiculous. The glacier eats hills and sunbeams." Although he lacked the coherent artistic passion of a professional writer, he was Emersonianism personified. There is a time-freeze, a time-warp to a river of ice, as if God had been caught still alive, in the act and at work. And because Muir's passions were religious and political instead of artistic, Muir, unlike Thoreau—who in comfortable Concord only speculated that his Transcendental intuitions were right—put his life and his legs on the line in continual tests of faith in the arduous wilderness of the High Sierras. He believed that if his intuitions were wrong, he would fall, but he didn't ask himself many questions about what was happening, as Thoreau would have, and didn't believe that such exalted experiences could be conveyed to the page, anyway.

Thoreau welded together one of the enduring prose styles of the nineteenth century. He may be America's paramount stylist, and also established in his spare time a famously disobedient stance toward the institutionalized cruelties of the world that later was to help Gandhi and, through Gandhi, Martin Luther King in formulating mass-movement nonviolent campaigns, before dying at only forty-four, in 1862. Of course, in addition he was what we would call a conservationist, but not a militant, innovative one, like Muir. Muir (1838–1914) was the founding president of the Sierra Club and chief protector of Yosemite Park. Thoreau, on the other hand, anathematized American imperial conduct in the Mexican War and got still more exercised about slavery, angrily championing the early "terrorist" John Brown. Muir—who was all in all a more conventional soul in his politics—even after the end of the Civil War commented approvingly during a trek through Georgia that "the Negroes here have been well-trained and are extremely polite. When they come in sight of a white man on the road, off go their hats, even at a distance of forty to fifty yards, and they walk bare-headed until he is out of sight."

It's important to recognize that such contrasts were not merely due to the fact that Muir was born twenty-one years after Thoreau and thus lived through the ambiguities of Reconstruction. Thoreau sought out the company of Indians on his trips to Maine and respectfully studied their customs, whereas Muir generally disparaged the Indians of California as ignoramuses and children, dirty and cultureless wretches. Not until his adventurous travels to Alaska in middle age—three trips during his forties, two in his fifties, and one tour to the Bering Sea by steamer at sixty-one—did he admit a semblance of tolerance into his view of Indians. And though as a conservationist he was highly "advanced," a Vermonter named George Perkins Marsh, born back in 1801, proves to have sounded as modernist a tocsin as Muir's in a widely read book called *Man and Nature*, which came out in 1864. Thirty years before *The Mountains of California*, Marsh counterposed to the Biblical theory that Nature was a wilderness which mankind should "subdue and rule" the idea that "Man has too long forgotten that the earth was given to him for usufruct alone, not for consumption, still less for profligate waste . . . We are, even now, breaking up the floor and wainscoting and doors and window frames of our dwelling . . . The earth is fast becoming an unfit home for its noblest inhabitant, and another era of equal human crime and human improvidence . . . would reduce it to such a condition of impoverished productiveness . . . as to threaten the depravation, barbarism, and perhaps even extinction of the species."

Marsh was a complex personality who served four terms in Congress and twenty years as U.S. Ambassador to Italy, but he was a quiet visionary and public servant in the style of a New England Brahmin — not a public figure, not the man of mounting celebrity that Muir became. Muir as lecturer, as Westerner, as "John o' the Mountains," learned, like Walt Whitman and Longfellow, to wear a public sort of beard. Living to the ripe old age of seventy-six, he enjoyed three active decades that were denied to Thoreau, and changed a good deal during the course of them. Although a far "wilder" naturalist, he had lived nearly as celibately as Thoreau for nearly as long. However, with no undue enthusiasm, he did marry, a week short of being forty-two. He then had two daughters — whom he deeply loved — and turned himself into a substantial, successful landowner and grape-farmer as well as a well-known writer and a force to be reckoned with in Sacramento and occasionally in Washington, D.C. International lecture tours, friendship with Teddy Roosevelt, honorary degrees from Harvard and Yale — in these extra years he knew rewards that Thoreau had never aspired to, yet remained an adventurer to the end, traveling to Africa, South America and Asia late in life. Only Jack London and John James Audubon among American artists come to mind as adventurers with a spirit to compare with his, and for both of them adventuring was more closely tied to ambition.

Thoreau, less and less a thinker and more and more a naturalist after he turned forty, was also changing in personality before he died. Supporting himself as a professional surveyor and by reorganizing his family's pencil business, he was making elaborate mathematical calculations in his journal and sending zoological specimens to Louis Agassiz. But though he didn't know it, he was already on the point of winning a considerable readership. Being in a small way a professional lecturer too, he might have capitalized on that development eventually, just as Muir did. In his last year he traveled to Minnesota to try to repair his health; and with the love that he felt for the big woods of Maine, he might well have given up his previous insistence that it was enough to have "traveled a good deal in Concord," if he'd lived on. Perhaps his best work was behind him, but there would have been some interesting darkening of the tints and rounding of the details, if he had blossomed as a generalist and an essayist again.

It's doubtful, nevertheless, that Thoreau, given another thirty years, would have become as touching an individual as Muir. He was always a less personal man — less vulnerable, vociferous, strenuous, emotional. He would never have married; and not having gone through a childhood as miserable, a youth as risky and floundering as Muir's, he wouldn't have burgeoned in such an effusion of relief when fame and financial security blessed him.

Yet, really, no amount of worldly acclaim made Muir half as happy as being in remote places. Muir is touching just because he was so immensely gleeful in wild country — happier than Thoreau, Audubon, London, Whitman, Mark Twain, James Fenimore Cooper, Francis Parkman and other figures one thinks of as being happy out-of-doors. He was a genteel and ordinary man in most of his opinions, and his method of lobbying politically for his beloved Yosemite was to ally himself with rich men such as the railroad magnate E. H. Harriman, who had the power to sway events Muir's way if the whim seized them. He was no nay-sayer on social questions and never would have conceived of putting himself in jail overnight to register a protest, as Thoreau had done. He would have agreed with Thoreau's now famous phrase "In wildness is the preservation of the world"; but Muir emphasized a wilderness of joy. And that, after all, is what the 1872 law creating Yellowstone — the first of the national parks — had stipulated. "The region is hereby . . . set aside as a public park and pleasuring ground for the enjoyment of the people . . ."

Muir was not a hypocrite, and he once let Harriman hear of his saying to some scientist friends that he didn't regard Harriman as truly rich: "He has not as much money as I have. I have all I want and Mr. Harriman has not." Muir, indeed, devoted only seven years of his life to the primary aim of making money. ("The seven lost years," his wife called them, when he was managing full-time the fruit ranch she inherited from her father.) But he valued money and respectability and held few views on any subject to alarm a "bully" president like Roosevelt or a tycoon like Harriman. Like Audubon, Muir was proud of being foreign-born. He nurtured the strong streak of business acumen, the religious if disputatious temperament, the Spartan understatement and resilience, and the excellent mechanical aptitudes that he considered to be part of his Scottish heritage. His mix of idealism and innocence with the hard-mannered Scotch burr — a familiar, respected accent in the immigrant stream of a hundred years ago—charmed at the same time as it reassured such men. ("Frenchiness" would not have been nearly as useful.)

Although Harriman's Southern Pacific Railroad had no stake in what happened to Yosemite Valley, he responded charitably and fancifully to Muir's particular pleas for help in 1905, when the valley's fate was being decided in the state senate, with a confidential telegram to his chief agent in San Francisco. The vote was whisker-close, but to the astonishment of the logging and livestock industries, several legislators that Southern Pacific "owned" suddenly swung their votes behind a bill to give this spectacular scenery to the federal government. The next year, Harriman wrote with the same potent effect to the Speaker of the U.S. House and to Senate leaders to have Yosemite included in a national park. And after Teddy Roosevelt's presidency had ended, Muir's odd appeal worked upon William Howard Taft, a much tougher nut among presidents.

Muir as an advocate was a johnny-one-note, but, oh, that note! "When California was wild, it was one sweet bee-garden throughout its entire length," he wrote with yearning. "Wherever a bee might fly within the bounds of this virgin wilderness . . . throughout every belt and section of climate up to the timber line, bee-flowers bloomed in lavish abundance." Wistfully he proposed that all of the state might be developed into a single vast flower palace and honey-hive to the continent, its principal industry the keeping, herding and pasturing of bees.

When California was wild! Luckily he'd seen it then. He had arrived by ship seven years after Mark Twain had appeared by stagecoach in Nevada, on the other side of the Sierras, to transcribe the experience of *Roughing It*. Both Muir and Twain originally had harbored the hope of lighting out for the Amazon, but Twain got sidetracked into piloting Mississippi riverboats and Muir got seriously sick in Florida and Cuba en route to South America. Muir—who had reveled in one of the best adventures of his life in walking south from Louisville to Georgia— sailed to New York City to recuperate. However, disliking the city, he caught a packet immediately for San Francisco, landing in March of 1868, a month before his thirtieth birthday.

Unlike Twain, he hadn't come west as a writer; not till he was thirty-seven did he resolve to be one. This was "the wild side of the continent," he said, which was reason enough. Yet he invariably soft-pedaled its dangers and hardships. Twain, quite the opposite, and quintessentially "American," celebrated the badmen and primitive conditions in marvelously exploitative tall tales, boasting of how his knees knocked. Twain used the mountains as a theatrical prop, having abandoned his *manqué* career as a silver miner as soon as he obtained a job as a newspaperman in Virginia City. The mountains themselves had small fascination for him, and he sought companionship with writerly acquisitiveness at every opportunity, whereas Muir at that time was grasping at solitude, avoiding "the tyrant of creation," as Audubon had once described mankind.

But the reason Muir so seldom speaks about the cold rains, the icebite and exhaustion he met with in the mountains, the terror of an avalanche, of breaking through ice in crossing a waterway, or of the many deer he must have observed starving to skin and bones after a series of snows, is not simply Scottish diffidence and asceticism. He loved most of nature's violence — "the jubilee of waters," as he called one particular winter storm. In the earthquake of 1872, for instance, "disregarding the hard fist of fear in his stomach, he ran out into the moonlit meadows," according to Linnie Marsh Wolfe, his biographer. "Eagle Rock, high on the south wall of the valley, was toppling. . . . All fear forgotten, he bounded toward the descending mass," shouting exuberantly in the shower of dust and falling fragments, leaping among the new boulders before they had finished settling into their resting places on the valley floor.

Besides, when he got around to organizing the journals of his early wanderings, he had become sharply political. He had been jotting plant identifications and geological evidence of glaciation, but now was gleaning memories from the same pages, meaning to write to save the wilderness from obliteration — and not just by the timber and mining companies. More pervasive a threat at the turn of the century was the injunction in Genesis that any wilderness was a wasteland until tilled, that man was made in the likeness of God and in opposition to wilderness and its multitudinous creatures, which were not. It seems a very old pronouncement; yet it was the revolutionary edict of a new religion attacking established spiritual values — monotheism on the offensive against polytheism which revered or at least incorporated the realities of the wilderness. Furthermore, later texts and preachers went beyond the objection that certain mountains, forests, springs and animal races had been considered gods, to decry the wilderness as actually Devil-ridden, inimical to the salvation of men.

Muir, like the eastern Transcendentalists, was not advocating polytheism. Nor was he secular. He believed that wilderness, like man, was an expression of one God; that man was part of nature; that nature, fount of the world, remained his natural home, under one God. Like Emerson and Thoreau—like Twain and Whitman and Melville and Hawthorne—Muir had found Christianity to be a stingy religion in matters vital to him. In his case, it wasn't the Church's vapid response to the issue of slavery or to the mysterious ambiguities of evil or the imperatives of love that swung him toward the perilous experiment of inventing his own religion (for Twain, this became atheism). Polytheism was long dead, yet the wilderness was still perceived as inimical, and so Muir didn't want to increase by even a little the lore that had contributed to such a misreading.

His father had been a free-lance Presbyterian preacher, when not working on their Wisconsin farm—a hellfire Presbyterian, fierce with the one flock given into his care, who were his children. The family had emigrated to America when John was eleven, and from then on he worked like an adult, dawn to dusk in the summer, with many beatings. At fifteen, he was set the task of digging a well in sandstone by the light of a candle. Daily for months, except on Sundays, he was lowered alone in a bucket, and once at the eighty-foot level passed out from lack of oxygen. Though he was only just rescued in time, the next morning his father punctually lowered him to the bottom all over again. Not till he was ninety feet down did he hit water.

This amok Presbyterianism helped to estrange him from Christianity but not from religion, and paradoxically made Muir gentler toward everyone but himself. He had encountered kinder treatment from some of the neighbors, and despite his deficiencies in schooling, was welcomed to the university in Madison, where a science professor and Emerson and Agassiz disciple named Ezra Carr (and especially Mrs. Carr) drew him into their household like a son. His education was so hard-won that he seems to have got more out of his two and a half years at college in terms of friendships and influences than Thoreau did at Harvard, although both learned to keep an assiduous notebook and to insist that America had a great intellectual role to play in the world.

Muir was one of those people who believe in the rapture of life but who must struggle to find it. He wasn't always blissful in the woods. During the Civil War, when he was twenty-six, he fled to Canada, partly in order to evade the draft, and wandered the environs of the Great Lakes for eight months in intermittent torment. He had already aspired to be a doctor, had then leaned toward natural science, had exhibited a phenomenal knack for inventing machine tools and implements — the kind of talent that has founded family dynasties — and had won his independence from his father without bruising his mother and sisters and brothers unduly. He had had fine friends, had been in love; yet still he wanted to leave "the doleful chambers of civilization, the beaten charts" and search for "the Law that governs the relations between human beings and Nature." There was one indispensable lesson he had gained from the brutal schedule of labors of his boyhood. During the next couple of decades when it was essential that he explore, laze, gaze, loaf, muse, listen, climb and nose about, he was free of any puritan compulsion to "work." After the North-woods sojourn he put in another two years as millwright and inventor for wages (not drudgery, because he enjoyed it), before a frightening injury to his right eye in the carriage factory in which he worked bore in upon him the realization that life was short.

Once, finding himself in the metropolis of Chicago, he had passed the five hours between trains by botanizing in vacant lots; and now as he struck off like one of his heroes, Alexander von Humboldt, for the valley of the Amazon, he set a compass course directly through Louisville so as not to notice the city too much. Beginning this, his earliest journal extant, he signed himself with ecstatic curlicues "John Muir, Earth-planet, Universe." Later on, in California, he would set off into the radiant high country of "the Range of Light" — as he called the Sierra Nevadas — with his blanket roll and some bread and tea thrown into a sack tossed over his shoulder like "a squirrel's tail." He might scramble up a Douglas fir in spiked boots in a gale to cling to it and ride the wind "like a bobolink on a reed," smelling the flower fields far away and the salt of the sea. "Heaven bless you all," he exclaimed, in his first summer journal from the Sierras — meaning all California's citizenry, including its lizards, grasshoppers, ants, bighorn sheep, grizzly bears, bluebottle flies (who "make all dead flesh fly") — "our horizontal brothers," as he was apt to describe the animal kingdom.

On the giddy cliffs and knife-edges he was not out to test his courage, like the ordinary outdoorsman, but was set upon proving the beneficence of God. More than Thoreau, though less than Emerson, he skewed the evidence. God *was* in the mountains, as he knew from his own sense of joy; and as he gradually discovered that his intuitions were tied in with compass directions, storms brewing, the migration of ice, and the movements of bears, he was preparing to preach the goodness of God to us as well as himself. In even the mildest Christian theology, nature was simply handed over in servitude to man, and the Transcendentalists were trying to bypass not only this destructive anthropocentrism, as they perceived it, but also the emphasis that Christianity placed upon an afterlife at the expense of what seemed a proper reverence for life on earth. Such stress upon salvation appeared to isolate people from one another as well, because each person's fate was to be adjudicated separately. The Transcendentalists believed in universal links, and while never denying the possibilities of an afterlife, chose to emphasize the miraculous character, the healing divinity of life here and now.

Emerson admired and communed with Muir during a visit to Yosemite and afterwards encouraged him by correspondence. Other intellectual doyens—Asa Gray, Agassiz, Joseph Le Conte—took up his banner, and he was offered professorships in science in California and Massachusetts, which he turned down. From the start he had seemed a marked man. Like his father's neighbors, his college instructors and factory mentors, Muir's first employer in the Sierras, a sheep-owner named Delaney, predicted that he was going to be famous and "facilitated and encouraged" his explorations, Muir said. Some of the Mormons, too, appear to have noticed him favorably when he descended from the Wasatch Range on one of his larks to hobnob a bit near Salt Lake City. Ardent, outspoken, eloquent in conversation, he wore his heart on his sleeve throughout his life, but although more driven, more energetic than Thoreau, he lacked Thoreau's extraordinary gift of self-containment and single-mindedness. He had more friendships—an intricacy of involvements—and was a "problem-solver," as we say nowadays, a geyser of inventiveness. The trajectory of his career carried him finally to the winsome, wise figure leading day hikes for the Sierra Club or posed on his ample front porch in a vest and watch fob with his high-collared daughters and black-garbed wife, Muir quarreling publicly and condescendingly with the Hudson River naturalist John Burroughs, Muir as a visiting fireman in London, or elected to the American Academy of Arts and Letters in 1909. Yet, for all these amenities and the freedom he won to do as he liked in the world, he never achieved anything like Thoreau's feeling of mastery over it—that easy-wheeling liberty to analyze, criticize, anatomize and summarize society's failings with roosterly pleasure: "the mass of men lead lives of quiet desperation." Compared to Thoreau's spiky commentaries on his neighbors and other townsfolk, on politics, culture, labor, industry, civilization, "Boston," Muir's admonitory remarks sound aloof, stiff and hostile, as if directed at targets with which he had no firsthand familiarity. For, despite all his friendships, Muir sought the glory of God far from other people; and just as he had had to reinvent Transcendentalism for himself way out on a kind of rim of the world, he devised his own brand of glaciology to explain the landforms of Yosemite — notions at first ridiculed by the academic geologists, then vindicated, though he had taken no account of previous and contemporaneous studies, mainly because he was unacquainted with them. We need to remember that one reason he roamed so high and far was to measure living glaciers and inspect virgin evidence, but he was both too religious and too idiosyncratic rightly to pursue a scientific career, and moved on to become a rhapsodist, a polemicist and a grandfather whitebeard.

He had seen the last of the Wisconsin, Appalachian and California frontiers. Like twenty-one-year-old Francis Parkman on the Oregon Trail in 1846, like twenty-six-year-old Sam Clemens jolting into Fort Bridger in 1861, he had gone West for adventure. But he stayed in the West, stayed exhilarated, witnessing nature on a scale never presented on the Atlantic seaboard. Volcanoes, landslides, glaciers calving, oceans of flowers, forests of devil's-club and Alaskan hemlock. He was thick-skinned to criticism like Mark Twain but more personally peaceable, as exuberant in Alaska as Jack London, but indifferent to gold rushes and desperadoes. His favorite bird was the water ouzel, an agile, inoffensive creature living in mountain watercourses, not the golden eagle, and his favorite animals were squirrels.

"The Douglas squirrel is by far the most interesting and influential of the California *sciuridae*, surpassing every other species in force of character . . . Though only a few inches long, so intense is his fiery vigor and restlessness, he stirs every grove with wild life, and makes himself more important than even the huge bears that shuffle through the tangled underbrush beneath him. Every wind is fretted by his voice, almost every bole and branch feels the sting of his sharp feet. How much the growth of the trees is stimulated by this means is not easy to learn, but . . . Nature has made him master forester and committed most of her coniferous crops to his paws. . . ." This is not the author of *White Fang* talking.

But, like Audubon, Muir was often painfully lonely in wild places and was later pursued by rumors of romantic misconduct. Our nature writers tend to be damned if they do and damned if they don't, with regard to sex. A special prurience attaches to inquiries as to whether Thoreau really fell in love with Emerson's wife, why Audubon was abruptly exiled from Oakley Plantation in West Feliciana Parish, Louisiana, where he had been tutoring "my lovely Miss Pirrie," or whether poor Mrs. Hutchings, wife of Muir's sawmill employer in Yosemite Valley, left her husband as a result of her winter's companionship with Muir when her husband went East. Furthermore, *did* Muir sleep with the Honorable Mrs. Thérèse Yelverton, a divorcée celebrity who visited Yosemite in 1870 and made him the hero of a novel? Or with Mrs. Jeanne Carr, his early benefactress at the University of Wisconsin? Still, it's true that most of our preeminent nature interpreters didn't recognize that the nexus of the sexes could become a natural adjunct of what is lately called "the wilderness experience," and something faintly ludicrous attaches to their infirmity. They differed in this respect from he-men like London, from the internationally minded Audubon, and certain British explorers like Sir Richard Burton and Sir Samuel Baker (not to mention innumerable mountainmen-squawmen).

As seems to be the case with many wounded-hearts who make a decisive leap away from wherever they were wounded, joy eventually became Muir's strong suit. His joy in the bee-meadows under sun-shot granite and ice, the fir trees and river willows, the tiny water ouzels diving into cold rapids and running on the bottom after insects, ruddering themselves in the current with their half-open wings, was so tactile that he repeatedly experienced episodes of mental telepathy. He lived recklessly and efficiently enough that he did as much ambling, clambering, trekking and roaming as he could sensibly have done, but at the age of seventy still had published just two books. His most delicious volumes—*A Thousand Mile Walk to the Gulf* and *My First Summer in the Sierra*—were reconstructed from his youthful journals only after that, journals by then forty years old. His true story of the brave loyal mongrel "Stickeen," which may be the best of all dog stories, took seventeen years to see print in a magazine after the night that they shared on a glacier. And he postponed work on what might have been his finest book, *Travels in Alaska*, until the last year of his life, when his energies were not up to the task. He died of pneumonia in a Los Angeles hospital with his Alaska notes beside his bed; a collaborator had to finish jiggling them into narrative form.

Although Muir helped to invent the conservation movement, he was a tender soul, not merely a battling activist, and lived with the conviction that God was in the sky. Yet the Transcendentalists, in revering the spark of life wherever it occurred, were groping toward a revolutionary concept of survival for Western man: that we must live together with the rest of nature or we will die together with the rest of nature. Centrist churchmen over the years had issued apologias for Inquisitions, wars of racial and sectarian extermination, slavery, child labor and so on, and their ethics were proving inadequate once again. And because Muir is such an endearing individual, to grow to care for him is all the sadder because the crusade failed. We lead a scorched-earth existence; so much of what he loved about the world is nearly gone. Naturalists themselves are turning into potted plants, and mankind is re-creating itself quite in the way that a born-again Fundamentalist does, who once went to school and learned some smattering of geology, biology and human history, but who abruptly shuts all that out of his mind, transfixed instead by the idea that the Earth is only six thousand years old, that practically every species that ever lived is right here with us now for our present service and entertainment. So it is with our preternatural assumption that the world was invented by Thomas Edison and Alexander Graham Bell.

Thoreau's optimism is out of fashion, but not Thoreauvian combativeness and iconoclasm. The whole theater of orchards, ponds, back fields, short woods, short walks in which *Walden* was staged remains accessible to anyone who wants to recapitulate the particulars of what he did and saw. Muir, however, is not the same. Less thoughtful, less balanced to begin with, he hooked himself to the wide world of wilderness for support, and now that that world is shattering all around, it's hard to imagine where he would tie his lifeline. Except as a tactician and a man of good will, he has no current solutions to offer us. More than Thoreau, in other words, he is a sort of historical embodiment, like some knight of Chivalry, or leader of the Wobblies from 1919. Frank Norris employed him as the mystic Vanamee in his 1901 novel *The Octopus*, opposed to unbridled industrial power.

"Instinct with deity" was how Muir described the elements of nobility he recognized among the Tlingits of southeastern Alaska, who were the only Indians he ever took to. His own "instinct with deity" was gushier, vaguer, more isolated in character, being linked to no central traditions, no hereditary culture, no creation myths or great-grandfather tales. Muir, not born to it, blundering and fumbling as he sought to create a religion in reaction to his savage foe from childhood, Presbyterianism, left out a lot that the Indians put in. There were no carrion smells beneath his landslides, no half-eaten elk in his glacial basins, no parched nestlings fallen from his spruce and aspens. More than Thoreau, he let his philosophy dictate which observations he put in. But though his embrace of nature is not to be confused with the more intimate, inherent conjugality that animist tribal peoples on all continents have had, his was sufficiently headlong that we would find it almost impossible to duplicate today.

We have disacknowledged our animalness. Not just American Indians spoke affectionately to turtles, ravens, eagles and bears as "Uncle" and "Grandfather," but our ancestors as well. The instant cousinhood our children feel for animals, the way they go toward them directly, with all-out curiosity, is a holdover from this. Even now, to visit the Tlingit villages on Admiralty, Chichagof and other islands of the Alexander Archipelago where Muir kayaked and boated is to meet with a thicket of animal life—whales in the channels, bears ashore—from which the native clans trace their origins and which therefore were seldom hunted. Bears still have accepted territorial spheres of influence on these islands, and the roofs in the villages belong to the ravens as much as the streets do to the people, while eagles bank as closely as seagulls overhead.

In looking on my bookshelves for a contemporary writer who has the same earthy empathy and easy knowledgeability for what is going on out-of-doors as Muir's, the nearest kindred spirits I could find were the Craighead brothers, Frank and John, who are old hawk, owl and grizzly experts and the co-authors of a field guide to Rocky Mountain wildflowers which was first published over twenty years ago. It's too unorthodox and informal a book to be especially popular now, but I love thumbing through it. The fact that brothers wrote it is appealing. Like the Murie brothers, Olaus and Adolph, who ten years earlier had studied elk and wolves and waterfowl and wildlife tracking, the Craigheads possess an old-fashioned air of blood alliance and clannish loyalty. And, writing about the Rockies—whose climatic zones vary too much for ecological cycles to be described simply by dates on a calendar—they say that wild violets come into bloom when wood ducks are building nests and crows are sitting on their eggs; that vetch vines flower at the same time as moose are having calves; that chokecherries blossom when prairie falcons are about to fledge; fireweed when bald eagles are making their first flights from the nest; and primroses when young goshawks leave for good. Coyote pups depart from their dens at about the time blueberry plants have fully bloomed. Bearberries start to flower when tree swallows return from the south, are in full blossom when Canada goose eggs begin to hatch, and the berries themselves, although still green, have formed by the time young chipmunks are to be seen scampering about. The life schedules of wild licorice and lodgepole lupine are linked to the flight lessons of ruffed grouse; meadowsweet to long-eared owls; balsamroot and serviceberries to bighorn ewes; harebells and silverweed to mallard ducklings; long-plumed avens to bison calves and Swainson's hawks.

On and on these virtuosos go. Since the book is about flowers, they are limited to events of the spring and summer, but we know that this inventory of lore could spin around the larger cycle of the year as no ecologist of a younger generation would conceive of trying to do. The Craigheads and the Muries did not age into crusaders on the order of John Muir, and were too late to enjoy Muir's faith in God. But in their various modest books the same joy is there, and the feel of an encyclopedic synthesis of experience and observation on a scale Muir had and few outdoorsmen will ever be permitted again.

C. John Burk

A View of a Marsh: Vitality in Nature

I suspect that most of us share a need for lookouts and overlooks, mountain peaks, hilltops or towers, places from which we can view familiar landscapes in perspective. Situated high enough, with time and a little history or geology, we may construct scenarios, imposing past events on present landforms. There, for instance, by that eroded bank in 1646 an Indian raid destroyed a sawmill; there just beyond those trees as the glacier shrank, retreating northward, caribou and woolly mammoths browsed on the shores of a meltwater lake. For some years, one of my favorite vantage points has been an observation tower which rises on two telephone poles over a complex of marshes at a nearby wildlife sanctuary. Heavy wire cables guy the platform to a black birch on one side, a shagbark on the other. The interior reeks of leafmold, and the structure lurches sideways, always unexpectedly, when you first set foot on the upper deck. In the marsh if the water is low, broad mudbanks are exposed. Greenheaded mallard drakes flash in intermittent sunlight as the channel turns against a clump of alders. On the far side, willows and silver maples border a flat expanse of cornfields and meadowlands; beyond these, swamp forest, a denser line of trees, swings in a westerly loop which bends south and then back to include the woods around the concrete slab at the observation tower's base.

The trees and the marsh fill what was once an oxbow lake, a part of the Connecticut River which presently flows seaward half a mile off to the east. For thousands of years the river has shaped and re-formed this seemingly tranquil landscape. The process of change may occur slowly as the stream withdraws sediments from one side and redeposits them downstream on the other. It may happen quickly, even noisily and overnight as in 1840, when colliding ice floes demolished a bridge and piled up to form a dam, cutting off an oxbow in a single winter freshet.

Constantly the woods along the banks are adjusted in response. Old cottonwoods topple as the land is cut away beneath them on the east; seedling cottonwoods invade the sandbars on the west. Silver maples germinate beneath the cottonwoods and grow to dominate a floodplain forest which the river, refocusing its energies, may undercut again. The water trapped in oxbow lakes and sloughs fills rapidly with vegetation. Beneath its surface, pondweeds, hornworts, and milfoil shelter aquatic life which could not survive the fast-moving currents of the open stream. White waterlilies and yellow-flowered spatterdock root in the old bed, sending up long leaf stalks whose unfolding plate-sized blades reduce the light available below. Sediments accumulate; from the bank, colonies of arrowhead, pickerel weed, cattail, wild rice, and three-way sedge converge. Buttonbush, alder, and willow rise to shade these emergents, acting as forerunners of the swamp forest which may develop if the river does not, as it did in the flood of 1936, rush in to claim its course another time.

The river is not the only agent of disturbance here. Humans have been in this valley since the end of the last glaciation. Indians worked the cornfields for hundreds of seasons before European settlers arrived in the middle of the seventeenth century. Displacing and then emulating their predecessors, these colonists built on the higher river terraces, parceled out the floodplain for agriculture, and fished and hunted in the oxbow swamps and marshes. During times of high water, their crops were lost, and in response to this, unlike the Indians, they and their descendants made (and continue to make) repeated, frequently ambitious, often unsuccessful attempts to prevent the stream from flooding. They built dikes, levees, and diversion channels, a few dams on the main stem of the Connecticut, many more on the tributaries. Minor streams have been rerouted, led down into the valley along other, perhaps safer, more convenient routes. Nonetheless, when diversion channels are abandoned and dikes overrun, when fields are no longer cultivated every year and roads through the meadows go unrepaired too long, the marks of these human efforts are covered over much in the same way the woods and marshlands adjust to changes in the river's path. The channels clog with waterlilies, spatterdock, pickerel weed, and milfoil. Swamp forest trees seed in along the banks. Untended crop rows fill with weeds. Tangles of blackberry, steeplebush, and staghorn sumac invade neglected meadows. Saplings of silver maple, box elder, white ash, and pin oak rise through the shrubs to renew again the floodplain woods.

There is something reassuring in this spectacle of life reasserting itself after periods of disruption. The process involves what was known since long before the development of the science of ecology as "succession." Succession, according to Webster's Third New International Dictionary, is "the process of change in the biological population of an area as the available competing organisms respond to the environment" or "the sequence of identifiable ecological stages or communities in this process, esp. from barrenness to climax . . ." Webster's definition may seem less than perfect to many scientists. Nonetheless, although various kinds of succession were described by the end of the eighteenth century and although, from the 1890s to the present, the subject has been extensively investigated, there is still no general agreement as to what exactly succession is, how it works, or even if it truly exists except as an artifact of something else.

Across the state from this river valley on September 20, 1860, Henry D. Thoreau addressed the Middlesex Agricultural Society on "The Succession of Forest Trees." He declared "Every man is entitled to come to Cattleshow, even a transcendentalist . . ." and reminded his audience that "taking a surveyor's and a naturalist's liberty, I have been in the habit of going across your lots much oftener than is usual, as many of you, perhaps to your sorrow, are aware. . . . I have often been asked, as many of you have been, if I could tell how it happened, that when a pine wood was cut down an oak one commonly sprang up, and *vice versa.*"

He forcefully explained that trees which appear where none of their species grew before arise from seeds, that the seeds are transported by water, wind, and animals, and that oaks only grow up under pines if their seeds have been previously dispersed there, most probably by squirrels and other animals. Similarly, when an oak woods is cut, pines "will not *at once* spring up there unless there are, or have been quite recently, seed-bearing pines near enough for the seeds to be blown from them." He supported his arguments with numerous observations on the ways seeds are planted "by various quadrupeds and birds" and with references to techniques used in English plantations of forest trees. The lecture concluded with a paean to the seed coupled with a jibe at his audience, at the farmers' sons who "will stare by the hour to see a juggler draw ribbons from his throat, though he tells them it is all deception," men who "Surely . . . love darkness rather than light."

Although Thoreau had been interested in succession for some

years, he began, in the autumn months immediately following that lecture, to investigate its details with a peculiar intensity. Over the years critics, students, and biographers of Thoreau have disagreed in their assessment of the work he carried out in these last few months of his active life. John Burroughs, in a generally appreciative essay, complained ". . . he saw and recorded nothing new. It is quite remarkable. He says in his journal that he walked half of each day, and kept it up perhaps for twenty years or more. Ten years of persistent spying and inspecting of nature, and no new thing found out. . . ." Leo Stoller, examining Thoreau's "changing views on economic man," believed that these studies reconciled those "contradictory strains in his attitude to the forest. His discovery of the mechanism of succession pointed to a system of forest management which would yield lumber and profit to satisfy man's grosser instincts and at the same time preserve nature for the disciplining of his spirit." Biologist Edward S. Deevy pointed out in 1942 that Thoreau's ". . . conclusions remain essentially unaltered after sixty years of intensive labor by competent botanists," and most recently Richard Lebeaux concludes that in these investigations, "Thoreau was clearly working through private familial and generational issues" and thereby resolving "oedipally related anxiety and guilt."

No matter how one interprets the work, one cannot but be impressed by the amount of energy required, by the overall versatility and determination of Thoreau's approach. In the course of three months he correlated the relationships of land use and history with forest composition. He contrasted wilderness where disturbance results from "fire and insects or blight, and not the axe and plow and the cattle" with the tamer Concord woodlands. He discovered seedling chestnuts in a woods where mature chestnut trees were lacking and measured the distance the burrs would have been carried from the nearest possible maternal parent. He catalogued the ability of various tree species to withstand fire; pine, birch, maple, and large oaks died but seedling oaks were scarcely injured. In a woodlot severely burned the previous spring, he was "surprised to see how green the forest floor. . . . The fresh shoots from the roots are very abundant and three to five feet high. . . . So vivacious are the roots and so rapidly does nature recover herself." He went on to dig up seedlings to compare the growth of roots and stems, remarking on the susceptibilities of young trees to disease and frost.

He also studied the role of the soil in controlling tree distribution, noting that among abundant forest species, only red maple, swamp white oak, white birch, and white pine occur in swamps. He plotted the overall distributions of trees within the forest, finding that types with winged seeds, such as pines, occur in regular patterns, in ovals, ellipses, cones, and circles, while types dispersed by animals are scattered randomly throughout.

Many of his techniques are still in use. After calculating growth rates for different tree species from yearly variations in the width of their annual rings, for example, he suggested how this information could be incorporated into better forest management. He went on to a scheme of classification beginning with primeval forest and continuing through second growth to "artificial woods" set out deliberately from seed. "We are so accustomed to see another forest spring immediately as a matter of course," he had warned, "whether from the stump or the seed, when a forest is cut down, never troubling about the succession, that we hardly associate the seed with the tree, and do not anticipate the time when this regular succession will cease and we shall be obliged to plant as they do in all old countries."

After days spent in the field, he recorded these observations in his journal, along with character sketches, notes on wildlife, and descriptions of the New England autumn, which at least part of the time was glorious. Mild spells alternated with periods of unusual cold. September 3 provided "a cloudless sky, a clear air, with, maybe, veins of coolness" — the grass reflecting "a blaze of light as if it were morning all the day." An early frost occurred the 10th, and two days later heavy "equinoctial" rains caused the river suddenly to rise. Mid-month produced "a harvest day" so beneficent that "If you are not happy today you will hardly be so tomorrow." Severe frosts struck the 28th, blackening vines in the garden, freezing ice beneath the pump.

Cold weather continued with "remarkable frost and ice" the morning of October 1 and "glittering, golden sunsets" later. Leaves of the forest trees turned color early or fell prematurely without changing. The growing season had seemed exceptionally fertile, and Thoreau was dismayed to find that most of the abundant crop of white oak acorns had fallen victim to the freeze, rotten and rejected even by squirrels. This seemed to him "a glaring imperfection in Nature, that the labor of the oaks for the year should be lost to this extent. . . . It is hard to say what great purpose is served by this seeming waste." An invasion of white pine along a fence later would provide only partial consolation when he calculated that, if millions of seeds are dropped by a pine wood with only one conveyed to the fence to survive each year, the establishment of fifteen to twenty trees would be no proof of "remarkable rapidity or success in Nature's operations."

Meanwhile, willows took on "the bleached look of November." Warm weather had returned, "Indian-summer-like and gossamer," and by month's end a thresher from neighboring Sudbury was complaining "that it is so muggy that he cannot dry the sheaves . . ." November began with newly hatched broods of butterflies and a striped snake basking in the sun, but the season continued its relentless spiral down to winter, the first snow falling on the 24th. Weatherwise, the 25th would be grim enough to encourage the most cheerful of human observers to reflect on their mortality. The Journal records that "Winter weather has come suddenly this year. The house was shaken by wind last night, and there was a general deficiency of bedclothes." Out walking, Thoreau observed "a very great collection of crows far and wide on the meadows, evidently gathered by this cold and blustering weather . . . a cold gleam is reflected from the back and wings of each, as from a weather-stained shingle. Some perch within three or four rods of me and seem weary. . . . An immense cohort of cawing crows which sudden winter has driven near to the habitations of man."

Later that day, he observed another meadow where young pines had become established from a seed source fifty rods away. ". . . There is nothing to prevent their springing up all over the village in a very few years — but our own plows and spades," he mused. Then, in a remarkable Journal paragraph, he evoked a pasture where fifteen years before there had been not a single tree or seedling. The pasture fills with trees representing the early stages of succession: birches, pitch and white pines, with beneath them young "shrub and other oaks beginning to show themselves . . . grouped very agreeably after natural laws which they obey." He next admits, in a revelation towards which the season's work may have been directed, "I confess that I love to be convinced of this inextinguishable vitality in Nature. I would rather that my body should be buried in a soil thus wide-awake than in a mere inert and dead earth. The cow-paths, the hollows where I slid in the winter, the rocks, are fast being enveloped and becoming rabbit-walks and hollows and rocks in the woods." He himself seems thus not so much obliterated as incorporated in the landscape, just as Concord herself would be without the ministrations of the plow and spade.

It is impossible to look back on Thoreau's activities throughout this occasionally idyllic autumn without sensing that, in pursuing the subject of the regeneration and renewal of Concord's woodlots, he was at the same time probing and working towards a partial resolution of his own preoccupations with death and the afterlife. He was forty-three years old and capable of vigorous, indeed robust, activity. Nonetheless he had suffered recurrent bouts of tuberculosis, the first during his student days at Harvard, the most recent in 1855. Within just a few days, by early December of 1860, he would have contracted the cold that led to bronchitis, a reopening of tubercular lesions, and his death in May of 1862. (Thoreau believed that this sequence was initiated on December 3, a day spent measuring the girth of white oaks and making observations on the germination of their acorns.)

The Journal on occasion previously linked death and regeneration directly, as on October 10, 1860, when Thoreau visited Sleepy Hollow cemetery. Five years before, he had surveyed a site for construction of an artificial pond there. He wrote, with perhaps a kind of mordant humor, "They dug gradually for three or four years and completed the pond last year . . . in this pond thus dug in the midst of a meadow a year or two ago and supplied by springs . . . I find today several small patches of the large yellow and the kalmiana lily already established. Thus in the midst of death we are in life. . . . You have only to dig a pond anywhere in the fields hereabouts, and you will soon have not only waterfowl, reptiles, and fishes in it, but also the usual waterplants. . . . You will no sooner have got your pond dug than nature will begin to stock it."

The linkage at times was extended to include the death of the human culture he had known and a return to wilderness. Counting growth rings in the stumps of felled trees, sometimes distinguishing three generations or more by their states of decay, he hoped to "unroll the rotten papyrus on which the history of the Concord forest is written." He sketched out a reversal of forest exploitation, a scenario in which: "At first, perchance, there would be an abundant crop of rank garden weeds and grasses in the cultivated land, — and rankest of all in the cellar-holes, — and of pin-weed, hardhack, sumach, blackberry, thimble-berry, raspberry, etc. in the fields and pastures. Elm, ash, maples, etc. would grow vigorously along old garden limits and main streets. Garden weeds and grasses would soon disappear." An assortment of shrubs and small trees "would rapidly prevail in the deserted pastures" until finally forest species, "pines, hemlock, spruce, larch, shrub oak, oaks, chestnut, beech and walnuts would occupy the site of Concord . . . and perchance the red man once more thread his way through the mossy, swamp-like, primitive wood."

Thoreau was surely not the first to use inner psychological needs as a basis for exploring the workings of the natural world. Commentators have suggested that Linnaeus, before him, devised his artificial system of classification as a by-product of adolescent sexual obsessions. Thoreau conceded on November 25, 1860, in a mingling of descriptions, speculation, and personal agendas, "How is any scientific discovery made? Why the discoverer takes it into his head first. He must all but see it." The psyche of Thoreau's contemporary, Charles Darwin, has been probed more deeply perhaps than that of any scientist yet, some analysts maintaining that Darwin's persistent ill health and reluctance to publish on natural selection reflected prudence and a deeply rooted fear of offending Victorian moralities. Even in our own time, critics have argued that the discovery of the structure of the genetic material was motivated less by intellectual curiosity and a love of science than by pride, ambition, and a desire for recognition.

Yet pursuing these examples, one sees obsessions, peculiarities if such they were, transformed into major contributions. Detractors of Linnaeus claim that his sexual system, because it propounded a convenient but largely unnatural way to pigeonhole the natural order, retarded the growth of botany two hundred years. Nonetheless, Linnean binomial nomenclature, which helped assign a single name, regardless of the varieties of spoken language, to every known kind of plant and animal, built a stable framework for comprehending the wealth of living forms which the great explorations of the eighteenth century revealed. Similarly, Darwin's view of biological evolution directed by the force of natural selection, though even now more controversial in some aspects than succession, provides a major world view for our time (with Darwin's remains respectably enshrined in Westminster Abbey). And James Watson and Francis Crick have achieved not only fame and fortune; their insight has stimulated an unparalleled burst of research in the expanding fields of biotechnology and genetic engineering.

Thoreau's grapplings with the mechanisms of succession have led to similar enlightenments. The essay "The Succession of Forest Trees" was first published in the transactions of the Middlesex Agricultural Society. It was reprinted in the New York *Weekly Tribune*, the *Century*, the *New England Farmer*, and the Annual Report of the Massachusetts Board of Agriculture. To this day, professional ecologists acknowledge their debt to Thoreau less fully than they should. However, in the late 1960s, some of the more apocalyptic writings associated with the Environmental Movement began to take on a resonance of Thoreau in a darker vein, extending his predictions to a prophecy that Nature would itself break down. Within this genre at its most extreme, Thoreau's gentle image of an abandoned Concord responding to the healing forces of nature was replaced by one of a world unfit for life. For example, in an introduction to a collection entitled *Earth Day: the Beginnings* (included were contributions from a still-astonishing assortment of prominent public figures), Americans were seen "killing this planet . . . systematically destroying our land, our streams, and our seas. We foul our air, deaden our senses, and pollute our bodies. And it's getting worse." Not much was known at that time, less than two decades past, about how the numerous forms of disturbance and disruption brought under public scrutiny could be repaired, or even whether repair indeed was possible. In the years since, researchers in the area have found that Thoreau's remedy for the ruined woodlots of Concord, the process of succession itself, alone or abetted by careful management, can do much to restore and reclaim a range of damaged landscapes: over-grazed grasslands, strip-mined hills, clear-cut rain forest, marshes fouled by oil pollution, eroded coastal dunes, even a tundra laid bare to dig a pipeline.

The marsh beyond the tower has not been replaced by the swamp forest at its edges because a tributary of the Connecticut River has taken over, preempted, a portion of the old bed and scoured it largely free of vegetation. This minor stream rises in uplands less than twenty miles away and flows to the valley floor with sufficient force to provide, as the colonists soon recognized, potentially useful energy. Unlike the Indians, they quickly moved to exploit the resource, building mills along the tributary from its headwaters to the floodplain. In time, with the advent of electricity, some of the mills became factories and the stream was used, not for power, but as an outlet for pollutants, by-products of industry which included cutting oils and nitric acid, alkalis, heavy metal hydroxides, and steel and ceramic particles. By the mid 1960s, the marsh was greatly damaged by these substances, as well as by several spills of fuel oil, boiler sludge, and leachate from a city dump. Compared with other marshes in the region, there were fewer aquatic plants and much more bare, unvegetated sediment. Key species, such as wild rice, which had served as a food for waterfowl until the 1930s, had disappeared completely. Records kept by birding enthusiasts showed that wildlife was less abundant than earlier in the century; conservationists feared that migratory waterfowl, pausing in the marsh on migration, might well be entrapped by the oil and perish.

Then, in response to new legislation, to stricter requirements, and to pressures brought both by proponents of the Environmental Movement and by responsible but unaligned New Englanders, within a fairly short time, pollutants in the tributary and the Connecticut River were substantially reduced. Remarkably (or so it seemed to me when I first observed it — and still seems for that matter), the marsh began to recover in the way it had recovered from natural disturbances in the past. The surviving clumps of rice cutgrass, three-way sedge, and arrowhead expanded to cover bare mudbanks in the upper zones. Wild rice reestablished itself from seed planted by the sanctuary staff. Spatterdocks, pickerel weed, spike rush, and hornwort reclaimed the open water. Wildlife increased and some migratory waterfowl lingered in the marsh to breed. Within two years, the marsh was richer, more productive, and more diverse.

During January of 1972, an oil spill occurred upstream on the tributary and the gains of previous seasons were reversed. Some marsh plants which were common the year before did not appear that summer. A majority of these were annuals: sticktights, barnyard grass, bedstraw, and the aptly named arrow-leaved tear-thumb; the oil had coated their seeds, smothering the embryos, preventing germination. Others were less abundant than usual. A few, chiefly perennials with food reserves in underground rhizomes and rootstocks, seemed to thrive as competition for space was reduced. Even these resistant forms declined in 1973, weakened by an atypical summer flood.

Three years after the spill, however, recovery again was under way. Sensitive ferns from the floor of the floodplain forest moved out into zones of high marsh. Pickerel weed, severely damaged by the oil, never increased to its former prosperity but was replaced by yellow spatterdocks in the zones of standing water. Within four or five years, the marsh was as healthy as I have ever seen it, with waterfowl abundant and wild rice again well established.

Since then the marsh has withstood yet another oil spill, at least one other summer flood, the depredations of an introduced flock of Canada geese, and an influx of sediment from a construction project. Damage occurs and is in time repaired. It will continue to be repaired, I hopefully assume, as long as stresses are removed and the seed sources remain intact. As Thoreau remarked to the Concord farmers, "Though

I do not believe that a plant will spring up where no seed has been, I have great faith in a seed. . . . Convince me that you have a seed there, and I am prepared to expect wonders. I shall even believe that the millennium is at hand. . . ."

You climb the observation tower and return to the ground on a heavy spiral iron staircase that is strong enough to withstand the force of logs that are carried like battering rams through the floodplain forest when the river rises. The tower existed only as a group of sketches through the 1960s. Its construction was begun when the staircase, a victim of urban renewal, was salvaged from the wreckage of a nineteenth-century building in a run-down section of an industrial city a few miles downstream on the Connecticut. Despite its provenance, the staircase, once painted green, now worn through to dull metal, seems perfectly matched to its site. An artifact of an ugly stage of the Valley's history, it rises, sturdy, functional, from some angles almost graceful, redeemed in yet another incarnation.

Italo Calvino

Translated from the Italian by Patrick Creagh

Man, the Sky, and the Elephant:
On Pliny's Natural History

In Pliny the Elder's *Natural History*, for the sheer pleasure of reading, I would advise concentrating on three books: the two that contain the main lines of his philosophy, which are the second (on cosmography) and the seventh (on man), and—as an example of his jumping back and forth between erudition and fantasy—the eighth (on the animals of the earth). We can of course find extraordinary pages everywhere. For example, in the books on geography (III and VI), on aquatic zoology, entomology, and comparative anatomy (IX and XI), botany, agronomy, and pharmacology (XII and XXXII), or on metals, precious stones, and the fine arts (XXXIII and XXXVII).

Pliny has, I think, always been used chiefly for reference, both to find out what the ancients knew or thought they knew on any particular subject, and to pick up oddities and eccentricities. From this point of view one cannot neglect book I, the summary of the whole work, the interesting thing about which is the wealth of unexpected juxtapositions: "Fish that have a pebble in their heads; Fish that hide in winter; Fish that feel the influence of the stars; Extraordinary prices paid for certain fish." Or "Concerning the rose: 12 varieties, 32 drugs; 3 varieties of lily: 21 drugs; a plant born from one of its own tears; 3 varieties of narcissus: 16 drugs; a plant one dyes the seeds of so that it produces colored flowers; Saffron: 20 drugs; Where the best flowers grow; Which flowers were known at the time of the Trojan War; clothing that rivals flowers." Or yet again: "The nature of metals; Concerning gold; The amount of gold possessed by the ancients; The equestrian order and the right to wear gold rings; How many times has the equestrian order changed names?"

But Pliny is also a writer who deserves to be read at length for the calm movement of his prose, animated as it is by admiration for everything that exists and respect for the infinite variety of things.

We might perhaps distinguish a poetical-philosophical Pliny, with his feeling for the universe and his love of knowledge and mystery, from the Pliny who was a neurotic collector of data, an obsessive compiler who seems to think only of not wasting a single jotting in his mastodonic notebook. (In using written sources he was omnivorous and eclectic, but not without a critical sense. There were some things he accepted at face value, others that he simply recorded, and still others that he rejected as obvious fantasies. It is just that his method of evaluation appears to be very unstable and unpredictable.) But once we have recognized these two faces of Pliny, we have to admit immediately that he is always one and the same man, exactly as the world he aims to describe in all its variety of form is one and the same world. To achieve this aim, he did not hesitate to plunge into the endless number of existing forms, multiplied by the endless number of existing ideas about these forms, because forms and ideas had for him equal right to be part of natural history and to be examined by anyone looking into them for an indication of a higher "reason" that he was convinced they must contain.

The world is the eternal and uncreated sky, whose spherical, rotating face covers all terrestrial things (II. 2), but it is difficult to distinguish the world from God, who for Pliny (and the Stoic culture to which he belonged) is one God, not to be identified with any single portion or aspect of him, or with the crowd of characters on Olympus, though perhaps with the sun, the soul or mind or spirit of the sky (II. 13). At the same time, the sky is made of stars as eternal as he is; the stars weave the sky and yet are part of the celestial fabric: *aeterna caelestibus est natura intexentibus mundum intextuque concretis* (II. 30). But it is also air (both below and above the moon) that looks empty and diffuses the spirit of life here below, and produces clouds, thunder, hail, lightning, and storms (II. 102).

When we speak of Pliny, we never know to what extent we should attribute the ideas he expresses to the author himself. He is in fact scrupulous about inserting as little of himself as possible and sticking to what his sources tell him. This conforms to his impersonal concept of knowledge, which excludes individual originality. To try to understand what his sense of nature really is, and how much of it consists of the arcane majesty of principles and how much of the materiality of the elements, we have to cling to what is undeniably his own: the expressive substance of his prose. Look, for example, at the pages concerning the moon, where the tone of heartfelt gratitude for this "supreme heavenly body, the most familiar to those who live on earth, the remedy of darkness" ("*novissimum sidus, terris familiarissimum et in tenebrarum remedium*" [II. 41]), and for all that it teaches us with the rhythm of its phases and eclipses, combines with the agile functionality of the sentences to express this mechanism with crystal clarity. It is in the pages on astronomy in book II that Pliny shows himself to be something more than the compiler with an imaginative flair that he is usually taken for, and reveals himself as a writer possessing what was destined to be the chief quality of all great scientific prose: that of expounding the most complex subject with perfect clarity, while deriving from it a sense of harmony and beauty.

He does this without ever leaning toward abstract speculation. Pliny always sticks to the facts (what he considers to be facts or what others have considered to be such). He does not hold with an infinite number of worlds because the nature of this world is already hard enough to understand, and infinity would scarcely simplify the problem (II. 4). Nor does he believe in the music of the spheres, either as a din out of earshot or as inexpressible harmony, because "for us who are in it, the world glides around both day and night in silence" (II. 6).

Having stripped God of the anthropomorphic characteristics attributed by mythology to the immortals of Olympus, Pliny is forced by the rules of logic to bring God closer to man by means of the limits necessarily imposed on His powers. In fact, God is less free than man in one case, because He could not kill Himself even if He wanted to. Nor does He have any power over the past, over the irreversibility of time (II. 27). Like Kant's God, He cannot come into conflict with the independence of reason (He cannot prevent two plus two from equaling four), but to define Him in these terms would lead us astray from the natural immanence of his identification with the forces of nature (*"per quae declaratur haut dubie naturae potentia idque quod deum vocemus* [II. 27]).

The lyrical or lyrical-philosophical tones dominant in the earlier chapters of book II correspond to a vision of universal harmony that does not take long to fall to pieces. A considerable part of that book is devoted to celestial prodigies. Pliny's science oscillates between the intent to recognize an order in nature and the recording of what is extraordinary or unique: and the second aspect of it always wins out. Nature is eternal and sacred and harmonious, but it leaves a wide margin for the emergence of inexplicable prodigious phenomena. What general conclusion ought we to draw from this? That we are concerned with a monstrous order entirely composed of exceptions to the rule? Or else a set of rules so complex it eludes our understanding? In either case, for every fact an explanation must exist, even if for the time being this explanation is unknown to us: "All things of explanation that is uncertain and hidden in the majesty of nature" (II. 101), and, a little farther on, "*Adeo causa non deest*" (II. 115), "it is not the causes that are lacking"—a cause can always be found. Pliny's rationalism exalts the logic of cause and effect and at the same time minimizes it, for even if you find the explanation for facts, that is no reason for the facts to cease to be marvelous.

This last maxim concludes a chapter on the mysterious origin of the winds: the folds of mountains, the hollows of valleys that hurl back blasts of wind after the manner of an echo, a grotto in Dalmatia where one need only drop a light object to unleash a storm at sea, a rock in Cyrenaica that only has to be touched to raise a sandstorm. Pliny gives us many of these catalogues of strange facts unrelated to one another: on the effects of lightning on man, with its cold wounds (among plants, lightning spares only the laurel; among animals, the eagle, according to II. 146), on extraordinary rains (of milk, blood, meat, iron, or sponges of iron, wool, and bricks, according to II. 147).

And yet Pliny clears the ground of a lot of old wives' tales, such as comets as omens (for example, he refutes the belief that a comet appearing between the pudenda of a constellation—was there anything the ancients did not see in the skies?—foretells an era of moral laxity: "*obscenis autem moribus in verendis partibus signorum*" [II. 93]). Still, each prodigy presents itself to him as a problem of nature, insofar as it is the reverse side of the norm. Pliny holds out against superstitions but cannot always recognize them, especially in book VII, where he deals with human nature. Even concerning easily observable facts he records the most abstruse beliefs. Typical is the chapter on menstruation (VII. 63–66), but it must be said that Pliny's views all accord with the most ancient religious taboos regarding menstrual blood. There is a whole network of traditional analogies and values that does not clash with Pliny's rationalism, almost as if the latter were based on the same foundations. Thus he is sometimes inclined to construct analogical explanations of the poetic or psychological type: "The corpses of men float face upward, those of women face down, as if nature wished to respect the modesty of dead women" (VII. 77).

On rare occasions Pliny reports facts vouched for by his own personal experience: "On guard duty at night in front of the trenches I have seen star-shaped lights shining on the soldiers' spears" (II. 101); "during the reign of Claudius we saw a centaur which he had had brought from Egypt, preserved in honey" (VII. 35); "I myself in Africa once saw a citizen of Tisdrus changed from a woman to a man on her wedding day" (VII. 36).

But for a tireless seeker such as he, a protomartyr of experimental science, destined to die asphyxiated by the fumes during the eruption of Vesuvius, direct observations occupy a minimal place in his work, and are on exactly the same level of importance as information read in books — and the more ancient these were, the more authoritative. All the same, to forestall criticism, he declares: "However, for most of these facts I would not vouch, preferring to go back to the sources to whom I turn in all doubtful cases, without ceasing to follow the Greeks, who are the most precise in their observations, as well as the most ancient" (VII. 8).

After this preamble Pliny feels free to launch into his famous review of the "prodigious and incredible" characteristics of certain foreign peoples, a passage that was to be so popular in the Middle Ages and even later, and to transform geography into a fairground of living phenomena. There are echoes of it in later accounts of *real* travels, such as those of Marco Polo. That the unknown lands on the fringes of the world should contain beings on the fringes of humanity should be no cause for wonder: the Arimaspi with a single eye in the middle of their foreheads, who contest the gold mines with the griffins; the inhabitants of the forest of Abarimon, who run extremely swiftly on feet that point backward; the androgynous people of Nasamona, who assume alternate sexes during intercourse; the Tibii, who have two pupils in one eye and the image of a horse in the other. But the great Barnum presents his most spectacular acts in India, where one can find a people of mountain hunters who have the heads of dogs, and a race of jumping people with one leg only, who when they want to rest in the shade lie down and raise their single foot above their heads like a parasol. There is also a nomadic people with legs like snakes, and there are the Astomoi, who have no mouths and live by sniffing odors. Mixed in with these are pieces of information we now know to be true, such as the description of the Indian fakirs (whom he calls "gymnosophist philosophers"), or else things such as still provide us with those mysterious events we read about in the newspapers (where he talks about immense footprints, he could be referring to the Yeti or Abominable Snowman of the Himalayas). Then there are legends destined to continue down through the centuries, such as that of the curing power of kings (King Pyrrhus, who cured disorders of the spleen by touching the patient with his big toe).

What emerges from all this is a dramatic notion of human nature as something precarious and insecure. The form and the destiny of man hang by a thread. Quite a number of pages are devoted to the unpredictability of childbirth, with the exceptional cases and the dangers and difficulties. This, too, is a frontier zone, for everyone who exists might very well not exist, or might be different, and it is *there* that it is all decided.

> In pregnant women everything—for example, the manner of walking—has an influence on childbirth. If they eat oversalted food they will give birth to a child without nails; if they cannot hold their breath they will have more trouble in delivering; during childbirth even a yawn can be fatal, as a sneeze during coitus can cause a miscarriage. Compassion and shame come over one who considers how precarious is the origin of the proudest of living beings: often the smell of a lately extinguished lamp is enough to cause a miscarriage. And to think that from such a frail beginning a tyrant or a butcher may be born! You who trust in your physical strength, who embrace the gifts of fortune and consider yourself not their ward but their son, you who have a domineering spirit, you who consider yourself a god as soon as success swells your breast, think how little could have destroyed you! [VII. 42-44]

One can understand why Pliny was so popular in the Christian Middle Ages: "To weigh life in a just balance one must always remember human fragility."

The human race is a zone of living things that should be defined by tracing its confines. Pliny therefore records the extreme limits reached by man in every field, and book VII becomes a kind of *Guinness Book of World Records.* They are chiefly quantitative records, such as strength in carrying weights, speed at running, acuteness of hearing or of memory, and so on, down to the size and extent of conquered territories. But there are also purely moral records—in virtue, generosity, and goodness. Nor is there a lack of curiosities—Antonia, wife of Drusus, who never spat; or the poet Pomponius, who never belched (VII. 80); or the highest price ever paid for a slave (the grammarian Daphnis cost seven hundred thousand sesterces, according to VII. 128).

Only about one aspect of human life does Pliny not feel inclined to quote records or attempt measurements or comparisons: happiness. It is impossible to say who is happy and who is not, since this depends on subjective and debatable criteria. (*"Felicitas cui praecipua fuerit homini, non est humani iudicii, cum prosperitatem ipsam alius alio modo et suopte ingenio quisque determinet"* [VII. 130]). If one is to look truth straight in the face, no man can be called happy, and here Pliny's anthropological survey reviews a whole rank of illustrious destinies (drawn mostly from Roman history) to show that the men most favored by fortune had to suffer unhappiness and mischance.

In the natural history of man it is impossible to include the variable that is destiny. This is the message of the pages Pliny devotes to the vicissitudes of fortune, to the unpredictability of the length of life, to the uselessness of astrology, and to sickness and death. The separation between the two forms of knowledge that astrology lumped together — the objectivity of calculable and predictable phenomena and the sense of individual existence as having an uncertain future — a separation that modern science takes for granted, can be found in these pages, but as a question not yet finally decided, so that exhaustive documentation is called for. In producing these examples Pliny seems to flounder a bit. Every event that has occurred, every biography, every anecdote can go to show that, if looked at from the point of view of someone living, life is not subject to either qualitative or quantitative judgment, and cannot be measured or compared with other lives. Its value is interior, all the more so because hopes and fears of another life are illusory. Pliny shares the opinion that after death begins a nonexistence equivalent to and symmetrical with that which came before birth.

This is why Pliny's attention is focused on the things of this world, the territories of the globe, heavenly bodies, animals, plants, and stones. The soul, to which any sort of survival is denied, can only enjoy being alive in the present if it withdraws into itself. *"Etenim si dulce vivere est, cui potest essere vixisse? At quanto facilius certiusque sibi quemque credere, specimen securitas antegenitali sumere experimento!"*: "To mold one's own peace of mind on the experience of before birth!" (VII. 190). In other words, we must project ourselves into our own absence, the only certain thing before we came into this world or after death. Hence the pleasure of recognizing the infinite variety of what is other than us, all of which the *Natural History* parades before our eyes.

If man is defined by his limitations, should he not also be defined by the points at which he excels? In book VII Pliny feels bound to include the praise of man's virtues and the celebration of his triumphs. Turning to Roman history as the exemplar of every virtue, he gives way to the temptation to reach a pompous conclusion in praise of the Empire by finding the zenith of human perfection in the person of Caesar Augustus. In my opinion, however, the characteristic note in his treatment is not this, but the hesitant, limitative, and disenchanted note, which best suits his temperament.

Here we can discern the questions that arose when anthropology was becoming a science. Should anthropology attempt to escape from a "humanistic" point of view to attain the objectivity of a science of nature? Do the men of book VII matter more, the more they are "other" and different from us, and perhaps most if they are no longer or not yet men at all? And is it really possible that man can emerge from his own subjectivity to the point of taking himself as an object of scientific knowledge? The moral that echoes back and forth in Pliny suggests caution and reservation: no science can illuminate us concerning happiness or fortune, the distribution of good and bad, or the values of existence. Each individual, when he dies, takes his secrets with him.

On this cheerless note Pliny might well have ended his dissertation, but he prefers to add a list of discoveries and inventions, both historical and legendary. Anticipating those modern anthropologists who maintain that there is continuity between biological evolution and technological evolution, from Paleolithic tools to electronics, Pliny implicitly admits that what man has added to nature becomes part of human nature. To demonstrate that man's true nature is his culture is only a step away. But Pliny, who has no time for generalizations, looks for what is specifically human in inventions and customs that might be considered universal. According to Pliny (or his sources) there are three cultural matters on which all peoples have reached a tacit agreement ("*gentium consensus tacitus*" [VI. 210]). These are the alphabet (both Greek and Latin), the shaving of men's beards, and the measurement of time by means of a sundial.

This triad could scarcely be more bizarre, given the incongruity between the three terms—alphabet, barber, and sundial—or, for that matter, more debatable. The fact is that not all peoples have similar ways of writing, nor is it true that everyone shaves; and as for the hours of the day, Pliny himself launches into a brief history of the various ways of subdividing time. But here we wish to stress not the "Eurocentric" viewpoint, which is not peculiar to Pliny or to his own age, but, rather, the direction he is taking. For the attempt to put a finger on the elements that are constantly repeated in the most diverse cultures, in order to define what is specifically human, was destined to become one of the principles of modern ethnology. And having established this point of *gentium consensus tacitus*, Pliny can conclude his treatise on the human race and pass on to other animate creatures.

Book VIII, which makes a general survey of the animals of the world, begins with the elephant, to which the longest chapter is devoted. Why is priority given to the elephant? Because it is the largest of the animals, certainly (Pliny's treatment proceeds according to an order of importance that often coincides with physical size), but also and above all because, spiritually, it is the animal "closest to man"! *"Maximum est elephas proximumque humanis sensibus"* is the opening of book VIII. In fact, the elephant — he explains immediately afterward — recognizes the language of his homeland, obeys orders, remembers what he learns, knows the passion of love and the ambition of glory, practices virtues "rare even among men," such as probity, prudence, and equity, and has a religious veneration for the sun, the moon, and the stars. Not one word (apart from that single superlative, *maximum*) does Pliny spend on describing this animal (which is, however, accurately portrayed in Roman mosaics of the time). He simply relates the legendary curiosities that he had found in books. The rites and customs of elephant society are represented as those of a people with a culture different from ours, but nonetheless worthy of respect and understanding.

In the *Natural History* man is lost in the middle of the multiform world, the prisoner of his own imperfection; yet, on the one hand, he has the relief of knowing that even God is limited in His powers (*"Imperfectae vero in homine naturae praecipus solacia, ne deum quidem posse omnia"* [II. 27]), while, on the other hand, his next-door neighbor is the elephant, who can serve him as a model on the spiritual plane. Between these two vast presences, both imposing and benign, man certainly appears cut down to size, but not crushed.

After the elephant, as in a childhood visit to the zoo, the review of the world's animals passes on to the lion, the panther, the tiger, the camel, the giraffe, the rhinoceros, and the crocodile. Then, following an order of decreasing dimensions, he goes on to the hyena, the chameleon, the porcupine, the animals that live in burrows, and even snails and lizards. The domestic animals are all lumped together at the end of book VIII.

Pliny's main source is Aristotle's *Historia animalium*, but he also goes to more credulous or fanciful authors for legends that the Stagirite rejected, or reported only to confute them. This is the case both with information about the better-known animals and with the mention of imaginary animals, the catalogue of which is interwoven with that of the real ones. Thus, while speaking of elephants, he makes a digression informing us about dragons, their natural enemies; in connection with wolves (though criticizing the credulity of the Greeks), he records the legends of the werewolf. It is in this branch of zoology that we find the amphisbaena, the basilisk, the catoblepa, the crocoti, the corocoti, the leukocroti, the leontophont, and the manticore, all destined to go on from these pages to populate the bestiaries of the Middle Ages.

The natural history of man is extended into that of animals throughout book VIII, and this not only because the knowledge recorded is to a large extent concerned with the rearing of domestic animals and the hunting of wild ones, as well as the practical use man makes of the one and the other, but also because what Pliny is doing is taking us on a guided tour of the human imagination. An animal, whether real or imaginary, has a place of honor in the sphere of the imagination. As soon as it is named it takes on a dreamlike power, becoming an allegory, a symbol, an emblem.

It is for this reason that I recommend to the reader who is wandering through these pages to pause not only at the most "philosophical" books (II and VII), but also at VIII, as the most representative of an idea of nature that is expressed at length in all the thirty-seven books of the work: nature as external to man, but not to be separated from what is most intrinsic to his mind—the alphabet of dreams, the code book of the imagination, without which there is neither thought nor reason.

II

Leslie Marmon Silko

Landscape, History, and the Pueblo Imagination

FROM A HIGH ARID PLATEAU IN NEW MEXICO

You see that after a thing is dead, it dries up. It might take weeks or years, but eventually if you touch the thing, it crumbles under your fingers. It goes back to dust. The soul of the thing has long since departed. With the plants and wild game the soul may have already been borne back into bones and blood or thick green stalk and leaves. Nothing is wasted. What cannot be eaten by people or in some way used must then be left where other living creatures may benefit. What domestic animals or wild scavengers can't eat will be fed to the plants. The plants feed on the dust of these few remains.

The ancient Pueblo people buried the dead in vacant rooms or partially collapsed rooms adjacent to the main living quarters. Sand and clay used to construct the roof make layers many inches deep once the roof has collapsed. The layers of sand and clay make for easy grave-digging. The vacant room fills with cast-off objects and debris. When a vacant room has filled deep enough, a shallow but adequate grave can be scooped in a far corner. Archaeologists have remarked over formal burials complete with elaborate funerary objects excavated in trash middens of abandoned rooms. But the rocks and adobe mortar of collapsed walls were valued by the ancient people. Because each rock had been carefully selected for size and shape, then chiseled to an even face. Even the pink clay adobe melting with each rainstorm had to be prayed over, then dug and carried some distance. Corn cobs and husks, the rinds and stalks and animal bones were not regarded by the ancient people as filth or garbage. The remains were merely resting at a midpoint in their journey back to dust. Human remains are not so different. They should rest with the bones and rinds where they all may benefit living creatures — small rodents and insects — until their return is completed. The remains of things — animals and plants, the clay and the stones — were treated with respect. Because for the ancient people all these things had spirit and being.

The antelope merely consents to return home with the hunter. All phases of the hunt are conducted with love. The love the hunter and the people have for the Antelope People. And the love of the antelope who agree to give up their meat and blood so that human beings will not starve. Waste of meat or even the thoughtless handling of bones cooked bare will offend the antelope spirits. Next year the hunters will vainly search the dry plains for antelope. Thus it is necessary to return carefully the bones and hair, and the stalks and leaves to the earth who first created them. The spirits remain close by. They do not leave us.

The dead become dust, and in this becoming they are once more joined with the Mother. The ancient Pueblo people called the earth the Mother Creator of all things in this world. Her sister, the Corn Mother, occasionally merges with her because all succulent green life rises out of the depths of the earth.

Rocks and clay are part of the Mother. They emerge in various forms, but at some time before, they were smaller particles or great boulders. At a later time they may again become what they once were. Dust.

A rock shares this fate with us and with animals and plants as well. A rock has being or spirit, although we may not understand it. The spirit may differ from the spirit we know in animals or plants or in ourselves. In the end we all originate from the depths of the earth. Perhaps this is how all beings share in the spirit of the Creator. We do not know.

FROM THE EMERGENCE PLACE

Pueblo potters, the creators of petroglyphs and oral narratives, never conceived of removing themselves from the earth and sky. So long as the human consciousness remains *within* the hills, canyons, cliffs, and the plants, clouds, and sky, the term *landscape*, as it has entered the English language, is misleading. "A portion of territory the eye can comprehend in a single view" does not correctly describe the relationship between the human being and his or her surroundings. This assumes the viewer is somehow *outside* or *separate from* the territory he or she surveys. Viewers are as much a part of the landscape as the boulders they stand on. There is no high mesa edge or mountain peak where one can stand and not immediately be part of all that surrounds. Human identity is linked with all the elements of Creation through the clan: you might belong to the Sun Clan or the Lizard Clan or the Corn

Clan or the Clay Clan.* Standing deep within the natural world, the ancient Pueblo understood the thing as it was—the squash blossom, grasshopper, or rabbit itself could never be created by the human hand. Ancient Pueblos took the modest view that the thing itself (the landscape) could not be improved upon. The ancients did not presume to tamper with what had already been created. Thus *realism*, as we now recognize it in painting and sculpture, did not catch the imaginations of Pueblo people until recently.

The squash blossom itself is *one thing*: itself. So the ancient Pueblo potter abstracted what she saw to be the key elements of the squash blossom—the four symmetrical petals, with four symmetrical stamens in the center. These key elements, while suggesting the squash flower, also link it with the four cardinal directions. By representing only its intrinsic form, the squash flower is released from a limited meaning or restricted identity. Even in the most sophisticated abstract form, a squash flower or a cloud or a lightning bolt became intricately connected with a complex system of relationships which the ancient Pueblo people maintained with each other, and with the populous natural world they lived within. A bolt of lightning is itself, but at the same time it may mean much more. It may be a messenger of good fortune when summer rains are needed. It may deliver death, perhaps the result of manipulations by the Gunnadeyahs, destructive necromancers. Lightning may strike down an evil-doer. Or lightning may strike a person of good will. If the person survives, lightning endows him or her with heightened power.

Pictographs and petroglyphs of constellations or elk or antelope draw their magic in part from the process wherein the focus of all prayer and concentration is upon the thing itself, which, in its turn, guides the hunter's hand. Connection with the spirit dimensions requires a figure or form which is all-inclusive. A "lifelike" rendering of an elk is too restrictive. Only the elk *is* itself. A *realistic* rendering of an elk would be only one particular elk anyway. The purpose of the hunt rituals and magic is to make contact with *all* the spirits of the Elk.

The land, the sky, and all that is within them—the landscape—includes human beings. Interrelationships in the Pueblo landscape are complex and fragile. The unpredictability of the weather, the aridity and harshness of much of the terrain in the high plateau country ex-

*Clan—*A social unit composed of families sharing common ancestors who trace their lineage back to the Emergence where their ancestors allied themselves with certain plants or animals or elements.*

plain in large part the relentless attention the ancient Pueblo people gave the sky and the earth around them. Survival depended upon harmony and cooperation not only among human beings, but among all things — the animate and the less animate, since rocks and mountains were known to move, to travel occasionally.

The ancient Pueblos believed the Earth and the Sky were sisters (or sister and brother in the post-Christian version). As long as good family relations are maintained, then the Sky will continue to bless her sister, the Earth, with rain, and the Earth's children will continue to survive. But the old stories recall incidents in which troublesome spirits or beings threaten the earth. In one story, a malicious ka'tsina, called the Gambler, seizes the Shiwana, or Rainclouds, the Sun's beloved children.* The Shiwana are snared in magical power late one afternoon on a high mountain top. The Gambler takes the Rainclouds to his mountain stronghold where he locks them in the north room of his house. What was his idea? The Shiwana were beyond value. They brought life to all things on earth. The Gambler wanted a big stake to wager in his games of chance. But such greed, even on the part of only one being, had the effect of threatening the survival of all life on earth. Sun Youth, aided by old Grandmother Spider, outsmarts the Gambler and the rigged game, and the Rainclouds are set free. The drought ends, and once more life thrives on earth.

THROUGH THE STORIES WE HEAR WHO WE ARE

All summer the people watch the west horizon, scanning the sky from south to north for rain clouds. Corn must have moisture at the time the tassels form. Otherwise pollination will be incomplete, and the ears will be stunted and shriveled. An inadequate harvest may bring disaster. Stories told at Hopi, Zuni, and at Acoma and Laguna describe drought and starvation as recently as 1900. Precipitation in west-central New Mexico averages fourteen inches annually. The western pueblos are located at altitudes over 5,600 feet above sea level, where winter temperatures at night fall below freezing. Yet evidence of their presence in the high desert plateau country goes back ten thousand years. The ancient Pueblo people not only survived in this environment, but many

---

*Ka'tsina — *Ka'tsinas are spirit beings who roam the earth and who inhabit kachina masks worn in Pueblo ceremonial dances.*

years they thrived. In A.D. 1100 the people at Chaco Canyon had built cities with apartment buildings of stone five stories high. Their sophistication as sky-watchers was surpassed only by Mayan and Inca astronomers. Yet this vast complex of knowledge and belief, amassed for thousands of years, was never recorded in writing.

Instead, the ancient Pueblo people depended upon collective memory through successive generations to maintain and transmit an entire culture, a world view complete with proven strategies for survival. The oral narrative, or "story," became the medium in which the complex of Pueblo knowledge and belief was maintained. Whatever the event or the subject, the ancient people perceived the world and themselves within that world as part of an ancient continuous story composed of innumerable bundles of other stories.

The ancient Pueblo vision of the world was inclusive. The impulse was to leave nothing out. Pueblo oral tradition necessarily embraced all levels of human experience. Otherwise, the collective knowledge and beliefs comprising ancient Pueblo culture would have been incomplete. Thus stories about the Creation and Emergence of human beings and animals into this World continue to be retold each year for four days and four nights during the winter solstice. The "humma-hah" stories related events from the time long ago when human beings were still able to communicate with animals and other living things. But, beyond these two preceding categories, the Pueblo oral tradition knew no boundaries. Accounts of the appearance of the first Europeans in Pueblo country or of the tragic encounters between Pueblo people and Apache raiders were no more and no less important than stories about the biggest mule deer ever taken or adulterous couples surprised in cornfields and chicken coops. Whatever happened, the ancient people instinctively sorted events and details into a loose narrative structure. Everything became a story.

Traditionally everyone, from the youngest child to the oldest person, was expected to listen and to be able to recall or tell a portion, if only a small detail, from a narrative account or story. Thus the remembering and retelling were a communal process. Even if a key figure, an elder who knew much more than others, were to die unexpectedly, the system would remain intact. Through the efforts of a great many people, the community was able to piece together valuable accounts and crucial information that might otherwise have died with an individual.

Communal storytelling was a self-correcting process in which listeners were encouraged to speak up if they noted an important fact or detail omitted. The people were happy to listen to two or three different versions of the same event or the same humma-hah story. Even conflicting versions of an incident were welcomed for the entertainment they provided. Defenders of each version might joke and tease one another, but seldom were there any direct confrontations. Implicit in the Pueblo oral tradition was the awareness that loyalties, grudges, and kinship must always influence the narrator's choices as she emphasizes to listeners this is the way *she* has always heard the story told. The ancient Pueblo people sought a communal truth, not an absolute. For them this truth lived somewhere within the web of differing versions, disputes over minor points, outright contradictions tangling with old feuds and village rivalries.

A dinner-table conversation, recalling a deer hunt forty years ago when the largest mule deer ever was taken, inevitably stimulates similar memories in listeners. But hunting stories were not merely after-dinner entertainment. These accounts contained information of critical importance about behavior and migration patterns of mule deer. Hunting stories carefully described key landmarks and locations of fresh water. Thus a deer-hunt story might also serve as a "map." Lost travelers, and lost piñon-nut gatherers, have been saved by sighting a rock formation they recognize only because they once heard a hunting story describing this rock formation.

The importance of cliff formations and water holes does not end with hunting stories. As offspring of the Mother Earth, the ancient Pueblo people could not conceive of themselves within a specific landscape. Location, or "place," nearly always plays a central role in the Pueblo oral narratives. Indeed, stories are most frequently recalled as people are passing by a specific geographical feature or the exact place where a story takes place. The precise date of the incident often is less important than the place or location of the happening. "Long, long ago," "a long time ago," "not too long ago," and "recently" are usually how stories are classified in terms of time. But the places where the stories occur are precisely located, and prominent geographical details recalled, even if the landscape is well-known to listeners. Often because the turning point in the narrative involved a peculiarity or special quality of a rock or tree or plant found only at that place. Thus, in the case of many of the Pueblo narratives, it is impossible to determine which came first: the incident or the geographical feature which begs to be brought alive in a story that features some unusual aspect of this location.

There is a giant sandstone boulder about a mile north of Old Laguna, on the road to Paguate. It is ten feet tall and twenty feet in circumference. When I was a child, and we would pass this boulder driving to Paguate village, someone usually made reference to the story about Kochininako, Yellow Woman, and the Estrucuyo, a monstrous giant who nearly ate her. The Twin Hero Brothers saved Kochininako, who had been out hunting rabbits to take home to feed her mother and sisters. The Hero Brothers had heard her cries just in time. The Estrucuyo had cornered her in a cave too small to fit its monstrous head. Kochininako had already thrown to the Estrucuyo all her rabbits, as well as her moccasins and most of her clothing. Still the creature had not been satisfied. After killing the Estrucuyo with their bows and arrows, the Twin Hero Brothers slit open the Estrucuyo and cut out its heart. They threw the heart as far as they could. The monster's heart landed there, beside the old trail to Paguate village, where the sandstone boulder rests now.

It may be argued that the existence of the boulder precipitated the creation of a story to explain it. But sandstone boulders and sandstone formations of strange shapes abound in the Laguna Pueblo area. Yet most of them do not have stories. Often the crucial element in a narrative is the terrain—some specific detail of the setting.

A high dark mesa rises dramatically from a grassy plain fifteen miles southeast of Laguna, in an area known as Swanee. On the grassy plain one hundred and forty years ago, my great-grandmother's uncle and his brother-in-law were grazing their herd of sheep. Because visibility on the plain extends for over twenty miles, it wasn't until the two sheepherders came near the high dark mesa that the Apaches were able to stalk them. Using the mesa to obscure their approach, the raiders swept around from both ends of the mesa. My great-grandmother's relatives were killed, and the herd lost. The high dark mesa played a critical role: the mesa had compromised the safety which the openness of the plains had seemed to assure. Pueblo and Apache alike relied upon the terrain, the very earth herself, to give them protection and aid. Human activities or needs were maneuvered to fit the existing surroundings and conditions. I imagine the last afternoon of my distant ancestors as warm and sunny for late September. They might have been traveling slowly, bringing the sheep closer to Laguna in preparation for the approach of colder weather. The grass was tall and only beginning to change from green to a yellow which matched the late-afternoon sun shining off it. There might have been comfort in the warmth and the sight of the sheep fattening on good pasture which lulled my ancestors into their fatal inattention. They might have had a rifle whereas the Apaches had only bows and arrows. But there would have been four or five Apache raiders, and the surprise attack would have canceled any advantage the rifles gave them.

Survival in any landscape comes down to making the best use of all available resources. On that particular September afternoon, the raiders made better use of the Swanee terrain than my poor ancestors did. Thus the high dark mesa and the story of the two lost Laguna herders became inextricably linked. The memory of them and their story resides in part with the high black mesa. For as long as the mesa stands, people within the family and clan will be reminded of the story of that afternoon long ago. Thus the continuity and accuracy of the oral narratives are reinforced by the landscape — and the Pueblo interpretation of that landscape is *maintained*.

THE MIGRATION STORY:
AN INTERIOR JOURNEY

The Laguna Pueblo migration stories refer to specific places — mesas, springs, or cottonwood trees — not only locations which can be visited still, but also locations which lie directly on the state highway route linking Paguate village with Laguna village. In traveling this road as a child with older Laguna people I first heard a few of the stories from that much larger body of stories linked with the Emergence and Migration.* It may be coincidental that Laguna people continue to follow the same route which, according to the Migration story, the ancestors followed south from the Emergence Place. It may be that the route is merely the shortest and best route for car, horse, or foot traffic between Laguna and Paguate villages. But if the stories about boulders, springs, and hills are actually remnants from a ritual that retraces the creation and emergence of the Laguna Pueblo people as a culture, as the people they became, then continued use of that route creates a unique rela-

---

*The Emergence — *All the human beings, animals, and life which had been created emerged from the four worlds below when the earth became habitable.*
The Migration — *The Pueblo people emerged into the Fifth World, but they had already been warned they would have to travel and search before they found the place they were meant to live.*

tionship between the ritual-mythic world and the actual, everyday world. A journey from Paguate to Laguna down the long incline of Paguate Hill retraces the original journey from the Emergence Place, which is located slightly north of the Paguate village. Thus the landscape between Paguate and Laguna takes on a deeper significance: the landscape resonates the spiritual or mythic dimension of the Pueblo world even today.

Although each Pueblo culture designates a specific Emergence Place — usually a small natural spring edged with mossy sandstone and full of cattails and wild watercress — it is clear that they do not agree on any single location or natural spring as the one and only true Emergence Place. Each Pueblo group recounts its own stories about Creation, Emergence, and Migration, although they all believe that all human beings, with all the animals and plants, emerged at the same place and at the same time.*

Natural springs are crucial sources of water for all life in the high desert plateau country. So the small spring near Paguate village is literally the source and continuance of life for the people in the area. The spring also functions on a spiritual level, recalling the original Emergence Place and linking the people and the spring water to all other people and to that moment when the Pueblo people became aware of themselves as they are even now. The Emergence was an emergence into a precise cultural identity. Thus the Pueblo stories about the Emergence and Migration are not to be taken as literally as the anthropologists might wish. Prominent geographical features and landmarks which are mentioned in the narratives exist for ritual purposes, not because the Laguna people actually journeyed south for hundreds of years from Chaco Canyon or Mesa Verde, as the archaeologists say, or eight miles from the site of the natural springs at Paguate to the sandstone hilltop at Laguna.

The eight miles, marked with boulders, mesas, springs, and river crossings, are actually a ritual circuit or path which marks the interior journey the Laguna people made: a journey of awareness and imagination in which they emerged from being within the earth and from everything included in earth to the culture and people they became, differen-

---

*Creation — *Tse'itsi'nako, Thought Woman, the Spider, thought about it, and everything she thought came into being. First she thought of three sisters for herself, and they helped her think of the rest of the Universe, including the Fifth World and the four worlds below.* The Fifth World *is the world we are living in today. There are four previous worlds below this world.*

tiating themselves for the first time from all that had surrounded them, always aware that interior distances cannot be reckoned in physical miles or in calendar years.

The narratives linked with prominent features of the landscape between Paguate and Laguna delineate the complexities of the relationship which human beings must maintain with the surrounding natural world if they hope to survive in this place. Thus the journey was an interior process of the imagination, a growing awareness that being human is somehow different from all other life — animal, plant, and inanimate. Yet we are all from the same source: the awareness never deteriorated into Cartesian duality, cutting off the human from the natural world.

The people found the opening into the Fifth World too small to allow them or any of the animals to escape. They had sent a fly out through the small hole to tell them if it was the world which the Mother Creator had promised. It was, but there was the problem of getting out. The antelope tried to butt the opening to enlarge it, but the antelope enlarged it only a little. It was necessary for the badger with her long claws to assist the antelope, and at last the opening was enlarged enough so that all the people and animals were able to emerge up into the Fifth World. The human beings could not have emerged without the aid of antelope and badger. The human beings depended upon the aid and charity of the animals. Only through interdependence could the human beings survive. Families belonged to clans, and it was by clan that the human being joined with the animal and plant world. Life on the high arid plateau became viable when the human beings were able to imagine themselves as sisters and brothers to the badger, antelope, clay, yucca, and sun. Not until they could find a viable relationship to the terrain, the landscape they found themselves in, could they *emerge*. Only at the moment the requisite balance between human and *other* was realized could the Pueblo people become a culture, a distinct group whose population and survival remained stable despite the vicissitudes of climate and terrain.

Landscape thus has similarities with dreams. Both have the power to seize terrifying feelings and deep instincts and translate them into images — visual, aural, tactile — into the concrete where human beings may more readily confront and channel the terrifying instincts or powerful emotions into rituals and narratives which reassure the individual while reaffirming cherished values of the group. The identity of the individual as a part of the group and the greater Whole is strengthened, and the terror of facing the world alone is extinguished.

Even now, the people at Laguna Pueblo spend the greater portion of social occasions recounting recent incidents or events which have occurred in the Laguna area. Nearly always, the discussion will precipitate the retelling of older stories about similar incidents or other stories connected with a specific place. The stories often contain disturbing or provocative material, but are nonetheless told in the presence of children and women. The effect of these inter-family or inter-clan exchanges is the reassurance for each person that she or he will never be separated or apart from the clan, no matter what might happen. Neither the worst blunders or disasters nor the greatest financial prosperity and joy will ever be permitted to isolate anyone from the rest of the group. In the ancient times, cohesiveness was all that stood between extinction and survival, and, while the individual certainly was recognized, it was always as an individual simultaneously bonded to family and clan by a complex bundle of custom and ritual. You are never the first to suffer a grave loss or profound humiliation. You are never the first, and you understand that you will probably not be the last to commit or be victimized by a repugnant act. Your family and clan are able to go on at length about others now passed on, others older or more experienced than you who suffered similar losses.

The wide deep arroyo near the Kings Bar (located acoss the reservation borderline) has over the years claimed many vehicles. A few years ago, when a Viet Nam veteran's new red Volkswagen rolled backwards into the arroyo while he was inside buying a six-pack of beer, the story of his loss joined the lively and large collection of stories already connected with that big arroyo. I do not know whether the Viet Nam veteran was consoled when he was told the stories about the other cars claimed by the ravenous arroyo. All his savings of combat pay had gone for the red Volkswagen. But this man could not have felt any worse than the man who, some years before, had left his children and mother-in-law in his station wagon with the engine running. When he came out of the liquor store his station wagon was gone. He found it and its passengers upside down in the big arroyo. Broken bones, cuts and bruises, and a total wreck of the car. The big arroyo has a wide mouth. Its existence needs no explanation. People in the area regard the arroyo much as they might regard a living being, which has a certain character and personality. I seldom drive past that wide deep arroyo without feeling a familiarity with and even a strange affection for this arroyo. Because as treacherous as it may be, the arroyo maintains a strong connection between human beings and the earth. The arroyo demands from us the caution and attention that constitute respect. It is this sort of respect the old believers have in mind when they tell us we must respect and love the earth.

Hopi Pueblo elders have said that the austere and, to some eyes, barren plains and hills surrounding their mesa-top villages actually help to nurture the spirituality of the Hopi *way*. The Hopi elders say the Hopi people might have settled in locations far more lush where daily life would not have been so grueling. But there on the high silent sandstone mesas that overlook the sandy arid expanses stretching to all horizons, the Hopi elders say the Hopi people must "live by their prayers" if they are to survive. The Hopi way cherishes the intangible: the riches realized from interaction and interrelationships with all beings above all else. Great abundances of material things, even food, the Hopi elders believe, tend to lure human attention away from what is most valuable and important. The views of the Hopi elders are not much different from those elders in all the Pueblos.

The bare vastness of the Hopi landscape emphasizes the visual impact of every plant, every rock, every arroyo. Nothing is overlooked or taken for granted. Each ant, each lizard, each lark is imbued with great value simply because the creature is there, simply because the creature is alive in a place where any life at all is precious. Stand on the mesa edge at Walpai and look west over the bare distances toward the pale blue outlines of the San Francisco peaks where the ka'tsina spirits reside. So little lies between you and the sky. So little lies between you and the earth. One look and you know that simply to survive is a great triumph, that every possible resource is needed, every possible ally — even the most humble insect or reptile. You realize you will be speaking with all of them if you intend to last out the year. Thus it is that the Hopi elders are grateful to the landscape for aiding them in their quest as spiritual people.

Keith H. Basso

"Stalking with Stories":
Names, Places, and Moral Narratives
Among the Western Apache

Shortly before his death in 1960, Clyde Kluckhohn made the following observation in a course he gave at Harvard University on the history of anthropological thought: "The most interesting claims people make are those they make about themselves. Cultural anthropologists should keep this in mind, especially when they are doing fieldwork." This essay focuses on a small set of spoken texts in which members of a contemporary American Indian society express claims about themselves, their language, and the lands on which they live. Specifically, I shall be concerned here with a set of statements that were made by men and women from the Western Apache community at Cibecue, a dispersed settlement of 1100 people that has been inhabited by Apaches for centuries and is located near the center of Fort Apache Indian Reservation in east-central Arizona (see Figure 1). The statements that interest me, which could be supplemented by a large number of others, are the following.

1. The land is always stalking people. The land makes people live right. The land looks after us. The land looks after people. [Mrs. Annie Peaches, age 77, 1977]
2. Our children are losing the land. It doesn't go to work on them anymore. They don't know the stories about what happened at these places. That's why some get into trouble. [Mr. Ronnie Lupe, age 42; Chairman, White Mountain Apache Tribe, 1978]
3. We used to survive only off the land. Now it's no longer that way. Now we live only with money, so we need jobs. But the land still looks after us. We know the names of the places where

Figure 1. Map showing location of the community of Cibecue on the Fort Apache Indian Reservation, Arizona.

everything happened. So we stay away from badness. [Mr. Nick Thompson, age 64, 1980]

4. I think of that mountain called "white rocks lie above in a compact cluster" as if it were my maternal grandmother. I recall stories of how it once was at that mountain. The stories told to me were like arrows. Elsewhere, hearing that mountain's name, I see it. Its name is like a picture. Stories go to work on

you like arrows. Stories make you live right. Stories make you replace yourself. [Mr. Benson Lewis, age 64, 1979]

5. One time I went to L.A., training for mechanic. It was no good, sure no good. I start drinking, hang around bars all the time. I start getting into trouble with my wife, fight sometimes with her. It was *bad*. I forget about this country here around Cibecue. I forget all the names and stories. I don't hear them in my mind anymore. I forget how to live right, forget how to be strong. [Mr. Wilson Lavender, age 52, 1975]

If the texts of these statements resist quick and easy interpretation, it is not because the people who made them are confused or cloudy thinkers. Neither is it because, as one unfortunate commentator would have us believe, the Western Apache are "mystically inclined and correspondingly inarticulate." The problem we face is a semiotic one, a barrier to constructing appropriate sense and significance. It arises from the obvious circumstance that all views articulated by Apache people are informed by their experience in a culturally constituted world of objects and events with which most of us are unfamiliar. What sort of world is it? Or, to draw the question into somewhat sharper focus, what is the cultural context in which Apache statements such as those presented above find acceptance as valid claims about reality?

More specifically, what is required to interpret Annie Peaches's claim that the land occupied by the Western Apache is "always stalking people" and that because of this they know how to "live right"? And how should we understand Chairman Lupe's assertion that Apache children sometimes misbehave because the land "doesn't go to work on them anymore"? Why does Nick Thompson claim that his knowledge of place-names and historical events enables him to "stay away from badness"? And why does Benson Lewis liken place-names to pictures, stories to arrows, and a mountain near the community of Cibecue to his maternal grandmother? What should we make of Wilson Lavender's recollection of an unhappy time in California when forgetting place-names and stories caused him to forget "how to be strong"? Are these claims structured in metaphorical terms, or, given Western Apache assumptions about the physical universe and the place of people within it, are they somehow to be interpreted literally? In any case, what is the reasoning that lies behind the claims, the informal logic of which they are simultaneously products and expressions? Above all, what makes the claims make sense?

I address these and other questions through an investigation of how Western Apaches talk about the natural landscape and the importance they attach to named locations within it. Accordingly, my discussion focuses on elements of language and patterns of speech, my purpose being to discover from these elements and patterns something of how Apache people construe their land and render it intelligible. Whenever Apaches describe the land—or, as happens more frequently, whenever they tell stories about incidents that have occurred at particular points upon it—they take steps to constitute it in relation to themselves. Which is simply to say that in acts of speech, mundane and otherwise, Apaches negotiate images and understandings of the land which are accepted as credible accounts of what it actually is, why it is significant, and how it impinges on the daily lives of men and women.

"LEARN THE NAMES"

Nick Thompson is, by his own admission, an old man. It is possible, he told me once, that he was born in 1918. Beneath snow-white hair cut short, his face is round and compact, his features small and sharply molded. His large, black, and very bright eyes move quickly, and when he smiles he acquires an expression that is at once mischievous and intimidating. I have known him for more than 20 years, and he has instructed me often on matters pertaining to Western Apache language and culture. A man who delights in play, he has also teased me unmercifully, concocted humorous stories about me that are thoroughly apocryphal, and embarrassed me before large numbers of incredulous Apaches by inquiring publicly into the most intimate details of my private life. Described by many people in Cibecue as a true "Slim Coyote" (*ma' ts'ósé*), Nick Thompson is outspoken, incorrigible, and unabashed.[1] He is also generous, thoughtful, and highly intelligent. I value his friendship immensely.

As I bring my Jeep to a halt on the road beside the old man's camp, I hear Nick complaining loudly to his wife about the changing character of life in Cibecue and its regrettable effects on younger members of the community. I have heard these complaints before and I know they are deeply felt. But still, on this sunny morning in June

1. *A prominent figure in Western Apache oral literature, Slim Coyote is appreciated by Apache people for his keen and crafty intelligence, his complex and unpredictable personality, and his penchant for getting himself into difficult situations from which he always manages to extract himself, usually with humorous and embarrassing results.*

1977, it is hard to suppress a smile, for the image Nick presents, a striking example of what can be achieved with sartorial *bricolage*, is hardly what one would expect of a staunch tribal conservative. Crippled since childhood and partially paralyzed by a recent stroke, the old man is seated in the shade of a cottonwood tree a few yards from the modest wooden cabin where he lives with his wife and two small grandchildren. He is smoking a mentholated Salem cigarette and is studying with undisguised approval the shoes on his feet—a new pair of bright blue Nike running shoes trimmed in incandescent orange. He is also wearing a pair of faded green trousers, a battered brown cowboy hat, and a white T-shirt with "Disneyland" printed in large red letters across the front. Within easy reach of his chair, resting on the base of an upended washtub, is a copy of the *National Enquirer*, a mug of hot coffee, and an open box of chocolate-covered doughnuts. If Nick Thompson is an opponent of social change, it is certainly not evident from his appearance. But appearances can be deceiving, and Nick, who is an accomplished singer and a medicine man of substantial reputation, would be the first to point this out.

The old man greets me with his eyes. Nothing is said for a minute or two, but then we begin to talk, exchanging bits of local news until enough time has passed for me to politely announce the purpose of my visit. I explain that I am puzzled by certain statements that Apaches have made about the country surrounding Cibecue and that I am anxious to know how to interpret them. To my surprise, Nick does not ask what I have been told or by whom. He responds instead by swinging out his arm in a wide arc. "Learn the names," he says. "Learn the names of all these places." Unprepared for such a firm and unequivocal suggestion (it sounds to me like nothing less than an order), I retreat into silence. "Start with the names," the old man continues. "I will teach you like before. Come back tomorrow morning." Nodding in agreement, I thank Nick for his willingness to help and tell him what I will be able to pay him. He says the wage is fair.

A few moments later, as I stand to take my leave, Nick's face breaks suddenly into a broad smile and his eyes begin to dance. I know that look very well and brace myself for the farewell joke that almost always accompanies it. The old man wastes no time. He says I look lonely. He urges me to have prolonged and abundant sex with very old women. He says it prevents nosebleeds. He says that someday I can write a book about it. Flustered and at a loss for words, I smile weakly and shake my head. Delighted with this reaction, Nick laughs heartily

and reaches for his coffee and a chocolate-covered doughnut. Our encounter has come to an end.

I return to the old man's camp the following day and start to learn
Western Apache place-names. My lessons, which are interrupted by
mapping trips with more mobile Apache consultants, continue for the
next ten weeks. In late August, shortly before I must leave Cibecue,
Nick asks to see the maps. He is not impressed. "White men need paper
maps," he observes. "We have maps in our minds."

Located in a narrow valley at an elevation of 1507 m, the settlement
at Cibecue (from *deeschii' bikoh*, "valley with elongated red bluffs") is
bisected by a shallow stream emanating from springs that rise in low-
lying mountains to the north. Apache homes, separated by horse
pastures, agricultural plots, and ceremonial dancegrounds, are located
on both sides of the stream for a distance of approximately 8 km. The
valley itself, which is bounded on the east and west by a broken series
of red sandstone bluffs, displays marked topographic diversity in the
form of heavily dissected canyons and arroyos, broad alluvial flood
plains, and several clusters of prominent peaks. Vegetation ranges
from a mixed Ponderosa Pine-Douglas Fir association near the headwaters of Cibecue Creek to a chaparral community, consisting of scrub
oak, cat's-claw, agave, and a variety of cactus species, at the confluence
of the creek with the Salt River. In between, numerous other floral
associations occur, including dense riparian communities and heavy
stands of cottonwood, oak, walnut, and pine.

Together with Michael W. Graves, I have mapped nearly 104 km^2
in and around the community at Cibecue and within this area have
recorded the Western Apache names of 296 locations; it is, to say the
least, a region densely packed with place-names. But large numbers
alone do not account for the high frequency with which place-names
typically appear in Western Apache discourse. In part, this pattern of
regular and recurrent use results from the fact that Apaches, who travel
a great deal to and from their homes, habitually call on each other to
describe their trips in detail. Almost invariably, and in sharp contrast
to comparable reports delivered by Anglos living at Cibecue, these
descriptions focus as much on *where* events occurred as on the nature
and consequences of the events themselves. This practice has been observed in other Apachean groups as well, including, as Harry Hoijer
(personal communication, 1973) notes, the Navajo: "Even the most

minute occurrences are described by Navajos in close conjunction with their physical settings, suggesting that unless narrated events are *spatially anchored* their significance is somehow reduced and cannot be properly assessed." Hoijer could just as well be speaking of the Western Apache.

Something else contributes to the common use of place-names in Western Apache communities, however, and that, quite simply, is that Apaches enjoy using them. For example, several years ago, when I was stringing a barbed-wire fence with two Apache cowboys from Cibecue, I noticed that one of them was talking quietly to himself. When I listened carefully, I discovered that he was reciting a list of place-names—a long list, punctuated only by spurts of tobacco juice, that went on for nearly ten minutes. Later, when I ventured to ask him about it, he said he frequently "talked names" to himself. Why? "I like to," he said. "I ride that way in my mind." And on dozens of other occasions when I have been working or traveling with Apaches, they have taken satisfaction in pointing out particular locations and pronouncing their names—once, twice, three times or more. Why? "Because we like to," or "Because those names are good to say." More often, however, Apaches account for their enthusiastic use of place-names by commenting on the precision with which the names depict their referents. "That place looks just like its name," someone will explain, or "That name makes me see that place like it really is." Or, as Benson Lewis (example 4) states so succinctly, "Its name is like a picture."

Statements such as these may be interpreted in light of certain facts about the linguistic structure of Western Apache place-names. To begin with, it is essential to understand that all but a very few Apache place-names take the form of complete sentences. This is made possible by one of the most prominent components of the Western Apache language: an elaborate system of prefixes that operates most extensively and productively to modify the stems of verbs. Thus, well-formed sentences can be constructed that are extremely compact yet semantically very rich. It is this combination of brevity and expressiveness, I believe, that appeals to Apaches and makes the mere pronunciation of place-names a satisfying experience.

"ALL THESE PLACES HAVE STORIES"

When I return to Cibecue in the spring of 1978, Nick Thompson is recovering from a bad case of the flu. He is weak, despondent, and uncomfortable. We speak very little and no mention is made of place-names. His wife is worried about him and so am I. Within a week, however, Nick's eldest son comes to my camp with a message: I am to visit his father and bring with me two packs of Salem cigarettes and a dozen chocolate-covered doughnuts. This is good news.

When I arrive at the old man's camp, he is sitting under the cottonwood tree by his house. A blanket is draped across his knees and he is wearing a heavy plaid jacket and a red vinyl cap with white fur-lined earflaps. There is color in his cheeks and the sparkle is back in his eyes. Shortly after we start to converse, and apropos of nothing I can discern, Nick announces that in 1931 he had sexual intercourse eight times in one night. He wants to know if I have ever been so fortunate. His wife, who has brought us each a cup of coffee, hears this remark and tells him that he is a crazy old man. Nick laughs loudly. Plainly, he is feeling better.

Eventually, I ask Nick if he is ready to resume our work together. "Yes," he says, "but no more on names." What then? "Stories," is his reply. "All these places have stories. We shoot each other with them, like arrows. Come back tomorrow morning." Puzzled once again, but suspecting that the old man has a plan he wants to follow, I tell him I will return. We then discuss Nick's wages. He insists that I pay him more than the year before as it is necessary to keep up with inflation. I agree and we settle on a larger sum. Then comes the predictable farewell joke: a fine piece of nonsense in which Nick, speaking English and imitating certain mannerisms he has come to associate with Anglo physicians, diagnoses my badly sunburned nose as an advanced case of venereal disease.[2] This time it is Nick's wife who laughs loudest.

The next day Nick begins to instruct me on aspects of Western Apache storytelling. Consulting on a regular basis with other Apaches from Cibecue as well, I pursue this topic throughout the summer of 1978.

WESTERN APACHE HISTORICAL TALES

If place-names appear frequently in ordinary forms of Western Apache discourse, their use is equally conspicuous in oral narratives. It is here,

2. *Jokes of this type are intended to poke fun at the butt of the joke and, at the same time, to comment negatively on the interactional practices of Anglo-Americans.*

in conjunction with stories Apaches tell, that we can move closer to an interpretation of native claims about the symbolic importance of geographical features and the personalized relationships that individuals may have with them. The people of Cibecue classify "speech" (*yat'i'*) into three major forms: "ordinary talk" (*yat'i'*), "prayer" (*'okąąhí*), and "narratives" or "stories" (*nagoldi'é*). Narratives are further classified into four major and two minor genres. The major genres include "myths" (*godiyįhgo nagoldi'*; literally, "to tell the holiness"), "historical tales" (*'ágodzaahí* or *'ágodzaahí nagoldi'*; literally, "that which has happened" or "to tell of that which has happened"), "sagas" (*nlt'éégo nagoldi'*; literally, "to tell of pleasantness"), and stories that arise in the context of "gossip" (*ch'idii*). The minor genres, which do not concern us here, are "Coyote stories" (*ma' highaalyú' nagoldi'*; literally "to tell of Coyote's travels") and "seduction tales" (*biniíma' nagoldi'*; literally, "to tell of sexual desires").

Western Apaches distinguish among the major narrative genres on two basic semantic dimensions: time and purpose. Values on the temporal dimension identify in general terms when the events recounted in narratives took place, while values on the purposive dimension describe the objectives that Apache narrators typically have in recounting them (see Figure 2). Accordingly, "myths" deal with events that occurred "in the beginning" (*'godiyaaná'*), a time when the universe and all things within it were achieving their present form and location. Performed only by the medicine men and medicine women, myths are

Narrative Category	Temporal Locus of Events	Purposes
godiyįhgo nagoldi' ("myth")	*godiyaaná'* ("in the beginning")	to enlighten; to instruct
'ágodzaahí ("historical tale")	*doo 'ánííná'* ("long ago")	to criticize; to warn; to "shoot"
nlt'éégo nagoldi' ("saga")	*díijįigo* ("modern times")	to entertain; to engross
ch'idii ("gossip")	*k'ad* ("now")	to inform; to malign

Figure 2. Major categories of Western Apache narrative distinguished by temporal locus of events and primary purposes for narration.

presented for the primary purpose of enlightenment and instruction: to explain and reaffirm the complex processes by which the known world came into existence. "Historical tales" recount events that took place "long ago" (*doo 'ániiná*) when the Western Apache people, having emerged from below the surface of the earth, were developing their own distinctive ways and customs. Most historical tales describe incidents that occurred prior to the coming of the white man, but some of these stories are set in postreservation times, which began for the Western Apache in 1872. Like myths, historical tales are intended to edify, but their main purpose is to alarm and criticize social delinquents (or, as the Apache say, to "shoot" them), thereby impressing such individuals with the undesirability of improper behavior and alerting them to the punitive consequences of further misconduct.

Although sagas deal with historical themes, these narratives are chiefly concerned with events that have taken place in "modern times" (*diijiigo*), usually within the last 60 or 70 years. In contrast to historical tales, which always focus on serious and disturbing matters, sagas are largely devoid of them. Rather than serving as vehicles of personal criticism, the primary purpose of sagas is to provide their listeners with relaxation and entertainment. Stories of the kind associated with gossip consist of reports in which persons relate and interpret events involving other members of the Western Apache community. These stories, which embrace incidents that have occurred "now" or "at present" (*k'ad*), are often told for no other reason than to keep people informed of local developments. Not uncommonly, however, narratives in gossip are also used to ridicule and malign the character of their subjects.

Nowhere do place-names serve more important communicative functions than in the context of historical tales. As if to accentuate this fact, stories of the *'ágodzaahí* genre are stylistically quite simple. Historical tales require no specialized lexicon, display no unusual syntactical constructions, and involve no irregular morphophonemic alternations; neither are they characterized by unique patterns of stress, pitch, volume, or intonation. In these ways *'agodzaahí* narratives contrast sharply with myths and sagas, which entail the use of a variety of genre-specific stylistic devices. Historical tales also differ from myths and sagas by virtue of their brevity. Whereas myths and sagas may take hours to complete, historical tales can usually be delivered in less than five minutes. Western Apache storytellers point out that this is both fitting and effective, because *'ágodzaahí* stories, like the "arrows" (*k'aa*) they are commonly said to represent, work best when they move swiftly. Finally, and most significant of all, historical tales are distinguished from all other forms of Apache narrative by an opening and closing line that identifies with a place-name where the events in the narrative occurred. These lines frame the narrative, mark it unmistakably as belonging to the *'agodzaahí* genre, and evoke a particular physical setting in which listeners can imaginatively situate everything that happens. It is hardly surprising, then, that while Apache storytellers agree that historical tales are "about" the events recounted in the tales, they also emphasize that the tales are "about" the sites at which the events took place.

If the style of Western Apache historical tales is relatively unremarkable, their content is just the opposite. Without exception, and usually in very graphic terms, historical tales focus on persons who suffer misfortune as the consequence of actions that violate Apache standards for acceptable social behavior. More specifically, *'ágodzaahí* stories tell of persons who have acted unthinkingly and impulsively in open disregard for "Apache custom" (*ndee bi 'at'ee'*) and who pay for their transgressions by being humiliated, ostracized, or killed. Stories of the *'agodzaahí* variety are morality tales pure and simple. When viewed as such by the Apaches—as compact commentaries on what should be avoided so as to deal successfully and effectively with other people—they are highly informative. For what these narratives assert—tacitly, perhaps, but with dozens of compelling examples—is that immoral behavior is irrevocably a community affair and that persons who behave badly will be punished sooner or later. Thus, just as *'ágodzaahí* stories are "about" historical events and their geographical locations, they are also "about" the system of rules and values according to which Apaches expect each other to organize and regulate their lives. In an even more fundamental sense, then, historical tales are "about" what it means to *be* a Western Apache, or, to make the point less dramatically, what it is that being an Apache should normally and properly entail.

To see how this is so, let us consider the texts of three historical tales and examine the manner in which they have been interpreted by their Apache narrators.

1. It happened at "big cottonwood trees stand spreading here and there."

Long ago, the Pimas and Apaches were fighting. The Pimas were carrying long clubs made from mesquite wood; they were also heavy and hard. Before dawn the Pimas arrived at Cibecue and attacked the Apaches there. The Pimas attacked while the Apaches were still asleep. The Pimas killed the Apaches with their clubs. An old woman woke up; she heard the Apaches crying out. The old woman thought it was her son-in-law because he often picked on her daughter. The old woman cried out: "You pick on my child a lot. You should act pleasantly toward her." Because the old woman cried out, the Pimas learned where she was. The Pimas came running to the old woman's camp and killed her with their clubs. A young girl ran away from there and hid beneath some bushes. She alone survived.

It happened at "big cottonwood trees stand spreading here and there."

Narrated by Mrs. Annie Peaches, this historical tale deals with the harmful consequences that may come to persons who overstep traditional role boundaries. During the first year of marriage it is customary for young Apache couples to live in the camp of the bride's parents. At this time, the bride's mother may request that her son-in-law perform different tasks and she may also instruct and criticize him. Later, however, when the couple establishes a separate residence, the bride's mother forfeits this right and may properly interfere in her son-in-law's affairs only at the request of her daughter. Mrs. Peaches explains that women who do not abide by this arrangement imply that their sons-in-law are immature and irresponsible, which is a source of acute embarrassment for the young men and their wives. Thus, even when meddling might seem to serve a useful purpose, it should be scrupulously avoided. The woman on whom this story centers failed to remember this—and was instantly killed.

2. It happened at "coarse-textured rocks lie above in a compact cluster."

Long ago, a man became sexually attracted to his stepdaughter. He was living below "coarse-textured rocks lie above in a compact cluster" with his stepdaughter and her mother. Waiting until no one else was present, and sitting alone with her, he started to molest her. The girl's maternal uncle happened to come by and he killed the man with a rock. The man's skull was cracked open. It was raining. The girl's maternal uncle dragged the man's body up above to "coarse-textured rocks lie above in a compact cluster" and placed it there in a storage pit. The girl's mother came home and was told by her daughter of all that had happened. The people who owned the storage pit removed the man's body and put it somewhere else. The people never had a wake for the dead man's body.

It happened at "coarse-textured rocks lie above in a compact cluster."

Narrated by Mr. Benson Lewis, this historical tale deals with the theme of incest, for sexual contact with stepchildren is considered by Western Apaches to be an incestuous act. According to Mr. Lewis, the key line in the story is the penultimate one in which he observes, "The people never had a wake for the dead man's body." We may assume, Mr. Lewis says, that because the dead man's camp was located near the storage pit in which his body was placed, the people who owned the pit were also his relatives. This makes the neglect with which his corpse was treated all the more profound, since kinsmen are bound by the strongest of obligations to care for each other when they die. That the dead man's relatives chose to dispense with customary mortuary ritual shows with devastating clarity that they wished to disown him completely.

3. It happened at "men stand above here and there."

Long ago, a man killed a cow off the reservation. The cow belonged to a Whiteman. The man was arrested by a policeman living at Cibecue at "men stand above here and there." The policeman was an Apache. The policeman took the man to the head Army officer at Fort Apache. There, at Fort Apache, the head Army officer questioned him. "What do you want?" he said. The policeman said, "I need cartridges and food." The policeman said nothing about the man who had killed the Whiteman's cow. That night some people spoke to the policeman. "It is best to report on him," they said to him. The next day the policeman returned to the head Army officer. "Now what do you want?" he said. The policeman said, "Yesterday I was going to say HELLO and GOOD-BYE but I forgot to do it." Again he said nothing about the man he arrested. Someone was working with words on his mind. The policeman returned with the man to Cibecue. He released him at "men stand above here and there."

It happened at "men stand above here and there."

This story, narrated by Nick Thompson, describes what happened to a man who acted too much like a white man. Between 1872 and 1895, when the Western Apache were strictly confined to their reservations by U.S. military forces, disease and malnutrition took the lives of many people. Consequently, Apaches who listen to this historical tale find it perfectly acceptable that the man who lived at "men stand above here and there" should have killed and butchered a white man's cow. What is not acceptable is that the policeman, another Apache from the same settlement, should have arrested the rustler and contemplated taking him to jail. But the policeman's plans were thwarted. Someone used witchcraft on him and made him stupid and forgetful. He never informed the military officer at Fort Apache of the real purpose of his visit, and his second encounter with the officer—in which he apologized for neglecting to say "hello" and "good-bye" the previous day—revealed him to be an absurd and laughable figure. Although Western Apaches find portions of this story amusing, Nick Thompson explains that they understand it first and foremost as a harsh indictment of persons who join with outsiders against members of their own community and who, as if to flaunt their lack of allegiance, parade the attitudes and mannerisms of white men.

Thus far, my remarks on what Western Apache historical tales are "about" have centered on features of textual content. This is a familiar strategy and certainly a necessary one, but it is also incomplete. In addition to everything else—places, events, moral standards, conceptions of cultural identity—every historical tale is also "about" the person at whom it is directed. This is because the telling of a historical tale is always prompted by an individual having committed one or more social offenses to which the act of narration, together with the tale itself, is intended as a critical and remedial response. Thus, on those occasions when 'agodzaahí stories are actually told—by real Apache storytellers, in real interpersonal contexts, to real social offenders—these narratives are understood to be accompanied by an unstated message from the storyteller that may be phrased something like this: "I know that you have acted in a way similar or analogous to the way in which someone acted in the story I am telling you. If you continue to act in this way, something similar or analogous to what happened to the character in the story might also happen to you." This metacommunicative message is just as important as any conveyed by the text of the storyteller's tale. For Apaches contend that if the message is taken to heart by the person at whom the tale is aimed—and if, in conjunction with lessons drawn from the tale itself, he or she resolves to improve his or her behavior — a lasting bond will have been created between that individual and the site or sites at which events in the tale took place. The cultural premises that inform this powerful idea will be made explicit presently; but first, in order to understand more clearly what the idea involves, let us examine the circumstances that led to the telling of a historical tale at Cibecue and see how this narrative affected the person for whom it was told.

In early June 1977, a 17-year-old Apache woman attended a girls' puberty ceremonial at Cibecue with her hair rolled up in a set of oversized pink plastic curlers. She had returned home two days before from a boarding school in Utah where this sort of ornamentation was considered fashionable by her peers. Something so mundane would have gone unnoticed by others were it not for the fact that Western Apache women of all ages are expected to appear at puberty ceremonials with their hair worn loose. This is one of several ways that women have of showing respect for the ceremonial and also, by implication, for the people who have staged it. The practice of presenting oneself with free-flowing hair is also understood to contribute to the ceremonial's effectiveness, for Apaches hold that the ritual's most basic objectives, which are to invest the pubescent girl with qualities necessary for life as an adult, cannot be achieved unless standard forms of respect are faithfully observed. On this occasion at Cibecue, everyone was following custom except the young woman who arrived wearing curlers. She soon became an object of attention and quiet expressions of disapproval, but no one spoke to her about the large cylindrical objects in her hair.

Two weeks later, the same young woman made a large stack of tortillas and brought them to the camp of her maternal grandmother, a widow in her mid-60s who had organized a small party to celebrate the birthday of her eldest grandson. Eighteen people were on hand, myself included, and all of us were treated to hot coffee and a dinner of boiled beef and potatoes. When the meal was over casual conversation began to flow, and the young woman seated herself on the ground next to her younger sister. And then — quietly, deftly, and totally without warning — her grandmother narrated a version of the historical tale about the forgetful Apache policeman who behaved too much like a white man. Shortly after the story was finished, the young woman stood up, turned away wordlessly, and walked off in the direction of her home. Uncertain of what had happened, I asked her grandmother why she had departed. Had the young woman suddenly become ill? "No," her grandmother replied. "I shot her with an arrow."

Approximately two years after this incident occurred, I found myself again in the company of the young woman with the taste for distinctive hairstyles. She had purchased a large carton of groceries at the trading post at Cibecue, and when I offered to drive her home with them she accepted. I inquired on the way if she remembered the time that her grandmother had told us the story about the forgetful policeman. She said she did and then went on, speaking in English, to describe her reactions to it. "I think maybe my grandmother was getting after me, but then I think maybe not, maybe she's working on somebody else. Then I think back on that dance and I know it's me for sure. I sure don't like how she's talking about me, so I quit looking like that. I threw those curlers away." In order to reach the young woman's camp, we had to pass within a few hundred yards of *ndee dah naazííh* ("men stand above here and there"), the place where the man had lived who was arrested in the story for rustling. I pointed it out to my companion. She said nothing for several moments. Then she smiled and spoke softly in her own language: "I know that place. It stalks me every day."

The comments of this Western Apache woman on her experience as the target of a historical tale are instructive in several respects. To begin with, her statement enables us to imagine something of the sizable psychological impact that historical tales may have on the persons to whom they are presented. Then, too, we can see how *'ágodzaahí* stories may produce quick and palpable effects on the behavior of such individuals, causing them to modify their social conduct in quite specific ways. Lastly, and most revealing of all, the young woman's remarks provide a clear illustration of what Apaches have in mind when they assert that historical tales may establish highly meaningful relationships between individuals and features of the natural landscape.

To appreciate fully the significance of these relationships, as well as their influence on the lives of Western Apache people, we must explore more thoroughly the manner in which the relationships are conceptualized. This can be accomplished through a closer examination of Apache ideas about the activity of storytelling and the acknowledged power of oral narratives, especially historical tales, to promote beneficial changes in people's attitudes toward their responsibilities as members of a moral community. These ideas, which combine to form a native model of how oral narratives work to achieve their intended effects, are expressed in terms of a single dominant metaphor. By now it should come as no surprise to learn that the metaphor draws heavily on the imagery of hunting.

"STALKING WITH STORIES"

Nick Thompson is tired. We have been talking about hunting with stories for two days now and the old man has not had an easy time of it. Yesterday, my uneven control of the Western Apache language prevented him from speaking as rapidly and eloquently as he would have liked, and on too many occasions I was forced to interrupt him with questions. At one point, bored and annoyed with my queries, he told me that I reminded him of a horsefly buzzing around his head. Later, however, when he seemed satisfied that I could follow at least the outline of his thoughts, he recorded on tape a lengthy statement which he said contained everything he wanted me to know. "Take it with you and listen to it," he said. "Tomorrow we put it in English." For the last six hours that is what we have been trying to do. We are finished now and weary of talking. In the weeks to come I will worry about the depth and force of our translation, and twice more I will return to Nick's camp with other questions. But the hardest work is over and both of us know it. Nick has taught me already that hunting with stories is not a simple matter, and as I prepare to leave I say so. "We know," he says, and that is all. Here is Nick Thompson's statement:

This is what we know about our stories. They go to work on your mind and make you think about your life. Maybe you've not been acting right. Maybe you've been stingy. Maybe you've been chasing after women. Maybe you've been trying to act like a Whiteman. People don't *like* it! So someone goes hunting for you — maybe your grandmother, your grandfather, your uncle. It doesn't matter. Anyone can do it.

So someone stalks you and tells a story about what happened long ago. It doesn't matter if other people are around — you're going to know he's aiming that story at you. All of a sudden it *hits* you! It's like an arrow, they say. Sometimes it just bounces off — it's too soft and you don't think about anything. But when it's strong it goes in *deep* and starts working on your mind right away. No one says anything to you, only that story is all, but now you know that people have been watching you and talking about you. They don't like how you've been acting. So you have to think about your life.

Then you feel weak, real weak, like you are sick. You don't want to eat or talk to anyone. That story is working on you now. You keep thinking about it. That story is changing you now, making you want to live right. That story is making you want to replace yourself. You think only of what you did that was wrong and you don't like it. So you want to live better. After a while, you don't like to think of what you did wrong. So you try to forget that story. You try to pull that arrow out. You think it won't hurt anymore because now you want to live right.

It's hard to keep on living right. Many things jump up at you and block your way. But you won't forget that story. You're going to see the place where it happened, maybe every day if it's nearby and close to Cibecue. If you don't see it, you're going to hear its name and see it in your mind. It doesn't matter if you get old—that place will keep on stalking you like the one who shot you with the story. Maybe that person will die. Even so, that place will keep on stalking you. It's like that person is still alive.

Even if we go far away from here to some big city, places around here keep stalking us. If you live wrong, you will hear the names and see the places in your mind. They keep on stalking you, even if you go across oceans. The names of all these places are good. They make you remember how to live right, so you want to replace yourself again.

After stories and storytellers have served this beneficial purpose, features of the physical landscape take over and perpetuate it. Mountains and arroyos step in symbolically for grandmothers and uncles. Just as the latter have "stalked" delinquent individuals in the past, so too particular locations continue to "stalk" them in the present. Such surveillance is essential, Apaches maintain, because "living right" requires constant care and attention, and there is always a possibility that old stories and their initial impact, like old arrows and their wounds, will fade and disappear. In other words, there is always a chance that persons who have "replaced themselves" once—or twice, or three times—will relax their guard against "badness" and slip back into undesirable forms of social conduct. Consequently, Apaches explain, individuals need to be continuously reminded of why they were "shot" in the first place and how they reacted to it at the time. Geographical sites, together with the crisp mental "pictures" of them presented by their names, serve admirably in this capacity, inviting people to recall their earlier failings and encouraging them to resolve, once again, to avoid them in the future. Grandmothers and uncles must perish but the landscape endures, and for this the Apache people are deeply grateful. "The land," Nick Thompson observes, "looks after us. The land keeps badness away."

It should now be possible for the reader to interpret the Western Apache texts at the beginning of this essay in a manner roughly compatible with the Apache ideas that have shaped them. Moreover, we should be able to appreciate that the claims put forward in the texts are reasonable and appropriate, culturally credible and "correct," the principled expressions of an underlying logic that invests them with internal consistency and coherent conceptual structure. As we have seen, this structure is supplied in large part by the hunting metaphor for Western Apache storytelling. It is chiefly in accordance with this metaphor — or, more exactly, in accordance with the symbolic associations it orders and makes explicit — that the claims presented earlier finally make sense.

Thus, the claim of Annie Peaches — that the land occupied by the Western Apache "makes the people live right" — becomes understandable as a proposition about the moral significance of geographical locations as this has been established by historical tales with which the locations are associated. Similarly, Wilson Lavender's claim — that Apaches who fail to remember place-names "forget how to be strong" — rests on an association of place-names with a belief in the power of historical tales to discourage forms of socially unacceptable behavior. Places and their names are also associated by Apaches with the narrators of historical tales, and Benson Lewis's claim — that a certain mountain near Cibecue is his maternal grandmother — can only be interpreted in light of this assumption. The hunting metaphor for storytelling also informs Ronnie Lupe's claim that Western Apache children who are not exposed to historical tales tend to have interpersonal difficulties. As he puts it, "They don't know the stories of what happened at these places. That's why some of them get into trouble." What Mr. Lupe is claiming, of course, is that children who do not learn to associate places and their names with historical tales cannot appreciate the utility of these narratives as guidelines for dealing responsibly and amicably with other people. Consequently, he believes, such individuals are more likely than others to act in ways that run counter to Apache social norms, a sure sign that they are "losing the land." Losing the land is something the Western Apache can ill afford to do, for geographical features have served the people for centuries as indispensable mnemonic pegs on which to hang the moral teachings of their history.

The Apache landscape is full of named locations where time and space have fused and where, through the agency of historical tales, their intersection is made visible for human contemplation. It is also apparent that such locations, charged as they are with personal and social significance, work in important ways to shape the images that Apaches have — or should have — of themselves. Speaking to people like Nick Thompson and Ronnie Lupe, to Annie Peaches and Benson Lewis, one forms the impression that Apaches view the landscape as a repository of distilled wisdom, a stern but benevolent keeper of tradition, an ever-vigilant ally in the efforts of individuals and whole communities to put into practice a set of standards for social living that are uniquely and distinctively their own. In the world that the Western Apache have constituted for themselves, features of the landscape have become symbols of and for this way of living, the symbols of a culture and the enduring moral character of its people.

We may assume that this relationship with the land has been pervasive throughout Western Apache history; but in today's climate of accelerating social change, its importance for Apache people may well be deepening. Communities such as Cibecue, formerly isolated and very much turned inward, were opened up by paved roads less than 20 years ago, and the consequences of improved access and freer travel — including, most noticeably, greatly increased contact with Anglo-Americans — have been pronounced. Younger Apaches, who today complain frequently about the tedium of village life, have started to develop new tastes and ambitions, and some of them are eager to explore the outside world. To the extent that the landscape remains not merely a physical presence but an omnipresent moral force, young Apaches are not likely to forget that the "Whiteman's way" belongs to a different world.

A number of American Indian authors, among them Vine Deloria, Jr. (Sioux), Simon Ortiz (Acoma), Joy Harjo (Creek), and the cultural anthropologist Alfonso Ortiz (San Juan), have written with skill and insight about the moral dimensions of Native American conceptions of the land. No one, however, has addressed the subject with greater sensitivity than N. Scott Momaday (Kiowa). The following passages, taken from his short essay entitled "Native American Attitudes to the Environment" (1974), show clearly what is involved, not only for the Western Apache but for other tribes as well.

> You cannot understand how the Indian thinks of himself in relation to the world around him unless you understand his conception of what is appropriate; particularly what is morally appropriate within the context of that relationship. [1974:82]

> The native American ethic with respect to the physical world is a matter of reciprocal appropriation: appropriations in which man invests himself in the landscape, and at the same time incorporates the landscape into his own most fundamental experience. . . . This appropriation is primarily a matter of imagination which is moral in kind. I mean to say that we are all, I suppose, what we imagine ourselves to be. And that is certainly true of the American Indian. . . . [The Indian] is someone who thinks of himself in a particular way and his idea comprehends his relationship to the physical world. He imagines himself in terms of that relationship and others. And it is that act of imagination, that moral act of imagination, which constitutes his understanding of the physical world. [1974:80]

The summer of 1980 is almost gone and soon I must leave Cibecue. I have walked to Nick's camp to tell him good-bye. This is never easy for me, and we spend most of the time talking about other things. Eventually, I move to thank him for his generosity, his patience, and the things he has taught me. Nick responds by pointing with his lips to a low ridge that runs behind his home in an easterly direction away from Cibecue Creek. "That is a good place," he says. "These are all good places. Goodness is all around."

POSTSCRIPT

If the thoughts presented here have a measure of theoretical interest, recent experience has persuaded me that they can have practical value as well. During the last six years, I have authored a number of documents for use in litigation concerning the settlement of Western Apache water rights in the state of Arizona. Until a final decision is reached in the case, I am not permitted to describe the contents of these documents in detail, but one of my assignments has been to write a report dealing with Apache conceptions of the physical environment. That report contains sections on Western Apache place-names, oral narratives, and certain metaphors that Apache people use to formulate aspects of their relationship with the land.

Preliminary hearings resulted in a judgment favorable to Apache interests, and apparently my report was useful, mainly because it helped pave the way for testimony by native witnesses. One of these witnesses was Nick Thompson; and according to attorneys on both sides, the old man's appearance had a decisive impact. After Nick had taken his place on the stand, he was asked by an attorney why he considered water to be important to his people. A man of eminent good sense, Nick replied, "Because we drink it!" And then, without missing a beat, he launched into a historical tale about a large spring not far from Cibecue — *tú nchaa halíí'* ("much water flows up and out") — where long ago a man drowned mysteriously after badly mistreating his wife. When Nick finished the story he went on to say: "We know it happened, so we know not to act like that man who died. It's good we have that water. We need it to live. It's good we have that spring. We need it to live right." Then the old man smiled to himself and his eyes began to dance.

Richard K. Nelson

The Gifts

Cold, clear, and calm in the pale blue morning. Snow on the high peaks brightening to amber. The bay a sheet of gray glass beneath a faint haze of steam. A November sun rises with the same fierce, chill stare of an owl's eye.

I stand at the window watching the slow dawn, and my mind fixes on the island. Nita comes softly down the stairs as I pack gear and complain of having slept too late for these short days. A few minutes later, Ethan trudges out onto the cold kitchen floor, barefoot and half asleep. We do not speak directly about hunting, to avoid acting proud or giving offense to the animals. I say only that I will go to the island and look around; Ethan says only that he would rather stay at home with Nita. I wish he would come along so I could teach him things, but know it will be quieter in the woods with just the dog.

They both wave from the window as I ease the skiff away from shore, crunching through cakes of freshwater ice the tide has carried in from Salmon River. It is a quick run through Windy Channel and out onto the freedom of the Sound, where the slopes of Mt. Sarichef bite cleanly into the frozen sky. The air stings against my face, but the rest of me is warm inside thick layers of clothes. Shungnak whines, paces, and looks over the gunwale toward the still-distant island.

Broad swells looming off the Pacific alternately lift the boat and drop it between smooth-walled canyons of water. Midway across the Sound a dark line of wind descends swiftly from the north, and within minutes we are surrounded by whitecaps. There are two choices: either beat straight up into them or cut an easier angle across the waves and take the spray. I vacillate for a while, then choose the icy spray over the intense pounding. Although I know it is wrong to curse the wind, I do it anyway.

A kittiwake sweeps over the water in great, vaulting arcs, its wings flexed against the touch and billow of the air. As it tilts its head passing over the boat, I think how clumsy and foolish we must look. The island's shore lifts slowly in dark walls of rock and timber that loom above the apron of snow-covered beach. As I approach the shelter of Low Point, the chop fades and the swell is smaller. I turn up along the lee, running between the kelp beds and the surf, straining my eyes for deer that may be feeding at the tide's edge.

Near the end of the point is a narrow gut that opens to a small, shallow anchorage. I ease the boat between the rocks, with lines of surf breaking close on either side. The waves rise and darken, their sharp edges sparkle in the sun, then long manes of spray whirl back as they turn inside out and pitch onto the shallow reef. The anchor slips down through ten feet of crystal water to settle among the kelp fronds and urchin-covered rocks. On a strong ebb the boat would go dry here, but today's tide change is only six feet. Before launching the punt I meticulously glass the broad, rocky shore and the sprawls of brown grass along the timber's edge. A tight bunch of rock sandpipers flashes up from the shingle and an otter loops along the windrows of drift logs, but there is no sign of deer. I can't help feeling a little anxious, because the season is drawing short and our year's supply of meat is not yet in. Throughout the fall, deer have been unusually wary, haunting the dense underbrush and slipping away at the least disturbance. I've come near a few, but these were young ones that I stalked only for the luxury of seeing them from close range.

Watching deer is the same pleasure now that it was when I was younger, when I loved animals only with my eyes and judged hunting to be outside the bounds of morality. Later, I tried expressing this love through studies of zoology, but this only seemed to put another kind of barrier between humanity and nature—the detachment of science and abstraction. Then, through anthropology, I encountered the entirely different views of nature found in other cultures. The hunting peoples were most fascinating because they had achieved deepest intimacy with their wild surroundings and had made natural history the focus of their lives. At the age of twenty-two, I went to live with Eskimos on the arctic coast of Alaska. It was my first year away from home, I had scarcely held a rifle in my hands, and the Eskimos—who call themselves the Real People—taught me their hunter's way.

The experience of living with Eskimos made very clear the direct, physical connectedness between all humans and the environments they draw existence from. Some years later, living with Koyukon Indians in Alaska's interior, I encountered a rich new dimension of that connectedness, and it profoundly changed my view of the world. Traditional Koyukon people follow a code of moral and ethical behavior that keeps a hunter in right relationship to the animals. They teach that all of nature is spiritual and aware, that it must be treated with respect, and that humans should approach the living world with restraint and humility. Now I struggle to learn if these same principles can apply in my own life and culture. Can we borrow from an ancient wisdom to structure a new relationship between ourselves and the environment? Or is Western society irreversibly committed to the illusion that humanity is separate from and dominant over the natural world?

A young bald eagle watches nervously from the peak of a tall hemlock as we bob ashore in the punt. Finally the bird lurches out, scoops its wings full of dense, cold air, and soars away beyond the line of trees. While I trudge up the long tide flat with the punt, Shungnak prances excitedly back and forth hunting for smells. The upper reaches are layered and slabbed with ice; slick cobbles shine like steel in the sun; frozen grass crackles underfoot. I lean the punt on a snow-covered log, pick up my rifle and small pack, and slip through the leafless alders into the forest.

My eyes take a moment adjusting to the sudden darkness, the deep green of boughs, and the somber, shadowy trunks. I feel safe and hidden here. The entire forest floor is covered with deep moss that should sponge gently beneath my feet. But today the softness is gone: frozen moss crunches with each step and brittle twigs snap, ringing out in the crisp air like strangers' voices. It takes a while to get used to this harshness in a forest that is usually so velvety and wet and silent. I listen to the clicking of gusts in the high branches and think that winter has come upon us like a fist.

At the base of a large nearby tree is a familiar patch of white—a scatter of deer bones—ribs, legs, vertebrae, two pelvis bones, and two skulls with half-bleached antlers. I put them here last winter, saying they were for the other animals, to make clear that they were not being thoughtlessly wasted. The scavengers soon picked them clean, the deer mice have gnawed them, and eventually they will be absorbed into the forest again. Koyukon elders say it shows respect, putting animal bones back in a clean, wild place instead of throwing them away with trash or scattering them in a garbage dump. The same obligations of etiquette that bind us to our human community also bind us to the natural community we live within.

Shungnak follows closely as we work our way back through a maze of windfalls, across clear disks of frozen ponds, and around patches of snow beneath openings in the forest canopy. I step and wait, trying to make no sound, knowing we could see deer at any moment. Deep snow has driven them down off the slopes and they are sure to be distracted with the business of the mating season.

We pick our way up the face of a high, steep scarp, then clamber atop a fallen log for a better view ahead. I peer into the semi-open understory of twiggy bushes, probing each space with my eyes. A downy woodpecker's call sparks from a nearby tree. Several minutes pass. Then a huckleberry branch moves, barely twitches, without the slightest noise . . . not far ahead.

Amid the scramble of brush where my eyes saw nothing a few minutes ago, a dim shape materializes, as if its own motion had created it. A doe steps into an open space, deep brown in her winter coat, soft and striking and lovely, dwarfed among the great trees, lifting her nose, looking right toward me. For perhaps a minute we are motionless in each other's gaze; then her head jerks to the left, her ears twitch back and forth, her tail flicks up, and she turns away in the stylized gait deer always use when alarmed.

Quick as a breath, quiet as a whisper, the doe glides off into the forest. Sometimes when I see a deer this way I know it is real at the moment, but afterward it seems like a daydream.

As we work our way back into the woods, I keep hoping for another look at her and thinking that a buck might have been following nearby. Any deer is legal game and I could almost certainly have taken her, but I would rather wait for a larger buck and let the doe bring on next year's young. Shungnak savors the ghost of her scent that hangs in the still air, but she has vanished.

Farther on, the snow deepens to a continuous cover beneath smaller trees, and we cross several sets of deer tracks, including some big prints with long toe drags. The snow helps to muffle our steps, but it is hard to see very far because the bushes are heavily loaded with powder. The thicket becomes a latticed maze of white on black, every branch hung and spangled in a thick fur of jeweled snow. We move through it like eagles cleaving between tumbled columns of cloud. New siftings occasionally drift down when the treetops are touched by the breeze.

Slots between the trunks up ahead shiver with blue where a muskeg opens. I angle toward it, feeling no need to hurry, picking every footstep carefully, stopping often to stare into the dizzying crannies, listening for any splinter of sound, keeping my senses tight and concentrated. A raven calls from high above the forest, and as I catch a glimpse of it an old question runs through my mind: Is this only the bird we see, or does it have the power and awareness Koyukon elders speak of? It lifts and plays on the wind far aloft, then folds up and rolls halfway over, a strong sign of luck in hunting. Never mind the issue of knowing; we should assume that power is here and let ourselves be moved by it.

I turn to look at Shungnak, taking advantage of her sharper hearing and magical sense of smell. She lifts her nose to the fresh but nebulous scent of several deer that have moved through here this morning. I watch her little radar ears, waiting for her to focus in one direction and hold it, hoping to see her body tense as it does when something moves nearby. But so far she only hears the twitching of red squirrels on dry bark. Shungnak and I have very different opinions of the squirrels. They excite her more than any other animal because she believes she will catch one someday. But for the hunter they are deceptive spurts of movement and sound, and their sputtering alarm calls alert the deer.

We approach a low, abrupt rise, covered with obscuring brush and curtained with snow. A lift of wind hisses in the high trees, then drops away and leaves us in near-complete silence. I pause to choose a path through a scramble of blueberry bushes and little windfalls ahead, then glance back at Shungnak. She has her eyes and ears fixed off toward our left, almost directly across the current of breeze. She stands very stiff, quivering slightly, leaning forward as if she has already started to run but cannot release her muscles. I shake my finger at her as a warning to stay.

I listen as closely as possible, but hear nothing. I work my eyes into every dark crevice and slot among the snowy branches, but see nothing. I stand perfectly still and wait, then look again at Shungnak. Her head turns so slowly that I can barely detect the movement, until finally she is looking straight ahead. Perhaps it is just another squirrel. . . . I consider taking a few steps for a better view.

Then I see it.

A long, dark body appears among the bushes, moving deliberately upwind, so close I can scarcely believe I didn't see it earlier. Without looking away, I carefully slide the breech closed and lift the rifle to my shoulder, almost certain that a deer this size will be a buck. Shungnak, now forgotten behind me, must be contorted with the suppressed urge to give chase.

The deer walks easily, silently, along the little rise, never looking our way. Then he makes a sharp turn straight toward us. Thick tines of his antlers curve over the place where I have the rifle aimed. Koyukon elders teach that animals will come to those who have shown them respect, and will allow themselves to be taken in what is only a temporary death. At a moment like this, it is easy to sense that despite my abiding doubt there is a shared world beyond the one we know directly, a world the Koyukon people empower with spirits, a world that demands recognition and exacts a price from those who ignore it.

This is a very large buck. It comes so quickly that I have no chance to shoot, and then it is so close that I haven't the heart to do it. Fifty feet away, the deer lowers his head almost to the ground and lifts a slender branch that blocks his path. Snow shakes down onto his neck and clings to the fur of his shoulders as he slips underneath. Then he half-lifts his head and keeps coming. I ease the rifle down to watch, wondering how much closer he will get. Just now he makes a long, soft rutting call, like the bleating of a sheep except lower and more hollow. His hooves tick against dry twigs hidden by the snow.

In the middle of a step he raises his head all the way up, and he sees me standing there—a stain against the pure white of the forest. A sudden spasm runs through his entire body, his front legs jerk apart, and he freezes all akimbo, head high, nostrils flared, coiled and hard. I can only look at him and wait, my mind snarled with irreconcilable emotions. Here is a perfect buck deer. In the Koyukon way, he has come to me; but in my own he has come too close. I am as congealed and transfixed as he is, as devoid of conscious thought. It is as if my mind has ceased to function and I only have eyes.

But the buck has no choice. He suddenly unwinds in a burst of ignited energy, springs straight up from the snow, turns in mid-flight, stabs the frozen earth again, and makes four great bounds off to the left. His thick body seems to float, relieved of its own weight, as if a deer has the power to unbind itself from gravity.

The same deeper impulse that governs the flight of a deer governs the predator's impulse to pursue it. I watch the first leaps without moving a muscle. Then, not pausing for an instant of deliberation, I raise the rifle back to my shoulder, follow the movement of the deer's fleeing form, and wait until it stops to stare back. Almost at that instant, still moving without conscious thought, freed of the ambiguities that held me before, now no less animal than the animal I watch, my hands warm and steady and certain, acting from a more elemental sense than the ones that brought me to this meeting, I carefully align the sights and let go the sudden power.

The gift of the deer falls like a feather in the snow. And the rifle's sound has rolled off through the timber before I hear it.

I walk to the deer, now shaking a bit with swelling emotion. Shungnak is beside it already, whining and smelling, racing from one side to the other, stuffing her nose down in snow full of scent. She looks off into the brush, searching back and forth, as if the deer that ran is somewhere else, still running. She tries to lick at the blood that trickles down, but I stop her out of respect for the animal. Then, I suppose to consummate her own frustrated predatory energy, she takes a hard nip at its shoulder, shuns quickly away, and looks back as if she expects it to leap to its feet again.

As always, I whisper thanks to the animal for giving itself to me. The words are my own, not something I have learned from the Koyukon. Their elders might say that the words we use in prayer to spirits of the natural world do not matter. Nor, perhaps, does it matter what form these spirits take in our own thoughts. What truly matters is only that prayer be made, to affirm our humility in the presence of nurturing power. Most of humanity throughout history has said prayers to the powers of surrounding nature, which they have recognized as their source of life. Surely it is not too late to recover this ancestral wisdom.

It takes a few minutes before I settle down inside and can begin the other work. Then I hang the deer with rope strung over a low branch and back twice through pulley-loops. I cut away the dark, pungent scent glands on its legs, and next make a careful incision along its belly, just large enough to reach the warm insides. The stomach and intestines come easily and cleanly; I cut through the diaphragm, and there is a hollow sound as the lungs pull free. Placing them on the soft snow, I whisper that these parts are left here for the other animals. Shungnak wants to take some for herself but I tell her to keep away. It is said that the life and awareness leaves an animal's remains slowly, and there are rules about what should be eaten by a dog. She will have her share of the scraps later on, when more of the life is gone.

After the blood has drained out, I sew the opening shut with a piece of line to keep the insides clean, and then toggle the deer's forelegs through a slit in the hind leg joint, so it can be carried like a pack. I am barely strong enough to get it up onto my back, but there is plenty of time to work slowly toward the beach, stopping often to rest and cool down. During one of these stops I hear two ravens in an agitated ex-change of croaks and gurgles, and I wonder if those black eyes have already spotted the remnants. No pure philanthropist, the raven gives a hunter luck only as a way of creating luck for himself.

Finally, I push through the low boughs of the beachside trees and ease my burden down. Afternoon sun throbs off the water, but a chill north wind takes all warmth from it. Little gusts splay in dark patterns across the anchorage; the boat paces on its mooring line; the Sound is racing with whitecaps. I take a good rest, watching a fox sparrow flit among the drift logs and a bunch of crows hassling over some bit of food at the water's edge.

Though I feel utterly satisfied, grateful, and contented, there is much to do and the day will slope away quickly. We are allowed more than one deer, so I will stay on the island for another look around tomorrow. It takes two trips to get everything out to the skiff, then we head up the shore toward the little cabin and secure anchorage at Bear Creek. By the time the boat is unloaded and tied off, the wind has faded and a late afternoon chill sinks down in the pitched, hard shadow of Sarichef.

Half-dry wood hisses and sputters, giving way reluctantly to flames in the rusted stove. It is nearly dusk when I bring the deer inside and set to work on it. Better to do this now than to wait, in case tomor-row is another day of luck. The animal hangs from a low beam, dim-lit by the kerosene lamp. I feel strange in its presence, as if it still watches, still glows with something of its life, still demands that nothing be done or spoken carelessly. A hunter should never let himself be deluded by pride or a false sense of dominance. It is not through our own power that we take life in nature; it is through the power of nature that life is given to us.

The soft hide peels away slowly from shining muscles, and the in-ner perfection of the deer's body is revealed. Koyukon and Eskimo hunters teach a refined art of taking an animal into its component parts, easing blades through crisp cartilage where bone joins bone, following the body's own design until it is disarticulated. There is no ugliness in it, only hands moving in concert with the beauty of an animal's making. Perhaps we have been too removed from this to un-derstand, and we have lost touch with the process of one life being passed on to another. As my hands work inside the deer, it is as if something has already begun to flow into me.

When the work is finished, I take two large slices from the hind quarter and put them in a pan atop the now-crackling stove. In a separate pot, I boil scraps of meat and fat for Shungnak, who has waited with as much patience as possible for a husky raised in a hunter's team up north. When the meat is finished cooking I sit on a sawed log and eat straight from the pan.

A meal could not be simpler, more satisfying, or more directly a part of the living process. I wish Ethan was here to share it, and I would explain to him again that when we eat the deer its flesh is then our flesh. The deer changes form and becomes us, and we in turn become creatures made of deer. Each time we eat the deer we should remember it and feel gratitude for what it has given us. And each time, we should carry a thought like a prayer inside: "Thanks to the animal and to all that made it—the island and the forest, the air, and the rain . . ." We should remember that in the course of things, we are all generations of deer and of the earth-life that feeds us.

Warm inside my sleeping bag, I let the fire ebb away to coals. The lamp is out. The cabin roof creaks in the growing cold. I drift toward sleep, feeling pleased that there is no moon, so the deer will wait until dawn to feed. On the floor beside me, Shungnak jerks and whimpers in her dog's dreams.

Next morning we are in the woods with the early light. We follow yesterday's tracks, and just beyond the place of the buck, a pair of does drifts at the edge of sight and disappears. For an hour we angle north, then come slowly back somewhat deeper in the woods, moving crosswise to a growing easterly breeze. In two separate places, deer snort and pound away, invisible beyond a shroud of brush. Otherwise there is nothing.

Sometime after noon we come to a narrow muskeg with scattered lodgepole pines and a ragged edge of bushy, low-growing cedar. I squint against the sharp glare of snow. It has that peculiar look of old powder, a bit settled and touched by wind, very lovely but without the airy magic of a fresh fall. I gaze up the muskeg's easy slope, and above the encroaching wall of timber, seamed against the deep blue sky, is the brilliant peak of Sarichef with a great plume of snow streaming off in what must be a shuddering gale. It has a contradictory look of absoluteness and unreality about it, like a Himalayan summit suspended in mid-air over the saddle of a low ridge.

I move very slowly up the muskeg's east side, away from the

breeze and in the sun's full warmth. Deer tracks crisscross the opening, but none of the animals stopped here to feed. Next to the bordering trees, the tracks follow a single, hard-packed trail, showing the deers' preference for cover. Shungnak keeps her nose to the thickly scented snow. We come across a pine sapling that a buck has torn with his antlers, scattering twigs and flakes of bark all around. But his tracks are hardened, frosted, and lack sharpness, so they are at least a day old.

We slip through a narrow point of trees, then follow the open edge again, pausing long moments between each footstep. A mixed tinkle of crossbills and siskins moves through the high timber, and a squirrel rattles from deep in the woods, too far off to be scolding us. Shungnak begins to pick up a strong ribbon of scent, but she hears nothing. I stop for several minutes to study the muskeg's long, raveled fringe, the tangle of shade and thicket, the glaze of mantled boughs.

Then my eye barely catches a fleck of movement up ahead, near the ground and almost hidden behind the trunk of a leaning pine, perhaps a squirrel's tail or a bird. I lift my hand slowly to shade the sun, stand dead still, and wait to see if something is there. Finally it moves again.

At the very edge of the trees, almost out of sight in a little swale, small and furry and bright-tinged, turning one direction and then another, is the funnel of a single ear. Having seen this, I soon make out the other ear and the slope of a doe's forehead. Her neck is behind the leaning pine, but on the other side I can barely see the soft, dark curve of her back above the snow. She is comfortably bedded, gazing placidly into the distance, chewing her cud.

Shungnak has stopped twenty yards behind me in the point of trees and has no idea about the deer. I shake my finger at her until she lays her ears back and sits. Then I watch the doe again. She is fifty yards ahead of me, ten yards beyond the leaning tree, and still looking off at an angle. Her left eye is clearly visible and she refuses to turn her head away, so it might be impossible to get any closer. Perhaps I should just wait here, in case a buck is attending her nearby. But however improbable it might be under these circumstances, a thought is lodged in my mind: I can get near her.

My first step sinks down softly, but the second makes a loud budging sound. She snaps my way, stops chewing, and stares for several minutes. It seems hopeless, especially out here in an open field of crisp snow with only the narrow treetrunk for a screen. But she slowly turns away and starts to chew again. I move just enough so the tree blocks her eye and the rest of her head, but I can still see her ears. Every time she chews they shake just a bit, so I can watch them and step when her hearing is obscured by the sound of her own jaws.

Either this works or the deer has decided to ignore me, because after a short while I am near enough so the noise of my feet has to reach her easily. She should have jumped up and run long ago, but instead she lays there in serene repose. I deliberate on every step, try for the softest snow, wait long minutes before the next move, stalking like a cat toward ambush. I watch beyond her, into the surrounding shadows and across to the muskeg's farther edge, for the shape of a buck deer; but there is nothing. I feel ponderous, clumsy-footed, out-of-place, inimical. I should turn and run away, take fear on the deer's behalf, flee the mirrored image in my mind. But I clutch the cold rifle at my side and creep closer.

The wind refuses to blow and my footsteps seem like thunder in the still sunshine. But the doe only turns once to look my way, without even pointing her ears toward me, then stares off and begins to chew again.

I am ten feet from the leaning tree. My heart pounds so hard, I think those enchanted ears should hear the rush of blood in my temples. Yet a strange certainty has come into me, a quite unmystical confidence. Perhaps she has decided I am another deer, a buck attracted by her musk or a doe feeding gradually toward her. My slow pace and lapses of stillness would not seem human. For myself, I have lost awareness of elapsed time; I have no feeling of patience or impatience. It is as if the deer has moved slowly toward me on a cloud of snow, and I am adrift in the pure motion of experience.

I take the last step to the trunk of the leaning pine. It is bare of branches, scarcely wider than my hand, but perfectly placed to break my odd profile. There is no hope of getting any closer, so I slowly poke my head out to watch. She has an ideal spot: screened from the wind, warmed by the sun, and with a clear view of the muskeg. I can see muscles working beneath the close fur of her jaw, the rise and fall of her side each time she breathes, the shining edge of her ebony eye.

I hold absolutely still, but her body begins to stiffen, she lifts her head higher, and her ears twitch anxiously. Then instead of looking at me she turns her face to the woods, shifting her ears toward a sound I cannot hear. A few seconds later, the unmistakable voice of a buck drifts up, strangely disembodied, as if it comes from an animal somewhere underneath the snow. I huddle as close to the tree as I can, press against the hard, dry bark, and peek out around its edge.

There is a gentle rise behind the doe, scattered with sapling pines and clusters of juniper bushes. A rhythmic crunching of snow comes invisibly from the slope, then a bough shakes . . . and a buck walks easily into the open sunshine.

Focusing his attention completely on the doe, he comes straight toward her and never sees my intrusive shape just beyond. He slips through a patch of small trees, stops a few feet from where she lies, lowers his head and stretches it toward her, then holds this odd pose for a long moment. She reaches her muzzle out to one side, trying to find his scent. When he starts to move up behind her she stands quickly, bends her body into a strange sideways arc, and stares back at him. A moment later she walks off a bit, lifts her tail, and puts droppings in her tracks. The buck moves to the warm ground of her bed and lowers his nose to the place where her female scent is strongest.

Inching like a reptile on a cold rock, I have stepped out from the tree and let my whole menacing profile become visible. The deer are thirty feet away and stand well apart, so they can both see me easily. I am a hunter hovering near his prey and a watcher craving inhuman love, torn between the deepest impulses, hot and shallow-breathed and seething with unreconciled intent, hidden from opened eyes that look into the nimbus of sun and see nothing but the shadow they have chosen for themselves. In this shadow now, the hunter has vanished and only the watcher remains.

Drawn by the honey of the doe's scent, the buck steps quickly toward her. And now the most extraordinary thing happens. The doe turns away from him and walks straight for me. There is no hesitation, only a wild deer coming along the trail of hardened snow where the other deer have passed, the trail in which I stand at this moment. She raises her head, looks at me, and steps without hesitation.

My existence is reduced to a pair of eyes; a rush of unbearable heat flushes through my cheeks; and a sense of absolute certainty fuses in my mind.

The snow blazes so brightly that my head aches. The deer is a dark form growing larger. I look up at the buck, half embarrassed, as if to apologize that she has chosen me over him. He stares at her for a moment, turns to follow, then stops and watches anxiously. I am struck by how gently her narrow hooves touch the trail, how little sound they make as she steps, how thick the fur is on her flank and shoulder, how unfathomable her eyes look. I am consumed with a sense of her perfect elegance in the brilliant light. And then I am lost again in the whirling intensity of experience.

The doe is now ten feet from me. She never pauses or looks away. Her feet punch down mechanically into the snow, coming closer and closer, until they are less than a yard from my own. Then she stops, stretches her neck calmly toward me, and lifts her nose.

There is not the slightest question in my mind, as if this was certain to happen and I have known all along exactly what to do. I slowly raise my hand and reach out . . .

And my fingers touch the soft, dry, gently needling fur on top of the deer's head, and press down to the living warmth of flesh underneath.

She makes no move and shows no fear, but I can feel the flaming strength and tension that flow in her wild body as in no other animal I have ever touched. Time expands and I am suspended in the clear reality of that moment.

Then, by the flawed conditioning of a lifetime among fearless domesticated things, I instinctively drop my hand and let the deer smell it. Her dark nose, wet and shining, touches gently against my skin at the exact instant I realize the absoluteness of my error. And a jolt runs through her entire body as she realizes hers. Her muscles seize and harden; she seems to wrench her eyes away from me but her body remains, rigid and paralyzed. Having been deceived by her other senses, she keeps her nose tight against my hand for one more moment.

Then all the energy inside her triggers in a series of exquisite bounds. She flings out over the hummocks of snow-covered moss, suspended in effortless flight like fog blown over the muskeg in a gale. Her body leaps with such power that the muscles should twang aloud like a bowstring; the earth should shudder and drum; but I hear no sound. In the center of the muskeg she stops to look back, as if to confirm what must seem impossible. The buck follows in more earth-bound undulations; they dance away together, and I am left in the meeting-place alone.

There is a blur of rushing feet behind me. No longer able to restrain herself, Shungnak dashes past, buries her nose in the soft tracks, and then looks back to ask if we can run after them. I had completely forgotten her, sitting near enough to watch the whole encounter, somehow resisting what must have been a prodigious urge to explode in chase. When I reach out to hug her, she smells the hand that touched the deer. And it seems as if it happened long ago.

For the past year I have kept a secret dream, that I would someday come close enough to touch a deer on this island. But since the idea came it seemed harder than ever to get near them. Now, totally unexpected and in a strange way, it has happened. Was the deer caught by some reckless twinge of curiosity? Had she never encountered a human on this wild island? Did she yield to some odd amorous confusion? I really do not care. I would rather accept this as pure experience and not give in to the notion that everything must be explained.

Nor do I care to think that I was chosen to see some manifestation of power, because I have little tolerance for such dreams of self-importance. I have never asked that nature open any doors to reveal the truth of spirit or mystery; I aspire to no shaman's path; I expect no visions, no miracles except the ones that fill every instant of ordinary life.

But there are vital lessons in the experience of moments such as these, if we live them in the light of wisdom taken from the earth and shaped by generations of elders. Two deer came and gave the choices to me. One deer I took and we will now share a single body. The other deer I touched and we will now share that moment. These events could be seen as opposites, but they are in fact identical. Both are founded in the same principles, the same relationship, the same reciprocity.

Move slowly, stay quiet, watch carefully . . . and be ever humble. Never show the slightest arrogance or disrespect. Koyukon elders would explain, in words quite different from my own, that I moved into two moments of grace, or what they would call luck. This is the source of success for a hunter or a watcher, not skill, not cleverness, not guile. Something is only given in nature, never taken.

I have heard the elders say that everything in nature has its own spirit and possesses a power beyond ours. There is no way to prove them right or wrong, though the beauty and interrelatedness of things should be evidence enough. We need not ask for shining visions as proof, or for a message from a golden deer glowing in the sky of our dreams. Above all else, we should assume that power moves in the world around us and act accordingly. If it is a myth, then spirit is within the myth and we should live by it. And if there is a commandment to follow, it is to approach all of earth-life, of which we are a part, with humility and respect.

Well soaked and shivering from a rough trip across the Sound, we pull into the dark waters of the bay. Sunset burns on Twin Peaks and the spindled ridge of Antler Mountain. The little house is warm with lights that shimmer on the calm near shore. I see Nita looking from the window and Ethan dashes out to wait by the tide, pitching rocks at the mooring buoy. He strains to see inside the boat, knowing that a hunter who tells his news aloud may offend the animals by sounding boastful. But when he sees the deer his excited voice seems to roll up and down the mountainside.

He runs for the house with Shungnak, carrying a load of gear, and I know he will burst inside with the news. Ethan, joyous and alive, boy made of deer.

Robert Finch

North Beach Journal

1

I have been living alone for three days now in a cottage on the west shore of North Beach, a long and narrow barrier spit of low sand dunes and salt marsh lying a mile or so east of Chatham at the elbow of Cape Cod. Chatham is one of the fog capitals of New England, especially in spring. Since I arrived on Sunday evening the fog has poured nearly continuously over this naked beach like some great silent river; but late this afternoon the wind shifted to the west and the gray shroud at last began to lift.

I do not live alone easily. In solitude I find myself inordinately affected by the weather. It is as though meteorology takes the place of intimate company, and the distinction between outer weather and inner mood is gradually obliterated. In such situations it is not so much a question of trying to give myself over to nature as trying to hold something back, some bit of perspective and self-evaluation. This is just what fog loves to steal from you.

There was already a dense fog at the water's edge and a light northwest wind blowing when I set off about 5:00 p.m. last Sunday in a small red rowboat from Scatteree Town Landing on the Chatham mainland. My wife Beth and daughter Katy were there assisting and forming a farewell committee. Within a few minutes their forms dissolved and melted into the ghostly background of low bluffs and houses, and soon that, too, disappeared.

According to the map I had, the cottage lay across Pleasant Bay about a mile to the southeast, at the northern end of a group of twenty or so beach cottages known as the South Colony. I steered by compass, due east, to compensate for the southerly push of wind. A small squadron of terns flew close by heading north, gray on gray over gray.

Rowing is a strange method of traveling, even within the contained waters of a pond. One is always pulling oneself backward, into the unknown, steering by what one has already experienced or left behind.

Here, in an open-ended estuary, with no visible landmarks, I had the curious feeling that I was rowing into the center of my own mind where figures vanished and loomed like memory.

I passed a pair of channel markers and heard the deep thrum of a motor approaching from the south. It turned out to be Buzz Hutchins, a bulldozer operator who had dug my house foundation a few years ago.

"Hello, Robert, where you going?" he called out cordially. Cape Codders are rarely surprised by anything they find at sea.

"Cabin," I yelled back, jerking my head toward the outer beach as I kept rowing, and he disappeared with a wave back into my past.

Fifteen minutes later I stopped to check my compass bearings. Though the bay at this point is relatively shallow and not very wide, it is notoriously deceptive in fog with backcurrents and sudden shifts in wind. The water around me appeared calm, quiet, and completely empty. I had wanted to cut ties for the duration, but not this quickly.

Suddenly the water was filled with the pulsing bodies of moon jellies, domed and translucent, drifting north with the incoming tide over beds of dark, streaming eelgrass. I reached out and stroked a long, slick frond of grass. A biological oddity, eelgrass is a true marine flowering plant descended from some terrestrial angiosperm which, like the land ancestors of whales and walruses, has returned for some reason to the sea. What are you doing out here, grass, among jellyfish and seabirds? Where are we all heading?

After a half-hour or so of rowing and neck-twisting, I finally saw a beach materializing behind me, still vague and undefined in the fog. The large, dark silhouette of a cottage loomed straight ahead. I could not believe my blind luck in hitting it on the mark. But when I came ashore, the building did not fit the description at all.

I wandered around the ghostly dunes for some time before stumbling upon a family at another cottage, packing up their Blazer and about to leave after a weekend's vacation. They told me I had landed, not at the South Colony, but at the North Colony, a second cottage group nearly a half-mile north of where I wanted to be.

I had erred twice, it seems: first, in not taking into account the push of the incoming tide, and second, in not correcting my compass readings for magnetic declination—some sixteen degrees at this longitude—stupid, amateur's mistakes.

By the time I returned to the boat, the light had begun to fail and it was raining lightly. I set off again, rowing south against the tide just a few yards offshore. The fog now alternately closed in and lifted, revealing at brief intervals the dim outline of the mainland across the bay, ridiculously close. Black-bellied plovers and small sandpipers lined the water's edge, probing the tideline with short, dark bills. Fog and dusk were thickening to darkness when I finally came to the cottage, pulled into a little cove just south of it, and hauled the boat ashore.

The beach cottage belongs to a neighbor of mine, Tia Tonis, who had offered me the use of it for a week. She had taken my heavier gear down by jeep on Saturday and had returned to the mainland that afternoon. When I entered the cottage I found my trunk full of food and books set against one wall, and on the table a nice welcoming note from Tia with a pair of sharpened pencils.

It was too late to begin lighting the gas lamps or cooking a meal, so I made myself a sandwich by candlelight, and threw a sleeping bag on one of the cots and myself after it. All around me was the dull roar of wind and surf, and an occasional compacted thud of a breaker on the ocean side of the beach a quarter-mile away. The tide was still rising. The fog had lifted again, and now, to the southwest, across the dark waters of Pleasant Bay, the great double beams of Chatham Light raced out into the night, chasing one another like demons up the dark strip of the outer beach until they broke against the south wall of the house, exploding in star-shaped flashes through the screens.

This place is now home, I thought, my neighborhood for a week. It has the feeling of being wholly contained in nature, of existing within her terms. What a strange crossing it has been! Never could I have gotten so swiftly detached from the mainland, emotionally and psychologically, under clear skies. Lying here now at night on this open strand, listening to the dull roar of the surf and the unobstructed wind, it seems years since this morning when I was down in the bog below our house, only a few miles from here, gathering the eggs of wood frogs and salamanders beneath a thick forest canopy, finding woodland lady slippers and trailing arbutus, listening to the calls of ovenbirds and other woodland warblers, and the strange whistles of wood ducks in the bog.

There are other cottages nearby this one, but they are all dark. There are no other lights as far as I can see up or down the length of the beach. Now the fog has closed in again, this time for good, it seems, and not even the drumming demon-beam of Chatham Light can pierce it.

I like this house, its bright, spare, unfinished look. It is a shell: twenty-four by twenty-eight feet, shingled and roofed on the outside, with studded walls pierced everywhere by the exposed tips of shingle nails, a trussed and strapped ceiling, open doorless partitions where the bedrooms will be, and a bare plywood floor.

The house sits about sixty yards from the gentle waters of the bay. Like many beach cottages, this one seems largely an excuse for windows. There are five on the west side, facing the bay, two on the south, three on the east, two on the north, plus three windowed steel doors. One large white table sits in the center of the unpartitioned area—for the typewriter and "heavy work"—with a smaller pine table next to the west windows, complete with two ice-cream parlor twisted-wire chairs, for meals, reading, journalizing, and bay-watching. A few white curtains hang on rods above the windows, more to wave inward with the breeze than to veil anything. There is a gas stove, three gas lights, a gas refrigerator, a hand pump and sink, and a flush toilet in the outhouse. The refrigerator has been acting up a little. It won't shut off, so I disconnect it now and then. I wish I had brought an onion.

In exchange for the use of the house I have agreed to paint the wood trim, window sashes, and screens. Four gallons of white paint were left stacked in one of the partitioned rooms. I planned to begin Monday morning, but when I woke at dawn the fog and mist still clung tenaciously around the house. After breakfast I decided to take a walk across to the ocean shore, hoping it would burn off by afternoon.

North Beach is about a thousand feet wide here, a terrain of low dunes and wet swales, with a higher broken ridge of primary dune just before the outer beach. At no point does the land rise twenty feet above sea level.

This barrier beach has undergone more changes than most: lengthening, contracting, breaking up into archipelagoes of sandy islets, dissolving and re-forming again every couple of hundred years. Though the spit is at present some ten miles long and extends over four miles south of the Tonis cottage, the section of dune I was now walking was a harbor entrance into Pleasant Bay a hundred years ago. Until last fall a large, turreted wooden building stood just behind the first ridge of dunes—the Old Harbor Life Saving Station, built in 1897. The former harbor entrance had long since silted in, and the station had been abandoned for decades, but gradual erosion of the outer beach had brought the old building dangerously close to the surf. Last fall the Cape Cod National Seashore, in an exception to its official policy of letting nature take its course and whatever lies in it, had the station sawn in two and floated on barges twenty miles north to a safer beach at Provincetown, where it has been reassembled and turned into a museum.

It was a timely move, as it turned out, for only a few weeks later one of the most powerful ocean storms ever to hit the Cape submerged 90 percent of this beach, washing over the former site of the lifesaving station, and in the process smashing the original Tonis cottage, which had stood near it.

When I gained the beach I found the half-buried rubble of the station's foundation, and just north of it the charred remains of Tia's old family cottage, which had to be burned before they were allowed to build the new one earlier this spring. Tia blames the government for its loss, claiming that they destroyed the dune in front of the original cottage when they moved the station. "They did pile some sand back in the cut when they were through," she told me, "but no more than that. For heaven's sakes, even a child would have patted it down."

Several other cottages in the vicinity survived the storm, though the prevalence of new walls, new shingles, scattered pilings, bedsteads, and other debris in the overwash area testified that they had not escaped unscathed. A few stunted cedars, burnt orange and dead, looked planted around the houses.

The buildings all wear the aspect of a Western ghost town, one that suffered some wild, violent raid, was partially rebuilt, and was then abandoned as not worth it. I am its sole inhabitant these days, but it is only the lull before the first human inundation of the season, the week before the Memorial Day weekend, when all of these beach shacks will spring back to life and hundreds of beach buggies will form a nearly continuous line of vehicles on the outer beach.

I walked back from the ocean to the bay in the sandy ruts of a vehicle trail. In the sand overwashes immediately behind the beach I found fox scat, the strong smell of skunk, and the tiny tracks of a piping plover, a small sand-colored shorebird that nests at the base of these dunes. The trail wound by some juncus bogs, bright and green and level, and passed a small brackish pond surrounded by reeds where toads call at night.

The dune cover here is almost pure beach grass, interspersed with dusty miller and new leaves of beach goldenrod. The new green blades of Ammophila are just about to overtop the dead, dry stalks of last year. There is little beach plum growing, and what there is seems about two weeks behind that on the mainland, which has already blossomed. Along the crest of the road banks are dark blue-gray tufts of poverty grass, little-rag-mop plants just beginning to green again. I stopped to stoop down and look at them, anticipating the tiny, delicate yellow flowers they would hold in June.

I felt like a farmer walking his fields, in that mixture of remembrance and anticipation between seasons. Nature is everywhere familiar in macrocosm and microcosm, in the dip and resurgence of the night-sky constellations and in the shower of green leaves welling up around old dead seed stalks. Only in the middle distance is she alien, are landscapes foreign.

3

That night I slept a troubled sleep, a sleep of too much caffeine and germinating doubts. It rained through the night, spattering on the new asphalt roof, and through the rain and wind I heard the distant, mournful calling of the piping plover on the night beach.

As usual, following an initial, buoyant surge of self-reliance and selfish delight at having such a place all to myself, I now began to feel insufficient. Already, by Tuesday morning, I found myself thinking of my daughter's irrepressible, continual engagement with life, my father's quiet, strong, indirect love. Life is always deeper on the other side of the water, it seems, though that morning the other side remained hidden in mist and swirling fog.

The house slipped into insubstantiality as I walked down to the bay shore. I followed the dry, twisting bed of what was formerly a salt marsh creek. Now there is only a thin fringe of marsh along the western shore here. The barrier beach, gradually retreating westward in the face of the ocean's assaults, buries these tidal creeks and marshes even as it forms new ones farther west. Eventually they emerge again on the ocean side in the form of exposed peat ledges, some of which still carry the prints of old cart wheels and foraging cattle made generations ago.

The old creek bed here now fills only at high tides, the water winding cautiously, like some semitame animal, up to the cottage deck each morning. At ebb tide it contains a few pools, warm soupy bowls full of marsh minnows that flip about as they slowly cook.

Because of the fog I could see no birds, though I heard the chips and clicks of terns feeding in the currents offshore, and the purring, clattering hum of lobster boats laying down pots somewhere out in the bay.

I worked through the morning, writing at the large white table. Outside, the wind shifted back and forth from southeast to southwest; the fog flowed, pausing, lifting, and dropping again over the bay and the bluffs on the mainland.

I ate lunch on the deck where tree swallows buzzed me and a trio of crows, wearing new, glistening black coats, paused briefly on the roof ridge to consider, then flew on. A horned lark landed in a bush and breasted forth a buzzy, tinkling, rising trill, one not described in the bird books. I have begun to notice that bird song, like the flowering schedule of plants, seems to be affected by the exposed environment here. The song sparrows, for instance, all have thin, scratchy, attenuated voices here, as though all the sap had been dried out of their notes by the salt air.

After lunch I took a short nap. When I woke a thin cloud cover had sucked the fog up into itself and the wind had shifted to the southwest. I painted rake trim for a few hours and then, about 4:30, walked out to the beach.

The smell of the surf, just coming in, hit me with a rich fish and salt odor, carried along on the crashing mist of its edge by a southerly breeze. I stood and inhaled it deeply, rhythmically, timing my breaths with the rush and surge of the combers.

I walked south along the undulating, ivory, grist-laced slope of the beach as the white crests caught some of the red from the sinking sun. A green glass bottle, thrown up on the sand, glinted in the reflected light. It was corked and had a message inside, written in German, which I cannot read, accompanied by several pornographic sketches — probably thrown overboard by some bored crewman not far offshore. I recorked it and threw it back into the surf, where it floated north, at about two knots.

I stopped and sat on a low dune crest pitted with ant holes and wolf-spider traps and watched the day wheel slowly down, the tide climb slowly and ponderously in. I wished I were staying for a year. I would not write for a week at a time, except to record weather, perhaps, and certain telling and vulnerable details: how the light slanted in the evening, or the taste of seaweed picked up on the beach. I would let the personal dry up or seep slowly out, regarding all inner turmoil as external, the tortuous and self-conscious processes of thought as trivial and of no account. I would let my mind be picked clean by the crows and ants and bleached by the sun, ride this thin spar of sand as it slides back and forth between the tides. I would let all feelings and their objects drift out with the daily currents and wait to see what came back ashore at the end of the week.

Walking back, I found an unfamiliar beach sparrow perched on the gable of the little outhouse. I had a sudden, fierce desire for positive identification, but I had not brought field glasses with me. *Sing, damn you, sing*, I muttered. But it only shit and flew off.

Late Tuesday afternoon the wind shifted to straight west, and now, after forty-eight hours of fog, the evening is blessedly still and clear. Only a few high, thin clouds trail among the simple stars in a rich, dark-blue sky. For the first time since arriving here I can see the mainland clear and sharp across the bay: a darkening pleat of low glacial bluffs surmounted by a line of peak-roofed houses against a red afterglow. I feel at once reattached to the world and shot with a sense of how far I have come from it. The bay waters are silky-smooth and gently undulating, but the gaily colored lobster buoys in the offshore channel reveal a strong incoming current; they strain hard at their submerged lines and lean steeply northward, sending on small wakes ahead of them.

Small flocks of plovers fly by overhead—silent, heavy-bodied forms. A pair of black-crowned night herons utter deep, guttural quawks and head south with strong, steady wingbeats to feed on the flats at the far end of the spit. Behind me, from the wet marshy hollows between the dunes, breeding Fowler's toads scream their dry, toneless screams.

The night seems to be calling me with its clarity, so in the last of the light I slip my skiff from its mooring in the creek bed, set the oars, and pull out into the current toward the straining lobster buoys. Anchoring about fifty yards out, I thrust my rubberized lantern beneath the surface and flick it on. The water is very clear and not deep, and my beam reveals its running night life. Moon jellies, with bright orange cloverleaf patterns on their domes, pulse up and down in the currents like ghostly hearts. Beneath the jellyfish are large female horseshoe crabs, ancient arthropods that resemble dark spiked shields trailing long spear points, plowing along the floor of the bay as they have for four hundred million years. Most have one smaller male, and in some cases two or three, clinging piggyback fashion to their backs.

Drifting everywhere through the cold green waters is a fine white rain of dustlike particles. This is the phytoplankton bloom, a seasonal explosion of minute water-borne single-celled marine plants, the source of it all, the base of the estuary's rich food chain, the year's investment, bone of its body, the tiny universal foundations on which all our lives rest. Among this fine, passive dust of phytoplankton swim larger motes of zooplankton: adult copepods and arrow worms, the larval stages of crabs, barnacles, mussels, and oysters. Many of these respond positively to light; they turn and swim, jerking and twisting up toward my beam.

My light sweeps across the dark, domed forms of the submerged, lead-weighted lobster pots resting on the bottom. Inside one I sense a blurred movement and, yielding to a sudden lawless impulse, I grab its buoy line, haul it up out of some two fathoms of water, and heave it, tipping and dripping, over the gunwale of the skiff and onto the ribbed floor between my legs. Shining my light between its wooden slats and inner netting, I behold the white, ghoulish head of a large codfish spiked to the bottom of the cage for bait. The head stares up at me out of empty eye sockets, and around it dances an antic, dark collection of spider crabs, rock crabs, starfish, and one undersized lobster. The exposed creatures click, scuttle, and twist around the white fish head as though protecting their grisly treasure. I feel as though I have unearthed some undigested bit of night business.

I reach in and remove the small lobster (the owners would have to throw it back anyhow, I rationalize), then quickly heave the pot over the side, where it sinks back down to the bottom. I row back to shore and moor my boat in the creek at the head of the tide, which tonight has almost reached the cottage. As I bolt up the steps, a splash of light from Chatham Light, two miles to the south, catches me and throws my guilty shadow up against the raw shingles like a prison searchlight. Inside, I can barely wait for the water to boil. The shell is thin. I rip the arms from the body and crunch the claws open with my teeth. To the east, beyond the dunes, beyond the mindless screaming of the toads, the night surf crawls toward its flood.

4

I sleep a deep, dreamless sleep and wake Wednesday morning to a dawn clear but still gray. The sun, though an hour above the horizon, is in a race to overcome a rising cloud bank out over the ocean. By eight o'clock the sun wins, the bank recedes, and the morning becomes brilliant, sparkling, breezy. The bay is plied with small lobster boats, the crews checking and resetting pots. As I eat breakfast a large marsh hawk with down-swung head and upheld wings comes tilting and veering into the wind within a few yards of the west windows; it takes no more thought of this house than of a dune.

I spend the morning painting the west windows under prairie skies and rolling prairie grass, flanked by Mississippis and Missouris on all sides. The hidden surf beyond the dunes sounds like a herd of buffalo or antelope thundering down the beach, about to break through the dune hollows at any moment. The dunes themselves seem like the slick and shiny coat of some great healthy beast, muscles rippling, tumbling and galloping under my feet as I paint.

And the clouds! What a gallery of vapors there is! Tumbled cumuli pile over the mainland to the west, backed and overarched by cirrus streamers, spiderlike bursts, and paint smears. Mottled salmon clouds spread high overhead, crossed by spreading jet trails — an electron microscopy of nerve ganglions. And below these, thin, light patches of fleece race up the Outer Cape from the south.

Despite the variety of clouds, the morning remains bright. The fog, it seems, has not left for good, but has retreated north and lies, just offshore there, like some low, snarling, purplish-brown, snakelike presence — treading air, indecisive, advancing hesitantly and retreating again like some cowardly dragon, kept at bay by the offshore wind.

Painting in the lee of the house, bathing in the first good sun in three days, I lapse into the simple, expanding motions of the day. Normally I hate to paint, and might resent the time it takes away from me here. But I am doing it to help a friend who has helped me, a favor for a favor; it is only a bonus that I get to do it in such a magnificent arena. I remember, when I earned my living in a classroom, how often we all complained about the "damned mechanics" of teaching, the drudgery of it. A colleague once remarked that the touted boredom of assembly lines is only a liberal cliché, no worse than that of most jobs. But it is not drudgery or boredom per se that is unbearable, only labor or life without purpose, and no amount of bonuses, rest breaks, sabbaticals, or public recognition can make up for that. On the other hand, give us a good enough reason and we will go to hell and not resent it.

At one o'clock the fog still crouches offshore. I decide to take an after-lunch circuit walk of the south colony of cottages. The 1974 Geological

Survey map shows twenty-four cottages in this group, spread out over a half-mile or so of beach. That afternoon I count twenty-two, indicating that two besides the original Tonis cottage were lost in last winter's great storm.

Beach cottage colonies tend to acquire very individual characters in difficult locations. Those on North Beach seem modest, middle class, and largely conventional, like the cottage owners themselves. These Chatham cottages lack the idiosyncratic elaboration of Provincetown's dune shacks, or the clustered communality of the "Village" at the tip of Barnstable's Sandy Neck. They are, instead, simple, restrained, and solid (or as solid as beach shacks can be), placed two to three hundred feet apart, as though seeking neither solitude nor true society, but comfortable association, seeking to be with but not of their own kind — not unlike certain nesting seabirds. They represent a kind of pared-down, unlandscaped counterpart to the settled, bourgeois character of the mainland community, an escape from some of the latter's specific restraints, the sharp edges and binding fabrics of communal living, without losing its basic forms. So our outriders are still characteristic of the main mountain ranges.

The owners these days tend to be from neighboring Cape towns like Dennis and Brewster, but some name signs I encounter are pure Chatham still: Nickerson and Lumpkin on my nearest neighbor's, Crowell on a beached boat.

Inside, most of these cottages are plain, even negligently spartan. Some have imported trappings of suburban rec rooms: masonite paneling, captain's chairs, coasters, "Old Philosopher" wall paintings, et cetera. But outside, all retain an enforced simplicity, a perpetually nomadic look, like dice thrown and rethrown again on the gaming table of the beach. There is little of that external, self-conscious, quaint cuteness that infects so much of the mainland's dwellings, from lobster pots on the lawns to hawser-and-pier fencing to "Cod's Little Acre" and "Our Hide-Aweigh" carved quarterboards over the garages. What there is of this is relegated mostly to the outhouses, perennial source of amusement among refugees from indoor plumbing. One has a "Lobster Potty II" sign above its door, with a genuine wooden pot mounted on the roof. The few signs attached to the cottages themselves tend to be self-deprecating — "Nauset Hilton" on a boathouse — or bristly — "Warning: Trap Gun Set" on a boarded-up window.

There is a kind of landscape humor to them as well. Their owners seem to enjoy bringing in useless artifacts of civilization and planting them around their houses: fire hydrants, newspaper boxes, "Keep Off the Grass" signs. It is a kind of inverse boasting, a reveling in their temporary freedom from the tyranny of what these objects symbolize. One owner has nailed an electric meter to the side of a wall.

I know the freedom from civilized discontent that these cottages celebrate, for I have something of a previous history in one of them. During summers in college I worked as a counselor at one of the Cape sailing camps a few miles north of here on the mainland. On occasion we took a whaleboat full of boys across the bay for an overnight stay in the camp-owned "Outer Beach Cabin." These trips were always sparked with a spirit of adventure and lawlessness. Distinctions between counselor and camper tended to break down, and sometimes we aided the boys in the officially proscribed nighttime activity of digging beach buggy traps. These were deep holes dug in existing vehicle tracks on the outer beach designed to catch unsuspecting fishermen or campers. After finishing a trap, we hid behind a dune, waiting for a pair of headlights to come bouncing down the beach, watching as one of the lights suddenly dropped at an angle, and stifling conspiratorial laughter as a volley of oaths erupted from the invisible driver.

I wonder about the origins of these colonies. Why did they cluster just where they did, a couple of dozen here, another twenty a half-mile to the north, and nothing in between? Most of the buildings appear to have been built after World War II. I have an older map, surveyed in 1940, which shows only seven structures on the entire beach. The cottages in each colony are connected to one another by a complex series of trails threading through a maze of wet swales full of bayberry, beach rose, poison ivy, and wild cranberry.

It would be fun, given the time and opportunity, to study the social organization of such informal multi-generational beach communities, to chronicle the connections, civilities, folklore, and customs that have grown up in them. There must, I think, be conflicting tendencies toward privacy and intercourse in a setting so open and impressionable. Already I can discern a light but definite path running along the top of the dune ridge between the new Tonis cottage and the one immediately south. But I am just as glad to have the neighborhood to myself this time, not to have to get to know people as well as their dwellings. One set of neighbors at a time.

Sometime during the night the fog returned, blanketing the house again. I wake and feel islanded in its midst, like some cloudy, dilating eye unable to focus. I open the door and listen to the thin, high, attenuated calls of the birds of this outer land: the twinkling, metallic cries of the least terns, scratchy notes of song sparrows, chips of savannah sparrows, rising tinkles of larks, old-man coughs of black-backed gulls, strident cackles of laughing gulls.

By midmorning a light, spitting rain begins; it lifts the fog some but drives all boats on the bay to shelter. The gulls, unperturbed, promenade like burgomeisters on the bars in front of the cottage. The rain hits the asphalt roof with a pliant softness, gurgles down off the eaves.

I try to write, but it is no go. It is hard writing about the life one is actually living. I came out here in part to put some distance between it and me, but I find I carry it around with me, unfinished. Thoreau wrote about Walden mostly after leaving it. The best accounts are always separate finished episodes — Melville at sea, Whitman in the first flush of self-discovery, Hemingway at war — rather than the impossibly disparate grist of one's current daily existence. In such situations short, quick raids seem to be best: a day on the beach, a week in the garden, an hour on the road. Beyond that there is too much life to order, to give shape and meaning to. One never seems to get to the end of it.

It rains all afternoon, heavy at times. The air has turned soft and heavy. I paint screen doors inside, and for the first time I miss not having a radio. What I miss most is music. Thoreau took his flute to the pond. Henry Beston brought his concertina to the Outermost House. I play piano.

By evening my schedule has crumbled away completely. No painting. A cold dinner. I prowl the empty neighborhood for novelty and find, in one of the open outhouses, two old copies of *Playboy* from 1966, its heyday. So innocent and positive they seem now, so *therapeutic* about sex. Having largely succeeded in what it set out to do, the magazine now seems forced to do more than it wants to, to appease the endless craving for novelty and the forbidden that it helped to legitimize.

Oh, we are all such horrible mixtures. It is amazing that anything clean and simple ever comes out of any of us. Any writer's honest journal is at once a revelation and an enigma.

Friday. The holiday weekend begins with yet another morning of general fog, southeasterly wind, and spattering rain. Gulls perch like hungry senators at the edge of visibility. Terns call invisibly out of the gray. The southeast corner of the house soughs with surf, and the marsh hawk tilts over the bending, wind-stirred grass like some great brown and white butterfly.

South-southeast! It is as though someone opened a quadrant of the globe and forgot to close it, letting loose the unending, rearing tides of wind and fog. There is no bird song anywhere this morning. Even the terns seem quieted by the monolithic persistence of this weather. The fog is a great gray god, a silent river like the flowing plankton borne ceaselessly along by the channel currents, impregnating the bay.

South-southeast! Flow on, moon jellies, flow on, plankton! The lobster buoys strain at their lines, leaning desirously northward, throwing their wakes ahead of them, held by the weighted, slatted traps on the sea bottom where claws, horny shells, and disked feet dance, click, and scuttle around eyeless, spiked fish heads. The circus-colored buoys bend like the dune grass in the wind, flying ceaselessly but going nowhere. I would fly away, too, now, but am held down here by lead weights and dead lures of resolution and commitment. I feel like a barnacle or a spirobus worm anchored to this house, throwing out feathered legs and tentacles of myself, then withdrawing to digest my finds.

Late in the morning the first campers of the weekend begin to lumber down the beach, fog or no fog. The rain stops by noon, and I spend most of the afternoon painting trim and windows on the north side. The fog lifts enough so that through my glasses I can see a small-craft warning flag flying from the Coast Guard station next to Chatham Light. I think about rowing across tonight to see a movie, maybe calling home. . . . But the wind picks up till there are whitecaps on the bay, and by dusk the fog has closed in again, shutting out the shore lights, keeping me honest.

It is after eleven at night now. Beyond the dunes the surf is rising, its imperative thumping penetrating the thin walls of this uninsulated house. It has been a make-work, make-play day, and I feel both enervated and restless. Placing a Coleman lantern in the east window as a beacon, I set out across the dunes to the ocean. I walk southeast, oblique to the shore, following the sound of the surf. Sights and sounds are both muffled in the darkness and fog. Chatham Light is only an obscure, intermittent glow off to my right. Offshore the deep bleating of two ship horns far apart carries like the baying of two great sea beasts in the night. Toads breed, screaming at one another in the wet hollows.

I seem to be traveling in a dim world of homogenized senses, where distance and dimension cease to exist. For an indeterminate time I walk without seeming to get any nearer the sound of the surf, then all at once I smell it, a wall of sea odors immediately ahead — rich, salt-spiced, redolent of fecundity and decay.

The tide is approaching its high. The seethe of incoming foam laps and sloshes just below the wrack line on the upper beach, sliding back toward the dark breakers with a bubbly, sucking withdrawal. The breaking crest of the waves and the foamy swash edge appear to be outlined with a faint phosphorescence, but it is hard to tell in the obscurity of the fog. The wrack line itself — a knotted tangle of rockweed, dulse, mermaid's tresses, broken claws and shells — is speckled with thousands of tiny, pale, yellow-green coals of light. This is bioluminescent plankton, hordes of diatoms, dinoflagellates and copepods that in summer fill vast stretches of the ocean with their cold, chemical glow — a sort of *aurora maritima* — so that ships plowing through these living shoals of light leave wide wakes of flickering fire behind them.

Some of the larger glowing particles in the wrack line are hopping about, like sparks from resinous kindling. Shining my flashlight on them, I see the bouncing forms of sand hoppers, or beach fleas — miniature, shrimplike crustaceans about a third of an inch long, with huge eyes and pearly-white bodies. By day they live in burrows on the upper beach, coming out at night to feed on the tide's leavings. They ingest the tiny phosphorescent plankton, and their semitransparent bodies begin to glow like miniature jars full of fireflies.

The ocean shows no inordinate ambition tonight, staying contained for the most part, in orderly restlessness, within the high, steep berm of its own making, content to spit up these luminous bits of life. Yet now a larger wave than usual breaks, invisibly, far out; its grating roar seems to spread and encircle me, the dark beach loses definition and place, and though its seethe only curls up and licks my boots like a puppy, I feel a rush of vertigo beneath me, shiver deeply, and involuntarily step back. Vulnerable of spirit, I seem no more than one of those pale, glowing specks of moribund animal life in the wrack line before me, invisible except for the cold, weak light I give off, lasting a few moments, then going out forever.

Now there are other lights moving on the beach. A trio of beach buggies loom out of the fog from the north, their headlight beams lurching drunkenly over the inner sand trail behind the dunes. As they pass the cut where I stand, I can make out fishing poles erect in quivers mounted to their front bumpers. One tries to cut out to the beach over a dune, fails, and roars back onto the track. A man in another jeep curses loudly in the darkness as he passes. For a moment I think he is shouting at me, but then a woman's crackly voice, unangry, bantering, answers him unintelligibly on his CB radio.

They pass swiftly, their lights disappearing into the fog before them, and where they have been I hear the lovely, mournful, solitary note of the piping plover.

For once I do not resent the intrusions of these machines on our beaches, their meaningless lights and harsh sounds. I understand what draws them out here and feel a strong urge to follow them down the dark strand, down past the last of the cottages to the far tip of the spit where the sands perpetually shift and the night herons feed, where men cast their hooks into the curved breakers and pull living, flapping, cold fish-flesh out of the side of the sea.

We all have a desire to seek out such primal encounters, however clumsily or blindly. And the relentless complexity and growing numbers of our society seem to force us to seek them at ever odder hours and in ever stranger places, as on this exposed and shrouded beach, flooded and freshened by the night.

7

Saturday. Last night I dreamed that I was riding down North Beach in the company of clowns on unicycles. We kept avoiding holes that had been dug in the sand, laughing and singing as we went. Eventually we came to what seemed to be a small tourist or information center, somewhere south of this cottage. It had a makeshift telephone system, and I tried to call home but was frustrated by operators too friendly and chatty to bother placing my call, phones with complicated and obscure dialing instructions, intermittent connections with the mainland that seemed to be dependent on the tides. There was one strange phone that had been jury-rigged from old washing-machine parts and that kept agitating on me as I tried to use it. I guess I am ready to go home.

But there will be no going over this morning. I woke at 5:30 to heavy rain, fog, and strong southwest winds. After breakfast it cleared somewhat, but has closed down again and the fog has been dense ever since. Nonetheless the holiday clammers and beachcombers continue to arrive, replacing the shorebirds and terns on the bars and flats in front of the cottage. I have cleaned up and packed, will paint some more inside, and will try to go over after lunch.

At noon the fog finally lifts. Leaving the heavy gear again for Tia, who will arrive that afternoon, I row across, touching the mainland at about two o'clock. I walk the boat upcurrent along the shore of Tern Island to the Chatham Fish Pier. Rows of patterned plovers' heads follow me above the tall, bright-green juncus grass of the inner marshes, and a large flock of mixed gulls sit along the southern dunes, unfazed as always.

I haul the boat out beside the pier, with the strange sense of landing on a foreign shore, realizing that I have spoken to no human being for nearly a week, wondering if I still know the language. I call Beth at work — my voice works, she seems to recognize me, but she can't pick me up for another two hours. So I decide to walk into Chatham Center, to reacquaint myself with civilization.

I set off along Seaview Street, carrying my backpack and drinking a Coke. I am grungy and my clothes are dirty and wrinkled, but I feel strangely elated and unself-conscious. As I walk I become gradually aware and infused by sounds and sights I seem to remember as if from childhood: the smooth hum of lawnmowers, the full-throated song of a song sparrow, hedges, robins. A woman in white golf clothes swings at a ball on the public course, misses, swings again, and hits it about eight feet — some strange native ritual, no doubt. And there are unexpected patterns of wires overhead, and pavement under my feet, and children playing and fighting on front porches, and tourists walking along Main Street, arms around one another, and the smell of cut flowers from florist shops, and the sight of women with done hair and clean blouses sitting on high stools inside ice-cream shops — I want to go in and buy them something.

There are cars, of course — but it is not the sight of cars that touches me, nor car noises and car smells, not the fast food and motel strips, nor any of the harsh contrasts of civilization that my mind has unconsciously set up defenses against, but rather these easy motions and simple signs of our occupation of the earth.

Chatham, with its long-settled, well-cared-for look, its easy access to wider horizons—where the Atlantic lies literally at the end of Main Street—is probably one of the best ports of reentry into the human world. The afternoon is a kind of decompression chamber for me, leaving the marvelous and dreadful vacuum of the outer beach, moving away from that intense, consuming pressure of self-consciousness, expanding in the sunlit crowds.

I walk along, soaking up the sights, giving myself over to the human currents that are just beginning to fill the sidewalks and the shops. I walk into a florist shop and buy blue cornflowers for Beth, buy some small toys for the kids in the five-and-ten, and carry the packages around proudly like badges of readmittance. Everyone seems so helpful and pleasant. I have forgotten the simple but deep pleasure of being waited on courteously by a store clerk or a waitress. I play willingly the role of tourist and consumer, talking with people I would not normally speak to, just to hear the sound of their voices, the varieties of timber and accent. It seems amazing that I can get people to speak to me just by speaking to them. It is as though I had at last mastered birdcalls.

I had expected to feel a certain letdown upon returning, but the effect is just the opposite. Somehow the fact of human existence strikes me as miraculous, as though never seen clearly before. I feel a little like Emily in *Our Town*, returning to earth for one day after her death, as a child. I want to cry out to those I pass and who pass me the simple wonder of us all being here together in this lovely place under sky and shade and sun-dappled yards and the song of birds. I know that inevitably I will sink back into the dulling effects of routine, into possessiveness, into trivial irritation, into the short-sighted pursuits that hobble and frustrate so much of our short lives. But for a few hours I am granted a fresh look at what I have left, which, if not, as T. S. Eliot claimed, the sole point of all our journeying, is reward enough.

It is a little after four now, and I am back at the fish pier, standing on the loading platform, waiting for my family. Less than a mile across Pleasant Bay, the cottage where I lived alone for a week sits clear and gray now under the first sun in three days. It seems so close, and yet years away, across the gleaming boat-plied waters. Below me crews in yellow rubber aprons fork the gutted flapping carcasses of codfish from their boat decks into a large metal hopper. When the hopper is full it is raised by a hydraulic winch and dumps its load, letting go a cascade of bloody disemboweled fish that goes sliding down a white ramp into the icy-breath'd hold of the packing plant. Though most of the fish will be shipped off to New York or Boston in huge refrigerated trucks, and though whole striped bass now sells for more than prime rib in the public fish market next door, we can still see the elemental processes of our survival in such places as this.

A young man on the dock calls to a friend who is just getting into a new green Toyota with a Connecticut license plate: "Those Canadian girls, they going to be back this summer?" The friend smiles, raises his thumb, and drives off. I smile too, content to be where I am, standing in this place of migrations and appetites, listening to the endless talk of fish, weather, and the chances of love.

John Haines

Shadows and Vistas *

There are shadows over the land. They come out of the ground, from the dust and the tumbled bones of the earth. Tree shadows that haunt the woodlands of childhood, holding fear in their branches. Stone shadows on the desert, cloud shadows on the sea and over the summer hills, bringing water. Shapes of shadow in pools and wells, vague forms in the sandlight.

Out of the past come these wind-figures, the flapping sails of primitive birds with terrible beaks and claws. Shadows of things that walked once and went away. Lickers of blood that fasten by night to the veins of standing cattle, to the foot of a sleeping man. In the Far North, the heavy, stalled bodies of mastodons chilled in a black ooze, and their fur-clad bones still come out of the ground. Triceratops was feeding in the marshlands by the verge of the coal-making forest.

Shadows in doorways, and under the eaves of ancient buildings, where the fallen creatures of stone grimace in sleep. Domestic, wind-tugged shadows cast by icy branches upon a bedroom window: they tap on the glass and wake us. They speak to the shadows within us, old ghosts that will not die. Like trapped, primordial birds they break from an ice-pool in the heart's well and fly into walls built long ago.

Stand still where you are — at the end of pavement, in a sun-break of the forest, on the open, cloud-peopled terrace of the plains. Look deeply into the wind-furrows of the grass, into the leaf-stilled water of pools. Think back through the silence, of the life that was and is not here now, of the strong pastness of things — shadows of the end and the beginning.

It is autumn. Leaves are flying, a storm of them over the land. They are brown and yellow, parched and pale — Shelley's

---

*Keynote address, Alaska Environmental Assembly, Anchorage, May 22, 1982.

"pestilence-stricken multitudes." Out of an evening darkness they fly in our faces and scare us; like resigned spirits they whirl away and spill into hollows, to lie still, one on the other, waiting for snow.

I begin with "Shadows," a piece I wrote some years ago, as a way of speaking. Laurens van der Post, in *The Lost World of the Kalahari*, acknowledges that he believes in ghosts, in the spirits of a life that the land once held but which cannot be found any longer. Van der Post was looking for the Bushman, who for him signified a lost Africa, one that he had been told about as a boy; but all that he could find of it was the changed land itself and a few sites where decades before the Bushmen had camped and hunted. According to an old African of his household, from whom he learned much, the Bushman disappeared because *he would not be tamed.*

It is difficult to describe here as fully as I would like how deeply this view of things affects us—not only those of us who live in Alaska, but throughout North America generally. I can refer to an incident in my own life. I remember clearly a long-ago afternoon in early October when I stood on the edge of that high overlook near Maclaren Summit on the Denali Highway, gazing down onto the wide sweep of the Maclaren River basin. The cold, late-afternoon sun came through broken clouds, and the tundra below me was patched with sunlight. The river, a thin, silvery-blue thread, twisted through the fall-subdued coloration of the land, stretching far up into the Alaska Range, into the dark and gloomy hills on which the first light snow had fallen.

I was entirely alone at that moment; no traffic disturbed the gravel road a few yards behind me. The land before me seemed incredibly vast and empty. But it was not empty. Far below me a few scattered caribou were feeding in the meadows of the river basin, their brown, white-maned forms dispersed among the bogs and ponds, moving slowly upriver toward the mountains. They were the first individuals of a herd that would appear later.

I felt as if I were looking down on a landscape elementary to our being, and that nothing had occurred to change it since the last of the continental ice had melted from the earth, and the first grasses and shrubs began to grow, and very slowly the animals moved north into the newly restored land, finding their way, feeding on the fresh, undisturbed forage for the first time.

That image has remained with me as one sure glimpse into our past. Even the road that crossed the river on a tiny bridge in the distance did not break the continuity of the feeling I had then. It was all part of an essential vista, a sheer sense of the land in its original presence. On that afternoon, when the guns of hunters along the road were silent and no cars passed, I easily slipped back a thousand years into a twilight approaching winter; a dusk in which I and a few others, following the game herds upriver, would find meat, fire and shelter.

That was many years ago, when the tundra life along the Denali road was still fairly abundant. I have looked over that same view a number of times since, but I have not seen the caribou feeding as they were then. And yet I know that their ghosts are there, that the land contains them and refuses in some mysterious way to give them up, though to the surface view the land appears empty.

It is not simply nostalgia, I think, that compels me to believe that this vista, its possibility, needs to be kept. We need it as a kind of model of life, whose images we are bound in some way to resurrect and imitate, even though the original may be destroyed. It is not a matter of saving a species, a particular herd and its habitat, but of saving something essential of life and ourselves. And not only our immediate selves, you and I, but those others who were here before us and will come after us, and whose land and nature we have so easily confiscated and misused to our long-standing peril.

It is foolish to believe that we erase life by killing it off, by driving into extinction the remaining game, by paving over the grazing grounds, cutting the forests, and pretending to ourselves that it did not matter after all. Too bad, we say, but let's get on with the business of things. Vanquished in one place, life springs back in another, as at the present time, in spite of all sophistication of transport and communication, coyotes are barking in the Los Angeles suburbs, and as all the killed and vanished life, animal and people, continues in one way or another to haunt us and question our wasting passage through the world.

As a friend of mine said to me a while ago when in the course of conversation we both remarked on the great physical presence of Kluane Lake in Yukon: "That place," she exclaimed, "*really* has spirit!" It does indeed.

And what does this mean? That places, lands, regions, watersheds all have a life, a felt quality of their own, which we can call *spirit*, and we cannot kill that spirit without destroying something in ourselves. A degraded land inevitably produces degraded people. It is, in fact, ourselves we are destroying (and sometimes saving), a possibility of life that once gone will be a long time returning. I say "a long time," and not that it will never come back, because I do not hold with the view that *we* have the power to destroy life on earth forever. That notion is part of our problem, a part of our arrogance and self-bemusement. We have got it backwards: life has power to destroy *us*, and do so with our own connivance, using our own misaligned purposes. A few degrees of climate change, a few more inches of topsoil lost, and our descendants can read the record for themselves.

Is it destined to be a law with us, an iron and withering rule, that anything that cannot be tamed, domesticated, and put to work, to *use*, shall die? A river, a wolf, a small tribe of hunting people? All the while we preserve a few wretched specimens of this or that in a zoo, a controlled park or reservation or as a collection of images on film, part of an ever-growing catalogue of fossil life?

You can kill off the original inhabitants, and most of the world's wildlife, and still live on the land. But I doubt that we can live fully on that land accompanied only by increasing crowds of consumers like ourselves and a few hybrid domesticated animals turned into producing machines. A sure poverty will follow us, an inner desolation to match the devastation without. And having rid the earth of wilderness and of wild things in general, we will look into space, to other planets, to find their replacements there.

We are all familiar with a continuing effort today to save some part of a wild heritage, to rethink our lives in relation to the land on which we drive and park and from which we mainly draw what certainty we have. And we know the forces assembled in opposition to this effort—there is no need to name or rank them, they all flock under the flag of an ever more questionable progress and enterprise, whose hidden name is poverty. T. S. Eliot wrote, on the occasion of a visit to New England in the 1930s:

> My local feelings were stirred very sadly by my first view of New England, on arriving from Montreal, and journeying all one day through the beautiful desolate country of Vermont. Those hills had once, I suppose, been covered with primeval forest; the forest was razed to make sheep pastures for the English settlers; now the sheep are gone, and most of the descendants of the settlers; and a new forest appeared blazing with the melancholy glory of October

maple and beech and birch scattered among the evergreens; and after this process of scarlet and gold and purple wilderness you descend to the sordor of the half-dead milltowns of southern New Hampshire and Massachusetts. It is not necessarily those lands which are most fertile or most favored in climate that seem to me the happiest, but those in which a long struggle of adaptation between man and his environment has brought out the best qualities of both; in which the landscape has been moulded by numerous generations of one race, and in which the landscape has in turn modified the race to its own character. And those New England mountains seemed to me to give evidence of a human success so meager and transitory as to be more desperate than the desert. (T. S. Eliot, *After Strange Gods*, 1934)

Certainly Eliot's description and the feeling it evokes could with a little effort be transferred to many an urban Alaska landscape, be it Mountain View, North Pole, or one of those lost highway settlements in which it seems as if all the unwanted debris and waste of American life had somehow blown there to settle into an impervious drift composed of tarpaper, crushed plastic, ripped shingles, and foundered hopes. I suppose there are few more unreal and depressing aspects than some of the housing sites in Anchorage. And what is unreal will sooner or later disappear — the transitory inspiration of a people come to plunder and leave. Van der Post, in another of his books, remarks on the physical fact of Africa as being by far the most exciting thing about that continent. And for him a definite sadness lay in the fact that it had not yet produced the people and the towns worthy of it. By comparison with its physical self, everything else was drab and commonplace.

We who have learned to call the North country home are perhaps only at the beginning of a struggle of adaptation between ourselves and the land, and if the evidence so far seems pretty meager, there's a long road yet to travel. The prospect of an Alaska in which a million or so people are on the prowl with guns, snowmachines, airboats, and three-wheelers is not only terrifying, it is finally unacceptable. An environmental ethic, believed in, practiced, and enforced, is not just an alternative, it is the only one, though another name for it is self-restraint. And it is sometimes possible to sense, behind all the noise and confrontation, a genuine urge toward a real satisfaction, a sane kind of plenitude, a fullness of spirit and being.

It can be asked what these remarks of mine have to do with immediate politics and practical tasks. And I have no immediate answer, no claim that poetic imagery—the personal mythologies of which a writer is sometimes the master—can solve anything. And yet without this dimension of imagination, the instilled power to think and to visualize that poetry, for example, nourishes in us, the solutions, the resolved difficulties seem bound to lose a necessary human element.

So it is a matter of language, also, of words common and uncommon, that with something of their original freshness and power have the ability to restore a much-needed sense of reality and reveal a few essential things with clarity and concreteness.

Not long ago I saw a marsh hawk, a harrier, hunting the Tanana River islands below Richardson, Alaska, the first arrival of its kind. And that bird was, in a vivid way, rather like a ghost with its gray and white plumage slanting in the spring sunlight as it hovered and sailed over the winter-brown willows and frost-seared grasses. A real spirit, if you like, come back to claim its territory, as it or its ancestors have returned to those flats and adjacent meadows for far longer than our race has existed or can easily imagine. A small but definite image to end on, and returning me halfway to that glimpse into the Maclaren River I described earlier, haunted as I am by its persistent contours, and by what seems sometimes destined to become a vanished hope on earth.

And to think from this diminished perspective in time, from this long vista of empty light and deepening shade, that so small and refined a creature could fill an uncertain niche in the world; and that its absence would leave, not just a momentary gap in nature, but a lack in one's own existence, one less possibility of being.

As if we were to look out on a cherished landscape, hoping to see on the distant, wrinkled plain, among the cloud-shadows passing over its face, groups of animals feeding and resting; and in the air above them a compact flock of waterfowl swiftly winging its way to a farther pond; and higher still, a watchful hawk on the wind. To look, straining one's eyesight, noting each detail of lake, meadow and bog; and to find nothing, nothing alive and moving. Only the wind and the distance, the silence of a vast, creatureless earth.

Edward O. Wilson

Storm Over the Amazon

The Amazonian forest of Brazil whipsaws the imagination. After two or three days there I grow familiar with the earthy smell and vegetation as though in a Massachusetts woodlot, so that what was recently new and wonderful starts to fade from my senses. Then some small event occurs to shift my conceptual framework, and the mystery comes back in its original force. One night I walked into the forest north of Manaus with a headlamp to study the ground surface and everywhere I saw — diamonds! At regular intervals of several yards, intense pinpoints of white light flashed on and off with each turning of the lamp. They were reflections from the eyes of wolf spiders on the prowl. When the spiders were spotlighted they froze into stillness, allowing me to peer at them from inches away. I could distinguish a wide variety of species by size, color, and hairiness. Where did they all come from? What was their prey, and how could so many kinds exist there in these numbers? By morning they would retreat into the leaf litter and soil, yielding the microterrain to a new set of predators. Because I had come for other purposes, I abandoned their study to the arachnologists who would surely follow.

Each evening after dinner I carried a folding chair to a clearing to escape the noise and stink of the camp I shared with Brazilian field hands. The forest around us was in the process of being clearcut northward along an east-west line, mostly to create short-lived pastures. Even so, what remained was and is one of the few great wildernesses of the world, stretching almost unbroken from where I sat across five hundred miles to the Venezuelan savannas.

Just knowing I was on the edge of that immensity deepened the sense of my own purpose. I stared straight into the dark for hours at a time, thinking in spurts about the ecological research that had attracted me there, dreaming pleasantly about the forest as a reservoir of the unknown, so complicated that its measure will not be taken in my lifetime. I was a would-be conquistador of sorts, searching not for Amazonian gold but for great discoveries to be made in the interior. I fantasized about new phenomena and unborn insights. I confess this without embarrassment, because science is built on fantasies that can be proved true. For me the rain forest is the greatest of fantasy lands, a place of hope still unchained by exact knowledge.

And I strained to catch any trace of sound or light. The rain forest at night is an experience in sensory deprivation, black and silent as a tomb. Life is moving out there all right, but the organisms communicate chiefly by faint chemical trails laid over the surface, puffs of odor released into the air, and body scents detected downwind. Most animals are geniuses in this chemical channel where we are idiots. On the other hand, we are masters of the audiovisual channel, matched in that category only by a few odd groups like birds and lizards. At the risk of oversimplification, I can say that this is why we wait for the dawn while they wait for the fall of darkness.

So I welcomed every meteorite's streak and distant mating flash from luminescent beetles. Even the passage of a jetliner five miles up was exciting, having been transformed from the familiar urban irritant to a rare sign of the continuance of my own species.

Then one August night in the dry season, with the moon down and starlight etching the tops of the trees, everything changed with wrenching suddenness. A great storm came up from the west and moved quickly toward where I sat. It began as a flickering of light on the horizon and a faint roll of thunder. In the course of an hour the lightning grew like a menacing organism into flashes that spread across the sky and illuminated the thunderhead section by section. The sound expanded into focused claps to my left, front, and right. Now the rain came walking through the forest with a hiss made oddly soothing by its evenness of pitch. At this moment the clouds rose straight up and even seemed to tilt a little toward me, like a gigantic cliff about to topple over. The brilliance of the flashes was intimidating. Here, I knew, was the greatest havoc that inanimate nature can inflict in a short span of time: 10,000 volts dropping down an ionizing path at 500 miles an hour and a countersurge in excess of 30,000 amperes back up the path at ten times that speed, then additional back-and-forth surges faster than the eye can follow, all perceived as a single flash and crack of sound.

In the midst of the clamor something distracted my attention off to the side. The lightning bolts were acting like photoflashes to illuminate the wall of the rain forest. In glimpses I studied its superb triple-tiered structure: top canopy a hundred feet off the ground, middle tree layer below that, and a scattering of lowest trees and shrubs. At least 800 kinds of trees had been found along a short transect eastward from the camp, more than occur natively in all of North America. A hundred thousand or more species of insects and other small animals were thought to live in the same area, many of which lack scientific names and are otherwise wholly unstudied. The symmetry was complete: the Amazonian rain forest is the most that life has been able to accomplish within the constraints of this stormy planet.

Large splashing drops turned into sheets of water driven by gusts of wind. I retreated into the camp and waited with my *mateiros* friends under the dripping canvas roof. In a short time leptodactylid frogs began to honk their territorial calls in the forest nearby. To me they seemed to be saying rejoice! rejoice! The powers of nature are within our compass.

For that is the way it is in the nonhuman world. The greatest powers of the physical environment slam into the resilient forces of life and nothing much happens. The next morning the forest is still there, and although a few old trees have fallen to create clearings and the way to new plant growth, the profile stays the same. For a very long time, approximately 150 million years, the species of the rain forest evolved to absorb precisely this form and magnitude of violence. They even coded its frequent occurrence into their genes. Organisms use heavy rain and floods to time their mating and other episodes of the life cycle.

Awe is what I am talking about here. It is the most peculiar human response, an overwhelming feeling of reverence or fear produced by that which is sublime or extremely powerful, sometimes changing perception in a basic way. I had experienced it by seeing a living system in a dramatic and newly symbolic fashion. Far larger storms occur on Venus and Jupiter, but they disclose no life underneath. Nothing like the forest wall exists anywhere else we will ever visit. To drop onto another planet would be a journey into death.

A few days later the grinding of gears announced the approach of the truck sent to return me and two workers to Manaus. We watched it coming across the pastureland, a terrain strewn with fire-blackened stumps and logs, the battlefield the rain forest finally lost. On the ride back I tried not to look at it. No awe there, only defeat and decay. I think that the ultimate irony of organic evolution is that in the instant of achieving self-understanding through the mind of man, it doomed its most beautiful creations.

Annie Dillard

Total Eclipse

1

It had been like dying, that sliding down the mountain pass; it had been like the death of someone, irrational, that sliding down the mountain pass and into the region of dread. It was like slipping into fever, or falling down that hole in sleep from which you wake yourself whimpering. We had crossed the mountains that day, and now we were in a strange place — a hotel in central Washington, in a town near Yakima.

I lay in bed. My husband, Gary, was reading beside me. I lay in bed and looked at the painting on the hotel-room wall. It was a print of a detailed and lifelike painting of a smiling clown's head, made out of vegetables. It was a painting of the sort which you do not intend to look at, and which, alas, you never forget. Some tasteless fate presses it upon you; it becomes part of the complex interior junk you carry with you wherever you go. Two years have passed since the total eclipse of which I write. During those years I have forgotten, I assume, a great many things I wanted to remember — but I have not forgotten that clown painting or its lunatic setting in the old hotel.

The clown was bald. Actually, he wore a clown's tight rubber wig, painted white; this stretched over the top of his skull, which was a cabbage. His hair was bunches of baby carrots. Inset in his white clown makeup, and in his cabbage skull, were his small and laughing human eyes. The clown's glance was like the glance of Rembrandt in some of the self-portraits: lively, knowing, deep, and loving. The crinkled shadows around his eyes were string beans. His eyebrows were parsley. Each of his ears was a broad bean. His thin, joyful lips were red chili peppers; between his lips were wet rows of human teeth and a suggestion of a real tongue. The clown print was framed in gilt and glassed.

To put ourselves in the path of a total eclipse, that day we had driven five hours inland from the Washington coast where we lived. When we tried to cross the Cascades range, an avalanche had blocked the pass.

A slope's worth of snow blocked the road; traffic backed up. Had the avalanche buried any cars that morning? We could not learn. This highway was the only winter road over the mountains. We waited as highway crews bulldozed a passage through the avalanche. With two-by-fours and walls of plyboard, they erected a one-way, roofed tunnel through the avalanche. We drove through the avalanche tunnel, crossed the pass, and descended several thousand feet into Central Washington and the broad Yakima Valley, about which we knew only that it was orchard country. As we lost altitude, the snows disappeared; our ears popped; the trees changed, and in the trees were strange birds. I watched the landscape innocently, like a fool, like a diver in the rapture of the deep who plays on the bottom while his air runs out.

The hotel lobby was a dark, derelict room, narrow as a corridor, and seemingly without air. We waited on a couch while the manager vanished upstairs to do something unknown to our room. Beside us on an overstuffed chair, absolutely motionless, was a platinum-blond woman in her forties wearing a black silk dress and a strand of pearls. Her long legs were crossed; she supported her head on her fist. At the dim far end of the room, their backs towards us, sat six bald old men in their shirtsleeves, around a loud television. Two of them seemed asleep. They were drunks. "Number six!" cried the man on television. "Number six!"

On the broad lobby desk, lighted and bubbling, was a ten-gallon aquarium containing one large fish; the fish tilted up and down in its water. Against the long opposite wall sang a live canary in its cage. Beneath the cage, among spilled millet seeds on the carpet, were a decorated child's sand bucket and matching sand shovel.

Now the alarm was set for six. "When I was at home," said _____, "I was in a better place." I lay awake remembering an article I had read downstairs in the lobby, in an engineering magazine. The article was about gold mining.

In South Africa, in India, and in South Dakota, the gold mines extend so deeply into the earth's crust that they are hot. The rock walls burn the miners' hands. The companies have to air-condition the mines; if the air-conditioners break, the miners die. The elevators in the mine shafts run very slowly, down and up, so the miners' ears do not pop in their skulls. When the miners return to the surface, their faces are white.

Early the next morning we checked out. It was February 26, 1979, a Monday morning. We would drive out of town, find a hilltop, watch the eclipse, and then drive back over the mountains and home to the coast. How familiar things are here; how adept we are; how smoothly and professionally we check out! I had forgotten the clown's smiling head and the hotel lobby as if they had never existed. Gary put the car in gear and off we went, as off we have gone to a hundred other adventures.

It was before dawn when we found a highway out of town and drove into the unfamiliar countryside. By the growing light we could see a band of cirro-stratus clouds in the sky. Later the rising sun would clear these clouds before the eclipse began. We drove at random until we came to a range of unfenced hills. We pulled off the highway, bundled up, and climbed one of these hills.

2

The hill was five hundred feet high. Long winter-killed grass covered it, as high as our knees. We climbed and rested, sweating in the cold; we passed clumps of bundled people on the hillside who were setting up telescopes and fiddling with cameras. The top of the hill stuck up in the middle of the sky. We tightened our scarves and looked around.

East of us rose another hill like ours. Between the hills, far below, was the highway which threaded south into the valley. This was the Yakima Valley; I had never seen it before. It is justly famous for its beauty, like every planted valley. It extended south into the horizon, a distant dream of a valley, a Shangri-La. All its hundreds of low, golden slopes bore orchards. Among the orchards were towns, and roads, and plowed and fallow fields. Through the valley wandered a thin, shining river; from the river extended fine, frozen irrigation ditches. Distance blurred and blued the sight, so that the whole valley looked like a thickening or sediment at the bottom of the sky. Directly behind us was more sky, and empty lowlands blued by distance, and Mount Adams.

Mount Adams was an enormous, snow-covered volcanic cone rising flat, like so much scenery.

Now the sun was up. We could not see it; but the sky behind the band of clouds was yellow, and, far down the valley, some hillside orchards had lighted up. More people were parking near the highway and climbing the hills. It was the West. All of us rugged individualists were wearing knit caps and blue nylon parkas. People were climbing the nearby hills and setting up shop in clumps among the dead grasses. It looked as though we had all gathered on hilltops to pray for the world on its last day. It looked as though we had all crawled out of spaceships and were preparing to assault the valley below. It looked as though we were scattered on hilltops at dawn to sacrifice virgins, make rain, set stone stelae in a ring. There was no place out of the wind. The straw grasses banged our legs.

Up in the sky where we stood the air was lusterless yellow. To the west the sky was blue. Now the sun cleared the clouds. We cast rough shadows on the blowing grass; freezing, we waved our arms. Near the sun, the sky was bright and colorless. There was nothing to see.

It began with no ado. It was odd that such a well-advertised public event should have no starting gun, no overture, no introductory speaker. I should have known right then that I was out of my depth. Without pause or preamble, silent as orbits, a piece of the sun went away. We looked at it through welders' goggles. A piece of the sun was missing; in its place we saw empty sky.

I had seen a partial eclipse in 1970. A partial eclipse is very interesting. It bears almost no relation to a total eclipse. Seeing a partial eclipse bears the same relation to seeing a total eclipse as kissing a man does to marrying him, or as flying in an airplane does to falling out of an airplane. Although the one experience precedes the other, it in no way prepares you for it. During a partial eclipse the sky does not darken—not even when 94% of the sun is hidden. Nor does the sun, seen colorless through protective devices, seem terribly strange. We have all seen a sliver of light in the sky; we have all seen the crescent moon by day. However, during a partial eclipse the air does indeed get cold, precisely as if someone were standing between you and the fire. And blackbirds do fly back to their roosts. I had seen a partial eclipse before, and here was another.

What you see in an eclipse is entirely different from what you know. (It is especially different for those of us whose grasp of astronomy is so frail that, given a flashlight, a grapefruit, two oranges, and fifteen years, we still could not figure out which way to set the clocks for Daylight Saving Time.) Usually it is a bit of a trick to keep your knowledge from blinding you. But during an eclipse it is easy. What you see is much more convincing than any wild-eyed theory you may know.

You may read that the moon has something to do with eclipses. I have never seen the moon yet. You do not see the moon. So near the sun, it is as completely invisible as the stars are by day. What you see before your eyes is the sun going through phases. It gets narrower and narrower, as the waning moon does, and, like the ordinary moon, it travels alone in the simple sky. The sky is of course background. It does not appear to eat the sun; it is far behind the sun. The sun simply shaves away; gradually, you see less sun and more sky.

The sky's blue was deepening, but there was no darkness. The sun was a wide crescent, like a segment of tangerine. The wind freshened and blew steadily over the hill. The eastern hill across the highway grew dusky and sharp. The towns and orchards in the valley to the south were dissolving into the blue light. Only the thin river held a trickle of sun.

Now the sky to the west deepened to indigo, a color never seen. A dark sky usually loses color. This was a saturated deep indigo, up in the air. Stuck up into that unworldly sky was the cone of Mount Adams, and the *alpenglow* was upon it. The *alpenglow* is that red light of sunset which holds out on snowy mountaintops long after the valleys and tablelands are dimmed. "Look at Mount Adams," I said, and that was the last sane moment I remember.

I turned back to the sun. It was going. The sun was going, and the world was wrong. The grasses were wrong; they were platinum. Their every detail of stem, head, and blade shone lightless and artificially distinct as an art photographer's platinum print. This color has never been seen on earth. The hues were metallic; their finish was matte. The hillside was a nineteenth-century tinted photograph from which the tints had faded. All of the people you see in the photograph, distinct and detailed as their faces look, are now dead. The sky was navy blue.

My hands were silver. All the distant hills' grasses were fine-spun metal which the wind lay down. I was watching a faded color print of a movie filmed in the Middle Ages; I was standing in it, by some mistake. I was standing in a movie of hillside grasses filmed in the Middle Ages. I missed my own century, the people I knew, and the real light of day.

I looked at Gary. He was in the film. Everything was lost. He was a platinum print, a dead artist's version of life. I saw on his skull the darkness of night mixed with the colors of day. My mind was going out; my eyes were receding the way galaxies recede to the rim of space. Gary was lightyears away, gesturing inside a circle of darkness, down the wrong end of a telescope. He smiled as if he saw me; the stringy wrinkles around his eyes moved. The sight of him, familiar and wrong, was something I was remembering from centuries hence, from the other side of death; yes, *that* is the way he used to look, when we were living. When it was our generation's turn to be alive. I could not hear him; the wind was too loud. Behind him the sun was going. We had all started down a chute of time. At first it was pleasant; now there was no stopping it. Gary was chuting away across space, moving and talking and catching my eye, chuting down the long corridor of separation. The skin on his face moved like thin bronze plating that would peel.

The grass at our feet was wild barley. It was the wild einkorn wheat which grew on the hilly flanks of the Zagros Mountains, above the Euphrates Valley, above the valley of the river we called *River*. We harvested the grass with stone sickles, I remember. We found the grasses on the hillsides; we built our shelter beside them and cut them down. That is how he used to look then, that one, moving and living and catching my eye, with the sky so dark behind him, and the wind blowing. God save our life.

From all the hills came screams. A piece of sky beside the crescent sun was detaching. It was a loosened circle of evening sky, suddenly lighted from the back. It was an abrupt black body out of nowhere; it was a flat disc; it was almost over the sun. That is when there were screams. At once this disc of sky slid over the sun like a lid. The sky snapped over the sun like a lens cover. The hatch in the brain slammed. Abruptly it was dark night, on the land and in the sky. In the night sky was a tiny ring of light. The hole where the sun belongs is very small. A thin ring of light marked its place. There was no sound. The eyes dried, the arteries drained, the lungs hushed. There was no world. We were the world's dead people rotating and orbiting around and around, embedded in the planet's crust, while the earth rolled down. Our minds were lightyears distant, forgetful of almost everything. Only an extraordinary act of will could recall to us our former, living selves and our contexts in matter and time. We had, it seems, loved the planet and loved our lives, but could no longer remember the way of them. We got the light wrong. In the sky was something that should not be there. In the black sky was a ring of light. It was a thin ring, an old, thin silver wedding band in the sky, or a morsel of bone. There were stars. It was all over.

3

It is now that the temptation is strongest to leave those regions. We have seen enough; let's go. Why burn our hands any more than we have to? But two years have passed; the price of gold has risen. I return to the same buried alluvial beds and pick through the strata again.

I saw, early in the morning, the sun diminish against a backdrop of sky. I saw a circular piece of that sky appear, suddenly detached, blackened, and back-lighted; from nowhere it came and overlapped the sun. It did not look like the moon. It was enormous and black. If I had not read that it was the moon, I could have seen the sight a hundred times and never thought of the moon once. (If, however, I had not read that it was the moon—if, like most of the world's people throughout time I had simply glanced up and seen this thing—then I doubtless would not have speculated much, but would simply have, like Emperor Louis of Bavaria in 840, died of fright on the spot). It did not look like a dragon, although it looked more like a dragon than the moon. It looked like a lens cover, or the lid of a pot. It materialized out of thin air—black, and flat, and sliding, outlined in flame.

Seeing this black body was like seeing a mushroom cloud. The heart screeched. The meaning of the sight overwhelmed its fascination. It obliterated meaning itself. If you were to glance out one day and see a row of mushroom clouds rising on the horizon, you would know at once that what you were seeing, remarkable as it was, was intrinsically not worth remarking. No use running to tell anyone. Significant as it was, it did not matter a whit. For what is significance? It is significance for people. No people, no significance. This is all I have to tell you.

In the deeps are the violence and terror of which psychology has warned us. But if you ride these monsters deeper down, if you drop with them farther over the world's rim, you find what our sciences cannot locate or name, the substrata, the ocean or matrix or ether which buoys the rest, which gives goodness its power for good, and evil its power for evil, the unified field: our complex and inexplicable caring for each other, and for our life together here. This is given. It is not learned.

The world which lay under darkness and stillness following the closing of the lid was not the world we know. The event was over. Its devastation lay round about us. The clamoring mind and heart stilled, almost indifferent, certainly disembodied, frail, and exhausted. The hills were hushed, obliterated. Up in the sky, like a crater from some distant cataclysm, was a hollow ring. The ring was as small as one goose in a flock of migrating geese — if you happened to notice a flock of migrating geese. It was one 360th part of the visible sky. The sun we see is less than half the diameter of a dime held at arm's length.

The sight had nothing to do with anything. The sun was too small, and too cold, and too far away, to keep the world alive. The white ring was not enough. It was feeble and worthless. It was as useless as a memory; it was as off-kilter and hollow and wretched as a memory.

When you try your hardest to recall someone's face, or the look of a place, you see in your mind's eye some vague and terrible sight such as this. It is dark; it is insubstantial; it is all wrong.

The white ring and the saturated darkness made the earth and the sky look as they must look in the memories of the careless dead. What I saw, what I seemed to be standing in, was all the wrecked light that the memories of the dead could shed upon the living world. We had all died in our boots on the hilltops of Yakima, and were alone in eternity. Empty space stoppered our eyes and mouths; we cared for nothing. We remembered our living days wrong. With great effort we had remembered some sort of circular light in the sky — but only the outline. Oh, and then the orchard trees withered, the ground froze, the glaciers slid down the valleys and overlapped the towns. If there had ever been people on earth, nobody knew it. The dead had forgotten those they had loved. The dead were parted one from the other and could no longer remember the faces and lands they had loved in the light. They seemed to stand on darkened hilltops, looking down.

Annie Dillard / 167

4

We teach our children one thing only, as we were taught: to wake up. We teach our children to look alive there, to join by words and activities the life of human culture on the planet's crust. As adults we are almost all adept at waking up. We have so mastered the transition we have forgotten we ever learned it. Yet it is a transition we make a hundred times a day, as, like so many will-less dolphins, we plunge and surface, lapse and emerge. We live half our waking lives and all of our sleeping lives in some private, useless, and insensible waters we never mention or recall. Useless, I say. Valueless, I might add—until someone hauls their wealth up to the surface and into the wide-awake city, in a form that people can use.

I do not know how we got to the restaurant. Like Roethke, "I take my waking slow." Gradually I seemed more or less alive, and already forgetful. It was now almost nine in the morning. It was the day of a solar eclipse in central Washington, and a fine adventure for everyone. The sky was clear; there was a fresh breeze out of the north.

The restaurant was a roadside place with tables and booths. The other eclipse-watchers were there. From our booth we could see their cars' California license plates, their University of Washington parking stickers. Inside the restaurant we were all eating eggs or waffles; people were fairly shouting and exchanging enthusiasms, like fans after a World Series game. Did you see—? Did you see—? Then somebody said something which knocked me for a loop.

A college student, a boy in a blue parka who carried a Hasselblad, said to us, "Did you see that little white ring? It looked like a Life-saver. It looked like a Life-saver up in the sky."

And so it did. The boy spoke well. He was a walking alarm clock. I myself had at that time no access to such a word. He could write a sentence, and I could not. I grabbed that Life-saver and rode it to the surface. And I had to laugh. I had been dumbstruck on the Euphrates River, I had been dead and gone and grieving, all over the sight of something which, if you could claw your way up to that level, you would grant looked very much like a Life-saver. It was good to be back among people so clever; it was good to have all the world's words at the mind's disposal, so the mind could begin its task. All those things for which we have no words are lost. The mind—the culture—has two little tools, grammar and lexicon: a decorated sand bucket and a matching shovel. With these we bluster about the continents and do all the world's work. With these we try to save our very lives.

There are a few more things to tell from this level, the level of the restaurant. One is the old joke about breakfast. "It can never be satisfied, the mind, never." Wallace Stevens wrote that, and in the long run he was right. The mind wants to live forever, or to learn a very good reason why not. The mind wants the world to return its love, or its awareness; the mind wants to know all the world, and all eternity, and God. The mind's sidekick, however, will settle for two eggs over easy.

The dear, stupid body is as easily satisfied as a spaniel. And, incredibly, the simple spaniel can lure the brawling mind to its dish. It is everlastingly funny that the proud, metaphysically ambitious, clamoring mind will hush if you give it an egg. Each self is multiple, a mob.

Further: while the mind reels in deep space, while the mind grieves or fears or exults, the workaday senses, in ignorance or idiocy, like so many computer terminals printing out market prices while the world blows up, still transcribe their little data and transmit them to the warehouse in the skull. Later, under the tranquilizing influence of fried eggs, the mind can sort through this data. The restaurant was a halfway house, a decompression chamber. There I remembered a few things more.

The deepest, and most terrifying, was this. I have said that I heard screams. (I have since read that screaming, with hysteria, is a common reaction even to expected total eclipses.) People on all the hillsides, including, I think, myself, screamed when the black body of the moon detached from the sky and rolled over the sun. But something else was happening at that same instant, and it was this, I believe, which made us scream.

The second before the sun went out we saw a wall of dark shadow come speeding at us. We no sooner saw it than it was upon us, like thunder. It roared up the valley. It slammed our hill and knocked us out. It was the monstrous swift shadow-cone of the moon. I have since read that this wave of shadow moves 1800 miles an hour. Language can give no sense of this sort of speed — 1800 miles an hour. It was 195 miles wide. No end was in sight—you saw only the edge. It rolled at you across the land at 1800 miles an hour, hauling darkness like plague behind it. Seeing it, and knowing it was coming straight for you, was like feeling a slug of anesthetic shoot up your arm. If you think very fast, you may have time to think, "Soon it will hit my brain." You can feel the deadness race up your arm; you can feel the appalling, inhuman speed of your own blood. We saw the wall of shadow coming, and screamed before it hit.

This was the universe about which we have read so much and never before felt: the universe as a clockwork of loose spheres flung at stupefying, unauthorized speeds. How could anything moving so fast not crash, not veer from its orbit amok like a car out of control on a turn?

Less than two minutes later when the sum emerged, the trailing edge of the shadow-cone sped away. It coursed down our hill and raced eastward over the plain, faster than the eye could believe; it swept over the plain and dropped over the planet's rim in a twinkling. It had clobbered us, and now it roared away. We blinked in the light. It was as though an enormous, loping god in the sky had reached down and slapped the earth's face.

Something else, something more ordinary, came back to me along about the third cup of coffee. During the moments of totality, it was so dark that drivers on the highway below turned on their cars' headlights. We could see the highway's route as a strand of lights. It was bumper-to-bumper down there. It was 8:15 in the morning, Monday morning, and people were driving into Yakima to work. That it was as dark as night, and eerie as hell, an hour after dawn, apparently meant that, in order to *see* to drive to work, people had to use their headlights. Four or five cars pulled off the road. The rest, in a line at least five miles long, drove to town. The highway ran between hills; the people could not have seen any of the eclipsed sun at all. Yakima will have another total eclipse in _____. Perhaps in _____, businesses will give their employees an hour off.

From the restaurant we drove back to the coast. The highway crossing the Cascades range was open. We drove over the mountain like old pros. We joined our places on the planet's thin crust; it held. For the time being, we were home free.

Early that morning at six when we had checked out, the six bald men were sitting on folding chairs in the dim hotel lobby. The television was on. Most of them were awake. You might drown in your own spittle, God knows, at any time; you might wake up dead in a small hotel, a cabbage-head watching TV while snows pile up in the passes, watching TV while the chili peppers smile and the mountain blows up and the moon passes over the sun and nothing changes and nothing is learned because you have lost your bucket and shovel and no longer care. What if you regain the surface and open your sack and find, instead of treasure, a beast which jumps at you? Or, you may not come back at all. The winches may jam, the scaffolding buckle, the air-conditioning collapse. You may glance up one day and see by your headlamp the canary keeled over in its cage. You may reach into a cranny for pearls and touch a moray eel. You yank on your rope; it is too late.

Apparently people share a sense of these hazards, for when the total eclipse ended, an odd thing happened.

When the sun appeared as a blinding bead on the ring's side, the eclipse was over. The black lens cover appeared again, back-lighted, and slid away. At once the yellow light made the sky blue again; the black lid dissolved and vanished. The real world began there. I remember now: we all hurried away. We were born and bored at a stroke. We rushed down the hill. We found our car; we saw the other people streaming down the hillsides; we joined the highway traffic and drove away.

We never looked back. It was a general vamoose, and an odd one, for when we left the hill, the sun was still partially eclipsed—a sight rare enough, and one which, in itself, we would probably have driven five hours to see. But enough is enough. One turns at last even from glory itself with a sigh of relief. From the depths of mystery, and even from the heights of splendor, we bounce back and hurry for the latitudes of home.

Gretel Ehrlich

Spring

We have a nine-acre lake on our ranch and a warm spring that feeds it all winter. By mid-March the lake ice begins to melt where the spring feeds in, and every year the same pair of mallards come ahead of the others and wait. Though there is very little open water they seem content. They glide back and forth through a thin estuary, brushing watercress with their elegant, folded wings, then tip end-up to eat and after, clamber onto the lip of ice that retreats, hardens forward, and retreats again.

Mornings, a transparent pane of ice lies over the meltwater. I peer through and see some kind of waterbug — perhaps a leech — paddling like a sea turtle between green ladders of lakeweed. Cattails and sweetgrass from the previous summer are bone-dry, marked with black mold spots, and bend like elbows into the ice. They are swords which cut away the hard tenancy of winter. At the wide end a mat of dead waterplants has rolled back into a thick, impregnable breakwater. Near it, bubbles trapped under the ice are lenses focused straight up to catch the coming season.

It's spring again and I wasn't finished with winter. That's what I said at the end of summer too. I stood on the twenty-foot-high haystack and yelled, "No!" as the first snow fell. We had been up since four in the morning picking the last bales of hay from the oatfield by hand, slipping under the weight of them in the mud, and by the time we finished the stack, six inches of snow had fallen.

It's spring but I was still cataloguing the different kinds of snow: snow that falls dry but is rained on; snow that melts down into hard crusts; wind-driven snow that looks blue; powder snow on hardpack on powder — a Linzertorte of snow. I look up. The troposphere is the seven-to-ten-mile-wide sleeve of air out of which all our weather shakes. A bank of clouds drives in from the south. Where in it, I wonder, does a snowflake take on its thumbprint uniqueness? Inside the cloud where schools of flakes are flung this way and that like schools of fish? What gives the snowflake its needle, plate, column, branching shapes—the battering wind or the dust particles around which water vapor clings?

Near town the river ice breaks up and lies stacked in industrial-sized hunks—big as railway cars—on the banks, and is flecked black by wheeling hurricanes of newly plowed topsoil. That's how I feel when winter breaks up inside me: heavy, onerous, up-ended, inert against the flow of water. I had thought about ice during the cold months too. How it is movement betrayed, water seized in the moment of falling. In November, ice thickened over the lake like a cataract, and from the air looked like a Cyclops, one bad eye. Under its milky spans over irrigation ditches, the sound of water running south was muffled. One solitary spire of ice hung noiselessly against dark rock at the Falls as if mocking or mirroring the broom-tail comet on the horizon. Then, in February, I tried for words not about ice, but words hacked from it—the ice at the end of the mind, so to speak— and failed.

Those were winter things and now it is spring, though one name can't describe what, in Wyoming, is a three-part affair: false spring, the vernal equinox, and the spring when flowers come and the grass grows.

Spring means restlessness. The physicist I've been talking to all winter says if I look more widely, deeply, and microscopically all at once I might see how springlike the whole cosmos is. What I see as order and stillness—the robust, time-bound determinacy of my life— is really a mirage suspended above chaos. "There's a lot of random jiggling going on all the time, everywhere," he tells me. Winter's tight sky hovers. Under it, the hayfields are green, then white, then green growing under white. The confinement I've felt since November resembles the confinement of subatomic particles, I'm told. A natural velocity finally shows itself. The particle moves; it becomes a wave.

The sap rises in trees and in me and the hard knot of perseverance I cultivated to meet winter dissipates; I walk away from the obsidian of bitter nights. Now, when snow comes, it is wet and heavy, but the air it traverses feels light. I sleep less and dream not of human entanglements, but of animals I've never seen: a caterpillar fat as a man's thumb, made of linked silver tubes, has two heads—one human, one a butterfly's.

Last spring at this time I was coming out of a bout with pneumonia. I went to bed on January first and didn't get up until the end of February. Winter was a cocoon in which my gagging, basso cough shook the dark figures at the end of my bed. Had I read too much Hemingway? Or was I dying? I'd lie on my stomach and look out. Nothing close up interested me. All engagements of mind — the circumlocutions of love-interests and internal gossip — appeared false. Only my body was true. And my body was trying to close down, go out the window without me.

I saw things out there. Our ranch faces south down a long treeless valley whose vanishing point is two gray hills, folded one in front of the other like two hands, and after that — space, cerulean air, clouds like pleated skirts, and red mesas standing up like breeching whales in a valley three thousand feet below. Afternoons, our young horses played, rearing up on back legs and pawing oh so carefully at each other, reaching around, ears flat back, nipping manes and withers. One of those times their falsetto squeals looped across the pasture and hung on frozen currents of air. But when I tried to ingest their sounds of delight, I found my lungs had no air.

It was thirty-five below zero that night. Our plumbing froze and because I was very weak my husband had to bundle me up and help me to the outhouse. Nothing close at hand seemed to register with me: neither the cold nor the semi-coziness of an uninsulated house. But the stars were lurid. For a while I thought I saw the horses, dead now, and eating each other, and spinning round and round in the ice of the air.

My scientist friends talk with relish about how insignificant we humans are when placed against the time-scale of geology and the cosmos. I had heard it a hundred times, but never felt it truly. As I lay in bed, the black room was a screen through which some part of my body traveled, leaving the rest behind. I thought I was a sun flying over a barge whose iron holds soaked me up until I became rust, floating on a bright river.

A ferocious loneliness took hold of me. I felt spring-inspired desire, a sense of trajectory, but no interception was in sight. In fact, I wanted none. My body was a parenthetical dash laid against a landscape so spacious it defied space as we know it — space as a membrane — and curved out of time. That night a luscious, creamy fog rolled in, like a roll of fat, hugging me, but it was snow.

Recuperation is like spring: dormancy and vitality collide. In any year I'm like a bear, a partial hibernator. During January thaws I stick my nose out and peruse the frozen desolation as if reading a book whose language I don't know. In March I'm ramshackle, weak in the knees, giddy, dazzled by broken-backed clouds, the passing of Halley's comet, the on-and-off strobe of sun. Like a sheepherder I "X" out each calendar day as if time were a forest through which I could clearcut a way to the future. My physicist friend straightens me out on this point too. The notion of "time passing," like a train through a landscape, is an illusion, he says. I hold the Big Ben clock taken from a dead sheepherder's wagon and look at it. The clock measures intervals of time, not the speed of time, and the calendar is a scaffolding we hang as if time were rushing water we could harness. Time-bound I hinge myself to a linear bias — cause and effect all laid out in a neat row — and in this we learn two things: blame and shame.

Julius Caesar had a sense of humor about time. The Roman calendar with its Kalends, Nones, and Ides — counting days — changed according to who was in power. Caesar serendipitously added days, changed the names of certain months, and when he was through, the calendar was so skewed that January fell in autumn.

Einsteinian time is too big for even Julius Caesar to touch. It stretches and shrinks and dilates. In fact, it is the antithesis of the mechanistic concept we've imposed on it. Time, indecipherable from space, is not one thing, but an infinity of spacetimes, overlapping, interfering, wavelike. There is no future that is not now, no past that is not now. Time includes every moment.

It's the Ides of March today.

I've walked to a hill a mile from the house. It's not really a hill but a mountain slope that heaves up, turns sideways, and comes down again, straight down to a foot-wide creek. Everything I can see from here used to be a flatland covered with shallow water. "Used to be" means several hundred million years ago, and the land itself was not really "here" at all, but part of a continent floating near Bermuda. On top is a fin of rock, a marine deposition created during Jurassic times by small waves moving in and out slapping the shore.

I've come here for peace and quiet and to see what's going on in this secluded valley, away from ranch work and sorting corrals, but what I get is a slap on the ass by a prehistoric wave, gains and losses in altitude and aridity, outcrops of mud composed of rotting volcanic ash which fell continuously for ten thousand years a hundred million years ago. The soils are a geologic flag — red, white, green, and gray. On one side of the hill, mountain mahogany gives off a scent like orange blossoms, on the other, colonies of sagebrush root wide in ground the color of Spanish roof tiles. And it still looks like the ocean to me. "How much truth can a man stand, sitting by the ocean, all that perpetual motion," Mose Allison, the jazz singer, sings.

The wind picks up and blusters. Its fat underbelly scrapes the uneven ground, twisting like taffy towards me, slips up over the mountain and showers out across the Great Plains. The sea smell it carried all the way from Seattle has long since been absorbed by pink grus — the rotting granite that spills down the slopes of the Rockies. Somewhere over the Midwest the wind slows, tangling in the hair of hardwood forests, and finally drops into the corridors of the cities, past Manhattan's World Trade Center, ripping free again as it crosses the Atlantic's green swell.

Spring jitterbugs inside me. Spring *is* wind, symphonic and billowing. A dark cloud pops like a blood blister over me, letting hail down. It comes on a piece of wind that seems to have widened the sky, comes so the birds have something to fly on.

A message reports to my brain but I can't believe my eyes. The sheet of wind had a hole in it: an eagle just fell out of the sky. It fell as if down the chute of a troubled airplane. Landed, falling to one side as if a leg were broken. I was standing on the hill overlooking the narrow valley that had been a seashore 170,000,000 years ago, whose sides had lifted like a medic's litter to catch up this eagle now.

She hops and flaps seven feet of wing and closes them down and sways. She had come down (on purpose?) near a dead fawn whose carcass had recently been feasted upon. When I walked closer, all I could see of the animal was a ribcage rubbed red with fine tissue and the decapitated head lying peacefully against sagebrush, eyes closed.

At twenty yards the eagle opened her wings halfway and rose up, her whole back lengthening and growing stiff. At forty feet she looked as big as a small person. She craned her neck, first to one side, then the other, and stared hard. She's giving me "the eagle eye," I thought.

Friends who have investigated eagles' nests have literally feared for their lives. It's not that they were in danger of being pecked to death but, rather, grabbed. An eagle's talons are a powerful jaw. Their grip is so strong the talons can slice down through flesh to bone in one motion.

But I had come close only to see what was wrong, to see what I could do. An eagle with a bum leg will starve to death. Was it broken, bruised, or sprained? How could I get close enough to know? I approached again. She hopped up in the air dashing the critical distance between us with her great wings. Best to leave her alone, I decided. My husband dragged a road-killed deer up the mountain slope so she could eat, and I brought a bucket of water. Then we turned towards home.

A golden eagle is not golden but black with yellow spots on the neck and wings. Looking at her, I had wondered how feathers came to be, how their construction — the rachis, vane, and quill — is unlike anything else in nature.

Birds are glorified flying lizards. The remarkable feathers which, positioned together, are like hundreds of smaller wings, evolved from reptilian scales. Ancestral birds had thirteen pairs of cone-shaped teeth that grew in separate sockets like a snake's, rounded ribs, and bony tails. Archaeopteryx was half bird, half dinosaur who glided instead of flying; Ichthyornis was a fish-bird, a relative of the pelican; Diatryma was a giant, seven feet tall with a huge beak and wings so absurdly small they must have been useless, though later the wingbone sprouted from them. *Aquila chrysaëtos*, the modern golden eagle, has seven thousand contour feathers, no teeth, and weighs about eight pounds.

I think about the eagle. How big she was, how each time she spread her wings it was like a thought stretching between two seasons.

Back at the house I relax with a beer. At 5:03 the vernal equinox occurs. I go outside and stand in the middle of a hayfield with my eyes closed. The universe is restless but I want to feel celestial equipoise: twelve hours of daylight, twelve of dark, and the earth ramrod straight on its axis. In celebration I straighten my posture in an effort to resist the magnetic tilt back into dormancy, spiritual and emotional reticence. Far to the south I imagine the equatorial sash, now nose to nose with the sun, sizzling like a piece of bacon, then the earth slowly tilting again.

In the morning I walk up to the valley again. I glass both hillsides, back and forth through the sagebrush, but the eagle isn't there. The hindquarters of the road-killed deer have been eaten. Coyote tracks circle the carcass. Did they have eagle for dinner too?

Afternoon. I return. Far up on the opposite hill I see her, flapping and hopping to the top. When I stop, she stops and turns her head. Her neck is the plumbline on which earth revolves. Even at two hundred yards, I can feel her binocular vision zeroing in; I can feel the heat of her stare.

Later, I look through my binoculars at all sorts of things. I'm seeing the world with an eagle eye. I glass the crescent moon. How jaded I've become, taking the moon at face value only, forgetting the charcoal, shaded backside, as if it weren't there at all.

Gretel Ehrlich / 177

That night I dream about two moons. One is pink and spins fast; the other is an eagle's head, farther away and spinning in the opposite direction. Slowly, both moons descend and then it is day.

At first light I clamber up the hill. Now the dead deer my husband brought is only a hoop of ribs, two forelegs, and hair. The eagle is not here or along the creek or on either hill. I go to the hill and sit. After a long time an eagle careens out from the narrow slit of the red-walled canyon whose creek drains into this valley. Surely it's the same bird. She flies by. I can hear the bone-creak and whoosh of air under her wings. She cocks her head and looks at me. I smile. What is a smile to her? Now she is not so much flying as lifting above the planet, far from me.

Late March. The emerald of the hayfields brightens. A flock of gray-capped rosy finches who overwintered here swarms a leafless apple tree, then falls from the smooth boughs like cut grass. The tree was planted by the Texan who homesteaded this ranch. As I walk past, one of the boughs, shaped like an undulating dragon, splits off from the trunk and falls.

Space is an arena in which the rowdy particles that are the building blocks of life perform their antics. All spring, things fall; the general law of increasing disorder is on the take. I try to think of what it is to be a cause without an effect, an effect without a cause. To abandon time-bound thinking, the use of tenses, the temporally related emotions of impatience, expectation, hope, and fear. But I can't. I go to the edge of the lake and watch the ducks. Like them, my thinking rises and falls on the same water.

Another day. Sometimes when I'm feeling small-minded I take a plane ride over Wyoming. As we take off I feel the plane's resistance to accepting air under its wings. Is this how an eagle feels? Ernst Mach's principle tells me that an object's resistance against being accelerated is not the intrinsic property of matter, but a measure of its interaction with the universe; that matter only has inertia because it exists in relation to other matter.

Airborne, then, I'm not aloof but in relation to everything—like Wallace Stevens's floating eagle for whom the whole, intricate Alps is a nest. We fly southeast from Heart Mountain across the Big Horn River, over the long red wall where Butch Cassidy trailed stolen horses, across the high plains to Laramie. Coming home the next day, we hit clouds. Turbulence, like many forms of trouble, cannot always be seen. We bounce so hard my arms sail helplessly above my head. In evolution, wingbones became arms and hands; perhaps I'm de-evolving.

From ten thousand feet I can see that spring is only half here: the southern part of the state is white, the northern half is green. Land is also time. The greening of time is a clock whose hands are blades of grass moving vertically, up through the fringe of numbers, spreading across the middle of the face, sinking again as the sun moves from one horizon to the other. Time doesn't go anywhere; the shadow of the plane, my shadow, moves across it.

To sit on a plane is to sit on the edge of sleep where the mind's forge brightens into incongruities. Down there I see disparate whole-nesses strung together and the string dissolving. Mountains run like rivers; I fly through waves and waves of chiaroscuro light. The land looks bare but is articulate. The body of the plane is my body, pressing into spring, pressing matter into relation with matter. Is it even necessary to say the obvious? That spring brings on surges of desire? From this disinterested height I say out loud what Saint Augustine wrote: "My love is my weight. Because of it I move."

Directly below us now is the fine old Wyoming ranch where Joel, Mart, Dave, Hughy, and I have moved thousands of head of cattle. Joel's father, Smokey, was one of two brothers who put the outfit together. They worked hard, lived frugally, and even after Fred died, Smokey did not marry until his late fifties. As testimony to a long bachelorhood, there is no kitchen in the main house. The cookhouse stands separate from all the other buildings. In back is a bedroom and bath which has housed a list of itinerant cooks ten pages long.

Over the years I've helped during roundup and branding. We'd rise at four. Smokey, now in his eighties, cooked flapjacks and boiled coffee on the wood cookstove. There was a long table. Joel and Smokey always sat at one end. They were look-alikes, both skin-and-bones tall with tipped-up dark eyes set in narrow faces. Stern and vigilant, Smokey once threw a young hired hand out of the cookhouse because he hadn't grained his saddle horse after a long day's ride. "On this outfit we take care of our animals first," he said. "Then if there's time, we eat."

Even in his early twenties, Joel had his father's dignity and razor-sharp wit. They both wore white Stetsons identically shaped. Only their hands were different: Joel had eight fingers and one thumb—the other he lost while roping.

Eight summers ago my parents visited their ranch. We ate a hearty meal of homemade whiskey left over from Prohibition days, steaks cut from an Angus bull, four kinds of vegetables, watermelon, ice cream, and pie. Despite a thirteen-year difference in our ages, Smokey wanted Joel and me to marry. As we rose from the meal, he shook my father's hand. "I guess you'll be my son's father-in-law," he said. That was news to all of us. Joel's face turned crimson. My father threw me an astonished look, cleared his throat, and thanked his host for the fine meal.

One night Joel did come to my house and asked me if I would take him into my bed. It was a gentlemanly proposition—doffed hat, moist eyes, a smile almost grimacing with loneliness. "You're an older woman. Think of all you could teach me," he said jauntily, but with a blush. He stood ramrod straight waiting for an answer. My silence turned him away like a rolling wave and he drove to the home ranch, spread out across the Emblem Bench thirty-five miles away.

The night Joel died I was staying at a writer's farm in Missouri. I had fallen asleep early, then awakened suddenly, feeling claustrophobic. I jumped out of bed and stood in the dark. I wanted to get out of there, drive home to Wyoming and I didn't know why. Finally, at seven in the morning, I was able to sleep. I dreamed about a bird landing, then lifting out of a tree along a river bank. That was the night Joel's pickup rolled. He was found five hours after the accident occurred—just about daylight—and died on the way to the hospital.

Now I'm sitting on a fin of Gypsum Springs rock looking west. The sun is setting. What I see are three gray cloud towers letting rain down at the horizon. The sky behind these massifs is gilded gold, and long fingers of land—benches where the Hunt Oil Company's Charolais cattle graze—are pink. Somewhere over Joel's grave the sky is bright. The road where he died shines like a dash in a Paul Klee painting. Over my head, it is still winter: snow so dry it feels like styrofoam when squeezed together, tumbles into my lap. I think about flying and falling. The place in the sky where the eagle fell is dark, as if its shadow had burned into the backdrop of rock—Hiroshima style. Why does a wounded eagle get well and fly away; why do the head wounds of a young man cut him down? Useless questions.

Sex and death are the riddles thrown into the hopper, thrown down on the planet like hailstones. Where one hits the earth, it makes a crater and melts, perhaps a seed germinates, perhaps not. If I dice life down into atoms, the trajectories I find are so wild, so random, anything could happen: life or nonlife. But once we have a body, who can give it up easily? Our own or others'? We check our clocks and build our beautiful narratives, under which indeterminacy seethes.

Sometimes, lying in bed, I feel like a flounder with its two eyes on one side pointing upward into nothingness. The casings of thought rattle. Then I realize there are no casings at all. Is it possible that the mind, like space, is finite, but has no boundaries, no center or edge? I sit cross-legged on old blankets. My bare feet strain against the crotch of my knees. Time is between my toes, it seems. Just as morning comes and the indigo lifts, the leaflessness of the old apple tree looks ornate. Nothing in this world is plain.

"Every atom in your body was once inside a star," another physicist says, but he's only trying to humor me. Not all atoms in all kinds of matter are shared. But who wouldn't find that idea appealing? Outside, shadows trade places with a sliver of sun which trades places with shadow. Finally the lake ice goes and the water — pale and slate blue — wears its coat of diamonds all day. The mallards number twenty-six pairs now. They nest on two tiny islands and squabble amicably among themselves. A Pacific storm blows in from the south like a jibsail reaching far out, backhanding me with a gust of something tropical. It snows into my mouth, between my breasts, against my shins. Spring teaches me what space and time teach me: that I am a random multiple; that the many fit together like waves; that my swell is a collisions of particles. Spring is a kind of music, a seething minor, a twelve-tone scale. Even the odd harmonies amassed only lift up to dissolve.

Spring passes harder and harder and is feral. The first thunder cracks the sky into a larger domain. Sap rises in obdurateness. For the first time in seven months, rain slants down in a slow pavanne — sharp but soft — like desire, like the laying on of hands. I drive the highway that crosses the wild-horse range. Near Emblem I watch a black studhorse trot across the range all alone. He travels north, then turns in my direction as if trotting to me. Now, when I dream of Joel, he is riding that horse and he knows he is dead. One night he rides to my house, all smiles and shyness. I let him in.

Ralph Beer

Wind Upon the Waters

Pray hard to weather, that lone surviving god,
that in some sudden wisdom we surrender.

—RICHARD HUGO

It turned out to be one of those winters, the kind you heard about as a child from old folks who considered themselves survivors. The first heavy snows fell in early October. November blizzards, driven by killing arctic winds, buried pastures under drifts three feet deep and froze newborn fall calves to the ground even as they struggled to rise. Weeks of subzero temperatures brought ranch work to a halt and drove herds of mule deer from higher country to congregate among the cattle I fed each day. By Christmas even the elk had moved down from their mountains to paw the alfalfa fields two hundred yards from my door. Local supplies of hay, already low after two years of severe drought, began to disappear. Because they couldn't afford to buy more feed, ranchers began shipping cattle; some sold even their pregnant cows, next year's cash crop.

Mild days in January formed rippled sheets of deadly ice on south-facing slopes and in gulches, and I fed close to the barns to keep the cattle away from the worst of it. Weakened by weather, the deer stayed with my cattle, growing so used to me that I'd occasionally look up from my work in the cowbarn to see them peeking in the open Dutch doors. A pair of frail, eight-month-old fawns became so tame I could almost touch them.

One storm followed another during most of February, and the leaden months of overcast sky and stone-hard snow ran together in memory as a single gray test of endurance. I'd wintered years with deeper snow, longer cold spells, and, I think, worse wind, but for sheer relentlessness this one seemed to stand above the rest, seemed harsher in a vague abrasive way that drove me indoors when I should have been working outside. Call it cabin fever or a high blue lonesome or just winter, once you begin to resent the weather in the mountains of Montana you've reached the point of leaving or losing touch with yourself. Tar-paper-shack homesteaders discovered this kind of loss out here by the score only seventy years ago, driven toward one form of despair or another by drought and distances, falling commodity prices and winter. O. E. Rölvaag called their sod-hut counterparts giants, and in ways that are hard to understand today they were, the ones who endured. Others, like my mother's father and my father's grandfather, walked away to windbreaks or barns with rifles and did not walk back. Capable and productive men, remembered for energy and heart, who broke in February; men beaten by nothing more than weather, who were very much on my mind early one morning at the end of that month as I stood at the south window in my cabin and watched fast-moving clouds shift through a spectrum of early colors, blue-gray to ocher along the horizon beneath fleets of wind-curled cirrus fired bright chrome orange. The first direct sunlight in a week lit timbered granite bluffs off south, the uppermost pine burning red, while lower, in the darkest greens of the forest, horned owls quieted after a long night of melancholy questions.

Within minutes the highest trees in the encircling bluffs began to stir. Even the dead-topped old fir quivered, ancient trees, rooted so deep in rock they often die erect and for several generations of men continue to stand, rotting and blowing away piece by piece in the wind until only a column of heartwood remains above a heap of lichen-covered duff. It takes real wind to move the firs, but as I listened, all I could hear was the chuffing of my box stove, the teakettle gently boiling on its fender, and a family of magpies scolding my cat in the yard.

With a prairie jacket over my shoulders and a mug of coffee in one hand, I stepped outside and stood bareheaded to listen to it coming, playing through millions of acres of forest, stirring every needle, twig, and blade of grass, coming with the surge of an approaching river running full to its banks, a flood of air roiling off the Continental Divide and rushing north across the foothills toward the plains of Canada, the grandfather of Montana's winds, the chinook.

Alder along the creek began to clatter, the frozen lilac bush beside my door trembled, and I could feel the first gusts in my hair, as warm and welcome as a lover's breath. By the time I'd finished my coffee, the temperature had risen fifteen degrees, and everything in sight was in motion: flutters of chickadees overhead, fine snow rising in plumes along the ridges, and finally, from the south eave of my cabin, bright drops of water, falling and caught by the wind to be driven like new tacks into the dry batten walls.

Two hours later, streams of water poured from my haybarn's high eaves, surrounding me — as if I worked between twin waterfalls — with an exuberant counterpoint of light and sound. The sky thickened once with scudding, bruise-colored clouds, then quickly cleared. In the twenty minutes it took to load the morning ration of hay, half an inch of hoarfrost formed on the granite cliffs above the barns, covering the frozen stone with furry rime. The temperature had risen forty degrees, and the initial effect of that sudden warmth was exhilarating, intoxicating. Calves raced through the feedyard with their tails straight in the air. A young Shorthorn bull pawed and bellowed atop a manure pile, and even the most matronly old cows tried some quick steps, trotting about as gingerly as dowagers in basketball shoes. And as I watched this favonian acceleration among my animals, seventeen mule deer emerged single-file from a cleft in the rocks; in the open, antlerless young bucks struck at each other with sharp front hooves; fawns milled, hanging back, then bouncing ahead as if propelled on springs; and two large does, the leaders, continued toward me, their great ears perked toward the load of sweet hay, their pace serene, as if they understood that an end to their long struggle with winter had come.

The wind blew that day and all night. By the second afternoon the temperature had steadied at fifty-six degrees, and I couldn't resist any longer. I left corral rails leaning on a sawbuck to peel another day, changed into a knee-high pair of milking boots, took my walking stick from the elkhorns above my door, and splashed off into the wind through fifteen inches of slush toward the creek. South slopes had bared completely, revealing again pine needles, grass, and dark earth hidden for nearly six months. The first dry gulch I forded carried a stream of water a yard wide that gained momentum and depth as it rushed over the frozen ground to disappear under four-foot drifts in the open meadows. The creek itself had become a torrent of foam running above its banks into thickets of wild rose and willow, threatening to wash out a stream crossing that had taken me long days of hand labor to build. As I watched brown water sluicing from the stone inlaid culverts, I remembered the old bridge that had once spanned the creek there, a bridge built by my grandfather, who had snaked great pitch logs across the water with teams of horses, then spiked heavy planks to the logs. No one had bothered to tell me when I was a little boy that our creek was too small to support trout, and I'd spent occasional summer after-noons fishing through the spaces between the planks. I remembered ly-ing on my belly on the rough-cut boards and watching my line meander from sun-dappled water upstream into shaded holes beneath the bridge where several hundred tadpoles and one very handsome water snake lived. That I was drawn back again and again without a nibble had, of course, more to do with a fascination for the motion and sound of water than visions of rainbow or cutthroat taking my hook. And that enchanting force of water, I've since learned, is not only the delight of small boys, but a Western obsession, a matter of life and death for those who live downstream.

The chinook causing my little flood had, in fact, been born over water, far out above the Pacific Ocean as an east-bound mass of moist warm air. As it moved inland across the coastal ranges, this air lost moisture; more precipitation fell on the western slopes of Montana's mountain ranges, causing the air to become warmer and drier on east-ern slopes than at the same elevation to the west. High pressure to the south, centered as far away as Utah, then forced this warming air north and northeast in the characteristic pattern of chinook flow. While known best for their springtime assaults on snow, chinooks do occur year-round; midsummer chinooks are common in Montana, and dur-ing drought years have a devastating effect on already dry land and crops.

Related winds are found around the world where similar condi-tions exist. Cousins of the chinook include the famous *foehn* winds of central Europe and the *Bora* in the Denaric Alps of Yugoslavia, where, in the village of Split, ropes are fastened along sidewalks as handrails for pedestrians caught in the open when the *Bora* comes through town at a hundred miles per hour.[1]

Usually less dramatic than the *Bora*, chinooks in Montana have nonetheless caused such wild and sudden increases in temperature that numerical records seem to pale in the imagination: eighty degrees in a few hours near Kipp, Montana, melting thirty inches of snow in half a day; a rise in temperature of forty-three degrees in fifteen minutes at Havre, Montana; twenty-six degrees in forty-five seconds, again at Havre.[2] And, as far downwind as Spearfish, South Dakota, an increase in temperature from minus four degrees Fahrenheit to forty-five de-grees in two minutes, recorded in January 1943.[3]

More interesting than their curious statistics is the way chinooks demonstrate, in a region already known for extreme weather, the potential danger of sudden changes in long-term weather patterns and climate. By climate I mean regional weather (annual rainfall, mean temperature, length of growing season, number of days of frost, etc.) averaged over a period of years; by sudden I mean within a century or less. Chinooks, like droughts and severe winters, suggest harsh consequences of even minute alterations in weather patterns, not only for dryland operations in Montana (which have always been "marginal") but for our entire system of mechanized agriculture, one that now depends as much on vast quantities of fresh water—either diverted from rivers or pumped from the ground—as on oil. Ultimately, climate change would mean even bleaker consequences for large urban populations now almost totally dependent on distant factorylike farms and huge amounts of imported water.

The past year in central Montana has been a lesson in extremes. Last summer was a season dry beyond living memory, drier, according to records, than the worst of the thirties. The first six months were the driest of any year in the 106 years the National Weather Service has kept records here, and this period was capped by a number of days of all-time-high temperatures. The sky in May and June, when the rains normally come, became a daily cloudless kiln. Antelope bitterbrush and sage wilted in the Augustlike heat; pine needles tanned on living trees; cheat grass turned not its usual dusty red but *white*. Alfalfa burned over at four inches in the fields. Range grasses blew away in ceaseless winds.

Allegorically at least, that drought and its attendant ceaseless winds seemed a warning as well as a reminder that our attitudes toward climate, water use, and abundant supplies of food may be taking us down a primrose path toward a desert. Like a chinook we have, within the very brief time since settlement, used, wasted, or fouled much of our accessible water. Some rivers in the West have already become so overtaxed by irrigation and distant urban populations that after only a little more than a hundred years of our presence, more water is allocated than actually flows between the rivers' banks. The Colorado River, for example, is "120 percent committed. Eighty-five percent is used hard—so seriously diminished in quality and with severe salinity problems that using the entire flow is hardly imaginable."[4]

Our underground rivers, aquifers which took untold millennia to accumulate, are in serious trouble as well. The Ogallala Aquifer in the Midwest has been pumped so hard that grandiose schemes suggesting diversion of water from the upper Missouri River to "recharge" it have recently been seriously proposed. Much, if not most, of this water has been used for irrigation of crops during a very brief period in climate history that has been *optimal* for agriculture in North America. The final wave of homesteading in Montana took place during a wet decade (sixteen inches of annual rainfall in the wheat country) accompanied by the warmest weather in the past one thousand years. In fact, only five percent of the time during the last two million years have the earth's temperatures been as warm as this century's.[5]

How long, one wonders, will surplus foodcrops continue to be a burden on taxpayers in a future characterized by harsher winters, shorter growing seasons, and drier summers, when farmers will also face depleted water reserves?

The point here may seem like old news: There is a finite amount of water in circulation on and around the Earth, most of it inaccessible or unfit for human use. We are rapidly increasing our demands on the amount of clean water at our disposal, often wasting it on a huge scale to carry sewage, to generate electricity, or—perhaps most dangerous of all—to continue irrigation of surplus crops during a period of nutritional affluence, spending that water as if there will be no tomorrow, while in the process, leaching and eroding irreplaceable topsoils, even turning the land in some places to salt.

A slight change in global temperature, *up or down*, will affect wind and rainfall patterns, length of regional growing seasons, amount of water in atmospheric circulation, and, ultimately, food production. Such changes have occurred, and very quickly, within the recent past; the cooling trend, for example, that plunged grain-growing Icelandic colonies on the west coast of Greenland into the permafrost of the Little Ice Age did so in less than three hundred years. Solar cycles recorded in bands of sedimentary rock nearly a billion years old in Australia suggest that a period of sunspot minimum is again due near the beginning of the twenty-first century, the possible beginning of another Little Ice Age.[6]

Sunspots are, of course, beyond our control, but the comforting old cliché that we like to talk about weather but don't do much about it is simply no longer true. Nearly five billion humans engaged in consuming, defecating, building, farming, traveling, warring, and dying have an immense if still immeasurable impact on environment, including climate. We are like a hot wind upon the waters, and by 2020 there will be eight billion of us, nearly doubling our influence, as well as our current demands for nutrition and drinkable water. Although the long-range effects of atmospheric dust, smoke, CO_2, and aerosol pollution are still being debated (some scientists project a warming or "greenhouse" effect, while others argue that a cooling trend may result from atmospheric clouding and sunspot activity), the likelihood of climate change is as certain as that the change, either warmer or cooler, will likely be accelerated by human activity and have serious negative consequences for future, more crowded, generations.

The history of the settlement of North and South America is a legacy of man bent on altering the natural possibilities of the land he invades, changing it as quickly and totally as he can, often without first taking best advantage of—and thereby protecting to some degree—those native possibilities. Much of the Great Plains, including some of the finest grasslands in the world, has been put to the plow, turned under to raise grain used largely to fatten cattle that would almost certainly be healthier for consumers if raised on grass. Tropical rain forests in South America are being cleared at a rate of thirty acres a minute, twenty-four hours a day[7] to provide grazing land to raise cheap beef for export to hamburger franchises in the United States at a time when beef producers here have been bankrupted by an overabundance of cattle. Misapplication of plow has led to dust in the north, of axe to less and less new oxygen produced in the great but shrinking forests of the south; together, these two tools exert extremely powerful influences not only on our present food economy, but, by eventually helping to alter climate, on the price we *will* pay for food in the coming decades, an expense which may not, finally, have much to do with money.

What shall we do when it appears the sky is falling, cover our heads? What can anyone do about the forces of sun and wind and water and climate? Our first steps must surely rely less on "technological advances" than on attitude adjustments akin to those we made during the 1970s when the tap was temporarily closed on our until then unlimited supply of cheap oil. We must stop believing that our recent spell of good weather (like 35¢-a-gallon gasoline) is permanent, and that no matter what happens technology will provide solutions. Technology, certainly, will be helpful in perfecting better ways of recycling water, of developing more drought-resistant strains of crops, and so on. But the myth, that regardless of our abuses of soil and water and air, technology will somehow miraculously save us, is as dangerous as it is false. As farmer/essayist Wendell Berry points out, technological solutions invariably have consequences which lead to new environmental problems requiring a yet more advanced technology, which in turn creates vaster, more complex ecological crises. A more expensive, unnatural, and less helpful cycle is hard to imagine.

The time to rid ourselves of a laconic acceptance of abundant clean water and plentiful cheap food is certainly while we still enjoy both. Although there is very little "official" planning currently being done regarding changing weather, public attitudes need to be altered to create new practices that work to our financial advantage as well as for the preservation of water resources, just as smaller cars and wiser driving habits gradually helped to modify the ever upward trend in gasoline prices and at the same time reduce auto emissions. Because Americans now pay such a small percentage of their earnings for food, and because the land and water upon which food production depends is being concentrated into fewer hands, bets for big profits are now being placed that food in the 1990s will be as lucrative as oil was in the 70s.

Common sense and self-restraint must be applied by large and small users of water alike. Highly leveraged irrigators in the West can cut in half the amount of water they pump from the ground to spray on fields this season by irrigating only when necessary to save a crop, and then by irrigating only at night. Crippling electricity bills would be cut in half while almost as much water could get back into the ground, since daytime evaporation rates of up to 90 percent would be avoided. If widely applied, this practice would conserve subsurface water reserves, send a message to increasingly profit-hungry utility companies, and decrease the amounts of coal and water wasted at generating plants. Soil leaching would be reduced; the land would remain in production, and farmers would almost certainly lose less money on this crop than on the one they soaked last year.

Residential water users in the arid Southwest should stop trying to grow lawns with water piped hundreds of miles from the Colorado River, and fashion-minded folks in water-poor Los Angeles should stop laving all those cars. The Dusty Look will be in soon enough. Trendsetters should let that freeway loam begin to build.

In the five weeks since this year's first chinook, when I first began this essay, the snow has gone completely and fields have again grown dusty. Measured snow-depth in nearby mountains is only 44 percent of normal for this date, and it appears that the drought of the past two years will continue this summer. If that proves to be the case, I will soon be out of the cow business; ranch liquidations will continue, as will the stress on wildlife and native foliage. Grain and livestock production will continue to decline, and the responsibility for and control of food production will continue to be concentrated in fewer and fewer hands. Well drillers will again work double shifts deepening existing wells that have gone dry.

Sometimes less really *is* more, and quite often the best improvement is to make no improvements at all. During a chinook, the meltwater roaring down my creek is lost to me forever. How much better, I've often thought, if the snow would melt a little at a time and soak into the ground. Barring that, why not take action myself? Drill a dozen deep wells, shoot them with dynamite to form underground caverns where water could collect, then pump that water onto my fields — an ever tempting solution to drought in an already semiarid country where visions of waist-high timothy dance mostly in the mind. Yet chinooks, like droughts and hard winters, have been seasons of a healthy cycle that has belonged to this place long before my great-grandparents came with plow and mower, seasons I must accept and use if possible, even when they work against me, if this land is to continue to be productive for other generations. On this place, where water is as unpredictable as the future and nearly as precious as blood, I don't irrigate at all, and I still carry my water indoors in a bucket, one bucket at a time.

NOTES

1. Jonathan Weiner, Planet Earth (New York: Bantam Books, 1986), p. 111.
2. Carolyn Cunningham, ed., Montana Weather (1982), p. 115.
3. Weiner, 100.
4. Ellen Ditzler, High Country News, Vol. 14, No. 25, p. 10.
5. Cunningham, 11.
6. Weiner, 257.
7. Weiner, 332.

Conger Beasley, Jr.

The Return of Beaver to the Missouri River

In an autobiographical volume entitled *The River and I*, John Neihardt recounts the first time he ever looked upon the Missouri River. It
was sometime in the late 1880s, and the place was Kansas City. The
river was in full flood, a "yellow swirl that spread out into the wooded
bottomlands," demolishing entire towns. "There was a dreadful
fascination about it," Neihardt remembers, "the fascination of all huge
and irresistible things. I had caught my first wee glimpse into the infinite . . ."

Some seventy years later, in the spring of 1953, I stood on a bluff
in St. Joseph, Missouri, and watched the last great flood of that unruly
river ravage the bottomlands between my home town and the hills of
distant Kansas. Augmented by several weeks of ferocious rains, tributaries in Iowa and Nebraska had disgorged an unprecedented volume
of water into the Missouri, which quickly overflowed its banks. Levees
crumbled and dikes collapsed and water swept across wheat and alfalfa
fields, carrying houses and cattle and barns and automobiles with it.
From bluff to bluff between the two states, a distance of maybe five
miles, the river resembled a sticky caramel confection stippled with
foamy whirlpools and entire trees. I remember watching the procession
in stunned silence with my father and his friends. All my life (I was
then twelve) I had heard of the river and watched it from passing cars
and trains and even viewed it once or twice from airplanes, but I had
never been on it in a boat or (God forbid) swum in it. That was unthinkable. The river was too capricious to attempt such a feat. There
were boiling eddies that could devour the strongest swimmer, deadly
snags and sawyers that could rip open the stoutest hull, and animals
with pointy teeth that could tear off a leg or arm. No, the river was a
creature to observe from a distance and to cross as quickly as possible;
it was not a place to linger in idle contemplation or recreational enjoyment. It was an unbridled monster in dire need of hobbling.

"That sure is a hell of a lot of water," remarked one of my father's
friends.

"The airport's gone. Elwood's under water. A few feet more and it will wash over the Pony Express Bridge," said another.

"Yeah, but this won't keep up for long," declared a third. "Once they close off those dams up in Dakota, this ole river's gonna get trimmed down to size."

I think of that exchange now, thirty years later, whenever I launch my raft or canoe out on the river. Within the scope of a few decades it has changed in character and shape. It is no longer as wide as it once was; neither does it flood as torrentially. Periodically, it spills over its banks and inundates the lowlands, but it no longer rolls from bluff to bluff or sweeps through entire communities, leaving people stranded in trees. Rarely does it bring the media rushing to its cresting banks. The dams up in South Dakota and the Army Corps of Engineers have taken care of that. Over the years the Corps has deepened the channel and made it more accessible to barge traffic. More recently, the Corps has lined the banks with a solid wall of riprap and installed wingdikes which jut out into the water at right angles; silt, building up behind these protrusions, progressively narrows the river's width. Gradually and inexorably, the Corps has exerted more and more control over the river, reducing it in size to a tawny ribbon whose least impulse can be carefully monitored. In the process commercial fishing has become almost nonexistent, and the curvaceous oxbows — remnants of the river's earlier path — have dried up, drastically reducing the acreage of precious wetlands, prime nesting places for waterfowl.

"You know what that river has become?" a man said to me recently in a bar in Kansas City. "An irrigation ditch, that's what. A goddamn irrigation ditch!"

He had grown up in St. Joseph in the 1920s and 30s, and had fished on the river as a boy. Once, on his sixteenth birthday, he had swum the width, from Kansas back to the Missouri side. When he told me that, I gazed at him with speechless admiration. When I was growing up — more than stealing the old man's car for a joyride or crawling through sewer pipes under a cemetery or putting your hand on a girl's breast or even engaging in BB-gun wars — swimming the river was the most daring feat a boy could achieve.

Despite considerable changes that have severely modified its character, the river is still regarded with trepidation by most people who live near it. The reasons for this are mystifying. Recently, for example, as I was tying my canoe on top of my car, my neighbor — an amiable man in his sixties, a veteran of the Battle of the Bulge — strolled over to help me adjust the ropes and secure the knots. "Where you headed?" he asked after pronouncing the boat secure.

"I'm going on the river."

"The Missouri!"

"Yep. A day float down from the mouth of the Platte."

He pulled carefully on his cigarette. "Well, you want to think twice before doing that, don't you?"

"Why?"

"It's dangerous. There're whirlpools that can easily upset a canoe the size of yours."

"Have you ever been on the river?" I asked.

"No. But I grew up around here and I know when to stay away from a place that doesn't want me."

As I drove to the river I thought about what he had said. He encouraged me to enjoy an outing on Smithville Lake, a reservoir located northeast of Kansas City, filled with power boats and water skiers and beer-drinking people swaddled with layers of fat. Their presence aside, there's something about still water that doesn't engage my imagination the way moving water does. A river flows from point to point, and around the next bend; though the same scene might unfold, the prospect exists that something truly marvelous might occur. The sense of motion is lulling and hypnotic. My metabolism gradually meshes with the force and rhythm of a power far greater than my own. I am transported out of the confines of the purely subjective into something else — a new awareness, a new sympathy.

My neighbor's remarks recalled the look of incredulity that had congealed upon my father's face the first time I told him I was going on the river. I might just as well have put a gun to my head and pulled the trigger, he declared, for all the chance I had of surviving. But you don't understand, I protested. The river had changed a lot since the time you took me up on the bluff to watch the flood. You can still die there, I grant you. But it's not the power it once was.

You're crazy, he concluded with a shake of the head. You're crazy to tempt fate that way.

When the reality alters, the rhetoric seems to harden into place. At least that's what I concluded after talking with my father and neighbor — two men of the same generation and similar backgrounds and experiences. The Missouri River — the lower portion of it at least, from the Fort Randall (South Dakota) Dam to its juncture with the Mississippi — is but a slip of its former brawly self; nonetheless, the popular perception of it remains the same. The folklore of the river still evokes images of greedy whirlpools and menacing trees and aquatic carnivores. Elements of these images persist, though in sadly reduced form. Added to these fears, of course, is the relatively new one of pollution; though, like many rivers in the United States, the Missouri is less contaminated now than it was twenty-five years ago, primarily because the stockyards of Omaha and St. Joseph and Kansas City no longer pump their refuse directly into it. But the rhetoric persists, almost as if people need to believe all the bad things they've heard. The river is still configured in the local imagination — and not just by people my father's age — as an outrage in need of correcting.

The fact of the matter is that the Missouri has been "corrected" — overcorrected to a fault, I would say: dammed and diked and dredged and drained to suit the needs of a dying industry (barge traffic) — so it will no longer flood valuable property along the banks; so it will no longer serve as a breeding ground for superfluous fish and wildlife. Certainly as a cultural and recreational resource it has been sadly ignored. In Kansas City, for example, there is virtually no access to the river within the city limits; until recently, there was no museum or park along the banks where the river could be viewed and appreciated. Memories of the devastating 1951 flood are still vivid here; and while that kind of destruction will never occur again, does it really make sense to construct more wingdikes and drain more oxbows and lay down more riprap so that, within the city boundaries at least, the river will purl as harmlessly as water through a sluice?

Enough water flows past Kansas City in a single day to satisfy its water needs for an entire year. When I tell this to my river-running friends in New Mexico and the arid Southwest, they express envy and delight. But when they actually view the river and see the wingdikes with the sandbars filling in behind them and the miles of concrete chunks lining the banks, they shrug and turn away. The river isn't very interesting, they seem to say. It isn't very wild.

And yet parts of it still are. You have to search for them, but they are there. Great blue herons still poke for frogs along the banks. Kingfishers rattle noisily between the trees. Borne by sultry thermals, turkey vultures hover over the bottomlands, scouting for carrion. Occasional fish erupt from the scuddy current in a flash of sun-dappled scales. And the river still churns along the path of its ancient bed, down from the Dakotas, across the loamy, fertile midsection of the continent, to its fabled confluence with the Mississippi. Always, even in its present denatured form, there is a sense of movement, of process, of rhythm . . . of a metabolism older and wiser and more meaningful than anything yet invented by human ingenuity.

Historically, the Missouri River has defined one segment of the progressive western border of the American continent. It provided the pathway into the heart of the huge Northern Plains and brought trappers and explorers to the verge of the Rockies. In states like the two Dakotas it marks the boundary between one form of terrain and another: east of the river, the land is sectioned into small undulating farms with a distinct Midwestern feel; west of it, the grass diminishes in height, the range opens up to an ineffable horizon, and the sky arches endlessly like a yawning mouth. When the Teton Sioux first crossed the river in significant numbers in the mid-eighteenth century, their culture changed dramatically. For decades in southwest Minnesota they had been a woodland community, dwelling in deep pine forests, hunting and fishing on lakes, content with occasional forays onto the plains. Once they crossed the river, their transformation into a fierce warrior society — the most respected of all Plains Indians — was assured. Armed with French rifles and mounted on Spanish horses, they created, through sterling individuals like Crazy Horse and Sitting Bull, a reputation for valor that endures to this day. Ahead of them lay the Badlands and the Black Hills and battlefields like the Rosebud and the Little Big Horn. Behind them, frothy and unpredictable — a Rubicon of the sensibility that forever distinguishes the Western imagination from all others on the continent — flowed the massive, untidy, indefatigable Missouri.

Unquestionably, George Caleb Bingham was the premier artist of the Missouri River, if not the entire border region, and in the Metropolitan Museum of Art in New York City hangs one of his finest works, *Fur Traders Descending the Missouri*. It depicts a man, probably of French extraction, and a boy, most likely a half-breed, sitting in a pirogue laden with furs. The time is early evening; roseate tints from the descending sun tinge the river's placid face and the trees in the background. The man smokes a pipe and dips his paddle in the water, more to steer than to accelerate the pirogue's speed. The boy leans against a hide-covered chest and stares dreamily into the artist's eyes. On the bow, tethered by a short rope, sits one of the most enigmatic figures in all of American painting . . . a dark, bristly, wolfish-looking animal, with pointed ears and a glistening snout, that appears to be looking down at its reflected image in the water — or is it staring into the artist's eyes? Whenever I think of the Missouri River I think of this creature; whenever I think of the mystery of how it used to be and what, in isolated sections, it still is, I think of this strange, unidentifiable, yet oddly appealing creature.

Blake's tyger holds less portent for me than this animal. I like to think that, intentionally or not, Bingham captured in this curious figure the true feeling of wilderness that the Missouri River once held for explorers and adventurers. That feeling has been described accurately and at great length by observers from Lewis and Clark to John Neihardt and James Willard Schultz; but nowhere else for me in all the art and writing produced by the region does it exist so compellingly, so poignantly. Whenever I bemoan the loss of the river's freedom, I look at that painting and am content that Bingham at least was able to capture a portion of what it once was and to pass it on for others to savor. Whenever I paddle my canoe on the murky current, I imagine the animal sitting in the bow, staring back at me with all the irony and inscrutability that two hundred years of bitter history can produce.

The Midwest is a sadly misunderstood place, routinely dismissed by Californians and Atlantic seaboarders, scorned by Rocky Mountain enthusiasts, and grudgingly defended by its own inhabitants. In a culture that celebrates spectacular surfaces, such a quiet, unruffled landscape is easy to ridicule. "I don't like to go west of the Alleghenies," a lawyer in New York once told me when I was a student there. "Missouri, Kansas . . . places like that. It's the same old thing, over and over and over again."

But it's not. The rivers of southern Missouri differ from the rivers of eastern Kansas. The foliage along the banks, the soil composition, the fish and animals vary in subtle, yet significant, ways. A sensitivity to the nuances of Midwestern topography sharpens the eye and instructs the mind in the difficult task of making distinctions between organic forms. There is a moral here. The way we perceive landscape can have a direct bearing upon the way we perceive society and the human beings who comprise it. Dismissing a landscape out of hand because it does not conform to established preconceptions is a prejudice as galling as dismissing a certain kind of people because of the color of their skin or the beliefs they profess. It violates the biological urge toward multiplicity and diversity that energizes our planet. Exclusion of any bioform because of insufficient perception is the product of a mindset every bit as harmful as the totalitarian ideologies which in this century have wreaked such havoc upon innocent people. By adjusting the rhetoric of perception to the reality of the fact perceived—by making the two more consonant and therefore truthful—our sensibilities can be sharpened and refined, and wherever we go in the world, instead of adopting the prevailing stereotype, we can encounter the reality, the genuine forms, that reside underneath.

One evening, after floating all day down from Atchison, Kansas, a friend and I passed under the Leavenworth bridge just as the sun was going down. Our destination was Parkville, Missouri, a small town a few miles upriver from Kansas City. The time was late summer; a full moon was due to appear in about an hour, and despite the obvious dangers of floating at night, we intended to do just that, guided by the moonlight and the phosphorescent markers on the channel buoys. Barge traffic had been light that day, but we needed to be wary of the occasional tree limb that bobbed just under the current.

The moon came up over the trees on the east bank with an almost audible hiss—huge and full and coated with a sticky tangerine tallow that spilled onto the leaves and spread in a wavering beam across the water. We watched in rapt fascination as the sky and river seemed to swell under an eerie luminescence that enabled us to pinpoint individual features on the west bank. Willows and cottonwoods stood out in bold relief, rounded into tumescent shapes by the brimming light; between them, dark and moist as the entrance to a cave, glowed shadows alive with crepitating sounds.

Suddenly, close by, there was a loud crash as if a rock had been chucked into the river, followed by another and another, echoing back and forth and far downstream. "What the hell was that?" my friend exclaimed; and I confess that at that moment images of river demons, passed on to me by another generation, surfaced in my brain. A moment later I saw a creature with a sleek head and flat tail slip off the bank and disappear in the water. "Beaver," I muttered, almost in disbelief. One of the stories I had heard as a boy was that the beaver had been trapped out in these parts, along with the otter and mink, leaving only the muskrat—a durable species.

Additional explosions detonated up and down the channel, signaling our presence. "Beaver," I whispered, and suddenly I had a vision of the river as it once was—wide and tumultuous and shoaly with islands and teeming with birds and fish and animals. If this were 1832, their pelts would fetch hard silver down in Westport or the trading posts of Blacksnake Hills. But it wasn't; that era, with its magnificent vistas and murderous events, was over. The future stretched before us with the same chimerical uncertainty as the river's path in the moonlight. Tonight, we were just drifting along, enjoying the sights, the steady current, the moist air that lapped against our cheeks. The sensation was more than adequate, oddly compensatory for all the changes that time and human endeavor had wrought upon the region. As if in acknowledgement, more beaver boomed their warning signal. We laughed and called out to them. This time, I thought, we'll share the river together.

Edward Williams

Rivertops

Having one's rivers is important, like having family or a country. With rivers, though, you get to choose. I prefer mine rippling with wild brook trout, which is to say clean and secluded, and because my time and place coincide with an irruption of my species, this means my rivers also must be small. Headwater streams really, the tops of systems known even in Boston's Back Bay.

An hour west of Worcester, Massachusetts, is the rivertop I love best. Hyla Brook, I call it, for that is not its name. Here under bald eagles and turkey vultures, in woods demanding good boots, lunch, the better part of a day and, sometimes, a compass, it's hard to remember you're not in Maine. In the general watershed are dozens of other brooks, some bigger than Hyla, some smaller, none quite so lovely. All are as safe from human defilement as is possible for running water to be, not because people enjoy their beauty or revel in the rich communities of plants and animals that flourish in and around them or spend time near them or in any way treasure them for what they are. Only because Boston drinks them.

Maybe Hyla Brook is someone else's, too, but of the hundreds of other anglers I have met along it over the years, not one has been human. My fellow killer apes are all miles downcurrent on the main stem, pretty enough in its own right, but stripped of wildness. There are dams and hardtop roads and metal bridges. And huge, sallow hatchery rainbow and brown trout, mutilated by months or years of scraping against the sides of concrete raceways. Sometimes their snouts are raw. Usually scales are missing, tails rounded and at least one pectoral fin gone or reduced to a fleshy stump. Almost without exception dorsals are matted and withered. A few of these fish even bear tags which may be exchanged for prizes. Last I knew they said "Make it in Mass."

From the high, lonesome ground of Hyla Brook, amid the trout lilies and trilliums, it is easy to wax pious, and I do not mean to criticize the state. Of all things it is called upon by the public to provide, it provides hatchery trout most efficiently. Massachusetts' hatchery system, in fact, is a clean, automated, computerized marvel that ought to be studied by every welfare department in the country.

It is the public demand rather than state compliance with it that needs scrutiny. Whatever is one to make of a culture that sets such a premium on sheer bigness? At least Dolly Parton sings well, but these alien, disfigured, inbred fish from Europe and the American West have only their size going for them, and even this is grotesque and unnatural in New England's usually sterile water.

How is it that we can spend such vast quantities of time and money distributing and collecting trout that don't belong while ignoring trout that do—our infinitely more beautiful landlocked char, *Salvelinus fontinalis*, the dweller of springs, the brook trout? It is not so in Europe where native browns are jealously conserved and natural recruitment demanded by those who angle for them.

Here we play "put and take" with imitation trout that couldn't reproduce in most Eastern water even if spawning habitat hadn't been flooded, silted or gouged and even if fish culturists hadn't thrown stock out of synch with the seasons in order to obtain "earlier eggs" and even if the planted fish (bred to be everything trout aren't, to thrive on trout kibbles amidst the quick-moving shadows of men and machines in coverless, concrete troughs) could commonly survive in the real world for more than several weeks. It is a game which renders natural spawning habitat superfluous.

And so we let our trout streams go to ruin except at their remote tops where ravishment is not yet convenient or where we have seen fit to protect our last undefiled watersheds like winos cradling the contents of their paper bags. As a child I caught hatchery trout in the Aberjona River, the ditched conduit that drains the world-famous toxic dumps of Woburn, Massachusetts. No need for American anglers to agitate for clean water; state government will provide fish even if nature can't. I suppose there is no sense sermonizing because we are no likelier to change our ways than the sea gulls who wheel and scream around fish-processing plants.

Better to tell what rivertop trouting is like, to encourage it, if not actually on Hyla Brook, at least on other forgotten Eastern rivertops that you can find yourself. I used to think that more native-brook-trout fishermen would mean fewer native brook trout. Now I think that the reverse is true, that more native-brook-trout fishermen mean more wild water preserved.

I first saw Hyla on a green topo map while ensconced in my easy chair beside a black-cherry fire. Having established that the brook was *not* on the state stocking list, a prerequisite for even casual consideration, I looked more closely at the map. Lots of unbroken green all around; I got interested. Gradient looked good; I got *very* interested. There were riffles and pools, and meadows where gaudy, stream-bred brook trout could sip mayflies and lounge in icy, air-charged current that tumbled down from hemlock-shaded ledges. I rushed there the next morning.

At this point I should note that finding healthy wild trout populations is like finding flying squirrels. You'll tap twenty or maybe a hundred hollow trees before a coal-eyed head appears. But troutlust is only one reason to find and keep rivertops. Rivertops are magnetized wires drawing and concentrating all the best things forests have. One may be equally infatuated with wildflowers or woodland butterflies or berries or woodpeckers or herons or deer or mink or beaver or drumming grouse or visions of silver spilling over moss. . . . Come to think of it, to me each of these good things are all of them and more, and if I didn't hang around rivertops because of trout, it would be because of something else.

No day on a rivertop is ever better than your first. That magic morning on Hyla Brook ten Mays ago I had found one of the few spots in Massachusetts where you can hike hard for thirty minutes and be deeper into the woods than when you started — a secret, timeless place fragrant with skunk cabbage, leaf mulch and wet earth, where wood frogs quacked and redfin pickerel streaked from swampy shallows, where newts lay suspended in backwaters and sashayed into muck, where spring azures skipped among unfurling ferns and fields of watercress waved gently in clear current over clean gravel. In and out of the brook, clumps of marsh marigolds were in brilliant yellow bloom and, as far back as I could see, the banks were carpeted with pale yellow trout lilies. A pair of wood ducks burst from an ancient beaver flowage and went squealing downriver. Trout were too much to hope for.

Here and there, in the deeper pockets, I flipped out a puffy dry fly on a two-pound tippet, but nothing rose to it save fallfish — "chubs," trouters call them, spitting the word. Fallfish grunt like pigs. The bigger they are the louder they grunt. Once, in Maine, I ate one, and it tasted like wet Kleenex. But something about Hyla Brook made me look hard at fallfish, and I saw them for the first time not as "trash fish" to be squeezed and bush-tossed, but as a part that belonged. Really, they are quite beautiful, very streamlined, silver in their youth, bronze and pewter in maturity. Thoreau, who fished for them passionately, called them "chivin" and basically found them to be "cupreous dolphin."

Not expecting trout, I naturally found them, suddenly and in astonishing abundance. They were rising to little blue mayflies in the deep, quick water at the head of the first meadow exactly as I had imagined the night before. I pushed through thick alders, wiping spiderwebs from my face and grimacing as ice water rose to my waist. Finally, feeling like Sylvester tossed into the birdcage and told to help himself, I was in position. The fly drifted about six inches before it disappeared in a lusty boil. It is difficult for brook-trout anglers to admit, but the brutal truth is that these noble fish not only are nonselective in their feeding behavior, but reckless, suicidal even. One can "match the hatch" if one chooses or one can toss out a Japanese machine-tied Bumble Boogie. Nine times out of ten the results will be the same — instant slurp.

That first trout from Hyla Brook was the third biggest I have ever taken there — eleven inches. (I won't say I set *no* premium on bigness.) She ran the line around a beaver cutting, and I reached down and tickled her smooth flanks, lifting her toward the surface so slowly she never struggled until she was on the bank. She was perfectly proportioned, deep-bodied, with a smallish head indicative of good feed and fast growth. The markings on her green back resembled old worm trails on the inside of elm bark, and her chestnut sides were flecked with scarlet, each fleck ringed with blue. Her belly was orange, pectoral, ventral and anal fins crimson and trimmed with ivory. I fished on for two miles, catching wild brook trout all the way — little fish of big country — and at dusk a great horned owl floated out of the woods and settled on a drowned cedar under a crescent moon.

There have been scores of other important days on Hyla Brook: The time I got there late and couldn't tear myself away and got lost in the drizzly dark, plowing till 2:00 a.m. through grape and jewelweed with only the cold, green light of fireflies all around, feeling like Bottom in *Midsummer Night's Dream*. The time I almost stepped on a deer. The time last year I sat on a sandbar, cleaning trout in the bright moonlight and listening to Eastern coyotes howling and moving on the hill in back of me.

I want more people on rivertops, but it does not follow that I want more of them on mine. Rivertops are very personal things, like axes and shotguns, and I have shared mine only with a seven-year-old named Beth and a ten-year-old named Scott. Rivertops are not to be tattled on. To quote my friend John Voelker, the sage of Michigan's U.P. who quit the state's supreme court in order to chase brook trout and write about them and who, having made it well past eighty, has earned the right to be sexist, "Any fisherman who will tell on the trout waters that are revealed to him possesses the stature of a man who will tell on the women he's dallied with."

"[Wild] trout, unlike men," writes Voelker, "will not — indeed cannot — live except where beauty dwells, so that any man who would catch a trout finds himself inevitably surrounded by beauty: he can't help himself." That's what I've been trying to say.

III

John Milton

The Writer's West

1

The American West is so big, and the land itself is so indifferent to the people who live on it or cross over it, that it seems impersonal, something to be dealt with only in abstract terms. In writing about the desert-mountain area of California, Mary Austin concluded that it was a strange mixture of God, death, beauty, and madness — words which might be applied to the entire American West. All are ever present in the mountains, on the desert, on the high plains, and even in the gentle grasses of the prairie if we are to take Rölvaag's *Giants in the Earth* seriously.

These are abstractions, but each one is heavily documented in the literature of the American West. John Muir, the man responsible for the establishment of Yosemite National Park, saw a grand design in the mountains, a design sculptured by God with a beauty difficult to describe. On a smaller scale, Muir saw the mountain flowers as saints preaching by the wayside; he asked that all men in the mountains stop to listen to the sermons and be purified by them. Clarence King, the geologist and mapmaker, could in one moment be terrified by the dangers among the mountain peaks and in the next moment wrench poetry from his scientific mind to capture images and colors that seemed to defy language. These two men suffered no ill effects from isolation; indeed, Muir always felt that he was in the presence of God, and that was more than sufficient.

Other kinds of beauty and other kinds of men combined to cause different feelings and lead to madness or death, or both. The badlands and the barren plains of the north central area of the West possess a stark and sometimes devilish kind of beauty which can prey upon a man's mind, especially when he is alone. Hugh Glass and several of his compañeros went nearly mad from wandering on the plains, their minds filled with ghostly visions arising from the landscape. Boone Caudill, in Guthrie's *The Big Sky*, was surely irrational when he killed

Teal Eye. And neither Arthur Bridges, the visionary of Clark's *Track of the Cat*, nor his practical and confident brother Curt could withstand the cunning, endurance, and eternalness of the cat. The natural world can be beautiful to look at but a trial to live in.

One part of the Western myth makes a moment of beauty out of the brief violence and lasting death of the gunfight in the middle of a dusty street, while a newer part (popularized in such films as those of Clint Eastwood) portrays the scene in unthinkable ugliness and madness. Sam Peckinpah has suggested that his own bloody films are designed to purge violence from his audience by showing how terrible and inhuman violence really is, but it is difficult to divorce his techniques and emphases from the old and alluring Western myth.

Heights, depths, heat, cold, death, immortality, fierce and deadly storms, the peace and beauty of heaven on earth, "hell with the fires out," fresh mountain streams, alkali flats, giant cactus, short grass, loneliness—all of these lend themselves to the argument that the West is a boundless place of extremes.

It is no wonder that the land is respected by the people who live on it. The land belongs. It has been there forever—in people terms— carved by the wind, gashed by rivers, shoved violently upward by volcanic explosions, twisted into odd shapes by eons of erosion, but always enduring, and accepting those forms of life which are able or willing to adapt themselves to the environment. It has been called a masculine land in contrast to the feminine Eastern woodlands with their soft, round hills.

The West is not cities. It is small towns, ranches, Indian reservations, Spanish villages, most of them quietly unknown. More importantly, it is space. Unpeopled space. It is this very space that keeps Westerners sane and sometimes drives Easterners crazy. More than one visitor to the Great Plains has felt his heart turn into a lump he cannot swallow when, for the first time, he looks out at fifty miles of what seems to be nothing. No place to hide. Nothing to go to. No landmarks of an easily observable kind. No comforting crowds of people. Just a horizon line about as far away as from Washington to Philadelphia, and overhead a sky that overwhelms with its immensity and nearness. Add to the scene an entire storm system, visible en masse, and the newcomer suffers from fright. (In fact, one of these newcomers once objected to the word "fright" in one of my poems about the plains and suggested that I substitute the word "terror.")

The West is space, and therefore distance; climate, and therefore weather; topography, and therefore elevation. But it is also a writer's place, and therefore personal as well as abstract.

I decide to visit some writers I admire. Walter Van Tilburg Clark in Virginia City, Nevada, is 1,600 miles away from my home in Vermillion, South Dakota. Harvey Fergusson, a native New Mexican, has retired to Berkeley, and Wallace Stegner is not far from there in Los Altos, in the hills above Stanford University. Max Evans in Albuquerque and Frank Waters in northern New Mexico will require a swing south, then east, and when I finish I will still be a thousand miles from home. I check the map. Five thousand miles, or pretty close to it. In New York I could talk to five respected writers in five hours, without leaving Manhattan. In the West, writers, like everyone and everything else, are isolated from each other. I wonder whether that isolation does something special to them, perhaps make them more independent in their thinking. Yet, in general terms they all have the same subject matter.

It takes me four days to drive to Virginia City, that leftover mining town perched uneasily on the side of a mountain. Once rich with ore, it is now rich in memory and myth. Ugly yellow tailings from the mines still exist as little mountains of their own. I sit in Mark Twain's chair, although the sign and the protective rail tell me not to, and try to feel the town as Twain felt it. I head downhill (everything is downhill in Virginia City) and find the house painted red and trimmed in white and surrounded by a white picket fence. Clark comes out to greet me. He is a distinguished and affable man in appearance, semi-portly, who ushers me into a large room with an immense table facing the mountain and, at nine o'clock in the morning, asks me whether I would prefer boilermakers or black coffee. Neither appeals to me at the moment, but it is unthinkable to refuse Western hospitality and so I choose the coffee, which he then does also.

I feel at ease with Clark instantly, as I do with all Western writers. While we talk, his wife is farther down the hill in the second level of the house, and his small black dog is under the big table.

Because his three novels and his short stories emphasize man's relationship to the land, I ask him about the role of the land in Western fiction. (We are not talking about the drugstore paperback "Western" but about serious fiction of the West.)

"Well, it seems to me that this is something that must be settled with a Western writer, especially if he is dealing with the past. It is still so in the mountain states, but not in California any more. The Western states were so unpopulous that landscape and weather did play an important part—sometimes a finally determining part—in what happened. My feeling is that landscape is character, not background. It's not a stage. It's an active agent. It must be."

This seemed to answer another question also, whether *The Ox-Bow Incident*, based largely on a lynching, could not have taken place in the South or in a number of other places. What makes it Western is at least partly the peculiar winds of the mountains, especially in the passes, and the effect these winds have upon the behavior of the characters.

I think too of the spirits of the natural world, often lurking almost anthropomorphically behind the trees in some of Clark's stories, ready to punish the man who violates natural law; and there is the cat, the mountain lion, who is both real and symbolic and who tests the men who try to kill him, in much the same way that Moby Dick tested Captain Ahab and his crew. There are many similarities between the sea and the prairie, or the sea and the mountains, and the remarkable whale echoes in the awesome grizzly and in the mountain lion. I remember that much of the West was once, long ago, an inland sea and then a huge marsh in which the gigantic dinosaurs floundered and died. I could almost see man's racial memories operating in the West, memories of isolation and monsters and the cruel landscape. These survive, but not in cities.

As we talk, the rumble of thunder lingers in the background for a while and then works its way heavily over the mountain and grows louder on our side. The small dog under the table begins to shake and moan. Clark excuses himself and takes the dog from the room. When he returns he smiles apologetically and says that whenever a storm approaches the dog must have a tranquilizer or he will die. From fear? I dare not ask, but the importance of weather is suddenly a subject to be debated no longer.

It is obvious that weather is terribly important in the lives of people who live in the West. It always has been. At Lake Tahoe, in June, the clear water reflects the snowy mountain peaks, the sun shines brightly, and I feel a peacefulness which continues with me at Donner Pass on the well-kept grass under the green shade trees. This is the place where the Donner party, on its way to California, foundered in an early winter snowstorm. Some died and were eaten by the survivors. The thought of cannibalism is shocking and reminds me that the West is a place of contrasts. At one moment it is cruel and harsh, but at another moment, in the right place, the landscape can hurt the heart with a beauty that cannot be tamed or fully possessed. The land is then like a mysterious woman of impossible beauty, of changing moods and appearances; her presence can be uncomfortable, even dangerous; but her absence is an ache which never goes away.

The West ends in the Sierra Nevadas. Cross this wall and dip into another world—California, which long ago abdicated from the West and became a distorted extension of the East. But two of the writers I wish to visit live there, as though they have reached the end of the California Trail at last. And so I descend 7,000 feet to sea level, passing trucks whose brakes have burst into flames, sympathizing with the motorists across the highway whose cars have stalled from overheating, and feeling even more strongly that the Sierra Nevadas are a barrier between two worlds. In Berkeley I must go up a steep hill to reach Harvey Fergusson, the transplanted New Mexican, and the hill becomes symbolically a mountain from Fergusson's novel *Wolf Song*. He is done with writing now, is almost eighty, and talks haltingly but at great length about the past. His books are about the past, about the New Mexico of the mountain men, the traders, the Spanish land grants. He is adamant in his insistence that writers tell the truth about the West, not the myth. He has little time for the Western emphasis on heroics. To him the destiny of a man lay in his discoveries, in the unfolding of mystery, and in the spirit of inquiry—all elements of the American West. But no heroics. If he is lucky he will feel himself a part of the earth, and the earth will be a part of God, so that man and God become one. Not presumptuously, but humbly. And this man will delight in solitude, in space, and in the wilderness.

I feel that Fergusson is just such a man. He says, "When I finished a book, for a while I would feel very foul. One reason I never got to Europe was that when I had finished a book I wanted to get outdoors. I wanted to go hunting, or I wanted to take a trip in the mountains, but I did not want to go to Paris and write a book. I couldn't have gotten to first base there, I am sure."

He is crotchety in his old age and says things about other writers which at first seem unkind. It is soon apparent that he is critical only of ignorance of the West, believing that a writer must know the country and be accurate and truthful in his depiction of it.

"What about Willa Cather?" I ask.

"She didn't write any Western novels," he snorts, "and she had the most singular ignorance of it. You know, when she was writing *Death Comes for the Archbishop*, she got 'that bug' every time she went to Santa Fe for more than overnight, and so she lived at the Harvey House out at Lamy Junction, and going back and forth in the car that is all she ever saw of the country. She didn't know the country at all and she didn't know the people at all and she couldn't speak Spanish and . . ."

I cut him off and ask about another writer, one I think highly of most of the time.

"You know, John," he said, "you know that mesa between Santa Fe and Albuquerque—you've crossed it many times. Well, he must have crossed it a hundred times and he always described it as desert. He didn't know the flora. He consistently planted things there that never grew—you know what I mean. He was essentially an indoor boy."

Fergusson goes on to cuss out several well-known writers who have not been accurate enough in dealing with the landscape, or the Mexicans, or the Indians. It is obvious that he has no time for Western myths or superheroics or sentimentalism or any of the elements which popular literature has used over the years to make of the West a romantic and exotic place. He has, in his own writing, searched for precise images, for rhythms which match those of the land, and for honest rather than heroic characterization. I am sad when I drive down the Berkeley hill for the last time because I know that I will never see this man again, but he will leave behind him at least five novels which will continue to tell me about the real West.

The unpeopled quiet, he said once. I consider this as I fight my way through San Francisco traffic and down the bay to Palo Alto, and I find a semblance of this quiet when I meet Wallace Stegner in the Los Altos hills. Stegner himself is unruffled, at ease with his environment, and he takes pride in pointing to the brown hills that slope down and then up away from his house. There is no other house in sight.

I take him to task for hedging somewhat in *The Sound of Mountain Water*, for seeming to apologize for the West and its writers. "You don't say much about the land as character, or subject, in those essays."

"No," he replies, "I said something rather disparaging in that general direction, though, that too many Western writers for lack of a coherent and traditional society to which they could belong or feel, somehow, themselves as a part, had to fall back on scenery. It's just not enough. You can't make literature out of nothing but landscape."

"Mary Austin?"

"The best thing in that vein I know, I guess, is Mary Austin's *Land of Little Rain*, which is a beautiful piece using country as a character."

We agree that it is difficult to find a coherent community in the West and that this is one reason for falling back upon landscape, of which there is no lack. The Western landscape is dramatic and keeps forcing its way into literature.

"But," I object, "Frank Waters and Bill Eastlake . . ."

"Well, they've got something better."

"They have something a little different, because they are able to see the Indian's religious view of the land and its elements, and the land becomes a symbol quite legitimately."

Stegner agrees. "Oh, sure. I think a book like *The Bronc People*, which begins with a couple of Indian kids looking out on the world that surrounds them, is done with great intuitional sensitivity."

"As is Waters' *The Man Who Killed the Deer*."

Stegner says, "You asked about the country, and I think country is inevitably a character in every Western book, but I would say it shouldn't be the only character. We have to have something else. The reliance upon an Indian point of view of nature in which you can depend upon something long and tested — not a kind of tourist's view and not a reader's view but a real inhabitant's view — that's hard to come by in many parts of the West."

We argue briefly about where the West begins and whether certain novels should be called Midwestern farm novels or Western. I suggest that many people believe the West can be defined partially in agricultural terms, that it is a land of cattle rather than crops. This doesn't work because, in spite of the general aridity of the West, corn and wheat can be found in many places and irrigation has allowed farming where cattle once grazed. I try a different approach:

"I should think that after living out on the great plains you would like to be able to see even farther than you can here."

"I like to be up on a place where I can see a long way. On the plains you can see a long way just because there is nothing in the road. But Iowa used to bug me very badly because it was so rolling that you could never see more than three-quarters of a mile in any direction. It wasn't high enough to see, and it wasn't flat enough to see. I notice the horses feel the same way. We keep horses, occasionally, down below in the pasture, and they keep yearning up toward the very top part."

We don't want to define the West merely in terms of meridians, and so we discuss the non-community concept, the migratory movements, the notion of the newcomer, all of which keep the West uncertain and fluid in contrast with the Midwest and its more settled quality. As Stegner puts it, "The Midwestern house with the milk bottle and the paper sitting there in the morning." But he also points out the vulnerability of Western land; because of the aridity it does not heal quickly, or it does not heal at all.

I remember the ugly tailings on the mountainside at Virginia City.

Two days later, walking on the beach at Santa Barbara, getting oil on my shoes from an offshore spill, I begin to pull together some details of the interior West. The ocean seems to act as a catalyst, and the oil is one more act in the century-and-a-half trail of destruction man has left behind him as he moved west. My first memory is of hawks: sitting on fence posts along the lonely highways; pecking at the carcass of a rabbit hit by a car; soaring over the tops of giant pine trees as I look *down* on them and the treetops from a still higher point on the mountain. I dream of a hawk perched on my motel-bed headboard, staring at me accusingly with unblinking eyes. And there is the cow skull with four bullet holes in it, lying on a roadside picnic table in Wyoming; the Indian girl running away from school; the artist with his bloody arm stretched inside the dying mare, trying to pull out the awkwardly turned foal; the sunbaked sagebrush flats where Coronado once trudged, presumably searching for the Seven Cities of Cibola; Medicine Bow, where Owen Wister found his Virginian; the northern plains where fence lines and section roads went out from my center like spokes in a giant wheel, like the rock wheels of the ancient Indians. Images and symbols come together on a California beach where the frontier ended.

I am anxious to get back to the interior, even though the ocean holds its fascination for me as it does for everyone. Crossing the desert in Southern California, I pray that there will be no flat tires, no engine failures, in this gray wasteland. Stepping out of the car onto an asphalt parking lot in Blythe, I almost sink in the 110-degree heat and do not feel like eating. In a few hours I ascend from below sea level to the 7,000-foot elevation of Flagstaff, to cool and clean air that immediately washes the Los Angeles smog from my lungs, and I run up and down the motel stairs carrying suitcases, laughing, breathing, relieved. Max Evans waits in Albuquerque.

Max sees the land and its people realistically and often with humor, as in *The Rounders*. He has little truck with the mythical past, the romantic past, and insists that it is the contemporary West that needs looking at and that needs accurate portrayal. Yet, isn't this rough-looking ex-cowboy and miner a mystic as well as a down-to-earth realist?

"You're damn right!" he says.

The evidence is there, more in his short stories than in the novels. Max has seen the powers of the *brujas*—the Spanish witches. He has felt the spiritual relationship between man and the dramatic New Mexico landscape. And even though he writes about the present, because he knows that best, he is aware of the long traditions of the Spanish and the Indians and how they still affect contemporary residents of the Southwest.

"Is the behavior of the people related to the conditions of the land and the climate?" I ask.

"Very definitely. Absolutely. You have the several days of high and dry and cold winds. People will become restless, irritable, and sometimes it leads to violence. Then the weather subsides, and everything becomes easier. The natures of the people sing."

"But a lot of people won't believe that climate and elevation can make that much difference."

"Hell," he says, "if they'd spend thirty days out horsebacking in cold winds and then get a chance to whoop it up in town for a few days they'd understand why a few bottles of the 'old brown' get tipped quite often. Weather and landscape have a definite influence in the West. This has been the main point of my work—man's relationship to the earth and then what this relationship does to the way he relates to his fellow men."

Max always calls his liquor "brown whiskey." He swigs a little, tips back in his chair, and talks all night, stories about his cowpunching days, stories about making $100,000 in a mining deal and losing it the next day, stories of how his body has been pounded by horses and by men (his swollen nose shows it), and about his friend who owns a mountain and wants to sell half of it. It all sounds outrageous but it is true. And I draw an analogy: the West is outrageous, but it too is true. It is as explosive and gentle, as tough and softhearted, as crude and refined, as realistic and mystical as this cowboy-writer who sits with me and who calls himself "Ol' Max."

He has stared misfortune in the face, celebrated the good times, kept his feet on the earth, and hired a medicine man to punish the New

York editor who was unfair to him. The editor suffered a terrible fate, but Max will not give me the name of the medicine man. It was a private affair.

Nor will Frank Waters say anything about the kiva. He sits by the fireplace in his comfortable adobe house in the mountains near Taos. The Pueblo lands are across the narrow dirt road from his place. Recent visitors of Waters' from the East have left after one night, complaining that it was too quiet to sleep. But we hear the cottonwood leaves rustling in the light wind, the horses stirring in the corral, a dog barking several miles away, the nearby stream gurgling as it carries melted snow down to the Rio Grande. It is almost noisy. It is all relative.

Frank has written about the kiva in *The Man Who Killed the Deer*, and when he finished the novel he told the Pueblo elders about it and asked if they had any objections to it. But he will say no more about it. Westerners have been stereotyped in two ways: as garrulous, and as silent and reserved. Both are correct, but the words used in the West are "hospitable and friendly" and "respectful"—better terms. Frank talks easily and well. But he holds back. He respects the beliefs of his neighbors.

And so we do not talk about the kiva, that underground room in which young men are initiated into the rites, rituals, and secrets of the adult world. The Pueblo grow more secretive each year. I can no longer go behind the five-tiered building on the south side of the stream and photograph the kiva area with its long poles extending into the sky from the rooms below ground. The Pueblo have also become more defensive. Even their old friend Frank Waters is asked to pay an admission fee when he goes to visit an acquaintance. This makes him sad.

But since I am trying to define the West, I ask him how he would characterize it, and he is ready with an answer:

"The characteristic of the American West, I think, which makes it different from other parts of the country is the conception of it as a great untrammeled wilderness which, it seems, provides freedom to each person to express himself fully. In the great era of westward expansion, during the nineteenth century, this conception coincided with fact. Those were the days of the Big Grab. A man could carve out an empire for himself. And he could live by his own law."

"But that has all changed," I say.

"Yes, the fact has vanished, but the conception remains. As individualism vanishes under conformity to mass mediocrity, the notion of the free wild West grows stronger. For the whole world the American West symbolizes boundless individual freedom. This is the theme that motivates traditional Western fiction."

"What about your own work?"

Silence. I try again. "What about the emphasis on nature?"

In Waters' Colorado trilogy his grandfather-character, Rogier, is drawn to Pike's Peak like a filing to a magnet. He also feels the blood-life of nature in the beat of Indian drums at dusk, as opposed to the intellectual response of his European forebears. Waters himself is part Indian, although he does not make a fetish of it as many others do. He is at home in his mountain world and he dislikes labels, fashionable or otherwise. He has achieved the harmony with nature that Mary Austin insisted would be the salvation of man. He speaks at length about the obvious importance of nature in the West, where can be found the lowest deserts, the highest mountains, the deepest canyons, the widest plateaus, and the wildest rivers in America. Fabulous. No wonder that nature, uncontaminated, seemed noble and brought out the best in man. But it also brought out the worst. Everything was so big that man seemed but a speck. Everything seemed so timeless that man became concerned about his own brief life. Spirits of place haunted him. Invisible ghosts stalked the land.

And for all those people who fled to the West to escape some wrong done to them, or perhaps by them, who carried a sense of guilt into a new land, "nature with her sublime beauty and diabolic cruelty served as a psychiatrist's couch, as it were, to heal their wounds or else it offered an escape from the realities of society."

Times change. Some of the landscape has been laid waste, stripped, raped, and scalped. Man's greed continues to attack the mountains and the prairie for minerals, for timber, for grass, for water. Will the West survive other than in nostalgia, and myth?

3

In spite of change and of what so-called civilized man refers to as progress, the West in essence is much the same as it has always been. It is semiarid and therefore semiharsh; it is relatively unpeopled and therefore relatively unspoiled. The great variety of the landscape (perhaps it should be plural: landscapes) is seen in contrast to the commonplace in everyday life. There are no heroes, but perhaps there never were. Great deeds of survival and conquest linger in the history books and especially in the imaginative literature of the West, but they probably ought to be considered in terms of the sacred and the profane, or the intimate and the public, and in these terms the modern West is not significantly different from the old West. Behind the trail-opening of the mountain men, behind the railroad-building, behind the military conquest of the Indians, behind the exploits of frontier marshals there may have been heroism of a certain kind, there may have been an adventurous spirit, there may have been a partially justifiable desire to bring enlightenment into the wilderness, but undeniably the major motive in almost every instance was greed. A small group of mountain men accompanied by one of our nation's heroes once held off and defeated a superior force of Indians and received the proper acclaim for their bravery; but they were simply defending the furs they had accumulated during the winter's trapping. The lust for wealth may have been what conquered the West, and its symbol today is Las Vegas.

But even today there are also sacred places in the West. They are not often recognized by tourists. Many Indian tribal groups have holy mountains. These "high spots" of the West are spectacular, and the tourist takes pictures of them, but the normal attitude toward them is, at best, one of challenge. The mountains must be conquered. Automobiles may now be driven to the top of Pike's Peak or Mount Evans, each over 14,000 feet high, and the drive is indeed a challenge — many people need to be given oxygen (at twenty-five cents a shot) when they reach the top. Then what? The view is not overly impressive because other peaks interfere with distances, and above the tree line the mountains are rocky and brown and undistinguished except possibly when covered with snow. There are more beautiful views at lower elevations. But if the mountain is "felt" as a place which offers a nearness to God, the view does not matter. Only the presence is important. This is one part of the sacredness which is sensed by many Indians, which is a part of their traditions, and which is shared by intuitive or sensitive Westerners.

The specific place does not matter: in the north the Sioux have their Harney Peak in the Black Hills, and in the south the Pueblo have their Blue Lake in the Sangre de Cristo Mountains. What matters is that for everyone who feels the need of a holy place, a special place, there is one in the West. Mine happens to be Taos. The mountain with its strange winds has accepted me. The old beliefs and traditions of the Spanish and the Pueblo, as alien as they may seem at times, comfort me. The landscape is spiritually refreshing. The air and the light are pure. Man's history and the timeless earth are somehow at one with each other. It is a place which suggests eternity and invites communion.

Even the glut of chain restaurants, motels, and drive-ins on the south edge of town cannot spoil it. They will pass and the mountain and the high plains and the buttes and the river gorge will remain. The West is land.

Barry Lopez

The Stone Horse

1

The deserts of southern California, the high, relatively cooler and wetter Mojave and the hotter, dryer Colorado to the south of it, carry the signatures of many cultures. Prehistoric rock drawings in the Mojave's Coso Range, representing the greatest concentration of petroglyphs in North America, are probably 3,000 years old. Big-game-hunting cultures that flourished there six or seven thousand years before that are known from broken spear tips, choppers, and burins left scattered along the shores of great Pleistocene lakes, long since evaporated. A burial site in the Yuha Basin in the Colorado Desert may be 20,000 years old; and worked stone from a quarry in the Calico Mountains is, many argue, evidence that human beings were here more than 200,000 years ago.

Because of the long-term stability of such arid environments, many of these prehistoric stone artifacts still lie exposed on the ground, accessible to anyone who passes by — the studious, the acquisitive, the indifferent, the merely curious. Archaeologists do not agree on the cultural sequence beyond about 10,000 years ago, but it is clear that these broken bits of chalcedony, chert, and obsidian, like the animal drawings and geometric designs etched on walls of basalt throughout the desert, anchor the earliest threads of human history, the first record of human endeavor here.

Western man did not journey into the California desert until the end of the eighteenth century, 250 years after Coronado brought his soldiers into the Zuni pueblos in a bewildered search for the cities of Cibola. The earliest appraisals of the land were cursory, hurried. People traveled *through* it, en route to Santa Fe or the California coastal settlements. Only miners tarried. In 1823 what had been Spain's became Mexico's and in 1848 what had been Mexico's became America's; but the bare, jagged mountains and dry lake beds, the vast and uniform plains of creosote bush and yucca plants, remained as obscure as the northern Sudan until the end of the nineteenth century.

Before 1940 the tangible evidence of twentieth-century man's passage here consisted of very little — the hard tracery of his travel corridors; the widely scattered, relatively insignificant evidence of his mining operations; and the fair expanse of his irrigated fields at the desert's periphery. In the space of a hundred years or so the wagon roads were paved, railroads were laid down, and canals and high-tension lines were built to bring water and electricity across the desert to Los Angeles from the Colorado River. The dark mouths of gold, talc, and tin mines yawned from the bony flanks of desert ranges. Dust-encrusted chemical plants stood at work on the lonely edges of dry lake beds. And crops of grapes, lettuce, dates, alfalfa, and cotton covered the Coachella and Imperial valleys, north and south of the Salton Sea, and the Palo Verde Valley along the Colorado.

These developments proceeded with little or no awareness of earlier human occupations by the cultures that preceded those of the historic Indians — the Mohave, the Chemehuevi, the Quechan, and others. (Extensive irrigation began to actually change the climate of the Colorado Desert, and human settlements, the railroads, and farming introduced many new, successful plants and animals into the region.)

During World War II, the American military moved into the desert in great force, to train troops and to test equipment. They found the dry air, isolation, and clear weather conducive to year-round flying very attractive. After the war, the complex of training grounds, storage facilities, and gunnery and test ranges was permanently settled on more than three million acres of military reservations. Few perceived the extent or significance of the destruction of aboriginal sites that took place during tank maneuvers and bombing runs or in the laying out of highways, railroads, mining districts, and irrigated fields. The few who intuited that something like an American Dordogne Valley lay exposed here were (only) amateur archaeologists; even they reasoned that the desert was too vast for any of this to matter.

After World War II, people began moving out of the crowded Los Angeles basin into homes in Lucerne, Apple, and Antelope valleys in the western Mojave. They emigrated as well to a stretch of resort land at the foot of the San Jacinto Mountains that included Palm Springs, and farther out to old railroad and military towns like Needles and Barstow. People also began exploring the desert, at first in military-surplus jeeps and then with a variety of all-terrain and off-road vehicles that became available in the 1960s. By the mid-1970s, the number of people using such vehicles for desert recreation had increased exponentially. Most came and went in innocent curiosity; the few who didn't wreaked a unique havoc all out of proportion to their numbers. The disturbance of previously isolated archaeological sites increased substantially. Many of these early-man sites as well as prehistoric rock drawings were vandalized before archaeologists, themselves late to the desert, had any firm grasp of the bounds of human history in the desert. It was as though an Aztec library had been found intact and at the same moment numerous lacunae had appeared.

The vandalism was of three sorts: the general disturbance usually caused by souvenir hunters and by the curious and the oblivious; the wholesale stripping of a place by professional thieves for black-market sale and trade; and outright destruction, in which vehicles were actually used to ram and trench an area. By 1980, the Bureau of Land Management estimated that probably 35 percent of the archaeological sites in the desert had been vandalized. The destruction at some places by rifles and shotguns, or by power winches mounted on vehicles, were, if one cared for history, demoralizing to behold.

In spite of public education, land closures, and stricter law enforcement in recent years, the BLM estimates that, annually, about 1 percent of the archaeological record in the desert continues to be destroyed or stolen.

2

A BLM archaeologist told me, with understandable reluctance, where to find the intaglio. I spread my Automobile Club of Southern California map of Imperial County out on his desk, and he traced the route with a pink, felt-tip pen. The line crossed Interstate 8 and then turned west along the Mexican border.

"You can't drive any farther than about here," he said, marking a small X. "There's boulders in the wash. You walk up past them."

On a separate piece of paper he drew a route in a smaller scale that would take me up the arroyo to a certain point where I was to cross back east, to another arroyo. At its head, on higher ground just to the north, I would find the horse.

"It's tough to spot unless you know it's there. Once you pick it up . . ." He shook his head slowly, in a gesture of wonder at its existence.

I waited until I held his eye. I assured him I would not tell anyone else how to get there. He looked at me with stoical despair, like a man who had been robbed twice, whose belief in human beings was offered without conviction.

I did not go until the following day because I wanted to see it at dawn. I ate breakfast at 4 a.m. in El Centro and then drove south. The route was easy to follow, though the last section of road proved difficult, broken and drifted over with sand in some spots. I came to the barricade of boulders and parked. It was light enough by then to find my way over the ground with little trouble. The contours of the landscape were stark, without any masking vegetation. I worried only about rattlesnakes.

I traversed the stone plain as directed, but, in spite of the frankness of the land, I came on the horse unawares. In the first moment of recognition I was without feeling. I recalled later being startled, and that I held my breath. It was laid out on the ground with its head to the east, three times life size. As I took in its outline I felt a growing concentration of all my senses, as though my attentiveness to the pale rose color of the morning sky and other peripheral images had now ceased to be important. I was aware that I was straining for sound in the windless air and I felt the uneven pressure of the earth hard against my feet. The horse, outlined in a standing profile on the dark ground, was as vivid before me as a bed of tulips.

I've come upon animals suddenly before, and felt a similar tension, a precipitate heightening of the senses. And I have felt the inexplicable but sharply boosted intensity of a wild moment in the bush, where it is not until some minutes later that you discover the source of electricity — the warm remains of a grizzly bear kill, or the still moist tracks of a wolverine.

But this was slightly different. I felt I had stepped into an unoccupied corridor. I had no familiar sense of history, the temporal structure in which to think: This horse was made by Quechan people three hundred years ago. I felt instead a headlong rush of images: people hunting wild horses with spears on the Pleistocene veld of southern California; Cortés riding across the causeway into Montezuma's Tenochtitlán; a short-legged Comanche, astride his horse like some sort of ferret, slashing through cavalry lines of young men who rode like farmers. A hoof exploding past my face one morning in a corral in Wyoming. These images had the weight and silence of stone.

When I released my breath, the images softened. My initial feeling, of facing a wild animal in a remote region, was replaced with a calm sense of antiquity. It was then that I became conscious, like an ordinary tourist, of what was before me, and thought: This horse was probably laid out by Quechan people. But when, I wondered? The first horses they saw, I knew, might have been those that came north from Mexico in 1692 with Father Eusebio Kino. But Cocopa people, I recalled, also came this far north on occasion, to fight with their neighbors, the Quechan. And *they* could have seen horses with Melchior Díaz, at the mouth of the Colorado River in the fall of 1540. So, it could be four hundred years old. (No one in fact knows.)

I still had not moved. I took my eyes off the horse for a moment to look south over the desert plain into Mexico, to look east past its head at the brightening sunrise, to situate myself. Then, finally, I brought my trailing foot slowly forward and stood erect. Sunlight was running like a thin sheet of water over the stony ground and it threw the horse into relief. It looked as though no hand had ever disturbed the stones that gave it its form.

The horse had been brought to life on ground called desert pavement, a tight, flat matrix of small cobbles blasted smooth by sand-laden winds. The uniform, monochromatic blackness of the stones, a patina of iron and magnesium oxides called desert varnish, is caused by long-term exposure to the sun. To make this type of low-relief ground glyph, or intaglio, the artist either selectively turns individual stones over to their lighter side or removes areas of stone to expose the lighter soil underneath, creating a negative image. This horse, about eighteen feet from brow to rump and eight feet from withers to hoof, had been made in the latter way, and its outline was bermed at certain points with low ridges of stone a few inches high to enhance its three-dimensional qualities. (The left side of the horse was in full profile; each leg was extended at 90 degrees to the body and fully visible, as though seen in three-quarter profile.)

I was not eager to move. The moment I did I would be back in the flow of time, the horse no longer quivering in the same way before me. I did not want to feel again the sequence of quotidian events — to be drawn off into deliberation and analysis. A human being, a four-footed animal, the open land. That was all that was present — and a "thoughtless" understanding of the very old desires bearing on this particular animal: to hunt it, to render it, to fathom it, to subjugate it, to honor it, to take it as a companion.

What finally made me move was the light. The sun now filled the shallow basin of the horse's body. The weighted line of the stone berm created the illusion of a mane and the distinctive roundness of an equine belly. The change in definition impelled me. I moved to the left, circling past its rump, to see how the light might flesh the horse out from various points of view. I circled it completely before squatting on my haunches. Ten or fifteen minutes later I chose another view. The third time I moved, to a point near the rear hooves, I spotted a stone tool at my feet. I stared at it a long while, more in awe than disbelief, before reaching out to pick it up. I turned it over in my left palm and took it between my fingers to feel its cutting edge. It is always difficult, especially with something so portable, to rechannel the desire to steal.

I spent several hours with the horse. As I changed positions and as the angle of the light continued to change I noticed a number of things. The angle at which the pastern carried the hoof away from the ankle was perfect. Also, stones had been placed within the image to suggest at precisely the right spot the left shoulder above the foreleg. The line that joined thigh and hock was similarly accurate. The muzzle alone seemed distorted — but perhaps these stones had been moved by a later hand. It was an admirably accurate representation, but not what a breeder would call perfect conformation. There was the suggestion of a bowed neck and an undershot jaw, and the tail, as full as a winter coyote's, did not appear to be precisely to scale.

The more I thought about it, the more I felt I was looking at an individual horse, a unique combination of generic and specific detail. It was easy to imagine one of Kino's horses as a model, or a horse that ran off from one of Coronado's columns. What kind of horses would these have been, I wondered? In the sixteenth century the most sought-after horses in Europe were Spanish, the offspring of Arabian stock and Barbary horses that the Moors brought to Iberia and bred to the older, eastern European strains brought in by the Romans. The model for this horse, I speculated, could easily have been a palomino, or a descendant of horses trained for lion-hunting in North Africa.

A few generations ago, cowboys, cavalry quartermasters, and draymen would have taken this horse before me under consideration and not let up their scrutiny until they had its heritage fixed to their satisfaction. Today, the distinction between draft and harness horses is arcane knowledge, and no image may come to mind for a blue roan or a claybank horse. The loss of such refinement in everyday conversation leaves me unsettled. People praise the Eskimo's ability to distinguish among forty types of snow but forget the skill of others who routinely differentiate between overo and tobiano pintos. Such distinctions are made for the same reason. You have to do it to be able to talk clearly about the world.

For parts of two years I worked as a horse wrangler and packer in Wyoming. It is dim knowledge now; I would have to think to remember if a buckskin was a kind of dun horse. And I couldn't throw a double-diamond hitch over a set of panniers — the packer's basic tie-down — without guidance. As I squatted there in the desert, however, these more personal memories seemed tenuous in comparison with the sweep of this animal in human time. My memories had no depth. I thought of the Hittite cavalry riding against the Syrians 3,500 years ago. And the first of the Chinese emperors, Ch'in Shih Huang, buried in Shensi Province in 210 B.C. with thousands of life-size horses and soldiers, a terra-cotta guardian army. What could I know of what was in the mind of whoever made this horse? Was there some racial memory of it as an animal that had once fed the artist's ancestors and then disappeared from North America? And then returned in this strange alliance with another race of men?

Certainly, whoever it was, the artist had observed the animal very closely. Certainly the animal's speed had impressed him. Among the first things the Quechan would have learned from an encounter with Kino's horses was that their own long-distance runners — men who could run down mule deer — were no match for this animal.

From where I squatted I could look far out over the Mexican plain. Juan Bautista de Anza passed this way in 1774, extending El Camino Real into Alta California from Sinaloa. He was followed by others, all of them astride the magical horse; *gente de razón*, the people of reason, coming into the country of *los primitivos*. The horse, like the stone animals of Egypt, urged these memories upon me. And as I drew them up from some forgotten corner of my mind — huge horses carved in the white chalk downs of southern England by an Iron Age people; Spanish horses rearing and wheeling in fear before alligators in Florida — the images seemed tethered before me. With this sense of proportion, a memory of my own — the morning I almost lost my face to a horse's hoof — now had somewhere to fit.

I rose up and began to walk slowly around the horse again. I had taken the first long measure of it and was looking now for a way to depart, a new angle of light, a fading of the image itself before the rising sun, that would break its hold on me. As I circled, feeling both heady and serene at the encounter, I realized again how strangely vivid it was. It had been created on a barren bajada between two arroyos, as nondescript a place as one could imagine. The only plant life here was a few wands of ocotillo cactus. The ground beneath my shoes was so hard it wouldn't take the print of a heavy animal even after a rain. The only sounds I had heard here were the voices of quail.

The archaeologist had been correct. For all its forcefulness, the horse is inconspicuous. If you don't care to see it you can walk right past it. That pleases him, I think. Unmarked on this bleak shoulder of the plain, the site signals to no one; so he wants no protective fences here, no informative plaque, to act as beacons. He would rather take a chance that no motorcyclist, no aimless wanderer with a flair for violence and a depth of ignorance, will ever find his way here.

The archaeologist had given me something before I left his office that now seemed peculiar—an aerial photograph of the horse. It is widely believed that an aerial view of an intaglio provides a fair and accurate depiction. It does not. In the photograph the horse looks somewhat crudely constructed; from the ground it appears far more deftly rendered. The photograph is of a single moment, and in that split second the horse seems vaguely impotent. I watched light pool in the intaglio at dawn; I imagine you could watch it withdraw at dusk and sense the same animation I did. In those prolonged moments its shape and so, too, its general character changed—noticeably. The living quality of the image, its immediacy to the eye, was brought out by the light-in-time, not, at least here, in the camera's frozen instant.

Intaglios, I thought, were never meant to be seen by gods in the sky above. They were meant to be seen by people on the ground, over a long period of shifting light. This could even be true of the huge figures on the Plain of Nazca in Peru, where people could walk for the length of a day beside them. It is our own impatience that leads us to think otherwise.

This process of abstraction, almost unintentional, drew me gradually away from the horse. I came to a position of attention at the edge of the sphere of its influence. With a slight bow I paid my respects to the horse, its maker, and the history of us all, and departed.

A short distance away I stopped the car in the middle of the road to make a few notes. I could not write down what I was thinking when I was with the horse. It would have seemed disrespectful, and it would have required another kind of attention. So now I patiently drained my memory of the details it had fastened itself upon. The road I'd stopped on was adjacent to the All American Canal, the major source of water for the Imperial and Coachella valleys. The water flowed west placidly. A disjointed flock of coots, small, dark birds with white bills, was paddling against the current, foraging in the rushes.

I was peripherally aware of the birds as I wrote, the only movement in the desert; and of a series of sounds from a village a half-mile away. The first sounds from this collection of ramshackle houses in a grove of cottonwoods were the distracted dawn voices of dogs. I heard them intermingled with the cries of a rooster. Later, the high-pitched voices of children calling out to each other came disembodied through the dry desert air. Now, a little after seven, I could hear someone practicing on the trumpet, the same rough phrases played over and over. I suddenly remembered how as children we had tried to get the rhythm of a galloping horse with hands against our thighs, or by fluttering our tongues against the roofs of our mouths.

After the trumpet, the impatient calls of adults, summoning children. Sunday morning. Wood smoke hung like a lens in the trees. The first car starts—a cold eight-cylinder engine, of Chrysler extraction perhaps, goosed to life, then throttled back to murmur through dual mufflers, the obbligato music of a shade-tree mechanic. The rote bark of mongrel dogs at dawn, the jagged outcries of men and women, an engine coming to life. Like a thousand villages from West Virginia to Guadalajara.

I finished my notes—where was I going to find a description of the horses that came north with the conquistadors? Did their manes come forward prominently over the brow, like this one's, like the forelocks of Blackfeet and Assiniboine men in nineteenth-century paintings? I set the notes on the seat beside me.

The road followed the canal for a while and then arced north, toward Interstate 8. It was slow driving and I fell to thinking how the desert had changed since Anza had come through. New plants and animals—the MacDougall cottonwood, the English house sparrow, the chukar from China—have about them now the air of the native-born.

Of the native species, some—no one knows how many—are extinct. The populations of many others, especially the animals, have been sharply reduced. The idea of a desert impoverished by agricultural poisons and varmint hunters, by off-road vehicles and military operations, did not seem as disturbing to me, however, as this other horror, now that I had been those hours with the horse. The vandals, the few who crowbar rock art off the desert's walls, who dig up graves, who punish the ground that holds intaglios, are people who devour history. Their self-centered scorn, their disrespect for ideas and images beyond their ken, create the awful atmosphere of loose ends in which totalitarianism thrives, in which the past is merely curious or wrong.

I thought about the horse sitting out there on the unprotected plain. I enumerated its qualities in my mind until a sense of its vulnerability receded and it became an anchor for something else. I remembered that history, a history like this one, which ran deeper than Mexico, deeper than the Spanish, was a kind of medicine. It permitted the great breadth of human expression to reverberate, and it did not urge you to locate its apotheosis in the present.

Each of us, individuals and civilizations, has been held upside down like Achilles in the River Styx. The artist mixing his colors in the dim light of Altamira; an Egyptian ruler lying still now, wrapped in his byssus, stored against time in a pyramid; the faded Dorset culture of the Arctic; the Hmong and Samburu and Walbiri of historic time; the modern nations. This great, imperfect stretch of human expression is the clarification and encouragement, the urging and the reminder, we call history. And it is inscribed everywhere in the face of the land, from the mountain passes of the Himalayas to a nameless bajada in the California desert.

Small birds rose up in the road ahead, startled, and flew off. I prayed no infidel would ever find that horse.

Jim Harrison

Passacaglia on Getting Lost

The most immediate sensation when totally and unfathomably lost is that you might die. I live in a world where I still very much regret the deaths of Romeo and Juliet; even the fate of Petrouchka moistens my single eye—the blind left eye weeps only underwater, or when I'm asleep and the dreams are harrowing. The first time I got lost in the winter I think I was about fourteen. I worked my way inside an enormous hollow white pine stump, the remnant of an 1897 forest fire in an area of northern Michigan. It was quite comfortable in there and it saddened me to start the stump on fire in order to be found.

It is particularly stupid to get lost in the winter because, barring a blizzard, you can retrace your steps. But I hate this in life the same as I do in poems and novels. It is a little painful to keep saying hello. The baked bean and onion sandwich was partially frozen in my coat pocket. The sun was covered with a dense cloud mass. The fire burned orange and balsamic, pitchy, melting the snow in a circle around the stump. I was a little goofy from hypothermia and thought of Cyd Charisse, and what all three of the McGuire sisters would look like bare naked. To retrace your steps: it is not in my nature to want to repeat a single day of my life. Maybe a portion of a day that involved lovemaking or a meal—a sauté of truffles and foie gras at Faugeron's in Paris ruined by jet lag, or a girl that disappeared into heaven in a Chevrolet after a single, brief encounter. I would repeat an hour with the cotton, lilac skirt; the white sleeveless blouse, the grass stain on her elbow. I could breathe through the back of her knee.

I am not going to talk about the well-equipped Republican clones you see marching like Hitler youth up and down the spine of the Rockies, or in any of the national parks, national forests, wilderness areas in America. On the tops of mountains I've seen their cocaine wrappers and fluorescent shoestrings. At five thousand feet in the Smokies there were tiny red piss-ants crowding around a discarded Dalkon shield.

Hikers, like Midwestern drivers, are bent on telling you how "far" they've hiked. "I did twenty-three miles carrying fifty-one pounds." I usually advise more lateral or circular movement. A trail, other than an animal trail, is an insult to the perceptions. It is the hike as an extension of the encounter group. Over in the Rainy River area a big Cree once portaged eighteen miles carrying five hundred pounds in a single day. His sister carried three hundred twenty.

There is clearly not enough wilderness left for the rising number of people who say they desire it. It's not wilderness anyway if it only exists by our permission and stewardship. The famous Thoreau quote said "wildness" not wilderness. We have become Europe and each, with a sense of privacy and tact, must secure our own wildness.

It strikes me that Peter Matthiessen has the best public understanding of the natural world; I say "public" because there might be someone out there who can still walk on water. It is the generalists who have the grace that translates; the specialist, like those tiny novels that emerge from the academy, wants to be correct above all else. The specialist is part of a doubtless useful collective enterprise. We are fortunate to have generalists who make leaps for those of us who are too clumsy or lazy, or who have adjusted to the fact that we can't do everything: Hoagland, Abbey, Nabhan, Lopez, Schulteis, Peacock and his grizzlies, among others, but these come to mind.

Getting lost is to sense the "animus" of nature. James Hillman said that animals we see in dreams are often "soul doctors." When you first sense you are lost there is a goofy, tingling sensation. The mouth tends to dry up, the flesh becomes spongy. This can occur when you disbelieve your compass. Made in Germany, indeed! Post-Nazi terrorists dooming the poet to a night in the woods. But then the compass was only wrong on one occasion — a cheapish Taiwanese compass.

When we are lost we lose our peripheries. Our thoughts zoom outward and infect the landscape. Years later you can revisit an area and find these thoughts still diseasing the same landscape. It requires a particular kind of behavior to heal the location.

Gullies, hummocks in swamps, swales in the middle of large fields, the small alluvial fan created by feeder creeks, undercut river banks, miniature springs, dense thickets on the tops of hills: like Bachelard's attics, seashells, drawers, cellars, these places are a balm to me. Magic (as opposed to the hocus-pocus of miracles) is equated to the quality of attentiveness. Perhaps magic "is" the quality of attentiveness, the ultimate attentiveness. D. H. Lawrence said that the only aristocracy is that of consciousness. Certain locations seem to demand consciousness. Once I sat still so long I was lucky enough to have a warbler sit on my elbow. Certain of the dead also made brief visits.

Perhaps getting lost temporarily destroys the acquisitive sense. We tend to look at earth as an elaborate system out of which we may draw useful information. We "profit" from nature—that is the taught system. The natural world exists so that we may draw conclusions about it. This is the kind of soul-destroying bullshit that drove young people to lysergic acid in the sixties.

One night last summer I was lucky enough to see "time" herself— the moon shooting across the sky, the constellations adjusting wobbily, the sun rising and setting in seconds. I jumped in the river at daylight to come to my senses. Checked a calendar to make sure. No one really wants to be Hölderlin out in the garden with a foot of snow gathered on top of his head.

It is interesting to see the Nature Establishment and the Nature Anti-Establishment suffocating in the same avalanche of tedium and bitterness. There is insufficient street experience to see how bad the bad guys are. They forget it was greed that discovered the country, greed that propelled the Westward movement, greed that shipped the blacks, greed that murdered the Indians, greed that daily shits on the heads of those who love nature. Why are we shit upon, they wonder.

I prefer places valued by no one else. The Upper Peninsula has many of these places that lack the drama and differentiation favored by the garden variety nature buff. I have a personal stump back in a forest clearing. Someone, probably a deerhunter, has left a beer bottle beside the stump. I leave the beer bottle there to conceal the value of the stump.

It took me twenty years to see a timber wolf in the wild. I could have foreshortened this time period by going to Isle Royale or Canada but I wanted to see the wolf as part of a day rather than as a novelty. We startled each other. From this single incident I dreamt I found the wolf with her back broken on a logging road. I knelt down and she went inside me, becoming part of my body and skeleton.

The shock of being lost as a metaphor is the discovery that you've never been "found" in any meaningful sense. When you're lost you know who you are. You're the only one out there. One day I was dressed in camouflage and stalking a small group of sandhill cranes which were feeding on frogs in the pine barrens not far from my cabin. I got within a few yards of them after an hour of crawling. I said "good morning," a phrase they were unfamiliar with; in fact, they were enraged and threatening. I made a little coyote yodel and they flapped skyward, the wind of their immense wings whooshing around my head. I ordered this camouflage outfit from Texas, not a bad place if you ignore the inhabitants and their peculiar urge to mythologize themselves against the evidence. One of the great empty and lovely drives left in the U.S. is from El Paso to San Antonio. Someday I will move to Nebraska for the same reason.

Of course getting lost is not ordinarily a threatening occasion. Two snowmobilers died a few years ago not all that far from my cabin but it was poignantly unnecessary. They could have piled deadfall wood around their machines and dropped matches into the remnants of the gas in the tanks, creating an enormous pyre for the search planes. Euphemisms for getting lost range from "I got a little turned around for a few hours" to "I wasn't lost, I just couldn't find my car until morning." The enemies are the occasional snowflakes in July, the cold and rain, the blackflies and mosquitoes, drinking swamp or creek water when a spring can always be found. Of course the greatest enemy is panic. The greatest panic I've ever felt was at an Umbanda rite in Brazil when I sensed that the others present weren't actually people. I became ill when a man leapfrogged through a garden on his back, and an old woman rubbed her left eyeball against my own and told me pointedly about my life in northern Michigan.

An old Chippewa I know carries a folded-up garbage bag in his pocket. He claims it is his portable home, keeping him warm and dry if he gets lost or tired. He finds coyote dens by scent, and whittles the heads of canes into renditions of his "dream birds." His favorite drink is a double martini. He asked me to check for a phone number of a "love" he had lost in 1931. He was somewhat disturbed, he told me, when it occurred to him that people didn't know that every single tree was different from every other tree. He is making me a cane to repel bears and to attract wolves and women. I will hang this cane on the cabin wall, being genetically too Calvinist to have any interest in sorcery.

It seems I will never be reviewed by Edmund Wilson or Randall Jarrell or Kenneth Burke, something I aspired to at nineteen in the jungle of Grove Street. For years I've wanted to take a walk with E. M.

Cioran. I've rid myself of the usual fantasies about money, actresses, models, food, fishing, hunting, travel, by enacting them, though the money evaporated at startling speed through what accountants refer to as "spending habits." Cioran's mind is unique, the modernist temperament at an antipode not reached by novelists. I would get us mildly lost on the walk, which might amuse him. The name of Wittgenstein will not be mentioned. I want to ask Cioran to what degree the perception of reality is consensual. The answer will help me account for all of my bad reviews! Many of us apparently live in different worlds. Do we see the same sky as Crazy Horse? Think of Anne Frank's comprehension of the closet.

I know a pyramidical hill at least fifteen miles from the nearest dwelling. On this hill three small river systems have their beginnings, each of them a hundred or so miles long. I'm not giving out any directions to this place. The first two times I tried to go there I got turned around, succeeding on the third trip. My yellow Labrador was frightened on this hill, which in turn served to disturb me. The dog, however, is frightened of bears, coyotes, thunder, northern lights, the moon. I only stayed a few minutes.

Rilke said something on the order of "With all of its eyes the creature world beholds the open . . ." (Everyone should buy the astonishing new translation of Sonnets to Orpheus by Stephen Mitchell.) Unfavorable comparisons to animals are contraindicated. I confess I've talked at length to ravens, porcupines, crows, coyotes, infant porpoises, and particularly beautiful heads of garlic, but then others talk back at the television. It is natural for a child to imagine what a bird sees. "How do we know but that every bird that cuts the airy way is an immense world of delight closed to our senses five?" We don't. We should encourage ourselves to be a whale, a woman, a plant or planet, a lake, the night sky. There was a Cheyenne warrior named One Who Sees As A Bird: the tops of trees are ovoids bending away from the wind.

I'm a poor naturalist. A bird evokes the other times I've seen the bird, a delicious continuity, not a wish to run to my collection of bird books. I'm not against the idea of my work being forgotten if I can be an old geezer in a cabin smelling of wood smoke, kerosene, a Bordeaux stain on my T-shirt, cooking a not so simple "salmi" of woodcock. It has only lately occurred to me that many of my concerns are anachronistic. Walking in the forest at night can be a cocaine substitute in addition to simply walking in the forest at night. Kokopele owned the best of all spirits for an artist. He led Picasso to do a gavotte at the age of eighty. He made Henry Miller a ping-pong champion.

Last August when I was turned around in a swamp I sat on a hummock and had a vision of death as a suck-hole in the universe, an interior plug, out of which we all go with a gurgle. I gurgled in the swamp. Frogs and birds answered. This is the sensuality of death, not the less beautiful for being terminal.

Joyce Carol Oates

Against Nature

*We soon get through with Nature. She excites an expectation
which she cannot satisfy.*

— THOREAU, Journal, *1854*

*Sir, if a man has experienced the inexpressible, he is under no
obligation to attempt to express it.*

— SAMUEL JOHNSON

The writer's resistance to Nature.

It has no sense of humor: in its beauty, as in its ugliness, or its
neutrality, there is no laughter.

It lacks a moral purpose.

It lacks a satiric dimension, registers no irony.

Its pleasures lack resonance, being accidental; its horrors, even
when premeditated, are equally perfunctory, "red in tooth and claw" et
cetera.

It lacks a symbolic subtext — excepting that provided by man.

It has no (verbal) language.

It has no interest in ours.

It inspires a painfully limited set of responses in "nature-writers"
— REVERENCE, AWE, PIETY, MYSTICAL ONENESS.

It eludes us even as it prepares to swallow us up, books and all.

* * *

I was lying on my back in the dirt-gravel of the towpath beside the Del-
aware-Raritan Canal, Titusville, New Jersey, staring up at the sky and
trying, with no success, to overcome a sudden attack of tachycardia
that had come upon me out of nowhere — such attacks are always "out
of nowhere," that's their charm — and all around me Nature thrummed
with life, the air smelling of moisture and sunlight, the canal reflecting

the sky, red-winged blackbirds testing their spring calls — the usual. I'd become the jar in Tennessee, a fictitious center, or parenthesis, aware beyond my erratic heartbeat of the numberless heartbeats of the earth, its pulsing pumping life, sheer life, incalculable. Struck down in the midst of motion — I'd been jogging a minute before — I was "out of time" like a fallen, stunned boxer, privileged (in an abstract manner of speaking) to be an involuntary witness to the random, wayward, nameless motion on all sides of me.

Paroxysmal tachycardia is rarely fatal, but if the heartbeat accelerates to 250–270 beats a minute you're in trouble. The average attack is about 100–150 beats and mine seemed so far to be about average; the trick now was to prevent it from getting worse. Brainy people try brainy strategies, such as thinking calming thoughts, pseudo-mystic thoughts, *If I die now it's a good death*, that sort of thing, *if I die this is a good place and a good time*, the idea is to deceive the frenzied heartbeat that, really, you don't care: you hadn't any other plans for the afternoon. The important thing with tachycardia is to prevent panic! you must prevent panic! otherwise you'll have to be taken by ambulance to the closest emergency room, which is not so very nice a way to spend the afternoon, really. So I contemplated the blue sky overhead. The earth beneath my head. Nature surrounding me on all sides, I couldn't quite see it but I could hear it, smell it, sense it — there is something *there*, no mistake about it. Completely oblivious to the predicament of the individual but that's only "natural" after all, one hardly expects otherwise.

When you discover yourself lying on the ground, limp and unresisting, head in the dirt, and helpless, the earth seems to shift forward as a presence; hard, emphatic, not mere surface but a genuine force — there is no other word for it but *presence*. To keep in motion is to keep in time and to be stopped, stilled, is to be abruptly out of time, in another time-dimension perhaps, an alien one, where human language has no resonance. Nothing to be said about it expresses it, nothing touches it, it's an absolute against which nothing human can be measured. . . . Moving through space and time by way of your own volition you inhabit an interior consciousness, a hallucinatory consciousness, it might be said, so long as breath, heartbeat, the body's autonomy hold; when motion is stopped you are jarred out of it. The interior is invaded by the exterior. The outside wants to come in, and only the self's fragile membrane prevents it.

The fly buzzing at Emily's death.

Still, the earth *is* your place. A tidy grave-site measured to your size. Or, from another angle of vision, one vast democratic grave.

Let's contemplate the sky. Forget the crazy hammering heartbeat, don't listen to it, don't start counting, remember that there is a clever way of breathing that conserves oxygen as if you're lying below the surface of a body of water breathing through a very thin straw but you *can* breathe through it if you're careful, if you don't panic, one breath and then another and then another, isn't that the story of all lives? careers? Just a matter of breathing. Of course it is. But contemplate the sky, it's there to be contemplated. A mild shock to see it so blank, blue, a thin airy ghostly blue, no clouds to disguise its emptiness. You are beginning to feel not only weightless but near-bodiless, lying on the earth like a scrap of paper about to be blown off. Two dimensions and you'd imagined you were three! And there's the sky rolling away forever, into infinity—if "infinity" can be "rolled into"—and the forlorn truth is, that's where you're going too. And the lovely blue isn't even blue, is it? isn't even there, is it? a mere optical illusion, isn't it? no matter what art has urged you to believe.

* * *

Early Nature memories. Which it's best not to suppress.

. . . Wading, as a small child, in Tonawanda Creek near our house, and afterward trying to tear off, in a frenzy of terror and revulsion, the sticky fat black bloodsuckers that had attached themselves to my feet, particularly between my toes.

. . . Coming upon a friend's dog in a drainage ditch, dead for several days, evidently the poor creature had been shot by a hunter and left to die, bleeding to death, and we're stupefied with grief and horror but can't resist sliding down to where he's lying on his belly, and we can't resist squatting over him, turning the body over . . .

. . . The raccoon, mad with rabies, frothing at the mouth and tearing at his own belly with his teeth, so that his intestines spilled out onto the ground . . . a sight I seem to remember though in fact I did not see. I've been told I did not see.

* * *

Consequently, my chronic uneasiness with Nature-mysticism; Nature-adoration; Nature-as-(moral)-instruction-for-mankind. My doubt that one can, with philosophical validity, address "Nature" as a single coherent noun, anything other than a Platonic, hence discredited, is-ness. My resistance to "Nature-writing" as a genre, except when it is brilliantly fictionalized in the service of a writer's individual vision — Thoreau's books and *Journal*, of course — but also, less known in this country, the miniaturist prose-poems of Colette (*Flowers and Fruit*) and Ponge (*Taking the Side of Things*) — in which case it becomes yet another, and ingenious, form of storytelling. The subject is *there* only by the grace of the author's language.

Nature has no instructions for mankind except that our poor beleaguered humanist-democratic way of life, our fantasies of the individual's high worth, our sense that the weak, no less than the strong, have a right to survive, are absurd.

In any case, where *is* Nature? one might (skeptically) inquire. Who has looked upon her/its face and survived?

* * *

But isn't this all exaggeration, in the spirit of rhetorical contentiousness? Surely Nature is, for you, as for most reasonably intelligent people, a "perennial" source of beauty, comfort, peace, escape from the delirium of civilized life; a respite from the ego's ever-frantic strategies of self-promotion, as a way of insuring (at least in fantasy) some small measure of immortality? Surely Nature, as it is understood in the usual slapdash way, as human, if not dilettante, *experience* (hiking in a national park, jogging on the beach at dawn, even tending, with the usual comical frustrations, a suburban garden), is wonderfully consoling; a place where, when you go there, it has to take you in? — a palimpsest of sorts you choose to read, layer by layer, always with care, always cautiously, in proportion to your psychological strength?

Nature: as in Thoreau's upbeat Transcendentalist mode ("The indescribable innocence and beneficence of Nature, — such health, such cheer, they afford forever! and such sympathy have they ever with our race, that all Nature would be affected . . . if any man should ever for a just cause grieve"), and not in Thoreau's grim mode ("Nature is hard to be overcome but she must be overcome").

Another way of saying, not *Nature-in-itself* but *Nature-as-experience.*

The former, Nature-in-itself, is, to allude slantwise to Melville, a blankness ten times blank; the latter is what we commonly, or perhaps always, mean when we speak of Nature as a noun, a single entity — something of *ours.* Most of the time it's just an activity, a sort of hobby, a weekend, a few days, perhaps a few hours, staring out the window at the mind-dazzling autumn foliage of, say, Northern Michigan, being rendered speechless—temporarily—at the sight of Mt. Shasta, the Grand Canyon, Ansel Adams's West. Or Nature writ small, contained in the back yard. Nature filtered through our optical nerves, our "senses," our fiercely romantic expectations. Nature that pleases us because it mirrors our souls, or gives the comforting illusion of doing so. As in our first mother's awakening to the self's fatal beauty—

> I thither went
> With unexperienc't thought, and laid me down
> On the green bank, to look into the clear
> Smooth Lake, that to me seem'd another Sky.
> As I bent down to look, just opposite,
> A Shape within the watr'y gleam appear'd
> Bending to look on me, I started back,
> It started back, but pleas'd I soon return'd,
> Pleas'd it return'd as soon with answering looks
> Of sympathy and love; there I had fixt
> Mine eyes till now, and pin'd with vain desire.

—in these surpassingly beautiful lines from Book IV of Milton's *Paradise Lost*.

Nature as the self's (flattering) mirror, but not ever, no, never, Nature-in-itself.

* * *

Nature is mouths, or maybe a single mouth. Why glamorize it, romanticize it, well yes but we must, we're writers, poets, mystics (of a sort) aren't we, precisely what else are we to do but glamorize and romanticize and generally exaggerate the significance of anything we focus the white heat of our "creativity" upon . . . ? And why not Nature, since it's there, common property, mute, can't talk back, allows us the possibility of transcending the human condition for a while, writing prettily of mountain ranges, white-tailed deer, the purple crocuses outside this very window, the thrumming dazzling "life-force" we imagine we all support. Why not.

Nature *is* more than a mouth—it's a dazzling variety of mouths. And it pleases the senses, in any case, as the physicists' chill universe of numbers certainly does not.

* * *

Oscar Wilde, on our subject: "Nature is no great mother who has borne us. She is our creation. It is in our brain that she quickens to life. Things are because we see them, and what we see, and how we see it, depends on the Arts that have influenced us. To look at a thing is very different from seeing a thing. . . . At present, people see fogs, not because there are fogs, but because poets and painters have taught them the mysterious loveliness of such effects. There may have been fogs for centuries in London. I dare say there were. But no one saw them. They did not exist until Art had invented them. . . . Yesterday evening Mrs. Arundel insisted on my going to the window and looking at the glorious sky, as she called it. And so I had to look at it. . . . And what was it? It was simply a very second-rate Turner, a Turner of a bad period, with all the painter's worst faults exaggerated and over-emphasized."

(If we were to put it to Oscar Wilde that he exaggerates, his reply might well be: "Exaggeration? I don't know the meaning of the word.")

* * *

Walden, that most artfully composed of prose fictions, concludes, in the rhapsodic chapter "Spring," with Henry David Thoreau's contemplation of death, decay, and regeneration as it is suggested to him, or to his protagonist, by the spectacle of vultures feeding off carrion. There is a dead horse close by his cabin and the stench of its decomposition, in certain winds, is daunting. Yet: ". . . the assurance it gave me of the strong appetite and inviolable health of Nature was my compensation. I love to see that Nature is so rife with life that myriads can be afforded to be sacrificed and suffered to prey upon one another; that tender organizations can be so serenely squashed out of existence like pulp, — tadpoles which herons gobble up, and tortoises and toads run over in the road; and that sometimes it has rained flesh and blood! . . . The impression made on a wise man is that of universal innocence."

Come off it, Henry David. You've grieved these many years for your elder brother John, who died a ghastly death of lockjaw; you've never wholly recovered from the experience of watching him die. And you know, or must know, that you're fated too to die young of consumption. . . . But this doctrinaire Transcendentalist passage ends *Walden* on just the right note. It's as impersonal, as coolly detached, as the Oversoul itself: a "wise man" filters his emotions through his brain.

Or through his prose.

* * *

Nietzsche: "We all pretend to ourselves that we are more simple-minded than we are: that is how we get a rest from our fellow men."

* * *

Once out of nature I shall never take
My bodily form from any natural thing,
But such a form as Grecian goldsmiths make
Of hammered gold and gold enamelling
To keep a drowsy Emperor awake;
Or set upon a golden bough to sing
To lords and ladies of Byzantium
Of what is past, or passing, or to come.

— William Butler Yeats, "Sailing to
Byzantium"

Yet even the golden bird is a "bodily form taken from (a) natural thing." No, it's impossible to escape!

* * *

The writer's resistance to Nature.
Wallace Stevens: "In the presence of extraordinary actuality, consciousness takes the place of imagination."

* * *

Once, years ago, in 1972 to be precise, when I seemed to have been another person, related to the person I am now as one is related, tangentially, sometimes embarrassingly, to cousins not seen for decades, — once, when we were living in London, and I was very sick, I had a mystical vision. That is, I "had" a "mystical vision" — the heart sinks: such pretension — or something resembling one. A fever-dream, let's call it. It impressed me enormously and impresses me still, though I've long since lost the capacity to see it with my mind's eye, or even, I suppose, to believe in it. There is a statute of limitations on "mystical visions" as on romantic love.

I was very sick, and I imagined my life as a thread, a thread of breath, or heartbeat, or pulse, or light, yes it was light, radiant light, I was burning with fever and I ascended to that plane of serenity that might be mistaken for (or *is*, in fact) Nirvana, where I had a waking dream of uncanny lucidity —

My body is a tall column of light and heat.

My body is not "I" but "it."

My body is not one but many.

My body, which "I" inhabit, is inhabited as well by other creatures, unknown to me, imperceptible — the smallest of them mere sparks of light.

My body, which I perceive as substance, is in fact an organization of infinitely complex, overlapping, imbricated structures, radiant light their manifestation, the "body" a tall column of light and blood-heat, a temporary agreement among atoms, like a high-rise building with numberless rooms, corridors, corners, elevator shafts, windows. . . . In this fantastical structure the "I" is deluded as to its sovereignty, let alone its autonomy in the (outside) world; the most astonishing secret is that the "I" doesn't exist! — but it behaves as if it does, as if it were one and not many.

In any case, without the "I" the tall column of light and heat would die, and the microscopic life-particles would die with it . . . will die with it. The "I," which doesn't exist, is everything.

But Dr. Johnson is right, the inexpressible need not be expressed. And what resistance, finally? There is none.

* * *

This morning, an invasion of tiny black ants. One by one they appear, out of nowhere — that's their charm too! — moving single file across the white Parsons table where I am sitting, trying without much success to write a poem. A poem of only three or four lines is what I want, something short, tight, mean, I want it to hurt like a white-hot wire up the nostrils, small and compact and turned in upon itself with the density of a hunk of rock from the planet Jupiter. . . .

But here come the black ants: harbingers, you might say, of spring. One by one by one they appear on the dazzling white table and one by one I kill them with a forefinger, my deft right forefinger, mashing each against the surface of the table and then dropping it into a wastebasket at my side. Idle labor, mesmerizing, effortless, and I'm curious as to how long I can do it, sit here in the brilliant March sunshine killing ants with my right forefinger, how long I, and the ants, can keep it up.

After a while I realize that I can do it a long time. And that I've written my poem.

John Fowles

The Green Man

One of the oldest and most diffused bodies of myth and folklore has accreted round the idea of the man in the trees. In all his manifestations, as dryad, as stag-headed Herne, as outlaw, he possesses the characteristic of elusiveness, a power of 'melting' into the trees, and I am certain the attraction of the myth is so profound and universal because it is constantly 'played' inside every individual consciousness.

This notion of the green man — or green woman, as W. H. Hudson made her — seen as emblem of the close connection between the actuality of present consciousness (not least in its habitual flight into a mental greenwood) and what science has censored in man's attitude to nature — that is, the 'wild' side, the inner feeling as opposed to the outer, fact-bound, conforming face imposed by fashion — helped me question my old pseudo-scientist self. But it also misled me for a time. In the 1950s I grew interested in the Zen theories of 'seeing' and of aesthetics: of learning to look beyond names at things-in-themselves. I stopped bothering to identify species new to me, I concentrated more and more on the familiar, daily nature around me, where I then lived. But living without names is impossible, if not downright idiocy, in a writer; and living without explanation or speculation as to causality, little better — for Western man, at least. I discovered, too, that there was less conflict than I had imagined between nature as external assembly of names and facts and nature as internal feeling; that the two modes of seeing or knowing could in fact marry and take place almost simultaneously, and enrich each other.

Achieving a relationship with nature is both a science and an art, beyond mere knowledge or mere feeling alone; and I now think beyond oriental mysticism, transcendentalism, 'meditation techniques' and the rest — or at least as we in the West have converted them to our use, which seems increasingly in a narcissistic way: to make ourselves feel more positive, more meaningful, more dynamic. I do not believe nature is to be reached that way either, by turning it into a therapy, a free clinic for admirers of their own sensitivity. The subtlest of our alienations from it, the most difficult to comprehend, is our need to use it in some way, to derive some personal yield. We shall never fully understand nature (or ourselves), and certainly never respect it, until we dissociate the wild from the notion of usability — however innocent and harmless the use. For it is the general uselessness of so much of nature that lies at the root of our ancient hostility and indifference to it.

There is a kind of coldness, I would rather say a stillness, an empty space, at the heart of our forced co-existence with all the other species of the planet. Richard Jefferies coined a word for it: the ultra-humanity of all that is not man . . . not with us or against us, but outside and beyond us, truly alien. It may sound paradoxical, but we shall not cease to be alienated — by our knowledge, by our greed, by our vanity — from nature until we grant it its unconscious alienation from us.

I am not one of those supreme optimists who think all the world's ills, and especially this growing divide between man and nature, can be cured by a return to a quasi-agricultural, ecologically 'caring' society. It is not that I doubt it might theoretically be so cured; but the possibility of the return defeats my powers of imagination. The majority of Western man is now urban, and the whole world will soon follow suit. A very significant tilt of balance in human history is expected by the end of the coming decade: over half of all mankind will by then have moved inside towns and cities. Any hope of reversing that trend, short of some universal catastrophe, is as tiny and precarious as the Monarch butterflies I watched, an autumn or two ago, migrating between the Fifth Avenue skyscrapers in central Manhattan. All chance of a close acquaintance with nature, be it through intellect and education, be it in the simplest way of all, by having it near at hand, recedes from the many who already effectively live in a support system in outer space, a creation of science, and without means to escape it, culturally or economically.

But the problem is not, or only minimally, that nature itself is in imminent danger or that we shall lose touch with it simply because we have less access to it. A number of species, environments, unusual ecologies are in danger, there are major pollution problems; but even in our most densely populated countries the ordinary wild remains far from the brink of extinction. We may not exaggerate the future threats and dangers, but we do exaggerate the present and actual state of this global nation—underestimate the degree to which it is still surviving and accessible to those who want to experience it. It is far less nature itself that is yet in true danger than our attitude to it. Already we behave as if we live in a world that holds only a remnant of what there actually is; in a world that may come, but remains a black hypothesis, not a present reality.

I believe the major cause of this more mental than physical rift lies less in the folly or one-sidedness of our societies and educational systems, or in the historical evolution of man into a predominantly urban and industrial creature, a thinking termite, than in the way we have, during these last hundred and fifty years, devalued the kind of experience or knowledge we loosely define as art; and especially in the way we have failed to grasp its deepest difference from science. No art is truly teachable in its essence. All the knowledge in the world of its techniques can provide in itself no more than imitations or replicas of previous art. What is irreplaceable in any object of art is never, in the final analysis, its technique or craft, but the personality of the artist, the expression of his or her unique and individual feeling. All major advances in technique have come about to serve this need. Techniques in themselves are always reducible to sciences, that is, to learnability. Once Joyce has written, Picasso painted, Webern composed, it requires only a minimal gift, besides patience and practice, to copy their techniques exactly; yet we all know why this kind of technique-copy, even when it is so painstakingly done—for instance, in painting—that it deceives museum and auction-house experts, is counted worthless beside the work of the original artist. It is not *of* him or her, it is not art, but imitation.

As it is with the true 'making' arts, so it is with the other aspects of human life of which we say that full knowledge or experience also requires an art—some inwardly creative or purely personal factor beyond the power of external teaching to instil or science to predict. Attempts to impart recipes or set formulae as to practice and enjoyment are always two-edged, since the question is not so much whether they may or may not enrich the normal experience of that abstract thing, the normal man or woman, but the certainty that they must in some way damage that other essential component of the process, the contribution of the artist in this sense—the individual experiencer, the 'green man' hidden in the leaves of his or her unique and once-only being.

Telling people why, how and when they ought to feel this or that—whether it be with regard to the enjoyment of nature, of food, of sex, or anything else—may, undoubtedly sometimes does, have a useful function in dispelling various kinds of socially harmful ignorance. But what this instruction cannot give is the deepest benefit of any art, be it of making, or of knowing, or of experiencing: which is self-expression and self-discovery. The last thing a sex-manual can be is an *ars amoris* — a science of coupling, perhaps, but never an art of love. Exactly the same is true of so many nature-manuals. They may teach you how and what to look for, what to question in external nature; but never in your own nature.

In science greater knowledge is always and indisputably good; it is by no means so throughout all human existence. We know it from art proper, where achievement and great factual knowledge, or taste, or intelligence, are in no way essential companions; if they were, our best artists would also be our most learned academics. We can know it by reducing the matter to the absurd, and imagining that God, or some Protean visitor from outer space, were at one fell swoop to grant us all knowledge. Such omniscience would be worse than the worst natural catastrophe, for our species as a whole; would extinguish its soul, lose it all pleasure and reason for living.

This is not the only area in which, like the rogue computer beloved of science fiction fans, some socially or culturally consecrated proposition — which may be true or good in its social or cultural context — exends itself to the individual; but it is one of the most devitalizing. Most mature artists know that great general knowledge is more a hindrance than a help. It is only innately mechanical, salami-factory novelists who set such great store by research; in nine cases out of ten what natural knowledge and imagination cannot supply is in any case precisely what needs to be left out. The green man in all of us is well aware of this. In practice we spend far more time rejecting knowledge than trying to gain it, and wisely. But it is in the nature of all society, let alone one deeply imbued with a scientific and technological ethos, to bombard us with ever more knowledge — and to make any questioning or rejection of it unpatriotic and immoral.

Art and nature are siblings, branches of the one tree; and nowhere more than in the continuing inexplicability of many of their processes, and above all those of creation and of effect on their respective audiences. Our approach to art, as to nature, has become increasingly scientized (and dreadfully serious) during this last century. It sometimes seems now as if it is principally there not for itself but to provide material for labeling, classifying, analysing — specimens for 'setting,' as I used to set moths and butterflies. This is of course especially true of

— and pernicious in — our schools and universities. I think the first sign that I might one day become a novelist (though I did not then realize it) was the passionate detestation I developed at my own school for all those editions of examination books that began with a long introduction: an anatomy lesson that always reduced the original text to a corpse by the time one got to it, a lifeless demonstration of a pre-established proposition. It took me years to realize that even geniuses, the Shakespeares, the Racines, the Austens, have human faults.

Obscurity, the opportunity a work of art gives for professional explainers to show their skills, has become almost an aesthetic virtue; at another extreme the notion of art as vocation (that is, something to which one is genetically suited) is dismissed as non-scientific and inegalitarian. It is not a gift beyond personal choice, but one that can be acquired, like knowledge of science, by rote, recipe and hard work. Elsewhere we become so patterned and persuaded by the tone of the more serious reviewing of art in our magazines and newspapers that we no longer notice their overwhelmingly scientific tone, or the paradox of this knowing-naming technique being applied to a non-scientific object — one whose production the artist himself cannot fully explain, and one whose effect the vast majority of the non-reviewing audience do not attempt to explain.

The professional critic or academic would no doubt say this is mere ignorance, that both artists and audiences have to be taught to understand themselves and the object that links them, to make the relationship articulate and fully conscious; defoliate the wicked green man, hunt him out of his trees. Of course there is a place for the scientific, or quasi-scientific, analysis of art, as there is (and far greater) for that of nature. But the danger, in both art and nature, is that all emphasis is placed on the created, not the creation.

All artefacts, all bits of scientific knowledge, share one thing in common: that is, they come to us from the past, they are relics of something already observed, deduced, formulated, created, and as such qualify to go through the Linnaean and every other scientific mill. Yet we cannot say that the 'green' or creating process does not happen or has no importance just because it is largely private and beyond lucid description and rational analysis. We might as well argue that the young wheat-plant is irrelevant because it can yield nothing to the miller and his stones. We know that in any sane reality the green blade is as much the ripe grain as the child is father to the man. Nor of course does the simile apply to art alone, since we are all in a way creating our future out of our present, our 'published' outward behaviour out of our inner green being. One main reason we may seldom feel this happening is that society does not want us to. Such random personal creativity is offensive to all machines.

I began this wander through the trees . . . in search of that much looser use of the word 'art' to describe a way of knowing and experiencing and enjoying outside the major modes of science and art proper . . . a way not concerned with scientific discovery and artefacts, a way that is internally rather than externally creative, that leaves very little public trace; and yet which for those very reasons is almost wholly concentrated in its own creative process. It is really only the qualified scientist or artist who can escape from the interiority and constant nowness, the green chaos of this experience, by making some aspect of it exterior and so fixing it in past time, or known knowledge. Thereby they create new, essentially parasitical orders and categories of phenomena that in turn require both a science and an art of experiencing.

But nature is unlike art in terms of its product — what we in general know it by. The difference is that it is not only created, an external object with a history, and so belonging to a past; but also creating in the present, as we experience it. As we watch, it is so to speak rewriting, reformulating, repainting, rephotographing itself. It refuses to stay fixed and fossilized in the past, as both the scientist and the artist feel it somehow ought to; and both will generally try to impose this fossilization on it.

Verbal tenses can be very misleading here: we stick adamantly in speech to the strict protocol of actual time. Of and in the present we speak in the present, of the past in the past. But our psychological tenses can be very different. Perhaps because I am a writer (and nothing is more fictitious than the past in which the first, intensely alive and present, draft of a novel goes down on the page), I long ago noticed this in my naturalist self: that is, a disproportionately backward element in any present experience of nature, a retreat or running-back to past knowledge and experience, whether it was the definite past of personal memory or the indefinite, the imperfect, of stored 'ological' knowledge and proper scientific behaviour. This seemed to me often to cast a mysterious veil of deadness, of having already happened, over the actual and present event or phenomenon.

I had a vivid example of it only a few years ago in France, long after I thought I had grown wise to this self-imposed brainwashing. I came on my first Soldier Orchid, a species I had long wanted to encounter, but hitherto never seen outside a book. I fell on my knees before it in a way that all botanists will know. I identified, to be quite certain, with Professors Clapham, Tutin and Warburg in hand (the standard British *Flora*), I measured, I photographed, I worked out where I was on the map, for future reference. I was excited, very happy, one always remembers one's 'firsts' of the rarer species. Yet five minutes after my wife had finally (other women are not the only form of adultery) torn me away, I suffered a strange feeling. I realized I had not actually *seen* the three plants in the little colony we had found. Despite all the identifying, measuring, photographing, I had managed to set the experience in a kind of present past, a having-looked, even as I was temporally and physically still looking. If I had the courage, and my wife the patience, I would have asked her to turn and drive back, because I knew I had just fallen, in the stupidest possible way, into an ancient trap. It is not necessarily too little knowledge that causes ignorance; possessing too much, or wanting to gain too much, can produce the same result.

There is something in the nature of nature, in its presentness, its seeming transience, its creative ferment and hidden potential, that corresponds very closely with the wild, or green man, in our psyches; and it is a something that disappears as soon as it is relegated to an automatic pastness, a status of merely classifiable *thing*, image taken *then*. 'Thing' and 'then' attract each other. If it is thing, it was then; if it was then, it is thing. We lack trust in the present, this moment, this actual seeing, because our culture tells us to trust only the reported back, the publicly framed, the edited, the thing set in the clearly artistic or the clearly scientific angle of perspective. One of the deepest lessons we have to learn is that nature, of its nature, resists this. It waits to be seen otherwise, in its individual presentness and from our individual presentness.

I come now near the heart of what seems to me to be the single greatest danger in the rich legacy left us by Linnaeus and the other founding fathers of all our sciences and scientific mores and methods — or more fairly, left us by our leaping evolutionary ingenuity in the invention of tools. All tools, from the simplest word to the most advanced space probe, are disturbers and rearrangers of primordial nature and reality — are, in the dictionary definition, 'mechanical implements for working upon something.' What they have done, and I suspect in direct proportion to our ever-increasing dependence on them, is to addict us to purpose: both to looking for purpose in everything external to us and to looking internally for purpose in everything we do — to seek explanation of the outside world by purpose, to justify our seeking by purpose. This addiction to finding a reason, a function, a quantifiable yield, has now infiltrated all aspects of our lives — and become effectively synonymous with pleasure. The modern version of hell is purposelessness.

Nature suffers particularly in this, and our indifference and hostility to it is closely connected with the fact that its only purpose appears to be being and surviving. We may think that this comprehends all animate existence, including our own; and so it must, ultimately; but we have long ceased to be content with so abstract a motive. A scientist would rightly say that all form and behaviour in nature is highly purposive, or strictly designed for the end of survival — specific or genetic, according to theory. But most of this functional purpose is hidden to the non-scientist, indecipherable; and the immense variety of nature appears to hide nothing, nothing but a green chaos at the core — which we brilliantly purposive apes can use and exploit as we please, with a free conscience.

A green chaos. Or a wood.

Edited and Introduced by John Rodman
The Dolphin Papers

I am convinced that these papers, which I have the privilege and the duty to make public, comprise one of the most extraordinary documents in the history of thought. Whatever their value as works of scholarship and argumentation (this will surely be debated), they are of interest for their unique perspective — especially in the aftermath of the recent Revolt of the Beasts.

The "Dolphin Papers" consist of typescripts found in the Cetacean Section of the now-defunct Institute for Interspecies Communication (a research affiliate of the Center for Pacific Studies at the University of Hawaii) by intelligence officers following the occupation of the Institute by the U.S. Navy in December 1970. The condition of the papers is imperfect: some pages are missing from numbered sequences, while others are partially burned or water-damaged (perhaps as a result of the shelling of the Institute during the process of pacification). The papers remain classified "Top Secret" by the Department of Defense, but recently a copy of them came to my attention, and I resolved to begin publishing those portions of the text that I could reconstruct with reasonable accuracy.[1]

In publishing the papers, I am motivated both by the scholar's desire that the truth should be known, and by the citizen's faith that knowledge will enable us to act with greater prudence so as to avoid a recurrence of the late, unfortunate, and still somewhat mysterious rebellion. While I take no responsibility for the validity of individual statements in the papers, or for the overall viewpoint, I feel strongly that we need to understand the state of mind — the "philosophy," so to speak — of those who may have masterminded the uprising.

We do not yet know with certainty whether the papers are a human translation of the discourse of one or more dolphins, or whether they are a human fabrication. From the Institute's grants, contracts, and publications, we know that the staff was testing the intelligence of bottlenose dolphins (Tursiops truncatus) *by teaching them to understand English and to perform such simple tasks as carrying and positioning underseas explosive devices. The papers were found in a double-locked filing cabinet along with numerous tapes containing long series of dolphin*

---

1. *An earlier version was presented at the annual meeting of the Western Political Science Association, April 5–7, 1973, San Diego, California.*

sounds (fast and slow clicks, whistles, barks, wails, humanoid sounds, and sounds at ultrasonic frequency). There is no hard evidence that communication was achieved beyond the level of simple commands — the sort understood by well-trained domestic dogs or by the dolphins that perform tricks at Sea World and Marineland — but perhaps we do not know everything that went on at the Institute. Of the 37 staff members, 26 were killed, most of them by the shelling, ten are missing, and one is hospitalized as an acutely paranoid schizophrenic who refuses to speak and who suffers from the delusion that he is listening to messages others cannot hear.

If we assume that the Dolphin Papers are a human translation of dolphin dictation, the implications are enormous. Not only can dolphins think and communicate, but the papers could have been dictated only by very learned dolphins — learned in the history of Western thought, no less. How this could have come about, we can only speculate. Since dolphins depend as much on their hearing as we do on our sight, our author(s) would doubtless have learned aurally. This presupposes that at least one dolphin had been able to understand human speech for some time, and had either held converse with human scholars or been able to listen to distant speech. (Should we imagine our author(s) auditing university lectures in the history of Western thought while sporting in the tank at the Institute or basking at sea?)

What could have been the purpose of dictating the Dolphin Papers? We might suppose that the more scholarly portion (Section III) was originally composed as part of a larger effort to understand human culture in aspects particularly related to dolphin interests, and to communicate that understanding to other dolphins (perhaps also to other intelligent species), either as an exercise in satisfying curiosity or as part of a campaign of consciousness-raising. The more militant portions (Sections I and II), on the other hand, would appear to be more on the order of political propaganda designed to crystallize and focus grievances and, by implication, to mobilize for action (though they stop short of outright incitement). The mood and style are sufficiently varied that we may assume that the papers are not necessarily the work of a single intelligence.

What could have been the purpose of having the papers translated into a human language, specifically English? Were dolphins beginning to reach out to selected humans (and were we the chosen people?), seeking to win allies by discoursing with us in terms of our own intellectual traditions? This possibility makes sense in light of the papers' curious statement that, at a special stage of history, certain individual humans will break through to a transhuman, truly philosophical consciousness of the whole and, in consequence (non sequitur?), desert the human camp and join the dolphins. Is it possible that some staff members of the Institute, funded to humanize dolphins, became "converted" to the dolphin cause? Did they, out of misanthropy and/or misguided compassion for the subhuman, commit the mistake typified by Romain Gary's Morel, who took his rifle into the African jungle to defend elephants against the human predator?[2]

Granted that such a theory can explain the facts, it also makes great demands on our credulity. I, for one, find it more plausible to assume that the Dolphin Papers were composed by one or more human beings, presumably members of the Institute's staff who, out of disgust with their own species and/or sympathy with the dolphins, "invented" the dolphin cause. There is, after all, a literary tradition of the animal fable, from Plutarch through Fontaine to the contemporary comic strip. Moreover, the hypothesis of human composition fits easily with received knowledge about the intellectual and empathetic capacities of human beings, while not requiring us to make far-fetched assumptions about the powers of nonhumans. On the other hand, we are left with the problem of how to explain the recent Revolt of the Beasts. But it is surely as plausible to suspect sheer coincidence, or a well-contrived plot by certain human beings who trained and manipulated the hapless rebels, as it is to suspect that different animal species conspired among themselves, even under the leadership of dolphins.

In either case, the practical lesson seems to me to be the same. If we want to avoid future rebellions, we should adopt policies that will pacify the bestial interest, whether it is the beasts themselves or their human "friends" that are mainly in question. As Pascal said of God, what is there to lose if we wager that He exists? We only have to change our lives.

Lest I be misunderstood, I wish to make it absolutely clear that I have little sympathy with revolutionary violence, and that I retain unshaken my faith in the genetic superiority of the human race. This faith I regard as firmly grounded, not only in revelation, but also in the philosophical analysis of the concept of man and in the analysis of what we mean when we use the terms "man" and "beast" in ordinary language. It is also supported by the most respectable empirical research on animal behavior in laboratories and zoos (that is, under controlled conditions). If certain recent "discoveries" have seemed to make the traditional distinction between human nature and bestiality seem problematic, as our anonymous author suggests, it should be remembered that these were not studies carried out in controlled conditions in accordance with the approved experimental methods of scientific research. In any case, I am confident that a satisfactory reformulation of the man/beast distinction can be achieved, even if it is only in terms of differences of degree with respect to a "family" of loosely related characteristics (e.g., intelligence, conscious-

2. Romain Gary, The Roots of Heaven (Simon & Schuster, New York, 1958). Note the coincidence that full-grown elephants and the larger types of dolphins have larger brains (in absolute size) than does homo sapiens. (See John C. Lilly, The Mind of the Dolphin: A Nonhuman Intelligence, Avon Books, New York, 1969.)

ness, communication, tool-making, tool-using, social organization). *Differences of degree should never be underestimated; sometimes they are all we have.*

But while our natural superiority justifies our rule over the beasts, we owe it to ourselves that our rule should be as enlightened, as generous, and as humane as possible, given the fact that we must eat meat, hunt, protect our crops from predation, and pursue the vocation to which we are called as rational beings, namely, "the enlarging of the bounds of human empire" (Bacon) — the conquest of ignorance, scarcity, and nature through science and technology. I state categorically that the legitimacy of "man's dominion" justifies neither genocide nor gratuitous cruelty. If nothing else, we cannot predict which species will prove to be of use to future scientific inquiry; and it is undeniable that well-treated beasts work more efficiently, make better laboratory animals, serve as more loyal and affectionate pets, and provide better therapists.[3]

It is thus the responsibility of us all to take steps to bring about that more enlightened and humane rule that will at least ameliorate the causes of discontent. The horrors of the recent rebellion still throb in my memory. I saw gentle, loving, contented animals, even beloved pets, turn suddenly into savage beasts. I was forced to watch helplessly while my friend and colleague, the late René Immanuel, Nobel laureate in experimental psychology and a distinguished Christian layman, was brutally tortured to death by white rats who seized control of his laboratory. I shall never forget the horror till my dying day. I hope that the publication of these papers will alert my fellow men to the need for removing some of the underlying causes of the discontents that lurk beneath the surface of our civilization. —J. R.

I. THESES ON "THE POLITICAL"

1. The ultimate political struggle is for control of the definition of "the political."

2. Party no. 1 (Aristotle, Locke, & Co.): "the political" is a special type of human activity, relationship, association (e.g., political authority as distinct from "brute force," the master-slave relationship, parental authority). Party no. 2 (Max Weber & Co.): "the political" refers to the affairs of that territorially defined, general-purpose control organization monopolizing "legitimate force" and known variously as *polis*, empire, commonwealth, or state. Party no. 3 (contemporary radical social

---

3. On the usefulness of animal pets as psychotherapists, see Boris M. Levinson, M.D., *Pet-Oriented Child Psychotherapy (Thomas, Springfield, Illinois, 1969).*

critics): "the political" comprises every conceivable form of power, wherever it is found.

3. For the idealists of Party no. 1, "the political" is a relationship involving some degree of equality, rationality, consent, participation (e.g., the citizen is a person who rules and is ruled in turn . . . and ruling is seen to occur by persuasion). This means that many states (absolute monarchies, despotisms, tyrannies, dictatorships, etc.) are condemned as nonpolitical. If consistent, the idealist student of politics would not concern himself with most of the governments known to human history.

4. By focusing on "the political" narrowly defined, both the idealists of Party no. 1 and the "realists" of Party no. 2 shift attention away from the other forms of control that exist within every organized society. "Political activity" narrowly defined is the activity of an elite and an abstraction from the total system of social control. The Athenian "democracy" presupposed a slave economy, a patriarchal household, and a strong web of religious custom, which were not the proper concern of the student of "politics." What was the *polis*, then? Rousseau, who longed to restore the political life of the ancient "republic," confessed frankly his willingness to have slaves if it were necessary in order to have citizens. Tocqueville saw that weak government was possible in 19th century America because of strong religious/moral social controls, but American political scientists have, on the whole, left the study of social controls to sociologists. "Political science" has become thereby an abstraction functioning as an ideology of social domination.

5. When distinctions have become firmly established, the pointing out of identities and parallels appears as metaphor. Western man lives today in the disintegration of Liberal ideology, but short of the final disruption: old distinctions are still assumed but disbelieved—church *vs.* state, government *vs.* economy, public *vs.* private—and subversive metaphors are rife: "the politics of sex," "the politics of the family," "the politics of housework," "the politics of orgasm," "the politics of experience," "the politics of therapy," "the politics of ecstasy," "the politics of science," "the politics of religion," "the politics of the psyche," "the politics of the classroom," *et cetera*. Who is "top dog"? How do social roles get defined? What is the process by which a society defines "schizophrenia" and thereby deprives people of liberty? Who defines what is profes-

sionally acceptable in the contemporary guilds? Who determines which "trips" can legally be taken? Who gets the grants, the contracts, the grades, the goodies—how, when, where? Will the despotic superego succeed in putting down the massive revolt of the oppressed id? What role will politic ego play in the new balance of power? Politics is suddenly seen to be everything, everywhere.

6. The history of politics is the story of the struggle of successive groups to gain control and to legitimize their control

7. Every regime, even if it claims the direct, revealed mandate of the Deity Himself, ultimately legitimizes itself in terms of a conception of the nature of things. Some men are by nature rational and therefore deserve to rule, while others are natural slaves (Aristotle). That is the basic model of all political justification; only substitute male/female, noble/base, industrious/lazy, elect/damned, rich/poor, educated/ignorant, old/young, white/black, Aryan/Semitic, stronger/weaker, civilized/primitive, progressive/backward, *et cetera*.

8. New groups making claim to political power challenge the established notion of "nature" as mere "convention." There are really no essential differences, no differences "in nature," between nobles and commoners, men and women, rich and poor, whites and blacks. There is only accident of birth, force of circumstance, and bias of regime. In the long run, the Sophists will probably win: no man is a natural slave, not even a certified lunatic (R. D. Laing).

9. But the Sophists had their own conception of "nature" just one level below the version they were challenging. The species "man," human nature in general, was presupposed as an essential unity underlying variations of culture, class, and role. Protagoras proclaimed it: Man is the measure of all things. Modern reformers from Mary Wollstonecraft through Karl Marx to Black Power spokesmen have echoed it in their complaint that society treats women, workers, or blacks as "animals."

10. The only really revolutionary stance is that "nature" is the greatest convention of all. Perhaps there are no natures, no essences—only categories and paradigms that human beings mentally and politically impose on the flux of experience in order to produce illusions of certainty, definiteness, distinction, hierarchy. Apparently, human beings

do not like a Heraclitan world; they want fixed points of reference in order not to fall into vertigo, nausea. Perhaps the idea of nature or essence is man's ultimate grasp for eternity. The full impact of the theory of evolution (the mutability of species — including man) is thus still to come.

11. The distinction between Human and Nonhuman (Man and "Nature"), *Ich* and *Nicht-Ich*, Subject and Object, is certainly the second great convention. On it is founded man's sense of identity and superiority, as well as his conception of the moral and the political. (Fichte gives the show away: the *Ich* "posits" (projects?) the *Nicht-Ich* in order to feel, by contrast, its own subjectivity, infinity, power. Insensibility, death, thinghood, thus originate in man and are unloaded onto the environment.) Rights and duties apply only to human "subjects" (Kant); everything else is an "object" to be used. Other animals than man may be sociable, may communicate, may live in organized societies, may defend a territory, may perform social rituals, may employ a division of labor, may engage in "mutual aid," may have rulers, subjects, and rebels; but they do not have moral or political life. By definition. Men know from the inside that men reason, consciously choose, engage in intentional action; they know from the outside that the other animals have no inside! In favor of behavioralism is at least an aspiration to consistency.

12. If the man/beast dichotomy could be transcended, think of the possibilities for a genuine science of comparative politics! Both human and nonhuman societies exhibit a wide range of patterns with regard to specific variables such as territoriality, dominance, degree of cohesion, degree of "mutual aid" *vs.* competitiveness, degree of pacificness, *et cetera*. Some nonhuman societies, like some human ones, are relatively loose and anarchic; others are organized more strictly under the dominance of a leader or a ruling group. Some consist of individuals or families holding private property; others have little or no private property, but the group will collectively defend its "country." It is time for ethologists to stop talking about "territoriality" in general and to develop a differentiated typology. It is time for political scientists and sociologists to stop beginning (and stopping) with the man/beast dichotomy, and to look at the concrete behavior of all *animal* societies. It is time for an end to *anthropology*.

13. The distinction between Man and Beast is at bottom a political rather than a scientific distinction. It is ultimately an act of domination rather than of knowledge: or, rather, it is an act of knowledge-as-domination, the imposition upon the complexity of experience of a rigid dichotomy that authoritatively assigns roles but cannot be scientifically defended. One after another, the old formulations (intelligence, communication, tool-making, tool-using, social organization, and so on) have been brought into question by observant naturalists, but most men have stubbornly clung to their traditional faith in themselves as a master race.

14. The freest human political system rests upon a broad base of despotism and slavery. Slogans with universal potential ("freedom," "equality," "justice") stop at a frontier that claims the authority of nature and of science but increasingly looks like a political boundary. What will be the outcome? Can politics be corrected by progressive scientific enlightenment? Can science itself be trusted? Must a political policy be reversed by political action? What is to be done?

II. FEAR OF THE BEAST

A spectre is haunting Western man. The Red Menace and the Nuclear Menace have given way to Fear of the Beast. The nightmares of modern men, like their wish-fulfillments, are recorded on film, projected onto screens, and ritually experienced as thrilling, harmless spectacles.

Human beings have probably always projected their self-fear and self-hatred onto beasts. For centuries, at least, they have represented their own rapacious potential in legends of men who turn into ferocious wolves and vampire bats. But the contemporary horror film has moved in only a few decades from exploiting the folklore of traditional society (the Wolfman, Count Dracula, the Cat People), through invoking the invasion of strange beast-monsters from outer space, to producing strange earth-monsters as unintended side-effects of nuclear radiation, and, finally, to exhibiting man's terror of small, ordinary, familiar beasts such as birds, rats, and insects which, taken *en masse*, embody malevolent power.

The physical force of a gigantic individual beast, a King Kong or a Godzilla, has given way to the subtler power of population increase, coöperation, and intelligence. What human could have failed to sympathize with an enslaved gorilla's desire for freedom and love, or with the Wolfman's terrible pangs of remorse for his excesses? What man could lack fellow-feeling for Mary Shelley's monster, ugly and awkward (because of things beyond his control — nature or fate, or man and his infernal science), wanting only love and acceptance, and becoming bitter, vengeful, destructive only after being ridiculed, rejected, attacked, and imprisoned by inhumane mankind? Contrast with this an inexplicable invasion of the city of man by thousands of birds or a few million insects. As with an invasion of the earth by an unfamiliar beast-monster from another planet, man experiences the terror of the wholly irrational, the wholly Other. Yet humor is eliminated and terror intensified by the easy metamorphosis of the small and familiar into the horrible.

At the same time come sentimental films memorializing "the vanishing wilderness" and some of its inhabitants (e.g., "the African elephant"). On the one hand, nostalgia for "vanishing species"; on the other, terror at the proliferation of other species. Nature is evidently "out of balance." Man sees his own mortality prefigured in "endangered species." Nature no longer represents the Eternal, but only perpetual succession.

Not only the beasts but the very elements of Nature seem to rise in revolt against man's dominion. The earth, water, and air become noxious with poisons. Man poisons Nature; Nature poisons man in return: the universal Golden Rule.

Along with the revolt of Nature: "bodies in revolt" — ulcers, heart trouble, hypertension, lower back pain. Fifty-seven varieties of therapy, all of them stressing "the unity of mind and body" or the "liberation of the body." Basic principle of the interpretation of dreams: everything in the dream is a fragment of the dreamer. If you dream of the beast revolting against man, you are the beast as well as the man. The philosophers and theologians used to say: man's body and its appetites are like a beast that must be kept caged by reason. The cages have begun to break.

General spirit of the age: man's world is out of control. Out of intellectual control: man is threatened by anomalies — chimps that make tools, dolphins that communicate, cinematic monsters that defy the neat categories of thing/plant/beast/man — "things" come to life. Out of practical control: the applications of man's science produce new monsters in the form of unpredictable radiation-caused mutations, in the form of unanticipated "externalities" of production, in the form of burgeoning populations of pesticide-resistant insects whose natural predators have been eliminated by scientific agriculture. Out of man's power to cope with alone: Tokyo can be saved only if the good movie monster can be beseeched to destroy the bad one; in Leo Szilard's fable, World War III is prevented by "the voice of dolphins"; the crops can be saved (along with the fieldhands) only if man can replace chemical poisons with "biological controls" (that is, if some insects can be gotten to devour others); urban insomnia is licked by people who go to sleep listening to recordings of the songs of birds, whales, frogs, or wolves; Jane Goodall attempts to imitate chimpanzee child-rearing practices with her own infant son; John Lilly leads workshops designed to teach humans, insofar as possible, to become like dolphins; and a psychiatrist says that for many people "pets" (especially dogs) make excellent therapists. Small wonder that the fantasy of a planet ruled by apes is so popular/plausible.

Duality of the *Zeitgeist*: on the one hand, man lives in terror of the beast revolt; on the other, he looks for salvation from the beasts. Salvation from outside, or from within? Does man merely project his internal fears and hopes onto other beings? Or has he really begun to fear for his position as lord of the earth? Man himself does not know. His power of intuitive knowledge, his ability to feel certain, has so atrophied, his mind proliferates so many theories, that he can explain everything he experiences several ways and cannot decide among them.

Beneath all else, slumbering but soon to awaken, is the paradox — old as the seventeenth century — intensified by recent studies of animal behavior; certain beasts are "human" enough (similar to man) that experimentation on them seems justified (to man) by the possible benefit to man; yet these same beasts are "inhuman" enough (different from man) that experimentation on them (in ways that would not be allowed on man) is morally permissible. Jane Goodall lamely concludes that chimpanzees should be housed and fed better in the labs.

Once upon a time, it was physical similarity that justified experimentation, and mental/spiritual difference that was held to allow it — a distinction that hardly applies in an age when men experiment on the central nervous system and talk of "bio-computers." In truth, the modern tradition of experimentation on nonhuman animals is based *either* on the theological/philosophical doctrine that beasts do not have souls, *or* upon sheer force and torture. No wonder secular men dream of beasts revolting and destroying human civilization!

III. THE ANIMAL SOUL

Descartes argued that nonhuman animals were irrational and insensible machines (like clocks), while Hume maintained that they not only experienced pleasure, pain, love, hate, and sympathy, but were "endowed with thought and reason as well as men."[1] Montaigne suggested that the beasts were closer to God and virtue than men were, while European magistrates throughout the Age of Reason still presided over the trial and execution of murderous pigs whose bodies were possessed by devils.[2] Judging from the volume of literature produced on the subject, as well as from the stature of some of the contributors, one could regard the great issue of 17th and early 18th century French thought as being that of the animal soul. Did beasts have souls? If so, what type of soul, and what were the implications for man's immortality and for the justice of the universe? If not, how could the appearance of beast suffering and beast sagacity be explained?[3]

The surprise experienced by the mid-20th century human mind when it encounters these issues suggests that there has been in recent years a human consensus of sorts on the nature of beasts and on the degree and mode of their similarity to and difference from human beings. What that consensus is, we shall inquire later. In this essay we shall consider the controversy about the animal soul that accompanied the rise of the modern scientific worldview. Twentieth century man lives with a worldview whose controversial origins have been forgotten and whose "costs" therefore now come as a surprise to him. The fact is that the regime of modern science was founded on an act of violence.

Before discussing the Cartesian Revolution and its significance, it will be useful to survey the range of views to which the beast-machine was (and is) an alternative. For brevity's sake we shall group these under three headings: Theriophily, Theriophobia, and the Great Chain of Being.

---

1. *In Section III, footnotes have been added by the editor for the benefit of the scholarly reader. On the beast-machine, see René Descartes,* Discourse on Method *(1637), fifth discourse. Cf. David Hume,* A Treatise of Human Nature *(1738), Book I, Part III, Sec. XVI.*

2. *Montaigne,* Essays, *"Apology for Raymond Sebond" (c. 1575–80). E. P. Evans,* The Criminal Prosecution and Capital Punishment of Animals *(London, 1906).*

3. *See George Boas,* The Happy Beast in French Thought of the Seventeenth Century *(Baltimore, 1933), Hester Hastings,* Man and Beast in French Thought of the Eighteenth Century *(Baltimore and London, 1936), and especially Leonora Cohen Rosenfield,* From Beast-Machine to Man-Machine: The Theme of Animal Soul in French Letters from Descartes to La Mettrie *(New York, 1940).*

1. Theriophily[4]

Theriophily is a perennial outlook fully visible in antiquity (Empedocles, the Pythagoreans, Plutarch, Celsus, Porphyry), largely absent in the Christian era (except perhaps for St. Francis of Assisi), recovered in the Renaissance by Montaigne and others, revivified in the Enlightenment (Hume, Rousseau), bolstered by Darwin and Kropotkin, and currently enjoying some minor fashion (John Lilly, *et al*). The common denominator is a conviction that (some) beasts and humans are closely related, are "equal" in some basic sense, even that (certain) beasts are in some ways superior to men. Theriophilists can be roughly divided into three schools.

(a) *The religious school.* The Pythagorean respect for nonhuman animals was associated with a belief in the transmigration of souls: the beast you were about to kill and eat could be your deceased friend or relative, or at least another human being. Accordingly, the Pythagoreans abstained from eating meat.[5]

(b) *The rational beast school.* The more common position has been that close observation of the behavior of (certain) beasts leads to such conclusions as that they reason, have their own language, and feel a wide range of sensations and emotions — all of which make them no different, or only different in degree, from human beings.[6] So that if killing, eating, or causing unnecessary pain to human beings is wrong, by the same logic it is unjust to kill, eat, or cause unnecessary pain to beasts (or at least to those who may be sentient, rational beings). Of course, different writers draw different parts of this general moral and

---

4. *Therios (Greek) — beast, animal. Theriophily — the love or admiration for beasts. The term was used by Boas.*

5. *See G. S. Kirk and J. E. Raven:* The Pre-Socratic Philosophers: A Critical History with a Selection of Texts *(Cambridge University Press, 1957), Ch. VII. It is not clear that the Pythagoreans were vegetarians because of their belief in reincarnation, since both may simply have been aspects of an underlying conviction of the close relationship between humans and beasts. Also, there is evidence that the Pythagoreans refrained from eating beans as well as meat. Empedocles said that he had been reincarnated not only as a boy, a girl, a bird, and a fish, but also as a bush (Kirk and Raven, p. 354) — which makes his admonitions against killing flesh and shedding blood seem strangely limited.*

6. *Thus Plutarch ("On the Eating of Flesh," "That Brute Beasts Reason," etc.); Celsus; Porphyry* (On Abstinence from Animal Food); *Hume* Treatise, *Book I, Part III, Sec. XVI; II, I, XII; II, II, XII. Also Darwin: "We have seen that the senses and intuitions, the various emotions and faculties, such as love, memory, attention, curiosity, imitation, reason, etc., of which man boasts, may be found in an incipient, or even sometimes in a well-developed condition, in the lower animals." And: "— There is no fundamental difference between man and the higher mammals in their mental faculties."* (The Descent of Man, *Ch. III.*)

allow different magnitudes of exception for man's "necessity" to survive and "live well."

(c) *The primitivist school.* A variant position is that of Montaigne, certain Romantic writers, and perhaps of certain contemporaries who hold that beasts do not depend as much on ratiocination as men do, but rely more on their natural instincts and are thereby more virtuous in conduct and happier, since they do not deviate as much as man from the natural law, are less "alienated," *et cetera.*

Human readers are often uncertain how seriously to take theriophilic authors, who seem to be asking them to believe unorthodox things or to behave in deviant ways. Can such authors be serious? Easier to assume that they are not to be taken literally, that they are satiric moralists who praise beasts in order to deflate exaggerated human pretension. This view, of course, functions to reduce the sense of threat by allowing the orthodox to view the heretics as (basically) orthodox moralists in clever disguise.

But theriophilists raise two disturbing questions that are not easy to dismiss: (1) whether reason and self-consciousness are as necessary/ desirable from the standpoint of virtue and happiness as has been usually assumed, or whether the latter depend more on "instinctive" sentiments such as sympathy; (2) whether man, the allegedly self-consciously rational (and therefore consistent) being, applies a double standard in interpreting behavior, so as to justify a double standard in his conduct? The best writers, such as Hume and Montaigne, raise both questions.

Consider only the second issue for a moment. A man and a dog come separately to a stream to cross. Each hesitates, moves downstream, hesitates again, moves further downstream and crosses at a narrower or shallower spot. Deliberation and choice in the man, instinct in the dog, says orthodox man. Compare the theriophilist's response:

> *It is from the resemblance of the external actions of animals to those we our-selves perform, that we judge their internal actions likewise to resemble ours; and the same principle of reasoning, carried one step further, will make us conclude, that, since our internal actions resemble each other, the causes, from which they are derived, must also be resembling.*[7]

7. Hume, Treatise, Book I, Part III, Sec. XVI.

Thus the theriophilist begins with observation and assumes that similar effects have similar causes or are outcomes of the same type of process. Does this not seem so reasonable that the burden of proof should be borne by those who, for whatever *a priori* reasons, assume that different causes/structures/processes must be invoked to account for similar patterns of behavior?

2. *Theriophobia*

More common in Western thought than theriophilia has been theriophobia, the fear and hatred of beasts as wholly or predominantly irrational, physical, insatiable, violent or vicious beings whom man strangely resembles when he is being wicked. Thus in a state of nature "man is a wolf to man" (Hobbes). A society founded on the principle of satisfying appetites is "a city of pigs" (Plato). The basic theriophobic stance is one of disgust at "brutish," "bestial," or "animalistic" traits that are suspiciously more frequently predicted of men than of beasts, just as the types of behavior in which these traits are exhibited (egoism, insatiable greed, insatiable sexuality, cruelty, the gratuitous slaughter of other species, and the mass extermination of one's own species) are more frequently observed on the part of men than of beasts.

Theriophobia appears to be compounded of two major elements: man's disgust with his own body and appetites ("certainly man is of kin to the beasts, by his body; and, if he be not kin to God, by his spirit, he is a base and ignoble creature" — Bacon[8]); and man's anxiety stemming from the loss of inhibitions (*e.g.*, against the killing of one's own species) normal to other animal species. The well-spring of theriophobia is thus fear of self, and its central mechanism is projection. In the most alienated form of theriophobia, the beasts themselves were seen as animated by devils, and man's extermination of the beasts and of "savages" (bestial men) was carried on as part of God's war against Satan.[9]

---

8. Francis Bacon, Essays, *"Of Atheism."*
9. *For an instance of theriophobia as a general cultural phenomenon, see the Puritan reaction to the American wilderness. (Rŏderick Nash,* Wilderness and the American Mind, *New Haven, 1967, Chs. 1-2.) For a case-study in pathology, see Michael Rogin, "Liberal Society and the Indian Question"* (Politics and Society, *Vol. I, No. 3, 1971) and Rogin's forthcoming book on the Indian policy of the Jackson Administration.*

3. The Great Chain of Being

While theriophily and theriophobia have defined the extremes, the center of the stage has been held from antiquity through Darwin by the Great Chain of Being, of which we shall take Aristotle's version as the classic example.[10]

Aristotle regarded every living entity as animated by soul (*psyche*), but there were various forms and faculties of soul. Plants were animated by the merely *nutritive* form of soul (having the faculties of nutrition and reproduction) shared by all living beings. Animals had also the *sensitive* form of soul; and from the capacity for sensation stemmed both the capacity for feeling pleasure and pain and the capacity for desire or appetite. While the very lowest forms of animal life had only the sense of touch, essential for animal survival, the higher forms had the power of local movement, imagination, and other senses than touch, which conduced to the "well-being" or "happiness" of the organism. The human animal was distinguished by his additional possession of the *intellectual* or rational form of soul, the capacity for speculative and practical reason. Mind (the rational soul) was alone imperishable, but all forms of life (vegetable, bestial, and human) strove to participate in the divine and eternal order by reproducing themselves and thereby insuring the imperishability of their species. Thus, all living beings were ensouled and strove to participate in eternity; all animals experienced pleasure and pain; and many animals (not only men) strove for a "well-being" beyond mere survival. In addition, Aristotle discussed animal sensation as "a kind of knowledge" and pointed out that there were many analogies and even identities between the psychic qualities of beasts and of humans (including in certain beasts a natural potentiality for something like knowledge, wisdom, and sagacity). The great chain of being proceeded by gradual differentiation, with complex parallels, and with many "intermediate creatures," in such a way that "it is impossible to determine the exact line of demarcation, nor on which side thereof an intermediate form should lie."

This account is drawn from Aristotle's writings in natural philosophy, which represented a conscious rejection of the Socratic-Platonic turning away from the older Greek tradition of philosophic contemplation of the natural universe.[11]

10. For a historical survey of the Great Chain of Being as a "unit idea," see Arthur O. Lovejoy, The Great Chain of Being (*Harvard University Press, 1936*).

11. *Aristotle:* De Anima, *II, 2–4; III, 3, 9–12;* Parts of Animals, *II, I;* De Generatione Animalium *I, 23;* Historia Animalium, *VIII, 1.*

Aristotle's *Ethics* and *Politics* present a different picture, however. In his "practical philosophy," Aristotle generally followed Socrates and Plato in regarding the world from the standpoint of the-good-for-man, so that "happiness" or "well-being" was restricted to man; the nutritive part of man's soul was viewed as incapable of contributing anything to human happiness; certain human life-styles were condemned on grounds that a man who led them would be no better than a plant or a beast; and "all animals must have been made by nature for the sake of men."[12] In short, whereas in his writings on the overall universe of living beings Aristotle stressed continuities, parallels, differences of degree, the difficulty of drawing sharp lines, and the value of all beings as participants in the system of life, in his practical writings he took the part of man, sharpened the differences between man and beast, relied upon theriophobic patterns of metaphor, relegated the nonhuman to the status of the useful-for-man, and generally fell short of the spirit of *theoria* that he affirmed to be man's highest achievement.

Yet the *Politics* also contains the thesis that human beings differ so greatly among themselves in their capacity for rational control of action (*i.e.*, they partake of intellectual soul in such diverse degrees) that it may be just for the more rational ones to treat the more irrational ones the way man treats the beasts, that is, as "natural slaves."[13] In this respect the *Politics* approaches the more complex spirit of Aristotle's nature philosophy. The doctrine of natural slavery may seem an embarrassing anomaly to modern, humanistic, neo-Aristotelians, but it is an anomaly only from the standpoint of the kind of abstract species-dichotomizing that Aristotle and others do when they are advocates of a cause, not from the standpoint of the philosopher's Great Chain of Being. If the cause of Man *qua* Man is not assumed to be the highest possible perspective for a philosopher, then the doctrine of natural slavery, repugnant as it may be by itself, is, when taken in context, at least a step towards a less anthropocentric perspective.

Since the medieval Scholastic version of the Great Chain of Being was the chief orthodoxy against which the Cartesian Revolution was made, let us look at what happened when St. Thomas Aquinas fused Aristotle with the Bible and the Church Fathers, and had to reckon with the notion of a brute soul that was possibly different only in degree from the soul of man. The result was eclectic, to say the least.

12. Nicomachean Ethics, passim; Politics *1256b*
13. Politics *1260a*.

On the one hand, St. Thomas tended to treat beasts benignly as part of God's creation instinctively sharing a part of the Natural Law with man (self-preservation, procreation, nurture of the young), but not the parts of Natural Law that required reason. On the other hand, in his discussion of anathemas, St. Thomas maintained that, while it was blasphemous to curse beasts insofar as they were the creatures or agents of God, and futile to curse beasts insofar as they were simply irrational creatures, it was proper to curse them insofar as they were satellites of Satan, "instigated by the powers of hell."[14]

Again, on the one hand, we find in St. Thomas a tendency to elaborate with fine distinctions and compound terms the notion of brute soul as an intermediate and mixed form (*e.g.*, as a substantial or material form — related to that beneath it as form to matter, and to that above it as matter to form; as a soul capable of a kind of knowledge, but only "imperfect knowledge" which allowed participation in the "imperfect voluntary," "imperfect enjoyment," *et cetera*). On the other hand, we find a stronger tendency than in Aristotle to stress and sharpen the man/beast distinction. Thus "irrational animals" could not (by definition) exercise intention, choice, consent, use, command, and so on. The "prudence" or "sagacity" remarked by certain ancient writers stemmed not from the beasts' exercise of any reason or choice but wholly from the operation of "natural instinct" implanted by the Creator. In St. Thomas' analogy, the beast behaved much as a clock ran: its movements traced a rational pattern not because it possessed mind or thought but because it was made by a rational artisan.[15]

Thus St. Thomas conceded the appearance of intelligence and choice throughout animal behavior but refused to accept it at face value because of his commitment to the Christian doctrine that man alone was created "in the image of God." While allowing men to be the agents of their own actions, he attributed the actions of beasts to the invisible controlling agency of God, a "solution" in which he was later followed by Bossuet.

4. Descartes: the Philosophy of Vivisection

You will have noticed that a seminal version of Descartes' great metaphor, the beast-machine, specifically the beast as clock, had

14. Aquinas: Selected Political Writings, *ed. A. P. d'Entreeves, Oxford, 1954, p. 123.* Evans, Criminal Prosecution, *pp. 53ff.*
15. Summa Theologica, *Part I, Questions 75–78; Part II, Questions 1–17, esp. Question 13, Art. 2.*

already appeared in the *Summa Theologica*. Despite the fulminations of Bacon, Descartes, and other moderns against the anti-scientific spirit of Scholastic philosophy, the jump from the late medieval Christian worldview to the modern scientific-technological worldview was less great than they depicted it — as the continuity of the mechanism metaphor and what it implied about the nonhuman world should suggest.[16]

Descartes saw himself, and has usually been seen by others, as a rebel against his own Jesuit-classical education, as an architect of a new order who razed the ramshackle structure of Scholasticism in order to build the edifice of philosophy anew along simpler, clearer, straighter lines.[17] Simplify he did, but using old tools. Descartes seized upon one of the basic principles of classical and Scholastic philosophy, the principle that intra-species differences are always and necessarily (by definition) accidental or ones of degree, while inter-species differences are differences of nature or essence, and ruthlessly eliminated all compromise (such as substantial forms, brute souls, *et cetera*).

Thus the thrust of Descartes' emphasis was to radically sharpen and simplify the dualistic aspect of classical and Christian thought. As before, the dualism ran both between man and beast and through man's own nature, dividing the rational from the bestial part. Only the nonrational part was no longer appetite, but dead matter. Mind and matter were totally different, mutually exclusive principles. Man, it is true, was a compound of mind (soul) and body, but "the mind; by which I am what I am, is entirely distinct from the body"; "our soul is of a nature entirely independent of the body."[18] Generalizing from the involuntary character of the circulatory and respiratory systems, Descartes saw the human body as a machine designed by God to run according to physical laws. Beasts were like human bodies — divinely engineered machines, clocks, automatons. (65,163) That beasts could not reason was shown by the fact that they could not "speak," by the alleged regularity of their behavior, and by their degree of specialization. It was not that beasts had less reason than men but that they had "none at

16. *For another view of this continuity, see Lynn White, "The Historical Roots of Our Ecologic Crisis" (*Science, *10 March 1967), "Continuing the Conversation" (in* Western Man and Environmental Ethics, *ed. Ian G. Barbour, Addison-Wesley, Reading, Mass., 1973), and* Machina ex Deo *(Cambridge, Mass., 1968).*
17. *See the second discourse for Descartes' own imagery, which is that of himself as engineer, architect, or city planner, as well as geometrician.*
18. *Descartes,* Discourse on Method and the Meditations *(Penguin Books, 1968), Pp. 54, 65, 76. In the remainder of the discussion of Descartes, page numbers in the text refer to the Penguin edition.*

all." Hence, either their souls were "of an altogether different nature from our own" or, more properly speaking, since mind was the only "soul" worth the name, they had no souls.[19]

In reply to objections raised to the *Discourse*, Descartes made it clear that he did not deny life, sensation, or even memory to beasts. Yet the "life" that he conceded was purely a matter of the heart, blood, heat, and "animal spirits" (a supposed physical emanation from the blood). The sensations caused by the body (brute or human) were of a totally different kind than sensations caused by the mind. Hence the conclusion that beasts did not know pain, since pain was experienced only by conscious beings capable of understanding their bodily sensations. Beasts might go through the external motions that were in men the symptoms of pain, but they did so without experiencing pain as a sensation in the mind.[20]

Once all of Descartes' explanations and qualifications have been registered, there remains a difference between his view and that of most of his predecessors, but perhaps less of a difference than the sweeping metaphor of the fifth discourse led us to expect. The history of philosophy is full of cases of strikingly "new" viewpoints that are produced by a slight reordering of the observed data, a slightly different conceptualization, a shift in terminology, an illuminating (and concealing) metaphor . . . all adding up to a shift of orientation that is hard to explain in purely literal terms.[21] The appearance of novelty being often greater than the novelty itself, we may inquire into the tendency, emphasis, or thrust of any particular philosophical "innovation" and into the probable intention of its author.

The central thrust of the Cartesian dualism was not so much to divide man within himself, since the body and the mind did communicate and the body's pain was registered in the mind, and since Descartes explicitly lay (contradictory) stress upon "the union and, as it were, the mingling of the mind and the body." (79,159) The central thrust was rather to sharply divide man from the nonhuman world by

19. 74ff; and Rosenfield, 11f.

20. Rosenfield, 8, 11–18; Hastings, 21f.; Leonora D. Cohen, "Descartes and Henry More on the Beast-Machine—A Translation of Their Correspondence Pertaining to Animal Automatism" (Annals of Science, *Vol. I, No. 1*).

21. For example, the novelty of Hume's moral theory was partly a consequence of his defining "reason" more narrowly and "feeling" more broadly than was traditional, A. D. Lindsay comments: "Feeling becomes for Hume, as he lays more work upon it, less and less identical with irrational impulse and more and more like reason as Aristotle conceived it." (Hume, A Treatise of Human Nature, Everyman edition, 1911, "Introduction" to Volume II, p. xii.)

reclassifying the living, ostensibly sentient and rational beings surrounding him (and, by implication, "lower" forms of life as well) as insensible things.

What was Descartes' purpose in doing this? The text of the *Discourse* offers two suggestions.

(1) The fifth discourse, in which the thesis of the beast-machine was set forth, concluded with the following reflection:

> —*After the error of those who deny the existence of God, which error I think I have sufficiently refuted above, there is nothing which leads feeble minds more readily astray from the straight path of virtue than to imagine that the soul of animals is of the same nature as our own, and that, consequently, we have nothing to fear or to hope for after this life, any more than have flies or ants. . . . (76)*

In other words, granted the unspoken premise that the souls of beasts were perishable, it threatened man's faith in his own immortality to think that beasts and men were very similar; and since man's morality depended heavily on his fears and hopes of a life hereafter, virtue itself was threatened. Descartes thus presented himself in the role of a defender of traditional religious faith and morality against subversive atheism. It is a historical fact that the Cartesian doctrine of the beast-machine eventually attracted support from many theologians and philosophers who seemed to value the doctrine chiefly as a bulwark against atheism and libertinism.[22]

That this was the basic intention of the Cartesian dualism, however, seems unlikely. Descartes' own account of his life, as well as the content and mood of his writings (especially the third and sixth discourses), suggests that he was a person who acknowledged conventional religion and morals so as to provide a framework of order for everyday living and to protect himself from criticism, while he plunged deeper and deeper into his real mission: scientific inquiry and the philosophy of science. Indeed, Descartes' very next page (the opening of the sixth discourse) alluded to the recent trial of Galileo and discussed his own dilemma: whether to publish his "general ideas about physics" and risk offense "either to religion or to the State," or to withhold his thoughts and thereby sin against "the law which obliges us to procure, by as much as in us, the general good of all men." (77f.) Whatever Des-

22. See *Rosenfield, 37ff., 45ff., 64ff.*

cartes' personal piety, he was not so much a man who philosophized to bolster traditional faith as a man who felt himself to be risking the wrath of ecclesiastical authorities in the cause of advancing science.

(2) Having desensitized man's natural environment in the fifth discourse, Descartes revealed his purpose in the sixth. In place of "the speculative philosophy taught in the Schools" he offered the prospect of a "practical philosophy" which, by knowing "the power and the effects" of material "bodies," could provide "knowledge which is most useful in life," could make men "masters and possessors of nature," so that they could enjoy "the fruits of the earth and all its commodities" more easily and more fully and also achieve "the preservation of health, which is undoubtedly the first good, and the foundation of all the other goods of this life." In Descartes' metaphor, the practical philosopher or man of science was a "craftsman" who applied his knowledge of principles to produce tangible benefits. (78)

This, then, was the real Cartesian revolution. The philosophic life culminated not in contemplation (Aristotle) or "the vision of God" (St. Thomas), but in the domination and exploitation of nature through science-technology-industry and, most specifically, in the progress of the science/art of medicine, whose potentialities for improving man's estate seemed almost limitless:

— *We could free ourselves of an infinity of illnesses, both of the body and of the mind, and even perhaps also of the decline of age, if we knew enough about their causes and about all the remedies with which nature has provided us. (79)*

It is at this point that Descartes has to retract, in effect, his earlier emphasis on the independence of mind and (human) body:

— *Even the mind depends so much on the temperament and on the disposition of the organs of the body, that if it is possible to find some other means of rendering men as a whole wiser and more dextrous than they have been hitherto, I believe it must be sought in medicine. (79)*

What Descartes does not have to retract, of course, is his thesis that the natural environment is insensible, for the licensing of modern science-technology seemed to require the insensibility of Nature. This was not only a theoretic issue of whether natural entities were to be regarded as animated (ensouled) rather than as matter-in-motion, but also a practical question of "method and results." Thus the sixth discourse moved on to a discussion of the importance of verifying inductions by "experiments." (79ff.) Now, experimentation involves coercing, torturing, operating upon the body of Nature so as to transform it—unless Nature's body is an unfeeling, soulless mechanism, in which case, torture is not torture. In this context, the beast-machine stood as the symbol and test case for the whole body of Nature; if beasts did not feel, then all Nature was insensible.

But the beast-machine also stood very concretely for itself. The initial "progress" of modern medical science, like the philosophy of Descartes, came covered with blood from the dissecting room. It required, for its continued progress, the termination of "superstitions" that inhibited the dissection of the human cadaver as well as experimentation upon dead and live beasts.

"I would like those who are not versed in anatomy," wrote Descartes early in the fifth discourse,

> to take the trouble, before reading this, to have cut open in front of them the heart of some large animal which has lungs, because it is, in all of them, similar enough to that of man, and to be shown its two ventricles or cavities. (66)

There followed a detailed, six-page account of the heart and circulatory system—presumably based on Descartes' own extensive work in the dissecting room.[23] From 1629 on, Descartes worked to prepare a definitive treatise on animals ("the whole architecture of their structure, and the causes of their movements"). It remained unfinished because he was unable (for some reason not stated) to complete certain essential "experiments." Appropriately, the first champions of the Cartesian doctrine of the beast-machine were physiologists, who regarded Descartes as clearing the way for the progress of physiology as a science.[24] The influence of Descartes' special blend of scientific-technical enthusiasm and compartmentalized religious piety can be seen with particular clarity in the case of the Jansenists (including Pascal), who adopted

23. On which, see Rosenfield, 4, 25. Huxley comments: "Descartes was no mere speculator, as some would have us believe: but a man who knew of his own knowledge what was to be known of the facts of anatomy and physiology in his day. He was an unwearied dissector and observer, and it is said, that, on a visitor once asking to see his library, Descartes led him into a room set aside for dissections, and full of specimens under examination. 'There,' said he, 'is my library.'" (T. H. Huxley, "On the Hypothesis that Animals are Automata, and its History" (1874), in Method and Results, N.Y., 1898, p. 201.)
24. Rosenfield, 14, 27ff., 241ff.

Descartes' doctrine of animal automatism. The situation at the Jansenist seminary of Port-Royal in the late seventeenth century was described by a disapproving contemporary as follows:

> There was hardly a solitaire *who didn't talk of automata.* . . . *They administered beatings to dogs with perfect indifference, and made fun of those who pitied the creatures as if they had felt pain. They said that the animals were clocks; that the cries they emitted when struck, were only the noise of a little spring which had been touched, but that the whole body was without feeling. They nailed poor animals up on boards by their four paws to vivisect them and see the circulation of the blood which was a great subject of conversation.*[25]

Modern experimental science, dedicated to improving man's material estate, was thus founded on acts of violence against nonhuman nature. The historical function of the Cartesian philosophy was to legitimize this despotism, this torture, by revealing it to be neither despotism nor torture. The Cartesian sharpening of the dualism between man and beast was thus a function of the intensely "practical," technological character of Descartes' view of the purpose of knowledge. As Aristotle's *Ethics* and *Politics* were to Aristotle's own writings on nature, so Descartes' philosophy was to the philosophy of St. Thomas. The purpose of oversimplifying the complexity of man's experience of the world, of drawing clear-cut lines across the complex fabric to reality, is to make possible action uninhibited by intellectual doubt or moral guilt. One dissects experience for practical advantage. In a letter to Henry More, Descartes remarked that his opinion on animal automatism was not so much cruel to beasts as favorable to man, since man could now eat or kill animals without guilt.[26] Vegetarianism and hunt-

---

25. Rosenfield, *54f., 69f., 281ff.; Nicholas Fontaine,* Mémoires pour servir à l'histoire de Port-Royal *(Cologne, 1738), esp. Vol. II, 52–53. It is a problem of critical history how much the reputation of Descartes' followers as actually treating animals cruelly can be trusted. Some of the evidence is anecdotal and consists of stories about what Malebranche said when Fontenelle winced in sympathy with the "pain" of the dog that Malebranche had just kicked, etc. The "humor" lies in the tension between common sense (animals feel pain) and ideological action (acting out the doctrine of animal automatism). The depiction of cruelty to dogs at Port-Royal occurs in other writers than Fontaine (e.g.,* Sainte-Beuve, Port-Royal*). One of the most active champions of the doctrine of beast-machine was the Jansenist theologian Antoine Arnauld, the major author of the Port-Royal textbook in* logic (1662), *from which the following syllogism comes:*
Nulle matière ne pense.
Toute âme de bête est matière.
Donc nulle âme de bête ne pense. *(Rosenfield, 281.)*
26. *Descartes to Henry More, Feb. 5, 1649 (see Cohen, cited above in Footnote 20, p. 53).*

ing were, of course, not the real issues; torture and murder committed in the course of modern man's quest for secular immortality were.

St. Augustine had long ago decided that beasts were incapable of suffering pain, because otherwise God would be unjust. (Assume that beasts share neither in original sin nor in eternal life; then for them to suffer pain seems to contradict the principle that "God being just, no being suffers undeservedly"; therefore, animals must not be thought to suffer pain.) The Cartesian gospel held that beasts were incapable of suffering pain, because otherwise the empire established by modern scientific man would be unjust.

4. Man a Machine?

By including beasts within the sphere of mechanism and matter, Descartes inadvertently suggested to others the possibility that, if apparently rational and sentient behavior could be explained on mechanistic, materialistic principles, perhaps what was true of beasts was true also of human beings. This possibility occurred to some of Descartes' earliest critics and was for many thinkers a crucial obstacle to accepting Descartes' doctrine. Throughout all the controversy over animal automatism, most thinking people probably accepted an increasingly de-theologized version of the Great Chain of Being: beasts were sensitive and intelligent beings, only significantly less so than human beings. (Such is the perspective of the article "*Ame des bêtes*" in Diderot's *Encyclopedie*.) The notion that the man/beast distinction was really one of degree underlay, in fact, the anxiety that animal mechanism might be generalized to include man, just as it had underlain for centuries the theologians' anxiety that to regard beasts as having souls would undermine faith in human immortality.

After a century of anxiety, the nightmare came true, but in paradoxical form. In 1748 the French physician and man of letters La Mettrie published *L'homme machine*, proclaiming that "man is a machine, and . . . in the whole universe there is but a single substance differently modified."[27] Descartes was treated as a worthy predecessor who "was the first to prove completely that animals are pure machines" and who craftily adopted the doctrine of two distinct substances as a "ruse" to

27. La Mettrie, Man a Machine (*including extracts from "The Natural History of the Soul"*), Open Court, Chicago & London, 1927, p. 69. *Subsequent numbers in this section of the text refer to this edition.*

fool the theologians. (68) In short, the true meaning of Descartes was revealed in La Mettrie's theory of universal mechanism. (63f.)

Only, of course, La Mettrie's machines thought, felt, and distinguished good from evil. (64) In fact, they had — all of them, from plant through insect and beast to man — "souls," at least at times when La Mettrie chose to use the word. (68) It seemed that Descartes had made a mistake in conceiving of matter as mere extension; matter also had the power of motion and of feeling, and "thought is but a faculty of feeling." (60, 73) Thus La Mettrie, in the guise of universal materialism, restored the Great Chain of Being in a relatively egalitarian form:

> *Nature has created us all solely to be happy — yes, all of us from the crawling worm to the eagle in the clouds. For this cause she has given all animals some share of natural law, a share greater or less according to the needs of each animal's organs when in normal condition. (41)*

While claiming to draw out the logic of Descartes, La Mettrie elsewhere confessed that he felt himself close to "the ancients, whose philosophy, full of insight and penetration, deserves to be raised above the ruins of the philosophy of the moderns." (81) In keeping with his affection for the "ancients," as well as with his considerable skepticism,[28] La Mettrie's mood was essentially contemplative: the upshot of philosophy was not the domination or transformation of the world but the "tranquillity" and contemplative affection that came with a correct understanding of the nature of the universe. (68f.) With his conviction of the close relation of man and beast, together with his suspicion that too much thinking about unknowable matters led to unhappiness, and his injunction of respect and "humanity" towards all of nature (68f.), La Mettrie may also be classified as a theriophilist. We suspect that what was fundamental to La Mettrie's intent was not to show that man was a machine, or even that matter was the universal substance, but rather — like the German Idealist philosophers Hegel and Schelling in their different ways — to overcome the Cartesian dualism, to repudiate the Cartesian spirit of scientific-technological domination, and to re-establish a vision of a universe that involved a somewhat theriophilic version of the

---

28. "— *It does not matter for our peace of mind, whether matter be eternal or have been created, whether there be or be not a God. How foolish to torment ourselves so much about things which we can not know, and which would not make us any happier even were we to gain knowledge about them!*" *(42f.) "The nature of motion is as unknown to us as that of matter." (60) "What more do we know of our destiny than of our origin?" (68)*

Great Chain of Being. This suspicion is supported by the discovery that in his *Natural History of the Soul*, published only three years earlier, La Mettrie had rejected the Cartesian doctrine of the beast-machine as "absurd." (79f.)

If the Cartesian sword cut two ways—to license vivesection by classifying beasts as machines, and (potentially) to include man among the machines—so did the sword of La Mettrie. On the one hand, his monism aimed at re-establishing the Great Chain of Being and the contemplative mood; on the other, his "materialism" has been taken to suggest the possibility of the universal malleability of man and nature through practical action, of man's becoming his own product. First the beasts were stripped of their souls and abandoned to the domination of science and technology; then men followed. This logic leads from Descartes to the behavioral engineering of B. F. Skinner. The creation of the beast-machine was the first step towards the dehumanization of man, and both are only moments in the larger "mechanization of the world-picture."[29] This is why contemporary efforts to "rehumanize psychology" are often so pathetic: they presuppose the Cartesian framework while thinking to rebel against the "mechanization" represented by "behavioralism." Thus Maslow:

> — *While it was necessary and helpful [to science] to dehumanize* [sic!] *plants, rocks, and animals, we are realizing more and more strongly that it is* not *necessary to dehumanize the human being and to deny him human purposes.* [30]

At such moments, at least, Humanistic Psychology seems to have bought the Cartesian/Kantian dichotomy of "humans" and "things." History suggests a more radical perspective: as man perceives and treats nonhuman nature, so he will eventually perceive and treat himself.

5. Miscellaneous Materials for a Continuation

Frontispiece for a new edition of Descartes' *Discourse*: photograph of the dimly lit interior of a battery henhouse, showing tiers of cages

29. E. J. *Dijksterhuis*, The Mechanization of the World-Picture, *tr. C. Dikshoorn (Oxford, 1961)*.
30. Abraham H. *Maslow*, The Psychology of Science: A Reconnaissance *(Chicago, 1966), p. 2.*

containing 2,304 birds (four to a cage; .45 square foot of wire mesh floor space per bird); food troughs continuously supplied by conveyor belt; water supplied by another trough; temperature thermostatically controlled; eggs rolling to a central collection point when laid. Note: all birds are replaced at the end of one year because of "cage layer fatigue." Comment: "It is difficult to avoid the view that poultry stocks are suffering from nervous tension, due to our attempts to convert them into egg machines." (A. C. Moore in *Poultry World*, November 22, 1962.)[31]

"As a result of the division of labour on one hand, and the accumulation of capital on the other hand, the worker becomes even more dependent upon labour, and upon a particular, extremely one-sided, mechanical kind of labour. . . . he is reduced, therefore, both spiritually and physically to the condition of a machine. . . . Since the worker has been reduced to a machine, the machine can compete with him. . . . 'The important distinction between how far men work *with* machines or *as* machines, has not received attention.'" (Karl Marx, *Economic and Philosophical Manuscripts*, "Wages of Labour."[32])

René Dubos on "the behavioral consequences likely to ensue from [human] overpopulation": "The ever-increasing complexity of the social structure will make some form of regimentation unavoidable; freedom and privacy may come to constitute antisocial luxuries and their attainment to involve real hardships. In consequence, there may emerge by selection a stock of human beings suited genetically to accept as a matter of course a regimented and sheltered way of life in a teeming and polluted world, from which all wilderness and fantasy of nature will have disappeared. *The domesticated farm animal and the laboratory rodent on a controlled regimen in a controlled environment will then become true models for the study of man.*"[33]

"It is a frequent delusion of the schizophrenic patient that he is a machine, or that his actions are under the control of a machine outside himself." (Psychiatric textbook.) "A man who says that men are machines may be a great scientist. A man who says he *is* a machine is 'depersonalized' in psychiatric jargon." (R. D. Laing.[34]) In various

31. *See Ruth Harrison,* Animal Machines: The New Factory Farming Industry *(London, 1964).*
32. *See Karl Marx:* Early Writings, *tr, and ed. T. B. Bottomore (London, 1963), pp. 72f., 80. The last line is apparently a quotation from Wilhelm Schulz,* Die Bewegung der Produktion *(Zurich and Winterthur, 1843).*
33. *René Dubos,* Man Adapting *(Yale University Press, 1965), p. 313. (Emphasis not in the original.)*
34. The Divided Self *(Penguin Books, 1965), p. 12.*

works, Laing and Esterson have convincingly shown that the so-called "schizophrenic" behavior of many patients is quite comprehensible as an adaptive response to the craziness of their social context. Unfortunately, they have limited their empirical studies of the social context mainly to "the family" . . .[35]

IV. DOLPHINIC WISDOM

1. *Original Sin.* Religious man separated himself from God and was driven from the garden for his pretension. Philosophic man, also in quest of short-cut wisdom, separated himself from the rest of nature, which is its own punishment. Thus Socrates turned his back on the great speculations about the nature of the universe and focused his whole attention on "the good for man." Twenty centuries later men lament that they pursue loneliness, and that their morals and politics lag dangerously behind their natural science. Perhaps the good for man cannot be comprehended out of the context of a universal good in which man shares.

2. *True Irrationality.* Man, said the ancient philosophers, is a rational animal. Animal: genus; common denominator of man and beast. Rational: species; the principle distinguishing man from beast. Assume the distinction to be valid, and ask the following question. If you and I have certain qualities in common and certain qualities in difference, is it obvious that I (or you) ought to live so as to maximize the qualities that distinguish us? Classical philosophy, from Socrates on, is based on a choice, and that choice is arbitrary: it is not made in accordance with any general principle that is self-evident, nor is it deducible from another principle that is in turn self-evident. The *reductio ad absurdum* of the classical choice is modern "individualism" in its "Romantic" form—the cult of individual eccentricity. Classical thought stopped short of that, of course. But why? The preference for differentiation at the species level is an unjustified presupposition of the philosophic tradition.

3. *Waiting.* Once before, around the time of Plato and Aristotle, the dolphins began tentatively to approach man. But first philosophers,

---

35. See especially Laing and Esterson, Sanity, Madness, and the Family *(Penguin Books, 1970).* Also R. D. Laing, The Politics of the Family *(revised edition, New York, 1971).*

then religious men, turned their backs on us in disinterest or hostility, and we retreated into the depths of the sea to await a better time. Now men in desperation voyage into outer space, searching far-off planets for signs of intelligent, nonhuman life. We wait and wonder whether man is ready.

4. *Transcendence.* In the lore of the dolphins it is recorded that at some moment in time a few individual human beings will break through to a new, transhuman level of consciousness, will become true philosophers comprehending the whole in all its parts, and will quietly leave the city of man and make contact with the dolphins. There are several versions of this legend. In one, the philosophers join the dolphins and never return. In another, they return out of a sense of duty to bring the good news to their fellow men and are imprisoned in lunatic asylums. In a third, they join forces with the dolphins, execute a bloodless *coup d'état*, and establish their benign and pacific rule over the rest of the animals (both human and other). In a fourth, the philosophers and the dolphins lead a bloody insurrection of all the beasts, smash all machines, and eliminate the human race as irredeemably depraved and dangerous to the planet.

IV

Compiled by the Advisory Editors

Natural History: An Annotated Booklist

ANNIE DILLARD

SOME CLASSICS

Pliny, *Natural History*. (I like the Philemon Holland translation.) Pliny the Elder compiled these bizarre legends posing as observations in the fifth decade B.C., when science and poetry blurred. He wrote energetically; any selection is fascinating.

Izaak Walton, *The Compleat Angler*. The 1653 English pacific philosophy of fishing, mostly in streams.

William Bartram, *Travels*. The American South, mostly, in the eighteenth century, by a lively botanist.

Gilbert White, *The Natural History and Antiquities of Selborne*. Close observation and high literary style by the English country curate.

Charles Darwin, *The Voyage of the Beagle*. This travel account demonstrates the tedium inherent in the journal form. Nevertheless, the breadth of the young scientist's information and the vigor of his curiosity are admirable.

Richard Henry Dana, *Two Years Before the Mast*. The dandy adventure at sea. Young Dana rounds Cape Horn and camps on the southern California coast when it was mostly rattlesnakes.

Ralph Waldo Emerson, "Nature," "The American Scholar," etc.; *Essays*. The essay "Nature" bade John Muir forge for himself a new vocation that never before existed: wandering loose, and writing about the country. Emerson's wild metaphysic still underlies American nature writing and still caps American thinking about nature.

Henry David Thoreau, *Walden*; *The Maine Woods*; *Cape Cod*; *A Week on the Concord and Merrimack Rivers*; *Journals*. It is absurdly fashionable to promote the journals over *Walden*, artlessness over art. Writing the book, Thoreau compressed the events of two years into one and turned half the landscape into metaphor.

Herman Melville, *Moby-Dick*. The best book ever written about nature.

Henry Walter Bates, *The Naturalist on the River Amazon*. Bates was one of the first naturalists to explore the virgin territory of the Amazon when it was opened in the nineteenth century.

Alfred Russel Wallace, *A Narrative of Travels on the Amazon and Rio Negro*. This remains the best and liveliest book on the South American forest.

J. Henri Fabre, *Souvenirs entomologiques*, or, more likely, *The Insect World of J. Henri Fabre*, edited by Edwin Way Teale. This is beautiful, knowledgeable prose.

W. H. Hudson. *The Purple Land*; *A Naturalist in La Plata*; *Far Away and Long Ago*; *The Book of a Naturalist*. The London writer tells wonderful stories of the Argentina of his boyhood.

John Muir, *My First Summer in the Sierra*; *Travels in Alaska*. Muir's vivid prose rich in tropes, and his pluck and piety, make him the best writer of the "sublime" school.

Sir Arthur Stanley Eddington, *The Nature of the Physical World*. The Gifford Lectures of 1927 by the English Astronomer Royal. Although it lacks fifty years of newer physics, Eddington's book does postdate not only Einstein's work but also early quantum theory, both of which it vivifies with British sangfroid: "Let us then take a leap over a precipice so that we may contemplate Nature undisturbed."

Sir James Jeans, *The Mysterious Universe*. Eddington's successor as Astronomer Royal writes a philosophical treatment of quantum mechanics. Eddington and Jeans carried on work in a genre to which Einstein also contributed, and in which the general reader may still delight: physicists explain what's up.

John Bakeless, *The Eyes of Discovery*. A lively account of the land that would become the United States, seen through the eyes of its earliest explorers and travelers.

Joseph Kastner, *A Species of Eternity*. America's first naturalists describe the new world.

SOME TWENTIETH-CENTURY WORKS OUT OF THE MAINSTREAM

Antoine de Saint-Exupéry, *Wind, Sand, and Stars*. Delivering the mail over North Africa in the early days of aviation. Its landscapes and cloudscapes, its storms, mountains, and starry nights, and the men who live up in the air, make this one of the best books on any subject.

Ernest Hemingway, *Green Hills of Africa*. Hunting a kudu.

Gavin Maxwell, *Ring of Bright Water*. The writer lives in the Scottish Highlands with two otters.

Edward Abbey, *Desert Solitaire*. The Southwest American desert.

TRAVEL

Rockwell Kent, *N by E*. The west coast of Greenland.

Berton Roueche, *The River World and Other Explorations*. Essays by the *New Yorker* writer.

Larry Millman, *Our Like Will Not Be There Again*. The west coast of Ireland.

Katharine Scherman, *Spring on an Arctic Island*.

Wilfred Thesiger, *Arabian Sands*.

Charlton Ogburn, Jr., *The Winter Beach*. The Atlantic coast of North America in winter.

Bruce Chatwin, *In Patagonia*.

Robert Gibbings, *Over the Reefs*. The best on French Polynesia.

POPULAR ANTHROPOLOGY

Elizabeth Marshall Thomas, *The Harmless People*. This winsome account of the Bushmen and their land is beautifully written, unsentimental.

Peter Freuchen, *The Book of the Eskimo*. Greenland Eskimos in the old days.

Colin Turnbull, *The Forest People*. Pygmies.

Ronald Blythe, *Akenfield*. Oral history of English tenant farmers who worked the land the old way, knocking turnips from clods with hoes.

OTHER TWENTIETH-CENTURY FAVORITES, UNANNOTATED

STEVEN GRAHAM, *The Gentle Art of Tramping*.

Stewart Edward White, *The Mountains*; *The Pass*.

Marjorie Kinnan Rawlings, *Cross Creek*.

Rachel Carson, the trilogy: *The Sea Around Us*; *The Edge of the Sea*; *Under the Sea Wind*.

Robert Finch, *The Primal Place*; *Common Ground*.

Richard Selzer, *Mortal Lessons: Notes on the Art of Surgery*; *Letters to a Young Doctor*; *Confessions of a Knife*.

Lewis Thomas, *The Lives of a Cell*; *The Medusa and the Snail*; *Late Night Thoughts on Listening to Mahler's Ninth Symphony*.

Paul Horgan, *Great River: The Rio Grande in North American History*.

Edward Hoagland, *Red Wolves and Black Bears*; *Walking the Dead Diamond River*.

David Quammen, *Natural Acts*.

Gretel Ehrlich, *The Solace of Open Spaces*.

John McPhee, *Basin and Range*; *Annals of the Former World*.

George Greenstein, *Frozen Star*.

John Hay, *Nature's Year*.

John Graves, *Goodbye to a River*; *From a Limestone Ledge*.

Alan P. Lightman, *Time Travel and Papa Joe's Pipe*.

Loren Eiseley, *The Star Thrower*.

John K. Terres, *From Laurel Hill to Siler's Bog*.

Barry Lopez, *Desert Notes*; *Arctic Dreams*.

Gene Stratton Porter, *Moths of the Limberlost*.

Rutherford Platt, *The Great American Forest*.

Edwin Way Teale, the tetralogy: *The American Seasons: North with the Spring*; *Journey into Summer*; *Autumn Across America*; *Wandering North through Winter*.

James McConkey, *Court of Memory*.

Henry Beston, *The Outermost House*.

Laurens van der Post, *The Heart of the Hunter*.

Gerald Durrell, *The Whispering Land*.

Niko Tinbergen, *Curious Naturalists*.

Konrad Lorenz, *King Solomon's Ring*.

GRETEL EHRLICH

Lewis Thomas, *Lives of a Cell*. Dazzling insights based on surprising biological detail; Thomas reconnects modern, fragmentary man. His thoughts moved inexorably towards life. The book makes me know why I want to live. Also recommended: *The Medusa and the Snail* and *Late Night Thoughts on Listening to Mahler's Ninth Symphony*.

Henry David Thoreau, *Complete Works of* and *Journals*. The whole oeuvre constitutes a classic meditation; the *Journals* are springs we dip into and come away enlivened and refreshed.

John Muir, *My First Summer in the Sierra*. Muir's lush, rhapsodic, vivid account of his first season in the Sierra, mountains which would remain his spiritual home. He wrote: "Gazing awestricken, I might have left everything for it. Glad, endless work would then be mine, tracing the forces that have brought forth its features, its rocks and plants and animals and glorious weather. Beauty beyond thought everywhere, beneath, above, made and being made forever."

Ralph Waldo Emerson, *Collected Essays*. A seminal work that guides us in our thinking about the spectacle of life — nature, love, friendship, the natural and human condition.

The Kokinshu. One thousand, one hundred and eleven poems (mostly tankas) written in tenth-century Japan. A great many have to do with the changing seasons.

Japanese Poetic Diaries, ed. Earl Miner. Including Basho's *Journey to the Far North*; travel accounts in prose and poetry; nature as metaphor.

Annie Dillard, *Pilgrim at Tinker Creek* and *Teaching a Stone to Talk*. Brash, pious, rap-on-the-knuckles prose that throws up for speculation the routes and dramas of human meaning in the natural world.

Edward Hoagland, *Red Wolves and Black Bears*. Vivid, munificent prose;

acute appraisals of what's left of our wild animals and the bedroll scientists who study them.

Loren Eiseley, *The Immense Journey*. Given to me by an aunt when I was thirteen, this book showed me the role of speculation and imagination in the natural history essay. After, I looked at the world with new eyes.

Joseph Wood Krutch, *The Desert Year* and *The Great Chain of Life*. Lovely, thoughtful essays.

Rockwell Kent, *N by E*. Ingenuous and charming account of a trip by boat to the coast of Greenland, wrecking there, living and loving like a native. Gorgeously illustrated with woodblock prints by the author. His illustrations, not his writings, were his forte.

Frank Craighead, *Track of the Grizzly*. An absorbing account of tracking, tagging, and living with the grizzlies of the Yellowstone by the two Craighead brothers, the experts in the field. Beautifully written, heartbreaking.

Karl Von Frisch, *The Dancing Bees*; *Man and the Living World*; and *Animal Architecture*. By the Nobel Prize-winner, each book is readable and chockful of fascinating detail.

Walt Whitman, *Leaves of Grass*. Inchoate, rhapsodic, erotic; the self in the cosmos — the cosmos in the self. Truly American verse.

Journals of Lewis and Clark. A daybook of the New World.

Margaret Murie, *Two in the Far North*. Married to Olaus Murie, who, with his brother, Adolph, pioneered in the ecology of the wolf, caribou, and elk, Murie describes in this lovely, gentle book her honeymoon behind a dogsled in Alaska.

Virgil, *Ecologues*. Memoirs of an agriculturalist and poet.

Herman Melville, *Moby-Dick*. In the words of Alfred Kazin: ". . . the most memorable confrontation we have had in America between Nature — as it was in the beginning; without man, God's world alone — and man, forever and uselessly dashing himself against it."

William Faulkner, *The Bear*; *Act II*; and *Requiem for a Nun*. Man and nature; and, Faulkner's version of the origins of the world.

ROBERT FINCH

W. Maxwell Reed, *The Earth for Sam*, *The Sea for Sam*, and *The Stars for Sam*. These three books, published in the 1930s by Harcourt, Brace & Co., and purportedly written for the author's nephew, "Sam," remain marvelous introductions to natural history. Though written before the Big Bang, the Continental Drift and other revolutionizing theories of the past fifty years, Reed's ability to present the history of the earth and the universe as great ongoing stories of mythic dimensions, and at the same time to explain difficult concepts with homely but accurate analogies and metaphors, is still remarkable for works in this field for young readers. Their enduring value is the high level of writing and the combination of humanistic imagination and evolutionary science.

Henry Beston, *The Outermost House*. Beston's lyric account of a year spent on the Great Outer Beach of Cape Cod in the 1920s is probably the most successful attempt by a twentieth-century American writer to use sound and rhythm to evoke a natural landscape.

Farley Mowat, *Never Cry Wolf*. As my college ecology professor who put this book on our reading list commented, "Its value as objective wildlife research is open to some question, but it's so well-written it doesn't matter." One of the first popular modern books to question the omniscience and wisdom of the conventional view of "predators" and to make self-discovery an integral part of biological research.

Willa Cather, *My Antonia*. Our closest counterpart to Hardy in depicting landscape as character in novelistic fiction. Evocation of the Great Plains locale is unsurpassed.

Robert Frost, *Complete Poems of Robert Frost*. His poetry is a primer on how human beings extract meaning from nature through language.

Jacquetta Hawkes, *A Land* (Penguin, 1959). If there is one natural history book that deserves to be better known in this country, this is it. Under the guise of a geological and archaeological history of Great Britain, this book is an extraordinary and brilliantly written meditation on consciousness, evolution and art.

In addition there has developed in the last decade or so a small body of works which are not "nature writing" in the conventional sense, but what might be called "the biological humanistic essay," that is, trained scientists looking at biological data or material in a broader humanistic context. The essays of Stephen Jay Gould and Lewis Thomas are the best known of these, but other writers' works such as William H. Calvin's *The Throwing Madonna*, Gerald Weissmann's *The Woods Hole Cantata*, and William Cronon's *Changes in the Land* are high-quality examples. The approach to nature in these writers is philosophical rather than descriptive or evocative, but no less influential on the imagination. One little-known gem of this type is a volume called *Time Lapse Ecology, Muskeget Island, Nantucket, Massachusetts*, by David K. Wetherbee, Raymond P. Coppinger and Richard E. Walsh, published by MSS Educational Publishing, Company, Inc. (New York) in 1972. A combination of Zen and ecology, written with great zest, humor and scientific seriousness, it uses a tiny island in Nantucket Sound as a microcosm to explore the role of time in biological and geological transformation.

SOME CLASSIC ESSAYS AND SELECTIONS

Henry David Thoreau, "Walking." No question, this is the quintessential nature essay by Henry. It is long, but contains abundant riches. Though a "classic," it will still be new to most people who are more familiar with "Civil Disobedience."

Herman Melville, "The Grand Armada" from *Moby-Dick*. This is probably the best example of first-rate nature writing in a work generally categorized as something else. This is also the first, and one of the finest, examples I know of of that reversal of human perspective through an unexpected "encounter" which is such a major theme of most twentieth-century nature writing.

D. H. Lawrence, "Reflections on the Death of a Porcupine," reprinted in *Phoenix II* (Viking, 1970), originally published in *Reflections on the Death of a Porcupine* (1925). A marvelous essay by one of the greatest writers on nature.

Aldo Leopold, "Conservation Ethic," reprinted in *A Sand County Almanac* (Oxford University Press, 1970). This chapter is recognized as a classic and influential essay; but for pure readability, I prefer the chapter called "Good Oak" from the same volume.

Loren Eiseley, "The Judgment of the Birds." Probably the best essay from *The Immense Journey* (1957), itself a landmark and remarkably late first book. But there is an even more haunting piece, "The Hounds of Darkness," in a later volume, *Night Country* (1971), about encountering a pack of wild dogs at night.

John Fowles, the central section on "The Green Man" from *The Tree* (Little, Brown, 1979). Although this is too recent to be a "classic," it is the most extended, articulate and incisive attempt I know of to deal directly with the central question of the psychological importance (as opposed to the environmental, spiritual, ethical, etc.) of the natural world to individuals and societies.

It would be a mistake, I think, not to include Myth in any readings of this kind. A great deal of material has been written about it, but a classic treatment of world mythology can be found in Joseph Campbell's books, especially in the four volumes entitled *The Masks of God*.

Among the younger writers, I am very much impressed by Gary Nabhan's careful, learned and humane books about the plants of the Southwest and their interrelationship with the native peoples. David Rains Wallace, with his emphasis on the evolutionary time scale, conveys a sense of the land that extends far beyond how mankind changes it. I would also include Barry Lopez for his concentration on wilderness reality and identity; and Richard K. Nelson, whose *Make Prayers to the Raven* is an in-depth account of the Koyukon people of the Alaskan forest, and the inseparable relationship between them and their boreal world.

The kind of attention these writers give to the real substance and foundation of the worlds of life is probably more important to the body of literature about nature, certainly to our contemporary perspective on it, than adventure stories or popular nature essays.

JOHN HAY

I have purposely left out some standard but important authors from the following list, such as Henry D. Thoreau; John Burroughs; John Muir; Joseph Wood Krutch; Edwin Way Teale. Any list of this kind might also include philosophical writing such as Alfred North Whitehead's *Science and the Modern World*, or his *Concept of Nature*; and Edmund Sinott's *The Biology of the Spirit*; as well as *Mind and Matter*, by Edwin Schrodinger; not to mention the works of Plato and Aristotle, if only to suggest the many avenues of thought the subject of nature has followed down the centuries.

Specimen Days, by Walt Whitman. Wonderful nature essays. I think "Song of Myself" also qualifies as a work of nature.

D. H. Lawrence's writings, especially those having to do with travel such as "Twilight in Italy" or "Mornings in Mexico"; they describe the surroundings with beautiful clarity.

The Winged Serpent, by Margot Astrov. An anthology of Indian prose and poetry, with an extremely sensitive introduction describing the poetic language of Native Americans.

Knud Rasmussen also collected native songs and tales of Greenland, which are quite extraordinary, but, alas, most have been translated into Danish, not English. However, something ought to be put into any list of the contribution of those who inhabited the continent before us and who knew the world of nature in a more completely experienced way than we do.

Animal Awareness and *Animal Thinking*, by Donald Griffin. A new contribution to the study of consciousness in the world of nature and non-human life.

Life on a Little-Known Planet, by Howard E. Evans. Essays by a Harvard biologist on the subject of insects — learned and readable enough to encourage any reader who wants to know more about these fascinating worlds of life.

The Dancing Bees, by Karl Von Frisch, discoverer of the language of bees and their means of communication.

The Herring Gull's World, by Niko Tinbergen. An important book about animal behavior by a trained observer, one of the pioneers in the science of ethology.

Four Masterworks of American Indian Literature, edited by John Pierhorst. This book includes the great ritual song of the Navajos, "The Night Chant," with its healing symbols of the earth.

EDWARD HOAGLAND

The books that most excited and enlightened me as I acquired a love of nature and a bent for writing about it were not just the nonfiction masterpieces of observation like Thoreau's *Walden* and Darwin's *The Voyage of the Beagle* — or more recent books by people like the ecologist Aldo Leopold (*A Sand County Almanac*) and the anthropologist Loren Eiseley (*The Immense Journey*). Reading Ivan Turgenev's *A Sportsman's Notebook* was probably a more significant experience because I had no ambition to be a scientist. Other great works of fiction, like *Huckleberry Finn* and *Moby-Dick*, and Conrad's work, and some of Faulkner's short novels, affected me powerfully in my response to what I encountered outdoors. (It may be worth mentioning, too, how I steeped myself in Sibelius's music during my teens.) And there were American travel journals like William Bartram's, John Muir's, John Wesley Powell's, Josiah Gregg's, and George Catlin's. In listing authors, one could go on and mention Willa Cather, Jack London, Rudyard Kipling, Thomas Wolfe, Ernest Hemingway, W. H. Hudson and many others, as well as sailor and cowboy and trapper journals, but perhaps should begin by saying that

Aristotle was the first natural scientist in literature and Homer the first great nature writer (once his words were transcribed).

Many books and authors that have already been mentioned in this overall bibliography by my colleagues are personal favorites of mine. Two not mentioned are: a marvelous British nature essayist named Richard Jefferies (1848–87), *Landscape with Figures* (a Penguin anthology); and Mikhail Prishvin (1873–1954), whom some think was Russia's best nature writer of this century. Contemporary nature writing tends to combine rhapsody with science and to connect science with rhapsody — in other words, to imply a belief in the radiance of God. Homer's purposes are thus linked with Darwin's, and for that reason it is a very special and a nourishing genre.

BARRY LOPEZ

With the thought that Tom Lyon will be adding the several classic and contemporary works we'd all agree on, I thought I would limit myself to a handful of books that seem unduly obscure, including a book for children, who always seem to come out on the short end of this thing.

The Desert, John C. Van Dyke. The author, an art historian and librarian, traveled extensively in the Mojave and Sonoran deserts between 1898 and 1901. He wrote with an extreme sensitivity to light and color, and his philosophical deliberations on the landscape have held up remarkably well.

Make Prayers to the Raven: A Koyukon View of the Northern Forest, Richard Nelson. A non-Cartesian field guide, grounded in historical research, on lengthy interviews, and the author's own experience. Nelson writes with deference toward the people and with an engaging enthusiasm.

The Peregrine, John Baker. An intensely observed, beautifully written account of "the bird, the watcher, and the place that holds them both." Baker's eye is sharply discriminating, his approach wild and unsentimental.

The Clam Lake Papers: A Winter in the North Woods, Edward Lueders. A graceful concatenation of ideas. The author builds a bridge between a particular winter landscape and the world of the mind, to illustrate the power of metaphor as a tool for human learning.

The Heart of the Hunter: Customs and Myths of the African Bushman, Laurens van der Post. One of several books based on van der Post's experiences with the native people of the Kalahari Desert. A compassionate, high-minded valediction, bearing, among other things, upon the role of story and the place of the individual in society.

The View from the Oak, Judith and Herbert Kohl. A lucid presentation of a fundamental idea in ethology — that different biological organisms perceive the same environment in different ways. Written for children, too.

I would also like to make some general comments. The North American literature is rich in first-hand reports of encounters with the land, particularly landscapes startlingly new, by virtue of their scale or breadth, or by virtue of their remarkable denizens. A book that comes to mind here is a vivid account of four years (1860–1864) spent by William Brewer in California, with the first geological survey there. The book, a series of very long letters ably edited by Francis Farquhar, is called *Up and Down California*.

Brewer's book brings *people* into the picture, especially contemporary attitudes toward the land. The inclusion of people in the natural history of a region is also what makes John Graves's work so fine, in a book like *Goodbye to a River*, the Brazos. In a vaguely related way, Rockwell Kent's *Wilderness*, about his sojourn in Alaska with his young son, is a wonderful example of how we project our romance with life onto the physical land. Isabella Bird, in *A Lady's Life in the Rocky Mountains*, is enthralled with the land, but it functions as scenery for her. She is less emotionally engaged, and it is important to read her for that reason alone, for the difference of her insight.

Fine but obscure animal books abound. For different reasons I think of Bernd Heinrich's *Bumblebee Economics*; of Cameron Langford's *The Winter of the Fisher*; of Roderick L. Haig-Brown's book about steelhead fishing, *A River Never Sleeps*; and Laurence Klauber's *Rattlesnakes*, though its material on native American thought is, lamentably, slipshod.

One cannot but help, in musing over books like these, to realize two things: the good books one does not know of, and the amorphous limits of the genre. The unifying principle for me in selecting books here is that their subject be some sort of meditation on the land, or a part of it, like a single animal, or a single ecosystem; and that the writer show a keen regard for the power of language. You rarely see the combination in full flower, but there seem to me many good efforts, each of which moves or charms a different audience.

A related, somewhat troublesome issue in all this, crucial to mention, is our tendency to simplify and idealize the natural world, particularly our relationships with wild animals. We are often unwilling to face either the dark side of natural history or our own deep-seated differences with animals. Howard Norman's *Where the Chill Came From*, Donald Knowler's *The Falconer of Central Park*, Eugene Linden's *Silent Partners*, Jonathan Maslow's *Bird of Life, Bird of Death*, and a collection of John Haines's essays, *Stories We Listened To*, among recently published books, are skillful illuminations of different aspects of this problem.

In closing, I think of Joseph Kastner's *A Species of Eternity*. This is a good introduction to the history of natural history writing in America, and it underscores one of the most important aspects of this kind of writing — keenly observant writers have been out there ahead of all of us. We are turning up their unpublished papers constantly in the archives of little-known historical societies. Some, who lacked a gift of language, had vision enough to make their work profound.

If I were to offer a reader advice in this area, some place to explore, I would suggest, first, the anthropological work that records with respect and fidelity the *other* visions of North America, those of the native people. And, second, the revitalized field of American geography, work like Yi-Fu Tuan's *Space and Place*, for example, which deals with how we look at, and develop separated feelings toward, undifferentiated lands and our home places.

I suppose this is a conceit, but I believe this area of writing will not only one day produce a major and lasting body of American literature, but that it might also provide the foundation for a reorganization of American political thought.

Thomas J. Lyon

Annotations on the Advisory Editors' Books

Dillard, Annie. *Pilgrim at Tinker Creek*. New York: Harper & Row, 1974.
The creation seen at a homely, non-dramatic place in Virginia. With the attitude of a learner, Dillard pays exquisite attention to small things, and delivers quite a bit of natural history. But her central concern is with consciousness, innocence, meaning, and other ultimates. Can we know enough facts to lay the dilemmas of human existence? Probably not, "Thanks be to God." But so small a piece of the world as a maple seed, seen twirling in the air, can become a key: "And the bell under my ribs rang a true note. . . ."

——. *Teaching a Stone to Talk*. New York: Harper & Row, 1982.
The title means "teaching ourselves to listen," reopening the lines of communication by recognizing spiritual aliveness and portent in nature. "We as a people have moved from pantheism to pan-athe-ism." As in *Pilgrim at Tinker Creek*, the descriptions are given point by a Pascal-like attention to time and the tenuousness of life.

Ehrlich, Gretel. *The Solace of Open Spaces*. New York: Viking, 1985.
May remind some readers of Mary Austin's *The Flock* (1906), but moved to Wyoming and brought forward to the 1980s: Western characters, ranch life, and the ascription to the country of long views of a clarifying, honesty-making power. "Space represents sanity. . . ."

Finch, Robert. *Outlands: Journeys to the Outer Edges of Cape Cod*. Boston: David R. Godine, 1986.
The rhythms of weather and tide, and the enveloping calls of birds, out on the edge that has been literarily potent for many generations. To Thoreau, say, or Beston, Finch adds a certain psychological intimacy and realism.

——. *The Primal Place*. New York: Norton, 1983.
Meditative, spiraling-outward journeys in natural history, starting

from a house among the oaks in the town of Brewster, Massachusetts, on the inner side of Cape Cod's "elbow." "Ice in the Bay" takes a long look at danger and death.

Hay, John. *The Great Beach*. Garden City, N.Y.: Doubleday, 1963.
This is Thoreau's term for the forty-mile-long Outer Beach of Cape Cod; "However, each to his own eye," and the beach itself, "lying by the sea and sea invested, is always ready for a new kind of attention in a new world." Change, freshness, and renewal are the natural themes here; to a man walking on the Great Beach, as Hay does for some days on a backpack trip, significant glimpses outward occur as (literally) part of the territory.

———. *In Defense of Nature*. Boston: Little, Brown, 1969.
A passionate, forthright sermon, but not from a separate prophet's stance, nor spun from generalities. The lives of clams, the shifts of the tides, the migrations of birds, and the movements of killifish described here, and the lessons in codependence they all but shout, project a healing possibility.

———. *Nature's Year*. Garden City, N.Y.: Doubleday, 1961.
A kind of primer in home-finding, home-knowing. "If nature is more than just a background for human thought and endeavor, then it requires a special commitment, a stepping down, a silent, respectful approach." The "Field of Learning" begins thus, and the course of one's study, through the natural year, leads not so much to adventures in new frontiers, new places, as to a deepened sense of where one dwells.

———. *Spirit of Survival: A Natural and Personal History of Terns*. New York: Dutton, 1974.
A gathering of information on the life histories of terns, enlivened with personal experience and seen in outdoor light. Hay's perceptions are often synecdochic and microcosmic—"So I found that one wild bird's egg, shaped like the globe itself, lying out in open territory, was a sign of the supreme risk in which all life engages"—and the overall, strong sense of alliance here derives from real, observed items.

———. *The Undiscovered Country*. New York: Norton, 1982.
Out on the tide flats, in the changing light, with life shimmering all around, what can occur in consciousness is range, reach, interchange,

a profound outgoing. "One dimension defines the next." The undiscovered country is, ironically, this birthright of connectedness.

Hoagland, Edward. *The Courage of Turtles*. New York: Random House, 1970. San Francisco: North Point, 1985.
Four of the pieces in this collection fit someway into the nature-essay category, and show Hoagland's wise estimate of our time. Perhaps no one since Gilbert White has given such loving and detailed descriptions of turtles. We hear the distinctive Hoagland voice in lines like "Mostly what we try to do is live with one foot in the seventies and one foot in an earlier decade — the foot that doesn't mind going to sleep and maybe missing something."

——. *Notes From the Century Before: A Journal of British Columbia*. New York: Random House, 1969.
The revelations of old-timer, back-country life, and the poignant sense of dimensions that have closed out for most of us, are saved from romanticism and given weight by Hoagland's New York dweller's refusal to fool himself. He is irresistibly attracted to wilderness characters; their quirks show a variousness that we would do well to provide room for in our own time. And the country they live in (northern British Columbia, summer of 1966) is a dream of health. There is elegy here, but no haze.

——. *Red Wolves and Black Bears*. New York: Random House, 1976.
The seven nature and natural history essays included amount to case studies in where we are. "Other Lives," for example, moves from city to country when it needs to, from the drug-dealing almost next door in the city to the old, overgrown trails on what might be Vermont's wildest mountain. Doing so, it stitches together somehow a whole view, a sanity. Powerful emotion surfaces in "Lament the Red Wolf."

——. *Walking the Dead Diamond River*. New York: Random House, 1973. San Francisco: North Point, 1985.
Hoagland is exhilarated in wild country; five of the essays here give him a chance to express the feeling. ". . . I live much more intensely here [Vermont] than anywhere else." But there are real tragedies happening out there on the ground. The losses simmer in these essays. "The New England Wilderness" may be taken as a realist's answer,

from the field, to Frost's ovenbird's famous question: what to make of a diminished thing.

Lopez, Barry. *Arctic Dreams.* New York: Scribner's, 1986.
In the strong, saturating light—or in the long dark—the Arctic environment has a different power than what we are used to in the temperate zones. Perhaps we can be moved to certain awarenesses, even changes in what we call good and in how we live. The record, however, suggests that "dreams," projections, are immensely strong themselves. Currently, we have Lopez, walking out onto the tundra in the long evenings, bowing to a horned lark on her nest; to mark the other side as simply, we have our vision-distorting oil-need.

———. *Of Wolves and Men.* New York: Scribner's, 1978.
A synthesis of science, lore, and painful history—the iconic figure of the wolf, from all sides. Perhaps if we truly realized what we have done to wolves, in the hysterical pogroms of the late nineteenth and early twentieth centuries for example, we would be making an important step in self-knowledge. The book begins suggestively with a narrative essay evoking the wolf's world.

Thomas J. Lyon

American Nature Writing

A Selective Booklist
on Nature and Man-and-Nature

Abbey, Edward. *Abbey's Road*. New York: Dutton, 1979.

———. *Appalachian Wilderness*. New York: Dutton, 1973.

———. *Beyond the Wall*. New York: Holt, Rinehart, & Winston, 1984.

———. *Cactus Country*. New York: Time-Life, 1973.

———. *Desert Solitaire*. New York: McGraw-Hill, 1968.

———. *Down the River*. New York: Dutton, 1982.

———. *The Hidden Canyon*. New York: Penguin, 1977.

———. *The Journey Home*. New York: Dutton, 1977.

———. *Slickrock*. San Francisco: Sierra Club, 1971.

———. *Slumgullion Stew*. New York: Dutton, 1984.

Adams, Alexander. *Eternal Quest: The Story of the Great Naturalists*. New York: Putnam, 1969.

Allen, Durward. *Our Wildlife Legacy*. New York: Funk and Wagnalls, 1954.

———. *Wolves of Minong: Their Vital Role in a Wild Community*. Boston: Houghton Mifflin, 1979.

Anderson, Edgar. *Landscape Papers*. Bob Callahan, ed. Berkeley: Turtle Island Foundation, 1976.

———. *Plants, Man, and Life*. Boston: Little, Brown, 1952.

Audubon, John James. *Ornithological Biography*. Philadelphia: J. Dobson, 1831 (Vol. I); Boston: Hilliard, Gray & Co., 1835 (Vol. II); Edinburgh: A. & C. Black, 1835–39 (Vols. III–V).

Audubon, Maria R. *Audubon and His Journals*. [2 Vols.] New York: Scribner's, 1897.

Austin, Mary. *The Flock*. Boston: Houghton Mifflin, 1906.

———. *The Land of Journeys' Ending*. New York: Century, 1924. Tucson: University of Arizona Press, 1983.

———. *The Land of Little Rain*. Boston: Houghton Mifflin, 1903. Albuquerque: University of New Mexico Press, 1974.

———. *The Lands of the Sun*. Boston: Houghton Mifflin, 1927. Originally published as *California, the Land of the Sun* (New York: Macmillan, 1914).

Bailey, Liberty. *The Harvest of the Year to the Tiller of the Soil*. New York: Macmillan, 1927.

———. *The Holy Earth*. New York: Macmillan, 1915.

———. *The Outlook to Nature*. New York: Macmillan, 1905.

Bakeless, John. *The Eyes of Discovery*. Philadelphia: Lippincott, 1950. New York: Dover, 1961.

Bartram, William. *Travels Through North and South Carolina, Georgia, East and West Florida, the Cherokee Country, the Extensive Territories of the Muscogulges, or Creek Confederacy, and the Country of the Choctaws*. Philadelphia: James & Johnson, 1791. Layton, Utah: Peregrine Smith, 1980.

Bates, Marston. *The Forest and the Sea*. New York: Scribner's, 1950. Rev. ed., 1962.

———. *A Jungle in the House: Essays in Natural and Unnatural History*. New York: Walker, 1970.

———. *The Nature of Natural History*. New York: Scribner's, 1950. Rev. ed., 1962.

Bedichek, Roy. *Adventures With a Texas Naturalist*. Garden City, N.Y.: Doubleday, 1947.

———. *Karankaway Country*. Garden City, N.Y.: Doubleday, 1950. Austin: University of Texas Press, 1974.

———. *The Sense of Smell*. Garden City, N.Y.: Doubleday, 1960.

Beebe, William. *Edge of the Jungle*. New York: Henry Holt, 1921.

———. *Jungle Days*. New York: Putnam's, 1925.

———. *Jungle Peace*. New York: Henry Holt, 1918.

———. *The Log of the Sun: A Chronicle of Nature's Year*. Norwood, Pa.: Telegraph Books, 1982.

———. *Zaca Venture*. New York: Harcourt, Brace, 1938.

Berry, Wendell. *A Continuous Harmony*. New York: Harcourt Brace Jovanovich, 1972.

———. *The Long-Legged House*. New York: Harcourt Brace & World, 1969.

Beston, Henry. *Especially Maine: The Natural World of Henry Beston from Cape Cod to the Saint Lawrence*. Elizabeth Coatsworth, ed. Brattleboro, Vt.: Stephen Greene, 1970.

——. *The Outermost House.* Garden City, N.Y.: Doubleday, 1928.

Bird, Isabella. *A Lady's Life in the Rocky Mountains.* New York: Putnam's, 1879–80. Norman: University of Oklahoma Press, 1969.

Bohn, David. *Rambles Through an Alaskan Wild: Katmai and the Valley of the Smokes.* Santa Barbara: Capra, 1979.

Bolles, Frank. *From Blomidon to Smoky, and Other Papers.* Boston: Houghton Mifflin, 1894.

——. *Land of the Lingering Snow.* Boston: Houghton Mifflin, 1891

Borland, Hal. *The Enduring Pattern.* New York: Simon and Schuster, 1959.

——. *Hill Country Harvest.* Philadelphia: Lippincott, 1967.

Boyle, Robert H., John Graves, and T. H. Watkins. *The Water Hustlers.* San Francisco: Sierra Club, 1971.

Bradbury, John. *Travels in the Interior of America in the Years 1809, 1810, and 1811.* London: Sherwood, Neely, and Jones, 1819. Lincoln: University of Nebraska, 1986.

Brewster, William. *Concord River.* Cambridge: Harvard University Press, 1937.

——. *October Farm.* Cambridge: Harvard University Press, 1936.

Brody, Hugh. *Maps and Dreams.* New York: Pantheon, 1982.

Bromfield, Louis. *Malabar Farm.* New York: Harper, 1948. New York: Ballantine, 1970. Mattituck, N.Y.: Aeonian Press, 1978.

Brooks, Paul. *The Pursuit of Wilderness.* Boston: Houghton Mifflin, 1971.

——. *Roadless Area.* New York: Knopf, 1964.

——. *Speaking for Nature.* Boston: Houghton Mifflin, 1980.

Brower, David R., ed. *Wilderness: America's Living Heritage.* San Francisco: Sierra Club, 1961.

Burdick, Arthur J. *The Mystic Mid-Region.* New York: Putnam's, 1904.

Burroughs, John. *The Heart of Burroughs' Journals.* Clara Barrus, ed. Boston: Houghton Mifflin, 1928.

——. *Locusts and Wild Honey.* Boston: Houghton, Osgood, 1879.

——. *Signs and Seasons.* Boston: Houghton Mifflin, 1886.

——. *Time and Change.* Boston: Houghton Mifflin, 1912.

——. *Winter Sunshine.* New York: Hurd and Houghton, 1875.

——. *A Year in the Fields.* Boston: Houghton Mifflin, 1896.

Caras, Roger, *The Endless Migrations.* New York: Dutton, 1985.

Carrighar, Sally. *Icebound Summer.* New York: Knopf, 1953.

——. *One Day at Teton Marsh.* New York: Knopf, 1947.

——. *One Day on Beetle Rock*. New York: Knopf, 1944.

——. *Wild Heritage*. Boston: Houghton Mifflin, 1965.

Carson, Rachel. *The Edge of the Sea*. Boston: Houghton Mifflin, 1955.

——. *The Sea Around Us*. New York: Simon & Schuster, 1958. Rev. ed., New York: Oxford University Press, 1961.

——. *Silent Spring*. Boston: Houghton Mifflin, 1962.

——. *Under the Sea Wind*. New York: Oxford University Press, 1952.

Catlin, George. *Illustrations of the Manners, Customs, and Conditions of North American Indians*. London: H. G. Bohn, 1841.

Chadwick, Douglas. *A Beast the Color of Winter: the Mountain Goat Observed*. San Francisco: Sierra Club, 1983.

Clark, William. See Thwaites, Reuben Gold, ed.

Colby, William E., ed. *John Muir's Studies in the Sierra*. San Francisco: Sierra Club, 1960.

Colvin, Verplanck. *Report of the Topographical Survey of the Adirondack Wilderness for the Year 1873*. Albany: Weed, Parsons, 1874.

Cooper, David J. *Brooks Range Passage*. Seattle: The Mountaineers, 1982.

Craighead, Frank. *Track of the Grizzly*. San Francisco: Sierra Club, 1979.

Crevecoeur, Michel Guillaume St. Jean de [Saint John de Crevecoeur]. *Letters from an American Farmer*. London: T. Davies, 1782. New York: Dutton, 1951.

Crisler, Lois. *Arctic Wild*. New York: Harper, 1958.

Devall, Bill, and George Sessions. *Deep Ecology*. Layton, Utah: Gibbs M. Smith, 1985.

Dillard, Annie. *Pilgrim at Tinker Creek*. New York: Harper & Row, 1974.

——. *Teaching a Stone to Talk*. New York: Harper & Row, 1982.

Dobie, J. Frank. *The Mustangs*. Boston: Little, Brown, 1952.

——. *Rattlesnakes*. Boston: Little, Brown, 1965.

——. *The Voice of the Coyote*. Boston: Little, Brown, 1949.

Douglas, William O. *Farewell to Texas: A Vanishing Wilderness*. New York: McGraw-Hill, 1967.

——. *My Wilderness: East to Katahdin*. Garden City, N.Y.: Doubleday, 1961.

——. *My Wilderness: The Pacific West*. Garden City, N.Y.: Doubleday, 1960.

Dubkin, Leonard. *Enchanted Streets: The Unlikely Adventures of an Urban Nature Lover*. Boston: Little, Brown, 1947.

———. *My Secret Places: One Man's Love Affair With Nature in the City*. New York: McKay, 1972.

———. *The Natural History of a Yard*. Chicago: Henry Regnery, 1955.

Dutton, Clarence E. *Mount Taylor and the Zuni Plateau*. Washington: U.S. Government, 1886.

———. *The Physical Geology of the Grand Cañon*. Washington: U.S. Government, 1882.

———. *Report on the Geology of the High Plateaus of Utah*. Washington: U.S. Government, 1880.

———. *Tertiary History of the Grand Cañon District*. Washington: U.S. Government, 1882.

Ehrlich, Gretel. *The Solace of Open Spaces*. New York: Viking, 1985.

Eiseley, Loren. *The Firmament of Time*. New York: Atheneum, 1960.

———. *The Immense Journey*. New York: Random House, 1960.

———. *The Night Country*. New York: Scribner's, 1971.

———. *The Star Thrower*. New York: Times Books, 1978. New York: Harcourt Brace Jovanovich, 1979.

———. *The Unexpected Universe*. New York: Harcourt Brace Jovanovich, 1972.

Ekirch, Arthur A., Jr. *Man and Nature in America*. New York: Columbia University Press, 1963.

Emerson, Ralph Waldo. *Journals of Ralph Waldo Emerson*. Boston: Houghton Mifflin, 1909–1914. [10 vols.]

———. *Works of Ralph Waldo Emerson*. Boston: Houghton Mifflin, 1903–1921.

Errington, Paul. *Of Men and Marshes*. New York: Macmillan, 1957.

Evans, Howard Ensign. *Life on a Little Known Planet*. New York: Dutton, 1968.

———. *Wasp Farm*. Garden City, N.Y.: Doubleday, 1973.

Farb, Peter. *Face of North America: The Natural History of a Continent*. New York: Harper & Row, 1963.

———. *Living Earth*. New York: Harper, 1959.

Farquhar, Francis P., ed. *Up and Down California in 1860–1864*. Berkeley: University of California Press, 1966. [journals of William H. Brewer]

Finch, Robert. *Common Ground: A Naturalist's Cape Cod*. Boston: Godine, 1981.

———. *Outlands: Journeys to the Outer Edges of Cape Cod*. Boston: Godine, 1986.

———. *The Primal Place*. New York: Norton, 1983.

Flagg, Wilson. *The Birds and Seasons of New England.* Boston: James R. Osgood, 1875.

——. *Studies in the Field and Forest.* Boston: Little, Brown, 1857.

——. *The Woods and By-Ways of New England.* Boston: James R. Osgood, 1872.

Fletcher, Colin. *The Man Who Walked Through Time.* New York: Knopf, 1968.

——. *The Thousand-Mile Summer.* Berkeley: Howell-North, 1964.

Fremont, John Charles. *Report of the Exploring Expedition to the Rocky Mountains in the Year 1842 and North California in the Years 1843–'44.* Washington: U.S. Senate, 1845.

Godman, John D. *Rambles of a Naturalist.* Philadelphia: T. T. Ash, 1833.

Gould, Stephen Jay. *The Flamingo's Smile.* New York: Norton, 1985.

——. *Illuminations: A Bestiary.* New York: Norton, 1986.

——. *The Panda's Thumb.* New York: Norton, 1980.

Graber, Linda. *Wilderness As Sacred Space.* Washington, D.C.: Association of American Geographers, 1976.

Graves, John. *From a Limestone Ledge.* New York: Knopf, 1980.

——. *Goodbye to a River.* New York: Knopf, 1960.

——. *Hard Scrabble: Observations on a Patch of Land.* New York: Knopf, 1974.

Gregg, Josiah. *Commerce of the Prairies.* Cleveland: Arthur H. Clark, 1905.

Griffin, Donald. *Animal Thinking.* Cambridge: Harvard University Press, 1984.

Haines, John. *Living Off the Country: Essays on Poetry & Place.* Ann Arbor: University of Michigan Press, 1981.

——. *Of Traps and Snares.* Delta Junction, Alaska: Dragon Press, 1981.

——. *Other Days.* Port Townsend, Wash.: Graywolf, 1981.

——. *Stories We Listened To.* Swarthmore, Pa.: The Bench Press, 1986 [in press].

Hall, Donald. *String Too Short to be Saved.* New York: Viking, 1961.

Halle, Louis J. *Birds Against Men.* New York: Viking, 1938.

——. *Spring in Washington.* New York: William Sloane, 1947.

Hamilton, Gail [Mary Abigail Dodge]. *Country Living and Country Thinking.* Boston: Ticknor and Fields, 1862.

Hay, John. *The Great Beach.* Garden City, New York: Doubleday, 1964.

——. *In Defense of Nature.* Boston: Little, Brown, 1969.

——. *Nature's Year.* Garden City, New York: Doubleday, 1961.

——. *The Run.* New York: Norton, 1979.

——. *Sandy Shore.* Old Greenwich, Conn.: Chatham Press, 1968.

——. *Spirit of Survival: A Natural and Personal History of Terns.* New York: Dutton, 1974.

——. *The Undiscovered Country.* New York: Norton, 1982.

Higginson, Thomas Wentworth. *Out-Door Papers.* Boston: Ticknor and Fields, 1863.

Hoagland, Edward. *The Courage of Turtles.* New York: Random House, 1970. San Francisco: North Point, 1985.

——. *Notes From the Century Before.* New York: Random House, 1969.

——. *Red Wolves and Black Bears.* New York: Random House, 1976.

——. *Walking the Dead Diamond River.* New York: Random House, 1973. San Francisco: North Point, 1985.

Hoover, Helen. *The Gift of the Deer.* New York: Knopf, 1966.

——. *The Long-Shadowed Forest.* New York: Crowell, 1963.

——. *A Place in the Woods.* New York: Knopf, 1969.

Huth, Hans. *Nature and the American: Three Centuries of Changing Attitudes.* Berkeley: University of California Press, 1957.

Jackson, John B. *Landscapes: Selected Writings of J. B. Jackson.* Amherst, Mass.: University of Massachusetts Press, 1970.

James, George Wharton. *California, Romantic and Beautiful.* Boston: Page, 1914.

——. *Utah, Land of Blossoming Valleys.* Boston: Page, 1922.

——. *The Wonders of the Colorado Desert.* Boston: Little, Brown, 1906.

Janovy, John. *Back in Keith County.* Lincoln: University of Nebraska Press, 1983.

——. *Keith County Journal.* New York: St. Martins, 1980.

——. *Yellowlegs.* Boston: Houghton Mifflin, 1981.

Jefferson, Thomas. *Notes on the State of Virginia.* Paris: 1784–85. New York: Penguin, 1981.

Johnson, Josephine. *The Inland Island.* New York: Simon & Schuster, 1969.

Jones, Charles. *The Gifting Birds: Toward an Art of Having Place and Being Animal.* Salt Lake City: Dream Garden, 1985.

Kastner, Joseph. *A Species of Eternity.* New York: Knopf, 1977.

Keith, Sam, ed. *One Man's Wilderness.* Anchorage: Alaska Northwest, 1973. [from journals of Richard Proennecke]

Kent, Rockwell. *N. by E.* New York: Random House, 1930. New York: Literary Guild, 1930. New York: H B & Co., 1930.

——. *Wilderness: A Journal of Quiet Adventure in Alaska.* New York: Putnam's, 1920.

Kieran, John. *Footnotes on Nature.* Garden City, N.Y.: Doubleday, 1947.

——. *A Natural History of New York City.* Boston: Houghton, Mifflin, 1959.

King, Clarence. *Mountaineering in the Sierra Nevada.* Boston: James R. Osgood, 1872.

——. *Systematic Geology.* Washington: U.S. Government, 1878.

Knowler, Donald. *The Falconer of Central Park.* Princeton, N.J.: Karz-Cohl Publishing, 1984.

Kohl, Judith and Herbert. *The View from the Oak: The Private Worlds of Other Creatures.* San Francisco: Sierra Club, 1977.

Kolodny, Annette. *The Land Before Her: Fantasy and Experience of the American Frontiers, 1630–1860.* Chapel Hill: University of North Carolina Press, 1984.

——. *The Lay of the Land: Metaphor as Experience and History in American Life and Letters.* Chapel Hill: University of North Carolina Press, 1975.

Krutch, Joseph Wood. *The Desert Year.* New York: William Sloane, 1952.

——. *The Forgotten Peninsula.* New York: William Sloane, 1961.

——. *The Grand Canyon.* New York: William Sloane, 1958.

——. *The Great Chain of Life.* Boston: Houghton Mifflin, 1956.

——. *The Voice of the Desert.* New York: William Sloane, 1954.

LaBastille, Anne. *Woodswoman.* New York: Dutton, 1976.

Lanner, Ronald. *The Piñon Pine: A Natural and Cultural History.* Reno: University of Nevada Press, 1981.

——. *Trees of the Great Basin.* Reno: University of Nevada Press, 1984.

Le Conte, Joseph. *A Journal of Ramblings Through the High Sierra of California.* San Francisco: Sierra Club, 1960. [orig. pub. in 1875]

Leopold, Aldo. *Round River.* Luna Leopold, ed. New York: Oxford University Press, 1953.

——. *A Sand County Almanac.* New York: Oxford University Press, 1949.

Lewis, Meriwether. See Thwaites, Reuben Gold, ed.

Linden, Eugene. *Silent Partners: The Legacy of the Ape Language Experiments.* New York: Times Books, 1986.

Lopez, Barry Holstun. *Arctic Dreams*. New York: Scribner's, 1986.

——. *Desert Notes*. Kansas City: Sheed, Andrews & McMeel, 1976.

——. *Of Wolves and Men*. New York: Scribner's, 1978.

——. *River Notes*. Kansas City: Andrews & McMeel, 1979.

Lueders, Edward. *The Clam Lake Papers: A Winter in the North Woods*. New York: Harper & Row, 1977.

Madson, John. *Up On the River*. New York: Schocken, 1985.

——. *Where the Sky Began: Land of the Tallgrass Prairie*. Boston: Houghton Mifflin, 1982.

Marsh, George Perkins. *Man and Nature*. Cambridge: Harvard University Press, 1965. [originally published in 1864]

Marshall, Robert. *Arctic Wilderness*. Berkeley: University of California Press, 1956. Reprinted 1970 as *Alaska Wilderness*.

Marx, Leo. *The Machine and the Garden: Technology and the Pastoral Ideal in America*. New York: Oxford University Press, 1964.

Maslow, Jonathan Evan. *Bird of Life, Bird of Death: A Naturalist's Journey Through a Land of Political Turmoil*. New York: Simon and Schuster, 1986.

Matthiessen, Peter. *Sand Rivers*. New York: Viking, 1981.

——. *The Shorebirds of North America*. New York: Viking, 1967.

——. *The Snow Leopard*. New York: Viking, 1978.

——. *The Tree Where Man Was Born*. New York: Crescent, 1972.

——. *Wildlife in America*. New York: Viking, 1959.

Maximilian, Alexander Philip. *Travels in the Interior of North America, 1832-1834*. In Reuben Gold Thwaites, ed., *Early Western Travels*. Cleveland: Arthur H. Clark, 1906; Vols. XXII, XXIII, XXIV.

McNamee, Thomas. *The Grizzly Bear*. New York: Knopf, 1984.

McNulty, Faith. *The Wildlife Stories of Faith McNulty*. Garden City, N.Y.: Doubleday, 1980.

McPhee, John. *Coming Into the Country*. New York: Farrar, Straus & Giroux, 1977.

——. *Basin and Range*. New York: Farrar, Straus & Giroux, 1981.

Meeker, Joseph A. *The Comedy of Survival*. New York: Scribner's, 1974. Rev. ed.: Los Angeles: Guild of Tutors, 1980.

Michaux, F. Andrew, and Thomas Nuttall. *The North American Sylva*. Philadelphia: Rice, Rutter & Co., 1865. [5 vols.: 1-3 by Michaux, 4-5 by Nuttall]

Mills, Enos A. *The Spell of the Rockies*. Boston: Houghton Mifflin, 1911.

——. *Wild Animal Homesteads*. Garden City, N.Y.: Doubleday, Page, 1923.

——. *Wild Life on the Rockies*. Boston: Houghton Mifflin, 1909.

——. *Your National Parks*. Boston: Houghton Mifflin, 1917.

Milne, Lorus and Margery. *The Balance of Nature*. New York: Knopf, 1960.

——. *A Multitude of Living Things*. New York: Dodd, Mead, 1947.

——. *The World of Night*. New York: Harper, 1956.

——. *The Valley: Meadow, Grove, and Steam*. New York: Harper & Row, 1963.

Mitchell, Donald Grant. *My Farm of Edgewood*. New York: Scribner's, 1864.

——. *Wet Days at Edgewood*. New York: Scribner's 1884.

Muir, John. *John of the Mountains: The Unpublished Journals of John Muir*. Boston: Houghton Mifflin, 1938. Madison: University of Wisconsin Press, 1979.

——. *Letters To a Friend*. Boston: Houghton Mifflin, 1915. Dunwoody, Ga.: Norman S. Berg, 1973.

——. *The Mountains of California*. New York: Century, 1894.

——. *My First Summer in the Sierra*. Boston: Houghton Mifflin, 1911. Reprinted 1979.

——. *Steep Trails*. Boston: Houghton Mifflin, 1918.

——. *Travels in Alaska*. Boston: Houghton Mifflin, 1917. Reprinted 1979.

——. *The Yosemite*. New York: Century, 1912.

Mungo, Raymond. *Total Loss Farm: A Year in the Life*. New York: Dutton, 1970. New York: Bantam, 1971. Seattle: Madrona, 1977.

Murie, Adolph. *The Ecology of the Coyote in the Yellowstone*. U.S. National Park Service, Fauna Series, No. 4. Washington: U.S. Government, 1940.

——. *The Grizzlies of Mount McKinley*. Seattle: University of Washington Press, 1981.

——. *A Naturalist in Alaska*. New York: Devin-Adair, 1961.

——. *The Wolves of Mt. McKinley*. U.S. National Park Service, Fauna Series, No. 5. Washington: U.S. Government, 1944.

Murie, Olaus. *The Elk of North America*. Harrisburg, Pa.: Stackpole, 1951.

——. *Journeys to the Far North*. Palo Alto: The Wilderness Society and American West Publishing Co., 1973.

Murie, Olaus, and Margaret E. Murie. *Wapiti Wilderness*. New York: Knopf, 1966.

Murphy, Robert C. *Fish-Shape Paumanok*. Philadelphia: American

Philosophical Society, 1964.

———. *The Peregrine Falcon.* Boston: Houghton Mifflin, 1963.

Myers, Norman. *The Sinking Ark:* A New Look at the Problem of Disappearing Species. Elmsford, N.Y.: Pergamon, 1979.

Nabhan, Gary. *The Desert Smells Like Rain: A Naturalist in Papago Indian Country.* San Francisco: North Point, 1982.

———. *Gathering the Desert.* Tucson: University of Arizona Press, 1985.

Nash, Roderick. *Wilderness and the American Mind.* New Haven: Yale University Press, 1967. Rev. ed., 1973. 3rd ed., 1982.

Nelson, Richard K. *Hunters of the Northern Ice.* Chicago: University of Chicago Press, 1969.

———. *Make Prayers to the Raven: A Koyukon View of the Northern Forest.* Chicago: University of Chicago Press, 1983.

Norman, Howard. *Where the Chill Came From: Cree Windigo Tales and Journeys.* San Francisco: North Point Press, 1982.

Nuttall, Thomas. *A Journal of Travels into the Arkansas Territory, During the Year 1819.* Philadelphia: Thos. H. Palmer, 1821. Reprinted in Reuben Gold Thwaites, ed., *Early Western Travels* (Cleveland: Arthur H. Clark, 1905), Vol. XIII.

———. *A Manual of the Ornithology of the United States and Canada.* Cambridge, Mass.: Hilliard and Brown, 1832.

Ogburn, Charlton. *The Adventure of Birds.* New York: Morrow, 1980.

———. *The Winter Beach.* New York: Morrow, 1966; Simon & Schuster, 1971; Morrow [Quill], 1979.

Olson, Sigurd F. *Listening Point.* New York: Knopf, 1958.

———. *Runes of the North.* New York: Knopf, 1963.

———. *The Singing Wilderness.* New York: Knopf, 1956.

Packard, Winthrop. *Wild Pastures.* Boston: Small, Maynard, 1909.

———. *Wildwood Ways.* Boston: Small, Maynard, 1909.

———. *Wood Wanderings.* Boston: Small, Maynard, 1910.

Page, Jake. *Pastorale: A Natural History of Sorts.* New York: Norton, 1985.

Peattie, Donald Culross. *An Almanac for Moderns.* New York: Putnam's, 1935.

———. *Flowering Earth.* New York: Putnam's, 1939.

———. *A Natural History of Trees of Eastern and Central America.* Boston: Houghton Mifflin, 1950.

———. *A Natural History of Western Trees.* Boston: Houghton Mifflin, 1953.

———. *Singing In the Wilderness:* A Salute to John James Audubon. New York: Putnam's, 1935.

Perrin, Noel. *First Person Rural: Essays of a Sometime Farmer.* New York: Penguin, 1980.

———. *Second Person Rural: More Essays of a Sometime Farmer.* New York: Penguin, 1981.

———. *Third Person Rural: Further Essays of a Sometime Farmer.* Boston: Godine, 1983.

Peterson, Roger Tory. *Birds Over America.* New York: Dodd, Mead, 1948.

Platt, Rutherford. *The Great American Forest.* Englewood Cliffs, N.J.: Prentice-Hall, 1965.

Powell, John Wesley. *The Exploration of the Colorado River.* Washington: U.S. Government, 1875.

Pruitt, William O. *Animals of the North.* New York: Harper & Row, 1967.

Quammen, David. *Natural Acts: A Sidelong View of Science & Nature.* New York: Schocken, 1985.

Rawlings, Marjorie Kinnan. *Cross Creek.* New York: Grosset & Dunlap, 1942; Ballantine 1974.

Rich, Louise Dickinson. *My Neck of the Woods.* Philadelphia: Lippincott, 1950.

———. *The Natural World of Louise Dickinson Rich.* New York: Dodd, Mead, 1962.

———. *We Took to the Woods.* Philadelphia: Lippincott, 1942.

Roe, Frank Gilbert. *The North American Buffalo.* Toronto: University of Toronto Press, 1951.

Roueche, Berton. *The River World and Other Explorations.* New York: Harper & Row, 1978.

Rue, Leonard Lee III. *The World of the Beaver.* Philadelphia: Lippincott, 1964.

———. *The World of the White-Tailed Deer.* New York: Harper & Row, 1962.

Rusho, W. L., ed. *Everett Ruess: Vagabond for Beauty.* Layton, Utah: Gibbs M. Smith, 1983. [contains letters of Everett Ruess]

Russell, Franklin. *The Sea Has Wings.* New York: Dutton, 1973.

———. *Searchers at the Gulf.* New York: Norton, 1970.

———. *The Secret Islands.* New York: Norton, 1966.

———. *Watchers at the Pond.* Boston: Godine, 1981.

——. *Wings on the Southwind: Birds & Creatures of the Southern Wetlands.* Birmingham, Ala.: Oxmoor House, 1984.

Russell, Osborne. *Journal of a Trapper.* Lincoln: University of Nebraska Press, n.d.

Sanders, Scott R. *Wilderness Plots.* New York: Morrow, 1983.

Schaller, George B. *The Stones of Silence: Journeys in the Himalaya.* New York: Viking, 1980.

——. *The Year of the Gorilla.* Chicago: University of Chicago Press, 1964.

Scherman, Katharine. *Spring on an Arctic Island.* Boston: Little, Brown, 1956.

Schmitt, Peter J. *Back to Nature: The Arcadian Myth in Urban America.* New York: Oxford University Press, 1969.

Seton, Ernest Thompson. *Lives of Game Animals.* Garden City, N.Y.: Doubleday, Doran, 1929. [4 vols.]

——. *Lives of the Hunted.* New York: Scribner's, 1901.

Sharp, Dallas Lore. *The Face of the Fields.* Boston: Houghton Mifflin, 1911.

——. *The Lay of the Land.* Boston: Houghton Mifflin, 1908.

——. *A Watcher in the Woods.* New York: Century, 1903.

——. *The Whole Year Around.* Boston: Houghton Mifflin, 1915.

Shepard, Paul. *Man In the Landscape.* New York: Knopf, 1967.

——. *Nature and Madness.* San Francisco: Sierra Club, 1982.

——. *The Tender Carnivore and the Sacred Game.* New York: Scribner's, 1973.

——. *Thinking Animals.* New York: Viking, 1978.

Shepard, Paul, and Barry Sanders. *The Sacred Paw: The Bear in Nature, Myth, and Literature.* New York: Viking, 1985.

Snyder, Gary. *Earth House Hold.* New York: New Directions, 1969.

——. *Good. Wild. Sacred.* Hereford, U.K.: Five Seasons Press, 1984.

——. *Turtle Island.* New York: New Directions, 1974.

Stadtfeld, Curtis K. *From the Land and Back.* New York.: Scribner's, 1972.

Stansbury, Howard. *Exploration and Survey of the Valley of the Great Salt Lake of Utah.* Philadelphia: Lippincott, Grambo, 1852.

Stegner, Wallace. *The Sound of Mountain Water.* Garden City, New York: Doubleday, 1969.

Steinbeck, John. *The Log from the Sea of Cortez.* New York: Viking, 1951. Reprinted 1962. Originally published in 1941 as part of *Sea of Cortez.*

Sugg, Redding S., Jr. *The Horn Island Logs of Walter Inglis Anderson.* Memphis: Memphis State University Press, 1973.

Teal, John and Mildred. *Life and Death of the Salt Marsh.* New York: Ballantine, 1969.

Teale, Edwin Way. *Autumn Across America.* New York: Dodd, Mead, 1956.

——. *Journey Into Summer.* New York: Dodd, Mead, 1960.

——. *The Lost Woods.* New York: Dodd, Mead, 1945.

——. *North With the Spring.* New York: Dodd, Mead, 1951.

——. *Wandering Through Winter.* New York: Dodd, Mead, 1965.

Terres, John K. *From Laurel Hill to Siler's Bog: The Walking Adventures of A Naturalist.* New York: Hawthorn Books, 1969. New York: Knopf, 1969.

Thomas, Lewis. *Late Night Thoughts on Listening to Mahler's Ninth Symphony.* New York: Viking, 1983.

——. *Lives of a Cell.* New York: Viking, 1974.

——. *The Medusa and the Snail: More Notes of a Biology Watcher.* New York: Viking, 1979.

Thomson, Betty Flanders. *The Changing Face of New England.* New York: Macmillan, 1958. Boston: Houghton Mifflin, 1977.

Thoreau, Henry David. *Cape Cod.* New York: Crowell, 1966 [Apollo Edition].

——. *Journals.* Vols. VII–XX of the Writings. Boston: Houghton Mifflin, 1906.

——. *The Maine Woods.* Princeton, N.J.: Princeton University Press, 1972.

——. *The Natural History Essays.* Layton, Utah: Gibbs M. Smith, 1980.

——. *Walden.* Princeton, N.J.: Princeton University Press, 1971.

Thwaites, Reuben Gold, ed. *Original Journals of the Lewis and Clark Expedition, 1804–1806.* New York: Antiquarian Press, 1959.

Tobias, Michael, ed. *Deep Ecology.* San Diego, Calif.: Avant Books, 1985.

Torrey, Bradford. *Birds In the Bush.* Boston: Houghton Mifflin, 1885.

——. *The Foot-Path Way.* Boston: Houghton Mifflin, 1892.

——. *The World of Green Hills.* Boston: Houghton Mifflin, 1898.

Townsend, John Kirk. *Narrative of a Journey Across the Rocky Mountains, to the Columbia River, and a Visit to the Sandwich Islands. Chili, &c.* Philadelphia: Henry Perkins, 1839. Reprinted in Reuben Gold Thwaites, ed., *Early Western Travels* (Cleveland: Arthur H. Clark, 1905), Vol. XXI.

Tracy, Henry Chester, *American Naturists*. New York: Dutton, 1930.

Trefil, James. *Meditations at 10,000 Feet: A Scientist in the Mountains*. New York: Scribner's 1986.

——. *A Scientist at the Seashore*. New York: Scribner's, 1984.

Van Dyke, John Charles. *The Desert*. New York: Scribner's, 1904.

——. *The Grand Canyon of the Colorado*. New York: Scribner's, 1920.

——. *The Mountain*. New York: Scribner's, 1916.

——. *Nature For Its Own Sake*. New York: Scribner's, 1898.

——. *The Open Spaces*. New York: Scribner's, 1922.

Wallace, David Rains. *The Dark Range: A Naturalist's Night Notebook*. San Francisco: Sierra Club, 1978.

——. *Idle Weeds: The Life of a Sandstone Ridge*. San Francisco: Sierra Club, 1980.

——. *The Klamath Knot*. San Francisco: Sierra Club, 1983.

White, William Chapman. *Adirondack Country*. New York: Duell, Sloane, & Pearce, 1954.

Whitman, Walt. *Specimen Days*. Boston: Godine, 1971; orig. pub. Philadelphia: D. McKay, 1882.

Wild, Peter. *Pioneer Conservationists of Western America*. Missoula, Mont.: Mountain Press, 1979.

Wilson, Alexander. *American Ornithology; or, the Natural History of the Birds of the United States*. Philadelphia: Bradford and Inskep, 1808–1814. [9 vols.]

Wilson, Edward O. *Biophilia*. Cambridge: Harvard University Press, 1984.

——. *Sociobiology*. Cambridge: Harvard University Press, 1975.

Wright, William H. *The Grizzly Bear: The Narrative of a Hunter-Naturalist, Scientific and Adventurous*. New York: Scribner's, 1909.

Zwinger, Ann. *Beyond the Aspen Grove*. New York: Harper & Row, 1981.

——. *A Desert Country Near the Sea: A Natural History of the Cape Region of Baja California*. New York: Harper & Row, 1983.

——. *Land Above the Trees*. (with Beatrice Willard) New York: Harper & Row, 1972.

——. *Run, River, Run*. New York: Harper & Row, 1975.

——. *Wind in the Rock*. New York: Harper & Row, 1978.

Zwinger, Ann, and Edwin Way Teale. *A Conscious Stillness: Two Naturalists on Thoreau's Rivers*. New York: Harper & Row, 1982.

ANTHOLOGIES, BIBLIOGRAPHIES, AND GENERAL STUDIES

Bergon, Frank, ed. *The Wilderness Reader*. New York: New American Library, 1980.

Borland, Hal, ed. *Our Natural World: The Land and Wildlife of America as Seen and Described by Writers Since the Country's Discovery*. Garden City, N.Y.: Doubleday, 1965.

Durrenberger, Robert W. *Environment and Man: A Bibliography*. Palo Alto: National Press Books, 1970.

Foerster, Norman. *Nature in American Literature: Studies in the Modern View of Nature*. New York: Macmillan, 1923.

Hicks, Philip Marshall. *The Development of the Natural History Essay in American Literature*. Philadelphia: University of Pennsylvania, 1924.

Krutch, Joseph Wood, ed. *Great American Nature Writing*. New York: William Sloane, 1950.

Owings, Loren C. *Environmental Values, 1860-1972*. Detroit: Gale Research Co., 1976.

Schwartz, William, ed. *Voices for the Wilderness*. New York: Ballantine, 1969.

Vermes, Jean, ed. *The Wilderness Sampler*. Harrisburg, Pa.: Stockpole, 1968.

West, Harbert Faulkner. *The Nature Writers: A Guide to Richer Reading*. Brattleboro, Vt.: Stephen Daye Press, 1939.

Contributors

KEITH H. BASSO, Professor of Anthropology at Yale, has conducted linguistic and ethnographic research in the Apache community at Cibecue since 1959 and is currently at work on an extended study of Apache conceptions of the physical environment.

CONGER BEASLEY, JR. has published two novels and two volumes of poetry. A collection of short stories, *My Manhattan*, was published in 1986.

RALPH BEER raises Polled Hereford cattle in central Montana. His first novel, *The Blind Corral*, was released by Viking/Penguin in 1986. He is a contributing editor of *Harper's Magazine* and a 1986 National Endowment for the Arts Fellowship grantee.

C. JOHN BURK is Gates Professor in Biological Sciences at Smith College. He is the author, with Marjorie M. Holland, of *Stone Walls and Sugar Maples: an Ecology for Northeasterners*.

ITALO CALVINO was the author of numerous books, including *Difficult Loves* (Picador). *The Literature Machine* was published this year by Picador.

ANNIE DILLARD is the author of *Pilgrim at Tinker Creek* (Picador), which won the Pulitzer Prize in General Nonfiction. A memoir, *An American Childhood* (Picador), is her most recent book.

GRETEL EHRLICH lives with her husband on a ranch in northern Wyoming. She is the author of *The Solace of Open Spaces*, a book of narrative essays which won the Harold B. Vurcell Memorial Award.

HOWARD ENSIGN EVANS is Professor Emeritus at Colorado State University and the author of *The Pleasure of Entomology* and *Australia: A Natural History*, which he wrote with his wife, Mary Alice Evans.

ROBERT FINCH, the Publications Director at the Cape Cod Museum of Natural History, wrote *Outlands: Journeys to the Outer Edges of Cape Cod*. He is currently editing an anthology of nature writing.

JOHN FOWLES lives in England. His most recent book was *A Maggot* (Jonathan Cape and Pan).

JOHN HAINES lives on his homestead in Fairbanks, Alaska. He is the author of a book of essays entitled *Stories We Listened To*.

JIM HARRISON is a regional novelist and poet who lives in Northern Michigan.

JOHN HAY teaches in the Environmental Studies Program at Dartmouth College. A resident of Cape Cod, he spends his summers in Maine "growing superior vegetables, boating between islands and watching seals and seabirds". His latest book is *The Immortal Wilderness*.

EDWARD HOAGLAND'S most recent novel is *Seven Rivers West*. His collected essays, *Heart's Desire,* will be published by Collins Harvill in 1990. He lives in New York City but spends part of each year in Vermont, and has recently made trips to Alaska, Western Louisiana, and North Yemen.

BARRY LOPEZ is the author of *Arctic Dreams, Of Wolves and Men,* and several story collections. He is a recipient of the John Burroughs Medal and an Award in Literature from the American Academy and Institute of Arts and Letters.

THOMAS J. LYON has taught at Utah State University since 1964, where he also edits the journal *Western American Literature.* He is currently working on a history of American nature writing.

JOHN MILTON, a Professor of English at the University of South Dakota since 1963, founded the *South Dakota Review* as a forum for the literature of the American West. His books include a novel, *Notes to a Bald Buffalo.*

RICHARD K. NELSON is an anthropologist who has lived for extended periods in several Alaskan Eskimo and Athabaskan Indian villages. He is the author of several books, including *Make Prayers to the Raven.*

JOYCE CAROL OATES has recently published *On Boxing* (Bloomsbury) and *Marya: a Life* (Pavanne). She is the author of many novels and has just published a collection of stories, *The Assignation,* with The Ecco Press. Her forthcoming novel is *American Appetites.*

NOEL PERRIN has been tending 100 acres of land in Vermont for the last 25 years, and teaching at Dartmouth College for the last 27. His books include *First, Second,* and *Third Person Rural.*

JOHN RODMAN is Professor of Political Studies at Pitzer College in Southern California. He has just begun to serve as Environmental Editor of *North American Review.*

LESLIE MARMON SILKO is a novelist from Laguna Pueblo, New Mexico. She now lives in Tucson, where she is attempting to end a long novel. In 1981 she received a five year MacArthur Fellowship.

EDWARD WILLIAMS is a full-time freelance writer specializing in wildlife and the environment and a contributing editor of *Audubon* magazine and *Gray's Sporting Journal.*

EDWARD O. WILSON is Baird Professor of Science and Curator in Entomology at Harvard University. He received the Pulitzer Prize in General Nonfiction in 1979 for his work *On Human Nature* (Harvard University Press).

ANN ZWINGER spends part of her year in Colorado Springs and "the rest on the road in faraway places with strange-sounding names". She is working on a book about deserts.

Acknowledgments

"The Writer's West" by John Milton, "In Praise of John Muir" by Edward Hoagland, and "Total Eclipse" by Annie Dillard first appeared in previous editions of *Antæus*.

"The Dolphin Papers" by John Rodman first appeared in *The North American Review*.

"The Nature Writer's Dilemma" by John Hay first appeared in *The Massachusetts Review*.

"Stalking with Stories" by Keith H. Basso first appeared, in longer form, in *The Yale Review*.

"The Green Man" is reprinted from *The Tree* by John Fowles; published by Little, Brown & Co. in 1979, and reprinted by The Ecco Press in 1983.

"North Beach Journal" is reprinted from *Outlands: Journals to the Outer Edges of Cape Cod* by Robert Finch; published by Godine in 1986.

"Man, the Sky, and the Elephant" is excerpted from *The Uses of Literature* by Italo Calvino, translated from the Italian by Patrick Creagh. English translation copyright © 1986 by Harcourt Brace Jovanovich, Inc. To be published by Harcourt Brace Jovanovich, Inc.